From Slavery to Freedom in Brazil

 **A series of course-adoption books on Latin America**

Independence in Spanish America: Civil Wars, Revolutions, and Underdevelopment (revised edition)—Jay Kinsbruner, Queens College

Heroes on Horseback: A Life and Times of the Last Gaucho Caudillos— John Charles Chasteen, University of North Carolina at Chapel Hill

The Life and Death of Carolina Maria de Jesus— Robert M. Levine, University of Miami, and José Carlos Sebe Bom Meihy, University of São Paulo

The Countryside in Colonial Latin America— Edited by Louisa Schell Hoberman, University of Texas at Austin, and Susan Migden Socolow, Emory University

¡Que vivan los tamales! Food and the Making of Mexican Identity— Jeffrey M. Pilcher, The Citadel

The Faces of Honor: Sex, Shame, and Violence in Colonial Latin America— Edited by Lyman L. Johnson, University of North Carolina at Charlotte, and Sonya Lipsett-Rivera, Carleton University

The Century of U.S. Capitalism in Latin America— Thomas F. O'Brien, University of Houston

Tangled Destinies: Latin America and the United States— Don Coerver, Texas Christian University, and Linda Hall, University of New Mexico

Everyday Life and Politics in Nineteenth Century Mexico: Men, Women, and War— Mark Wasserman, Rutgers, The State University of New Jersey

Lives of the Bigamists: Marriage, Family, and Community in Colonial Mexico— Richard Boyer, Simon Fraser University

Andean Worlds: Indigenous History, Culture, and Consciousness Under Spanish Rule, 1532–1825— Kenneth J. Andrien, Ohio State University

The Mexican Revolution, 1910–1940— Michael J. Gonzales, Northern Illinois University

Quito 1599: City and Colony in Transition— Kris Lane, College of William and Mar

Argentina on the Couch: Psychiatry, State, and Society, 1880 to the Present—Edited by Mariano Plotkin, CONICET (National Council of Scientific Research, Argentina), and Universidad Nacional de Tres de Febrero, Buenos Aires, Argentina.

A Pest in the Land: New World Epidemics in a Global Perspective—
Suzanne Austin Alchon, University of Delaware

The Silver King: The Remarkable Life of
the Count of Regla in Colonial Mexico—
Edith Boorstein Couturier, Ph.D., Professor Emerita

National Rhythms, African Roots:
The Deep History of Latin American Popular Dance—
John Charles Chasteen, University of North Carolina at Chapel Hill

The Great Festivals of Colonial Mexico City:
Performing Power and Identity—
Linda A. Curcio-Nagy, University of Nevada at Reno

The Souls of Purgatory: The Spiritual Diary of
a Seventeenth-Century Afro-Peruvian Mystic, Ursula de Jesús—
Nancy E. van Deusen, Western Washington University

Dutra's World: Wealth and Family in Nineteenth-Century Rio de Janeiro—
Zephyr L. Frank, Stanford University

Death, Dismemberment, and Memory:
Body Politics in Latin America—
Edited by Lyman L. Johnson, University of North Carolina at Charlotte

Plaza of Sacrifices: Gender, Power, and Terror in 1968 Mexico—
Elaine Carey, St. John's University

Women in the Crucible of Conquest:
The Gendered Genesis of Spanish American Society, 1500–1600—
Karen Vieira Powers, Arizona State University

Beyond Black and Red: African-Native Relations in Colonial Latin America—
Edited by Matthew Restall, Pennsylvania State University, University Park

Mexico OtherWise: Modern Mexico
in the Eyes of Foreign Observers—Edited and translated by Jürgen
Buchenau,
University of North Carolina at Charlotte

Local Religion in Colonial Mexico—
Edited by Martin Austin Nesvig, University of Miami

Malintzin's Choices: An Indian Woman in the Conquest of Mexico—
Camilla Townsend, Rutgers University

Slaves, Subjects, and Subversives: Blacks in Colonial Latin America—
Edited by Jane G. Landers, Vanderbilt University, and Barry M.
Robinson, Samford University

Series advisory editor:
Lyman L. Johnson, University of North Carolina at Charlotte

View of São Salvador, Courtesy of João Mauricio Rugendas, Viagem Pitoresca Através do Brasil (Rio de Janeiro/São Paulo/Brasilia: A casa do Livro, 1972 [1835]), plates unpaginated.

FROM SLAVERY TO FREEDOM IN BRAZIL

Bahia, 1835–1900

Dale Torston Graden

UNIVERSITY OF NEW MEXICO PRESS

ALBUQUERQUE

10 09 08 07 06   1 2 3 4 5

Library of Congress Cataloging-in-Publication Data

Graden, Dale Torston, 1952–
From slavery to freedom in Brazil : Bahia, 1835–1900 / Dale Torston Graden.
p. cm. — (Diálogos)
Includes bibliographical references and index.
ISBN-13: 978-0-8263-4051-1 (pbk. : alk. paper)
ISBN-10: 0-8263-4051-2 (pbk. : alk. paper)
1. Slavery—Brazil—Bahia (State)—History—19th century.
2. Slaves—Emancipation—Brazil—Bahia (State)—History—19th century.
I. Title. II. Diálogos (Albuquerque, N.M.)
HT1129.B33G72 2006
306.3'62098109034—dc22
2006007649

DESIGN AND COMPOSITION: *Mina Yamashita*

To my mother,
Laura Ann Jacobson Graden,
and in memory of my father,
Thurston Harold Graden

Contents

LIST OF ILLUSTRATIONS / x

ACKNOWLEDGMENTS / xiii

INTRODUCTION / xv

CHRONOLOGY / xxvii

Part One: 1850–51: Two Perspectives on the End of the International Slave Trade to Bahia

CHAPTER ONE: Suppression of the Slave Trade / 1

CHAPTER TWO: "There Are Too Many Slaves in T his Port City of Salvador!": Slave Resistance and the End of the Slave Trade to Bahia / 17

Part Two: 1871: Two Perspectives on Passage of the Law of the Free Womb

CHAPTER THREE: War and Peace: A First Phase of Abolition in Bahia, 1850s–71 / 53

CHAPTER FOUR: Castro Alves / 83

Part Three: 1888: Three Perspectives on Abolition in Bahia

CHAPTER FIVE: Candomblé / 103

CHAPTER SIX: A Second Phase of Abolition, 1871–79 / 133

CHAPTER SEVEN: Liberation, 1880–88 / 159

Part Four: 1888–1900: Freedom

CHAPTER EIGHT: The Aftermath / 199

CONCLUSION / 225

GLOSSARY / 231

ARCHIVES / 235

NOTES / 237

INDEX / 289

List of illustrations

Tables and Graphs

Table 1.1:   Volume of Transatlantic Slave Arrivals by Region of
             Arrival, 1519–1867 / 2

Table 2.1:   Estimates of Slave and Total Population in Brazil,
             1798–1890 / 20

Table 2.2:   Estimates of Largest Provincial Slave Populations in Brazil,
             1864 / 21

Table 2.3:   Arrests of Fugitive African and Crioulo Slaves in Salvador,
             1849–85 / 46

Graph 2.1:   Arrests of Fugitive Slaves in Salvador, 1849–80 / 47

Table 3.1:   Arrests of Fugitive Slaves in Salvador, 1863–1870 / 68

Table 6.1:   Police Records of Slaves Transported from Salvador,
             1853–78 / 135

Table 6.2:   Arrests of Fugitive Slaves in Salvador, 1870 to 1878 / 143

Table 7.1:   Slave Populations in Bahia, Pernambuco, Rio de Janeiro,
             and São Paulo Provinces, 1864–87 / 186

Table 8.1:   Free and Slave Population in the Municipalities Influenced
             by the Presence of Antônio Conselheiro / 219

Maps

Map 1.1:   Important ports and regions tied to the slave trade between
           Africa and Brazil / 3

Map 2.1:   Map of Brazil in the late nineteenth century / 19

Map 2.2:   Map of the Bay of All Saints and Bahian Recôncavo / 23

Map 6.1:   Provinces and regions of nineteenth-century Brazil / 137

Map 8.1:   Canudos region, 1893–97 / 217

Figures

Frontispiece: View of São Salvador. Lithograph produced by João Mauricio Rugendas in 1825; published in 1835.

Figure 1.1: "Negros in the Bottom of a Slave Ship" / 9

Figure 2.1: Arabic document sent by police of Recife, requesting translation / 30

Figure 2.2: Arabic document sent by police of Recife, requesting translation / 31

Figure 3.1: Statue of Luís Gama / 73

Figure 3.2: The newspaper *O Alabama* / 78

Figure 5.1: The orixá Omolu / 112

Figure 5.2: Spectacular orixás stand above the dike of Tororó / 120

Figure 5.3: A *Baiana* "cleansing" the spirit of a believer in front of the Church of Saint Lazarus in Salvador / 124

Figure 6.1: Statue of Luiz Tarquínio / 155

Figure 7.1: "The Monster of 28 September 1885" / 173

Figure 7.2: A shackled slave observing the rise of the "Sun of Liberty" / 185

Figure 8.1: "Long Live Carnaval" / 203

Figure 8.2: Photo of children who survived the destruction of Canudos / 223

Acknowledgments

Learning about the history of Salvador and Bahia and Brazil has been a fulfilling journey.

Many institutions and individuals helped me to research and write this book. The Fulbright Commission of Brazil and the United States first awarded me a grant for dissertation research and subsequently a Senior Fulbright award to teach and research at the Federal University of Bahia. The National Endowment for the Humanities, the Departments of History at the University of Connecticut and the University of Idaho, and the University of Idaho Research Council all provided financial support.

In the United States and Canada, my thanks go to George Reid Andrews, Richard D. Brown, E. Bradford Burns (deceased), Nancy Dafoe, Anani Dzidzienyo, David Eltis, John Kicza, Hendrik Kraay, Laura Guedes, Hugh M. Hamill (deceased), A. William Hoglund, Elizabeth Mahan, James Martin and Patricia Catoira, Randy Matory, Abilio and Beth Monteiro, Jeffrey Needell, Jennifer O'Laughlin, Eugenio Piñero, Miguel Ramírez, Raúl Sánchez, Francisco Scarano, David Sheinin, Irene Silverblatt, Thomas Skidmore, Donald Spivey, Lynn Sweet, Robert W. Vrecenak, Thomas Whigham, Dick Wilson, Dennis and Joan West, and Daniel Zirker.

In Brazil, my thanks to Carlos Alencar, Henriques Alencar, *a família* Alencar, Lina Aras, Jeferson Bacelar, Fláviodos Santos Gomes, *a família* Guedes, Silvia Hunold Lara, Luiz Mott, Anna Amélia Vieira Nascimento, Antônio Olavo, Paulo César Oliveira, José Gabriel da Costa Pinto (deceased), Maria Ligia Prado, João José Reis, James Riordan, Angela Hormazabal Santibañez, Consuelo Pondé de Sena, *a família* Pondé, Eduardo Silva, Renato da Silveira, and Ana Tachard.

At the University of New Mexico Press, thanks to David Holtby, Sonia Dickey, and Alex Giardino, for her meticulous editing. *Obrigado também* to Lyman Johnson for his *gentileza* in helping me to write this book.

Jason Burke and Clara Chaffin, graduate students in the Department of Geography at the University of Idaho, prepared three of the maps.

Thanks to the staffs of the Instituto Histórico e Geográfico Brasileiro, the National Archives of Brazil, and the National Library of Brazil (institutions in Rio de Janeiro), and the Public Archive of the State of Bahia, the Instituto Geográfico e Histórico da Bahia, Centro de Estudos Afro-Orientais, and the Clemente Mariani Foundation (all in Salvador).

Segments of this book were previously published in the journals *Hispanic American Historical Review*, *Brazil/Brasil: A Journal of Brazilian Literature*, *Review of Latin American Studies*, and *Estudos Afro-Asiáticos*, and the book edited by Hendrik Kraay, *Afro-Brazilian Culture and Politics: Bahia, 1790s to 1990s* (Armonk, NY, and London England: M. E. Sharpe, 1998). ▨

Introduction

Three big themes pervade the historiography of international abolition. One is related to the spread of Enlightenment and Christian thought in Europe from the second half of the eighteenth century. Churchgoers from diverse backgrounds, including Quakers, Anglicans, evangelical Methodists and Baptists, found appeal in such ideals. Beginning in the 1780s, this led to a heightened awareness of the slave trade between Africa and the Americas; it eventually led to a call to end the trade. It also coincided with working-class petition campaigns demanding the abolition of slavery in the British Empire. These events in England inspired abolitionist agitation in the United States and other regions in the Americas. A second theme posits that expanding capitalism linked to the Industrial Revolution acted as a force for social change in the nineteenth century. A free labor ideology associated with this capitalist transformation condemned slavery as inefficient and inhumane. A third theme focuses on slave resistance as playing a major role in causing the demise of the international slave trade and slavery across the Americas in the nineteenth century.

Three Perspectives on International Abolition

Religious and intellectual ferment in England from the 1770s to 1833 helped transform criticism of the slave trade and slavery into a full-fledged political movement. Quakers played a central role in this process. During the eighteenth century, Quakers became increasingly alienated by the exploitation and suffering endured by enslaved Africans. In 1787, nine Quakers joined with three others to found the Committee for Effecting the Abolition of the Slave Trade in London. An influential Anglican member of this group was Thomas Clarkson (1760–1846). In early summer of that year, Clarkson set out on a five-month journey in

England to gather information to present to the committee. He visited the port cities of Bristol and Liverpool where he inspected a slave ship and interviewed several thousand sailors who had been employed on slaving voyages. With support of the Quaker James Phillips, Clarkson published *A Summary View of the Slave Trade and of the Probable Consequences of Its Abolition* in 1787. The following year, Parliament established a committee for the first time to investigate the slave trade.

In response to mounting protests, British politicians William Wilberforce, George Canning, Charles Fox, and William Pitt forged a political agenda aimed at ending British involvement in the slave trade. Yet, seven proposals submitted to Parliament from 1780 to 1805 to accomplish this goal were defeated. Finally, in March 1807, Parliament passed an enactment that made the traffic in slaves illegal for British subjects after May 1, 1807. On January 1, 1808, the U.S. government outlawed the transport of slaves to the United States.[1]

Events in England had repercussions throughout the Atlantic world. In the eighteenth century, British ships carried the largest number of slaves to the Americas. At century's end, the British government underwent a dramatic shift by becoming the leading advocate of ending the African slave trade. From 1808, England signed several antislave trade treaties with various European nations and Brazil. For the next six decades, Great Britain sought to put a halt to all trading in slaves from Africa. The British West Africa Squadron and its allies captured 1,982 slave vessels out of 8,238 slave ships that set out from Africa between 1808 and 1870. (these numbers confirmed to date; certainly there were other slave voyages not recorded.)[2] This effort helped to end the international slave trade to Brazil (1850–51) and Cuba (1870), the two countries receiving the largest number of African slaves from 1808 through the late 1860s.

From the second half of the eighteenth century, a major change in international economy influenced antislavery discourse. In his seminal book *Capitalism and Slavery* (1944), Eric Williams claimed that this transition from mercantile to industrial capitalism doomed slavery in the British Caribbean islands. Williams alleged that British government policy endorsed the antislavery cause when Caribbean sugar plantations could no longer provide big returns on investments. In other words, economics caused the downfall of slavery in the British Caribbean; humanitarian concern, according to Williams, played a minimal role in this process.

Subsequent studies of international abolition have challenged the Williams thesis. Seymour Drescher posits that trends in the international economy did little to doom slavery in the British Caribbean or elsewhere at the beginning of the nineteenth century. Instead, evidence suggests a rise in output and profits from sugar production in the Caribbean encouraged owners to retain their slaves. Termination of England's involvement in the slave trade (1807) followed by slave emancipation in the British Caribbean (1833), therefore actually proved detrimental to the financial interests of British planters and investors. Passage of these two laws constituted a form of "econocide."[3] Analyzing the origins of antislavery mobilization at the end of the eighteenth century, Drescher contends that the key source of this upsurge can be traced to urban working-class protests in Great Britain, specifically the city of Manchester, commencing in 1787–88.[4]

Another critic of *Capitalism and Slavery*, David Brion Davis, depicted Williams's portrayal of the rise and fall of Caribbean slavery as "cynical reductionism."[5] Davis suggests that expanding capitalism during the "age of revolution" (1770–1823) brought with it a heightened moral sensibility critical of slavery. British capitalists joined with activists of all sorts—Africans like Olaudah Equiano and other free blacks who resided in England, workers, reformers associated with churches, intellectuals— to condemn slavery in distant colonies. Seldom are individuals motivated solely by humanitarian concern; this was certainly the case with British entrepreneurs and owners of factories. By focusing on the abuses of slavery, they sought to deflect attention from exploitative labor relations in England.[6]

Williams, Drescher, and Davis have provided major contributions for understanding the forces that led to the downfall of slavery in the Americas. Nevertheless, they have considered slave resistance as playing a secondary or marginal role in causing international abolition.

Slave resistance, the third theme or interpretation of abolition, emphasizes that the actions of slaves created all sorts of problems for owners and investors. Resistance took many forms, the most visible and commented on being revolts, assassinations of owners and managers of estates, and escapes. Less visible manifestations of slave resistance included day-to-day subversion and deflecting to the demands of owners. Urban slaves joined brotherhoods and protested unacceptable labor policies or police activities that infringed on hard-won freedoms. Rural slaves employed various strategies to preserve their physical and mental health and to undermine the capacity of owners to coerce their slave property. Given the difficulties of analyzing and measuring slave resistance, historians have minimized this third theme when analyzing the hundred-year process to end slavery (1780s–1888) across the Americas.

Since the 1980s, slave resistance has gained attention as a factor in ending the international slave trade and the institution of slavery. Slave resistance in the Caribbean Basin has been situated in a regional and international context. Studies of the Haitian Revolution (1791–1804) have offered insights on participants, impact, and legacy. The subversive effects of "Haitianism" became of utmost concern to masters throughout the Americas.[7] Slave resistance in the North American British colonies and independent United States (1619 to 1865) and in Brazil (1520s to 1888) have become major fields of study.[8] Slaves were agents of their own liberation. They employed a wide range of strategies and tactics in their quest to be free, often receiving the aid of free persons. Abolition has been shown to be a process far more complex than merely the handing down of laws by enlightened leaders and parliaments or progressive sentiments inexorably linked to a widening international capitalism.

Pressures in Bahia to End the Slave Trade and End Slavery

Each of the three abolitionist themes has relevance to Bahian history in the nineteenth century. From the sixteenth century to the early 1850s, Brazil's northeastern province of Bahia received at least 1.2 million slaves from Africa. Thousands of these slaves passed through the city of Salvador, the central port of the province and capital of Brazil until 1763. By the beginning of the nineteenth century, Salvador was the second-largest city in Brazil after Rio de Janeiro, located 750 miles to the southwest.

Salvador gained notoriety as the largest slave entrepôt in the Americas.

A huge province nearly the size of France, Bahia's economy depended on slave labor. African slaves transported to Bahia labored on sugar plantations situated in a region known as the Recôncavo, a fertile strip of land some sixty miles long and thirty miles wide surrounding the huge bay at Salvador known as Baía de Todos os Santos (Bay of All Saints). Slaves also cultivated lands that produced coffee and tobacco in the Recôncavo and cocoa in the south of the province. Slaves worked on large estates, midsized farms, and small farms. They sailed on boats that plied the Bay of All Saints and unloaded goods in the port of Salvador. Slaves carried materials and people throughout the city of Salvador. Urban and rural owners, those who owned many slaves or a few, white, mixed-race and black owners, all exploited African and *crioulo* (born in Brazil) slaves to their benefit.

The slaves of Salvador made a marked impression on the Portuguese royal family when they arrived to the city on January 22, 1808. Fleeing twenty-three thousand French troops loyal to Napoleon that had invaded Portugal, the Braganza family stepped on Brazilian soil with pomp and ceremony. Salvador was too much an African city for their tastes; a month later the royal entourage headed to Rio de Janeiro, where they settled permanently. Prince Regent João became João VI, "King of the United Kingdoms of Portugal, Brazil, and the Algarves," in 1816. Five years later in 1821, João VI returned to Portugal, leaving his twenty-three-year-old son, Prince Pedro, as head of the internal affairs Portugal's colony of Brazil. In 1822, Pedro declared independence from Portugal, and soon after he was declared Emperor of Brazil. Dom Pedro I ruled during the First Empire until his abdication from the throne in 1831. This event was followed by a period of political instability and five major provincial revolts.

In 1840, the Brazilian-born son of Pedro I was crowned King Pedro II at age fourteen. Dom Pedro II brought stability to the empire by taking power away from provincial legislatures and placing all police forces under his control. The emperor reestablished the Council of State as a way to further strengthen centralized rule in Rio de Janeiro.

Pedro appointed seventy-two councilors from 1842 to 1889, fourteen of whom originated in Bahia, this number second only to the seventeen councilors selected from the province of Rio de Janeiro. Pedro II headed the Second Empire for forty-nine years until a military coup in 1889. Influential planters, believing that Pedro had failed to act in their best interests during the final years of the slave regime (1880–88), helped to bring about his downfall.[9]

In the years immediately following independence from Portugal in 1822–23, Brazil's imperial government desired diplomatic recognition from Great Britain and the benefits of unimpeded trade. To achieve these ends, Brazilian officials signed treaties and passed a law (in 1831) to outlaw the slave trade. These had little impact in Bahia. Describing Salvador as a "port of pirates," the Bahian historian Ubiratan Castro de Araújo has examined how Portuguese, British, and Bahian merchants invested in and facilitated slave voyages for two more decades (1831–51).[10] Hundreds of individuals profited from the trade, including shipbuilders, owners of ships, crews, captains, farmers, along with civil and military officials. In spite of the many tentacles of the slave trade, British naval patrols in the Atlantic Basin helped to force an end to slave importations into Bahia by 1850–51.

An economic interpretation of the ending of slavery in the northeastern provinces of Brazil has influenced numerous descriptions of nineteenth-century Bahia. The demise of slavery in Bahia has been closely linked to the decreasing profitability of sugar production in the province.[11] Recent studies have shed new light on the ways in which Bahia's regional economy impacted attitudes and slaveholding. These demonstrate the prominent role of slaves in Bahian agriculture right up until the emancipation decree of 1888.[12] Such analysis debunks the myth that the institution of slavery simply faded away in Bahia due to transformations caused by the international economy. This also signals the need for more research focusing on the final years of slavery in Bahia.

Slave resistance has particular relevance in Bahia. From 1807 to 1835, more than twenty slave revolts shook Salvador and the Recôncavo. These upheavals culminated in the 1835 Malês Revolt, the largest urban slave rebellion in the history of the Americas. Disturbances involving free persons, including anti-Portuguese protests, military revolts, and federalist rebellions, added to the tensions of the period. Provincial officials viewed with trepidation the possibility that African slaves might join with crioulo slaves or with lower-class free persons to threaten elite interests. Although no slave revolts occurred after 1835 in Bahia or Brazil of the magnitude of the Haitian Revolution or the revolt of the Malês, in no way does this mean that African and crioulo slaves weakened in their quest for liberation. Slaves became, in the words of the Brazilian historian Jacob Gorender, "intimately associated with the abolitionist movement [composed] of free men."[13]

Slave Resistance and Activists in Bahia

While British condemnation of the slave trade and the spread of capitalist values in the Atlantic world played important roles in ending the slave trade and ultimately slavery itself in Bahia, this book pays special attention to the role of slave resistance in compelling abolition in the province. It demonstrates that the Africans of Salvador—slaves, freedpersons (former slaves who had attained their freedom, known as *libertos*), and "liberated Africans" (*Africanos livres*)—helped bring a halt to the African slave trade to Bahia and Brazil in 1850–51.[14] Slave resistance combined with the actions of a small group of abolition activists in Bahia contributed to passage of subsequent abolitionist legislation at two critical junctures: in 1871 with passage of the Law of the Free Womb; and in May 1888 when Brazil's parliament voted to end slavery in Brazil.

An important question to pose at the outset regards how the actions of slaves in Bahia after 1835 differed from the manifestations of slave resistance in Brazil during the previous three centuries. Various hypotheses can be suggested. First, slaves in Salvador and throughout Bahia knew about and remembered well the revolt of the Malês in 1835. This event became embedded in their historical memory and gave them inspiration. Second, slaves observed the British antislavery squadron along the Bahian coast. British sailors rescued several thousand Africans from slave ships and deposited them on Brazilian soil as "liberated Africans." Africans who survived shared their story with slaves and others in Salvador. Third, slaves commonly understood and paid close attention to the debates about emancipation that swirled around them. On numerous occasions from the 1830s to 1888, slaves and their free allies articulated their desires for freedom and dissatisfaction with slavery in myriad ways. Political discourse associated with antislavery legislation influenced the strategies underpinning such acts of resistance.

The book is divided into four parts. Part 1 focuses on the ending of the slave trade to Bahia. International pressures and infectious disease (Chapter 1) combined with slave resistance in Bahia (Chapter 2) to force an abrupt decline in slave importations into Bahia by 1851. In Part 2, a first phase of the abolitionist movement is traced from the early 1850s up through passage of the Law of the Free Womb in 1871. Popular alienation with the war against Paraguay, slave resistance, and protests led by African Brazilian intellectuals and activists fueled tensions that led to the antislavery legislation of 1871 (Chapter 3). The writings and public activities of the Bahian poet Castro Alves helped cause abolition to become a major political debate during this period (Chapter 4). Part 3 focuses on the final years of slavery in Bahia. It emphasizes the role of African Candomblé (Bahian term denoting African Brazilian religion) in fomenting abolitionist expression (Chapter 5). During the second phase of abolition that occurred between 1871 and 1879 (Chapter 6) and the third phase from 1880 to 1888 (Chapter 7), slave resistance combined with the actions of a small group of radicals helped to bring an end to slavery in Bahia. Events in Bahia significantly influenced political discourse and imperial decisions in Rio de Janeiro. Part 4 (Chapter 8) demonstrates how former slaves seized opportunities and protected hard-won freedoms after liberation from 1888 to 1900.

This book adds to our understanding of the process of abolition in Bahia and Brazil in five key ways. First, slave resistance played a decisive role in causing an end to the international slave trade to Bahia. By dominating commercial transport in small boats in the harbor of Salvador, African slaves gained control over a key strategic location in the city. Planned, organized actions by slaves in Salvador caused major problems for slave traders by 1850. These included collusion between slaves and liberated Africans left in Bahia by the British squadron, sharing of information about British anti-slave trade activities, and preparations for a revolt. Furthermore, slaves and their allies, particularly those situated in Salvador, inspired antislavery and abolitionist protests from 1850 to 1888 in Bahia. "Organized collective acts" of slave resistance as a manifestation of abolitionist protest appeared in Bahia from the 1860s, comparable to more publicized episodes in Brazil's central-southern provinces (especially those of the 1880s).[15] These latter regions have received close attention by historians seeking to understand the ties between slave resistance and abolition, especially the provinces of Rio de Janeiro and São Paulo. This book expands on these insightful contributions.

Second, an abolitionist movement led by black and mixed-race Bahians emerged in the early 1860s and continued until abolition in 1888. Its origins can be traced to the writings and actions of the former slave Luís Gama, whose work began to appear in the late 1850s. Based in Salvador, this movement included both intellectuals and hardened protestors. Their mobilization contributed to the significant decline in the number of slaves present in Salvador by 1878–79. In the decade that followed (to May 1888), Africans and their descendants contributed to the effort to bring an end to slavery in Bahia.

Third, the war with Paraguay had a devastating impact on Bahia. Hundreds of men refused to be shipped off to the front, and several thousand troops returned to Bahia at war's end poor and angry. Concern that this free underclass might align with slaves in Bahia impacted provincial politics in the late 1860s and after. Tensions at war's end caused by lower-class free persons, slaves, and abolitionists contributed to passage of the Law of the Free Womb in September 1871. Memory of the war would affect Bahian politics for the next three decades.

Fourth, by the mid-1880s, abolitionist agitators attracted a devoted following among lower-class free people in the Recôncavo of Bahia. These common folk participated in public demonstrations and subversive activities. At this same time a charismatic figure named Antônio Conselheiro (Anthony the Counselor) gained renown in the arid northeastern interior of the province as a leader who appealed to the shared class interests of slaves and rural folk. Antônio Conselheiro's growing influence and power undermined the capacity of planters to control their slaves. In 1893, he founded a settlement in the interior of Bahia that became known as Canudos. The outcome was a cataclysm: the total destruction of Canudos in 1897 by federal troops, the death of Antônio Conselheiro, and the deaths of thousands of his followers.

Fifth, this book sheds a special light on the Bahians Antônio Castro Alves and Eduardo Carigé, who made extraordinary efforts on behalf of slaves. As intellectuals, both paid homage to the contributions of Africans and their descendants to Brazilian society. As radical activists, both denounced slavery in their home province of Bahia and throughout the empire. In the final verse of "Tragedy at Sea: The Slave Ship" (1868), one of the first and most famous abolitionist statements in Brazil, Castro Alves made clear his sentiments:

> Atrocity that crushes the soul!
> Blot out this filthy brig
> From the trail opened by Columbus
> Like a rainbow on the uncharted seas—
> Against this infamy
> Rise up, heroes of the New World!
> Andrada, tear this flag from the wind!
> Columbus, close the doors of your seas![16]

Remembering the horrors of the slave trade and condemning slavery in his home country of Brazil, the poet calls on Africans to "rise up," to rebel against their enslavement. Alves invokes the memory of José Bonifácio de Andrada e Silva (1765–1838), a major figure during the independence period and one of Brazil's first critics of slavery. The poem resonated with slaves and abolitionists alike. From the mid-1860s when Castro Alves began penning and publicly reciting his abolitionist poetry until the declaration of emancipation in 1888, Eduardo Carigé and others paid heed to these calls for action. With unceasing determination and courage, they ultimately succeeded in destroying a scourge that surrounded them.

Definitions and Money

A final note concerns definitions and money. Following the example of Celia Maria Marinho de Azevedo, I make a distinction between the words "antislavery" and "abolitionist." Antislavery can be defined as a "generalized posture of opposition to slavery that did not necessarily look toward and fight for abolition." An abolitionist, by contrast, sought to critique all aspects of the institution of slavery and "stressed the need to end slavery, whether gradually or immediately."[17]

Scholars differ in their choice of terms to describe nonwhite Brazilians descended from African ancestors. Some employ the term "person of color."[18] Others prefer African Brazilian or, in the case of Bahians descended from Africans, African Bahian.[19] In both delineations, nonwhites are included in a single category. Such a description might be considered simplistic given the wide range of racial categories employed in nineteenth-century Brazil and Bahia, for example, black (*prêto/prêta, negro/a,* and *crioulo/a*), a mixed-race person of combined African and European origins (*mulatto/a* or *pardo/parda*), or a mixed-race person of Indian and European origins (*caboclo*). When the racial characteristic of a nonwhite person is known, I employ the term that was used. When it is not, I use the term person of color.

The word crioulo had two meanings in nineteenth-century Bahia. First, the term implied one's place of birth. A crioulo slave meant that a slave had been born in Brazil to distinguish him or her from a slave born in Africa. With the ending of the international slave trade to Brazil in 1850–51, few Africans entered Brazil. Hence, a second usage evolved that defined a crioulo as a Brizilian-born Black. In the second half of the nineteenth century, it was a word commonly used both verbally and in writing. The term crioulo continues to be used in twenty-first-century Brazil as a pejorative word or as a racial slur.

In the nineteenth century, the Brazilian monetary unit was the *real* (plural *réis*). One *real* had little worth, so that the most common monetary unit was the *milréis*, or 1,000 réis, this amount denoted as 1$000 in the documents of the nineteenth century. I have used 1$ to denote one milréis here. In 1835, it is estimated that 10$ could purchase fifteen kilos of beef jerky, twenty-four liters of beans, or five liters of manioc flour.[20] Income for a day's labor in Salvador in 1849 ranged from 320 réis (US 17 cents) to 1$384 réis (US 73 cents).[21] In the 1880s, a daily newspaper cost between 40 and 100 réis (US 2 to 4 cents), and a standard wage for one day of urban labor was 2$ (US 80 cents).[22] The value of 1$ varied over the course of the nineteenth century, from about US $1.00 in the early 1820s to 79 cents in 1834 to 52 cents in 1849 to 19 cents in 1900.[23] The purchasing power of one U.S. dollar in the 1860s (for goods such as foodstuffs, basic metal goods, commodities, and so on) was approximately seven times greater than one dollar in 2005. ▣

Chronology

1500: Europeans arrive in Brazil. An estimated 2 to 8.5 million Indians are living in Brazil.

1510s–1870: An estimated 15 million or more slaves are transported from Africa to the Americas.

1520s–1850s: African slave trade to Brazil; an estimated 4.5 million slaves are transported to Brazil from various parts of Africa.

1791–1804: The Haitian Revolution.

1807: England prohibits the international slave trade to its Caribbean colonies.

1808: The United States prohibits the international slave trade to the United States, as stipulated in Article 1, Section 9 of the U.S. Constitution, passed in 1787.

1790s–1860: An internal slave trade that sends an estimated 1 million slaves out of the upper South and into the deep South and western United States continues into the early 1860s.

September 1822: Independence declared in Brazil.

July 1823: Independence attained in Brazil with defeat of Portuguese troops in Bahia.

1823–69: Abolition of slavery in mainland Spanish America.

1831: The "Baptist Revolt" in the British colony of Jamaica.

1833: Emancipation declared in the British colonies, resulting in the liberation of 800,000 slaves.

1835: Revolt of the Malês in Salvador, Bahia.

1848: Karl Marx and Frederick Engels publish *The Communist Manifesto*.

September 1850: Brazil's General Assembly passes the Eusébio de Queiroz Law, which outlaws the slave trade; enforcement of the law results in a precipitous decline in the number of African slaves imported to Brazil.

1830s–81: An internal slave trade in Brazil transfers at least 222,500 slaves from the provinces of the North-Northeast to the Center-South.

1861–65: U.S. Civil War.

1864–70: War of the Triple Alliance, also known as the Paraguayan War.

1865–75: Reconstruction in the U.S. South.

1870: End of the slave trade to Cuba.

1870: Passage of the Law of the Free Womb in Cuba and Puerto Rico.

September 1871: The Law of the Free Womb, also known as the Rio Branco Law, passes in Brazil.

1873: Slavery ends in Puerto Rico.

1886: Slavery ends in Cuba.

May 1888: An imperial decree is signed, ending slavery in Brazil, the last nation to end slavery in the Americas.

November 1889: A military coup d'état ends the monarchy; the First Republic is established.

1893–97: The town known as Canudos is created in northeastern Bahia by the followers of a charismatic leader named *Antônio Conselheiro* (Anthony the Counselor). The town attracts common folk of the interior and former slaves, and within four years its population grows to 25,000 inhabitants, making it the second-largest city in the state of Bahia. Viewed as a threat to the new Republic and the planter elite of Bahia, in September and October 1897, military troops destroy the city and kill most of its inhabitants.

PART ONE
1850–51

Two Perspectives on the

End of the International Slave Trade to Bahia

CHAPTER ONE

Suppression of the Slave Trade

International pressures played a key role in ending the international slave trade to Bahia. British seizures of Bahian ships commenced soon after Prince Regent João of Portugal signed a treaty of alliance with England. By this 1810 treaty, the regent, who resided in Rio de Janeiro after being forced to depart from Portugal in the wake of Napoleon's invasion of 1807, agreed to the "gradual abolition of the slave trade." He also agreed that Brazilian traders could only purchase slaves from regions in Africa under Portuguese control. Subsequent treaties and laws permitted the British squadron to seize slaving ships destined for Bahia. It is undeniable that these British actions contributed to the permanent demise of the slave trade to Bahia and to the rest of Brazil by 1850–51.

Other events helped bring an end of the slave trade, as well. These included outbreaks of infectious diseases in Salvador and other Brazilian ports along with African resistance on the African coast. Inspired by the halt in slave importations and the example of abolitionist initiatives in other regions of the Americas (British, French and Danish Caribbean, Spanish America, the U.S. North), Bahian activists founded the first abolitionist societies in Salvador at midcentury.

The Culmination of the Slave Trade to Brazil in the Nineteenth Century

Slave ships carried at least 4,430,900 African slaves to Brazil during more than three centuries (1520s–1850s).[1] This calculation represents close to 40 percent of the total number of slaves transported from Africa to the Americas. During the first half of the nineteenth century, the importation reached some of its highest annual and decadal levels.

TABLE 1.1. VOLUME OF TRANSATLANTIC SLAVE ARRIVALS BY REGION OF
ARRIVAL, 1519–1867 (IN THOUSANDS) (2006)

	Northeast Brazil	Bahia	Southeast Brazil	Spanish Caribbean
1519–1600	18.6	5.9	4.5	0.0
1601–1650	121.0	115.9	80.4	0.0
1651–1675	47.4	84.8	61.3	0.8
1676–1700	84.7	102.1	71.5	0.0
1701–1725	114.3	186.1	120.4	2.9
1726–1750	75.6	231.5	150.1	1.2
1751–1775	99.1	176.1	204.5	18.6
1776–1800	119.7	223.8	270.4	55.7
1801–1825	227.4	256.9	498.7	252.2
1826–1850	95.4	171.5	761.7	348.7
1851–1867	0.4	1.9	3.6	156.3
All years	1003.6	1556.5	2227.2	836.3
% OF TOTAL SLAVE TRADE	9.4	14.6	20.9	7.8

Source: David Eltis, "A Reassessment of the Supply of African Slaves to
the Americas," Paper Presented at the American Historical Association Meeting,
Philadelphia, Pennsylvania, January 2006. Courtesy of David Eltis.

Various factors contributed to this upsurge in the nineteenth century.
With the destruction of plantations on the Caribbean island of Saint
Domingue during the Haitian Revolution (1791–1804), sugar and coffee
prices surged upward and planters in Brazil sought to supply markets
with increased output from their estates. To satisfy their need for more
workers, planters purchased slaves. In Bahia, slave imports reached their
pinnacle in the decades of the 1820s and 1840s. Ships also disembarked
African slaves in unprecedented numbers south of Bahia to satisfy rising
demand for workers. As a result, more slaves arrived along the Brazilian

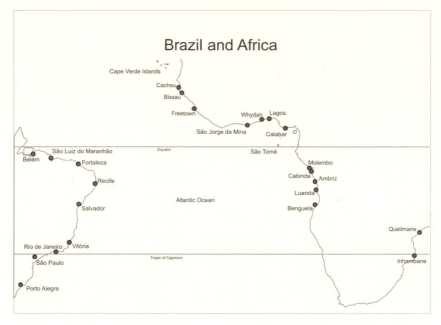

Map 1.1 Brazil and Africa. Important ports and regions tied to the slave trade between African and Brazil.

coast north and south of the city of Rio de Janeiro from 1821 to 1850 than in all other regions in the Americas combined.[2]

Another reason for the increase in slave imports at this juncture can be traced to investor responses to British efforts to suppress the traffic. Treaties between Great Britain and Portugal (in 1810, 1815, and 1817), as well as a treaty between Great Britain and Brazil in 1826 (after Brazilian independence in 1822), placed various legal restrictions on slave traders. Ratification of the 1826 treaty by the British Parliament in 1827 stipulated that the slave trade to Brazil would become illegal three years later (in 1830). A law passed in November 1831 by the Brazilian General Assembly reaffirmed the illegality of importing slaves into Brazil. The 1831 Brazilian law stated that any slave entering the nation would be free; it also gave police the right to penalize individuals found guilty of involvement in the trade. Due to the influence of slave traders, however, locally elected officials and juries did little to enforce the 1831 law.[3]

Inadequate enforcement by Brazilian imperial authorities and widespread demand undermined British efforts to stem the huge influx of African slaves to Brazil after 1831. To address this problem, the British parliament passed the Aberdeen Act in 1845. This act deemed that slave ships were pirate ships. It allowed British cruisers to seize slave ships wherever they were encountered, whether on the high seas or on the Brazilian coast. The Aberdeen Act demonstrated the continued determination of a small group of British politicians to halt the slave trade to Brazil. But such initiatives only encouraged the major participants in the slave trade—Brazilian, Portuguese, British, and U.S. citizens—to transport to Brazil as many slaves as possible in case suppression efforts succeeded. (This was similar to what had occurred in the late 1820s before the 1830 deadline agreed on between England and Brazil went into effect.)[4] In May 1846, for example, a British consul in Salvador wrote that the ship *Três Amigos* had landed some 1,350 slaves on the Bahian coast. Fifty Africans died during the voyage.[5] The consul attributed the "massive importations" of these months to Salvadoran companies composed of individuals who purchased shares in slaving ventures.[6]

As the leading advocate of a new "global moralism," in the words of the French-born historian and anthropologist Pierre Verger, England sought to destroy the operations of slave traders.[7] In its suppression efforts from 1811 to the mid-1850s, British cruisers captured at least 238 ships owned by investors based in Bahia and involved in slave trading.[8] Such initiatives strained relations between the British and Brazilian governments. British officials and ship crews commonly criticized Bahian authorities as being unwilling or incapable of ending the slave trade. Many Bahians viewed the British as arrogant and intrusive.

The presence of the British squadron along the Bahian coast and in the harbor of Salvador necessarily provoked conflicts. In the mid-1820s, uniformed Brazilian soldiers and sailors assaulted British merchants and sea captains. Similar incidents continued into the 1830s and 1840s. In late April 1848, for example, the British sloop *Grecian* accompanied the captured Brazilian slaving vessel *Bella Miquelina* with 517 Africans on board into the port of Salvador. On the night of April 29 a "large party of armed men [from Salvador] in two country boats" attempted to board the slave ship. An officer and the ship's crew successfully held off the fifty to sixty attackers, at least two of whom died in the assault.[9]

In one episode in 1851, the captain and crew of the British ship *Rifles* came on shore in Salvador. Dressed in formal attire, the commander dined at the house of the British vice consul. When he attempted to board a boat to return to the ship, a group of rowdies pelted him with stones. The British vice consul accused seamen who plied the bay in small boats selling food and wares as responsible for this "outrage."[10] Bad feelings toward the British for their efforts to suppress the slave trade and disquiet over the presence of British ships in the harbor of Salvador were at the root of these outbreaks.

U.S. diplomats also harassed slave traders and their associates. Although representing a nation that allowed the slave regime to flourish in the U.S. South, numerous representatives abroad sought to halt the slave trade. These included southerners who supported slavery and secession from the Union, for example, the Virginian Henry A. Wise, U.S. minister to Brazil in the 1840s. On the one hand, such individuals considered southern planters as caring owners who treated their slaves in a kind manner. On the other hand, they viewed the slave trade as inhumane and the use of the U.S. flag on slave ships seeking to escape from British cruisers immoral (U.S. policy would not allow British warships to search and seize U.S. ships until 1862). Furthermore, U.S. diplomats were aware of the rebelliousness of newly arrived African slaves, particularly in Brazil and Cuba, and viewed with trepidation the "Africanization" of these two countries if the slave trade continued uninterrupted.[11]

In 1845, the U.S. consul at Salvador Alexander Tyler demanded that two U.S. captains accused of involvement in the slave trade be arrested. Tyler informed the chief of police of Salvador of plans to send captains John Woodbury of Boston and Thomas Duling (who used an alias of Thomas Darling in Salvador to hide his identity) of Philadelphia to the United States to stand trial for illegal participation in the slave trade, based on a U.S. law in 1800 that made it illegal for U.S. citizens to engage in the transport of slaves from one foreign country to another. Responding to the pleas of the U.S. consul, the police detained the two men. In the words of John Gillmer, a U.S. businessman with investments in the slave trade between Salvador and Africa and who subsequently gained appointment as U.S. consul to Bahia (1850–62), "In this disgraceful manner were two respectable Americans citizens at the mere whim and caprice of Mr. Tyler [U.S. consul], conducted through the most public street of this city in open day, and in the presence of a great number of spectators, native and foreign, to the common prison at the Dockyard, where vagrants only are generally sent." Seeking a quick resolution to this affair, the chief of police released the two captains, and Duling immediately departed from Salvador on a ship bound for Long Island, New York.[12] Another U.S. consul named George Gordon stationed at Rio de Janeiro during these months also enraged slave traders by his public condemnation of the slave trade. Gordon received several threats in response to his protests. He claimed that his enemies had been opening his mail and were trying to run him out of office.[13]

British and U.S. diplomats sought to take advantage of opportunities that they believed might impede further slave importations. In late 1848, the British chargé d'affaires in Rio de Janeiro, James Hudson, encouraged his government to incite slave rebellion in Brazil. Hudson called for a naval blockade and occupation of Bahia, writing, "It is almost certain that the negros will not let such an occasion of securing their freedom escape." Hudson predicted "the existence of slavery itself in other portions of Brazil would be vitally affected."[14] Fomenting slave violence in Brazil, however, would not have boded well with British investors seeking markets to export British and European goods in the recently opened transatlantic steamship trade.[15] For this reason and others, the British Foreign Office rejected such a plan for more subtle initiatives. These included British financial support for newspapers critical of the slave trade published in Salvador (*O século*) and Rio de Janeiro (*O Brasil* and *Correio da Tarde*).[16]

Some Bahians joined in the effort to bring a permanent end to the international slave trade. In two episodes in late 1851, provincial officials intervened with slaving vessels. One illegal landing of an estimated six hundred slaves occurred in early September on the southern coast of

Bahia near Ilhéus. To destroy evidence that the ship had transported slaves to Bahia, the crew sank the vessel *Ultimação* and then fled into the interior. Soon after arriving on the scene, police encountered 112 Africans, including 60 adults and 47 children (we do not know the ages of the 5 other Africans who died). The officials transported this group of survivors to Salvador. Hidden by unscrupulous investors and planters, the remainder of the Africans ended up enslaved on estates in the region.[17]

Nearly two months later on October 29, 1851, the Brazilian warship *Itapagipe* intercepted the *Relâmpago* (built in Baltimore, Maryland, and previously named the *Empério*) twenty miles south of Salvador near the coastal town of Jaguaripe. It was a horrific affair, with sixty Africans drowning during a hasty attempt by the crew to land them on shore before apprehension. A battle erupted inland between the traffickers and the police, leaving dead two free blacks who had attempted to flee with slaves in their possession. Police took into custody 312 African slaves; another 100 had perished during the transatlantic voyage from the west coast of Africa. After their return to Salvador, African survivors from the voyage of the *Relâmpago* helped police to identify members of the crew. A judge sentenced thirty persons involved in this smuggling venture to prison terms.[18]

Violent resistance by Africans on the African coast further contributed to a hardening of outlook among Bahian investors with regards to resumption of the slave trade. The U.S. brig *Mary Adeline* departed from Rio de Janeiro in April 1852 destined for the coast of Angola. After having been visited by the British steamship *Fire Fly* investigating evidence of slave trading, the *Mary Adeline* ran aground on a sandbar at Shark's Point near the mouth of the Congo River. Within hours an estimated fifteen hundred to three thousand Africans attacked the boat. They used muskets, spears, oars, and cutlasses as weapons, along with hooks and poles to climb the side of the ship. The small crew of the *Mary Adeline* fought back by shooting a six-pound cannon that killed several of the Africans. Only with the help of the British ships *Fire Fly* and the *Dolphin* did the *Mary Adeline* manage to break free and anchor in deep water. News of the battle spread quickly. Couriers capable of running fifty to sixty miles a day surely carried this information along the African coast.[19] Inhabitants of Salvador learned of the attack after the return of the *Mary Adeline* to Salvador in late July. A planned attack by Africans of a slaving vessel helped to convince Bahians and foreigners resident in Salvador that a resumption of the slave trade would pose significant and unwanted risks. The notion that ship crews would have to fight armed warriors when trying to load Africans on to slaving vessels appealed to no one. Furthermore, it was doubtful that Africans who witnessed violent confrontations on the African coast would be passive slaves once landed in Salvador.[20]

The British became a symbol of beneficence to African and crioulo slaves in Salvador and other Brazilian ports. Examples abound. In the late afternoon darkness of Thursday, December 30, 1824, the British ship *Ascension* destined for Germany encountered a shipwreck five hundred miles off the coast of Bahia. Seeing Africans in the water holding on to the main mast, the captain of the *Ascension* kept his vessel close by. At 5:00 a.m. the next morning, two small boats sent out from the *Ascension* successfully picked up thirty-one Africans (the crew had abandoned the slave ship). Hearing muffled sounds from inside the capsized ship, carpenters cut openings on the side and helped extricate ten more Africans who had survived. The British captain estimated that two hundred slaves had perished in the wreck. The *Ascension* then changed its course and returned to Bahia. Although we do not know the fate of the survivors, descriptions of what had occurred spread among fellow Africans in the port city of Salvador.[21] The survivors certainly did not hesitate in sharing such information, nor did British representatives, who had an interest in publicizing anti-slave trade activities and humanitarian acts.

More than two decades later, in early May 1848, a black man managed to get on board the British ship *Grecian* while it was anchored in the port of Salvador. Conversing in fluent English, the man introduced himself as John Freeman, a native of Sierra Leone and a subject of the British crown. Freeman stated that he had been kidnapped the year before at the port of Popó (located in present-day Republic of Benin) on the coast of West Africa and was then transported to Salvador as a slave.

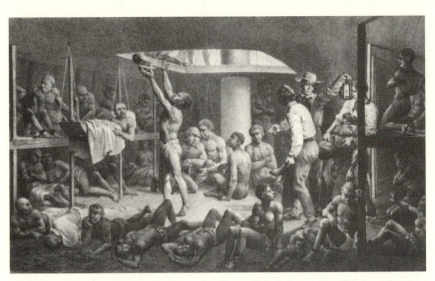

Figure 1.1 "Negros in the Bottom of a Slave Ship." Courtesy of João Mauricio Rugendas, *Viagem Pitoresca Através do Brasil* (Rio de Janeiro/São Paulo/Brasilia: A Casa do Livro, 1972[1835]), plates unpaginated.

For five months he had been enslaved, having been purchased by a black slave owner in the city. Freeman asked for help. Commander L. S. Tindal agreed to allow Freeman to remain on board until he spoke to the British consul.[22] Such gestures of kindness contrasted with the responses of most Europeans and Brazilians to African and crioulo slaves. The actions and words of British and U.S. diplomats and officials influenced the worldview and strategies of slaves, freedpersons, and liberated Africans in Salvador, Rio de Janeiro, and other port cities of Brazil.[23]

Epidemics

In October 1849, a yellow-fever epidemic spread quickly through Salvador and the interior of Bahia. The British consul believed that the virus had been passed from slaving vessels that entered the port.[24] A Commission of Public Hygiene specially appointed to investigate the yellow-fever epidemic in Bahia concurred. In its report submitted on December 23, 1849, the commission concluded:

Many prophylactic measures must be instituted to wipe out these foci of pests, which everyone knows exist in our city due to the barbarous and immoral traffic in Africans. The Africans [slaves] have been imported here by men who, for their own [financial] interest have sacrificed human beings, [actions] which are against the law, against medicine and against religion. They [the traffickers] have kept the Africans in tightly packed groups at depots with complete disregard of all [forms] of personal hygiene.[25]

President Francisco Gonçalves Martins (the president was the equivalent of governor of the province) admitted that the fever had caused serious problems. Although Martins (president with interruptions from October 1848 to May 1852) made no direct reference to the slave trade, his comments reflected both personal and elite concern about a decreasing capacity to maintain order. Ships remained anchored in the port for extended periods, less food arrived in Salvador from the interior, and troops deserted from the military arsenals and the National Guard.[26] President Martins estimated that one hundred thousand Bahians had been infected in a few months, noting that not more than one thousand slaves and free blacks (*escravos e negros livres*) died. Martins theorized that perhaps blacks possessed a special ability to resist infection.[27] In spite of residing in the more salubrious upper part of the city, well-to-do inhabitants became ill. Among these was the U.S. consul Thomas Turner, who succumbed to the sickness. This first outbreak of the epidemic subsided by April 1850. Nevertheless, the yellow-fever virus persisted in Bahia for almost four years; in May 1853, Bahians would face another outbreak.[28]

In seeking the sources of the epidemic, medical investigators found plenty of evidence to demonstrate that one source of the yellow fever had been people on board ships entering Brazilian ports. Some health officials argued that the yellow fever could be traced to the slavers. They subscribed to the ideas of the French physician M. F. M. Audouard, who wrote in a series of articles published from the 1820s to the early 1850s that the filthy conditions on slave ships facilitated the transmission of yellow fever. Brazilian medical doctors paid close attention to the "human cargo" who survived the transatlantic voyage from Africa, speculating that Africans possessed a special capacity for carrying yellow-fever germs in their bodies.[29]

The questions raised in 1850 over the origins of the yellow-fever epidemic contributed to the imperial government's decision to halt the slave trade. Influential politician (former minister of finance and prime minister) Manoel Alves Branco declared in a speech that he considered it quite "probable" that one of the principal reasons for the arrival of yellow fever could be traced to the slave trade.[30] Senators attributed the fact that the epidemic had missed Pernambuco due to the halt in the slave trade to that province.[31] In August, free citizens of Recife appeared at dockside to protest the arrival of a ship from Salvador for fear that its enslaved passengers would bring yellow fever. They questioned the origins of the slaves on board (whether recently imported from Africa or Brazilian-born), in spite of being assured by Recife's chief of police that all passports had been closely inspected with no irregularities discovered.[32]

Similarly, an outbreak of a cholera epidemic in Brazil further undermined the efforts of large investors who sought to return to the "golden age" of the slave trade (during the three decades previous to 1850).[33] In May 1855, the first signs of cholera appeared in the northern port city of Belém, Pará. Passengers on a ship soon carried the intestinal infection to Bahia; within six months it spread to the provinces of Sergipe, Alagoas, Rio Grande do Norte, Paraíba, and Pernambuco. Doctors did not know the specific reasons for the outbreak, but some asserted that cholera was a contagious virus that could be transmitted between persons.[34] Distinct from the earlier outbreak of yellow fever, free blacks and slaves bore the brunt of the cholera epidemic. One reason for this can be traced to unsanitary conditions (for example, bad meat and bad water) that engulfed the majority of people of color in both city and countryside.

The cholera epidemic devastated the province of Bahia. The estimated 46,000 persons who died included thousands of slaves in the townships of Santo Amaro and Cachoeira in the Recôncavo, regions with numerous

sugar *engenhos* (sugar mills; in Brazil it also means sugar plantations).[35]
A description of the period offers an estimate that 9,332 inhabitants
died in Salvador between August 1855 and May 1856.[36] One logical
response to this crisis in terms of the available workforce would have
been to import more African slaves, no matter the dangers involved. Yet
Brazilians recognized the arrival of more "unseasoned" Africans could
easily lead to the further spread of the dreaded cholera morbus. Even
the most ambitious planters could not disregard this threat. A future
resumption of the international slave trade might result in consequences
far worse than monetary loss, public humiliation, or British incursions
into Brazilian ports. The cholera epidemic of 1855–56 helped to seal the
fate of the transatlantic slave trade to Brazil.

In the midst of the epidemic, a schooner seeking to disembark
African slaves appeared off the coast of Brazil. One of at least 430
ships constructed in the United States involved in a transatlantic slave
voyage, the *Mary E. Smith* embarked from Boston on August 25,
1855.[37] Previous to its departure, the ship raised the suspicions of U.S.
and British authorities due to materials taken on board known to be
used on slaving vessels (for example, extra wood planks to construct a
slave deck, metal shackles, a large number of water casks). Fending off
arrest by a U.S. deputy marshal and a handful of men in his employ who
boarded the *Mary E. Smith* as it was pulled out of Boston harbor by a
tugboat, Captain Vincent D. Cranotick forced the intruders off the boat
and set sail eastward with a destination of Africa.[38]

After a voyage to the Congo region of Africa, where it took on 400
to 450 Africans between the ages of fifteen and twenty, the *Mary E.
Smith* arrived near São Mateus (the northern coast of the province of
Espírito Santo) in January 1856. Informed of a possible attempt to leave
African slaves on the coast, the British steamship *Olinda* seized the vessel
and escorted it to Salvador. Port authorities there estimated that at least
seventy-one Africans had died from sickness picked up on board the ship
between the time of interception off the Brazilian coast on January 20
and arrival in Salvador on January 31.

Bahian officials condemned the *Mary E. Smith* and brought the surviving Africans into the city. This act "caused terror among the population of the city," spurred by the belief that the presence of ill Africans would further spread the cholera epidemic. Bahian doctors and health officials offered medical care and provided food, which supposedly improved the Africans' health. In spite of such measures, one hundred more of the Africans who had arrived on the ship died during the following two weeks. By February 14, out of two hundred thirteen Africans who survived, eighty-eight remained desperately ill, suffering from a variety of sicknesses, including cholera morbus.[39] Incidents of infection markedly increased in the city in February. Inhabitants attributed the spread of cholera during that month to the Africans from the *Mary E. Smith* and the decision to allow them to disembark.[40]

Abolitionist Stirrings

Aware of an aggressive British naval squadron and international condemnation of the slave trade and slavery, reformers in Salvador established two abolitionist societies at midcentury. One was named the "Philanthropic Society of Bahia to Benefit those Brazilians who had the Misfortune to be Born Slaves." It included among its members slaves and free persons. The Philanthropic Society sought recognition of its statutes in early 1850, in a petition the chief of police promptly rejected. Chief of police André Corsino Pinto Chichôrro da Gama wrote that dangerous persons of the lowest classes who joined such an organization would quickly become "fanaticized" in a liberation movement.[41] The Philanthropic Society disappeared after a few months.

In 1852 a group at Salvador's famed Faculty of Medicine organized in support of abolition, named the "Second of July Emancipation Society." The group's name celebrated the date that Bahian forces successfully assured Brazil's independence in 1823 by defeating the last contingents of Portuguese troops in the nation. Similar to law schools in the cities of Recife and São Paulo, faculty members and students at the medical school in Salvador called for an end to slavery in Bahia.[42] Given the elevated social status of the group's members, police officials did little to impede them from holding their meetings. Nevertheless, when the Second of July

Emancipation Society dissolved after a few months, having accomplished little, provincial officials welcomed the society's demise.[43] They did not want individuals or organized groups of any sort questioning the right of Bahians to own slaves at this critical juncture. Nevertheless, professors and students at the Faculty of Medicine, including Luís Anselmo da Fonseca, Jerônimo Sodré, Francisco Alvares dos Santos, Eduardo Carigé, and Manoel Victorino, went on to play a leading role in the abolitionist movement in Bahia.

Conclusions

In their study of the "Hidden History of the Revolutionary Atlantic," Peter Lindbaugh and Marcus Rediker trace the spread of revolutionary vectors through turbulent port cities of the Americas. One of these ideological currents included British abolitionist thought and protest commencing in the 1780s.[44] For Brazilians, efforts to end the international slave trade became the most obvious manifestation of the shift in British attitudes and official policy. From 1811 to the mid-1850s, the British navy intercepted slaving ships with ties to Salvador throughout the Atlantic Basin. Bahians with investments in the slave trade vehemently protested, for example, in a letter signed by Bahian merchants to the king of England in 1845 complaining of the "aggressions inflicted [*violências que soffrem*] on Brazilian ships by English cruisers."[45] The appearance of the British navy along the Bahian coast and in the Bay of All Saints made an indelible impression on inhabitants of Salvador, indicating clearly diminished support for slavery in the Atlantic world.

"Subversive news networks" associated with maritime trade that flourished during the first half of the nineteenth century quickly disseminated details of such episodes.[46] Evidence abounds. Slaves laboring in the port of Salvador and in boats along the coast willingly spread news. Slaves transporting goods from Salvador to the Recôncavo on boats shared information with slaves residing in the interior of the province about British activities. Slaves and free persons involved in domestic and international travel disseminated firsthand accounts about events, persons, and resistance related to international abolition.

In spite of British and U.S. efforts to suppress the slave trade since the early nineteenth century, traffickers continued to land Africans on Bahian beaches and in Salvador through the early 1850s. By midcentury, thousands of recently imported African and crioulo slaves resided in Salvador and in other parts of Bahia. Their presence caused discomfort and fear among the free population of Bahia, even as their labor enriched planters. Outbreaks of infectious disease and attacks on slave ships along the African coast added to the tensions of those years. To gain a fuller picture of the closure of the slave trade and the first stirrings of an organized abolitionist movement, the African world in Bahia calls for our attention. Most importantly, we need to evaluate the role of slave resistance in causing Bahian officials to act with unprecedented commitment and effectiveness from the late 1840s. ▣

CHAPTER TWO

"There Are Too Many Slaves in This Port City of Salvador!"

Slave Resistance and the
End of the Slave Trade to Bahia

In 1850, former Chargé d'Affaires at the British consulate in Rio de Janeiro William Gore Ouseley appeared before the House of Lords in Great Britain. A diplomat with long experience in Brazil (he was head of the consulate from 1832 to 1836 and 1838 to 1841, and then visited Brazil again in 1845 and 1848), Ouseley commented on the manner in which Brazilians had responded to British efforts to suppress the international slave trade to Brazil. He stated:

> When I first went out to Rio de Janeiro, there was no hope whatever of inducing the Brazilians to look upon suppressive measures against the Slave Trade, otherwise than as a mere fiscal regulation, as far as their own Government was concerned, and as dictated by jealousy and the competition of the British Colonies on the part of our Government, without any regard to humanity. No enlarged ideas of policy, nor any question of the injurious influence it might have upon Brazil, had ever entered into their heads, with the exception of one or two distinguished men, such as the Andrades, who opposed it on moral grounds and those of justice and humanity, and some others, who considered the trade in a political light as fraught with danger. Subsequently an insurrection occurred in Bahia [in 1835], which induced the Brazilian government to look with some anxiety to the increase of the Negro population, and the danger arising from it.[1]

In June 1852, Brazil's minister of justice, José Ildefonso de Sousa Ramos, reflected on why his government acted with uncharacteristic determination to end the international slave trade after 1850. Brazil had signed a treaty with Great Britain in 1830 that outlawed the transport of African slaves to Brazil. Suppression efforts during the two decades that followed (1830 to 1850) did little to halt the importation of thousands of slaves all along the coast. Sousa Ramos wrote:

> The imperial government [of Brazil] helped to bring about the complete extinction of the traffic as a measure of social convenience, of civilization, of national honor, and even of public security. [Such initiatives] show to be true a fact of great importance—that the government of Brazil has enough force to carry out its searches and to execute effectively its laws.[2]

This statement by a high-ranking official raises important questions. To what extent did memories of the 1835 insurrection in Bahia influence attitudes and political decisions among Brazilians to end the international slave trade fifteen years later in 1850? And what about the minister's use of the words public security? Did Sousa Ramos mean that the actions of the British Navy—which included confiscation of slave ships, incursions into Brazilian ports like Salvador's Bay of All Saints in 1850–51, and even searches of estates along the coast—had threatened the sovereignty and security of the Brazilian state, thereby forcing imperial ministers to act? Did he echo a belief held by both United States and British diplomats that such interventions by the British might jeopardize the stability of the slave regime?[3]

Public security in Brazil had been threatened by the rebellious acts of slaves and by the fears engendered by this turbulence had instilled in the Brazilian elite by the late 1840s. Slave resistance, and social tensions closely related to it, influenced Brazilian imperial officials in their decision to support complete termination of the slave trade between Africa and Brazil. Several important events helped to bring about this decision. A major slave rebellion in 1835 in Salvador known as the Malês (Muslims)

Map 2.1 Nineteenth-Century Brazil.

Revolt left the master class deeply concerned about the ability of slaves and freedpersons to organize a revolt during the following two decades. The arrival of African slaves through the ports of Salvador and Rio de Janeiro added to elite fears that more slave revolts would occur.

This chapter focuses on the way in which internal pressures contributed to Brazil's final suppression of the slave trade. This perspective in no way diminishes British contributions to this endeavor.[4] Conditions within Brazil, particularly the presence of several thousand recently arrived Africans in the ports of Salvador and Rio de Janeiro, also played a significant role in ending the slave trade. This chapter sheds light on the question of why popular and official opinion in Brazil shifted quickly in 1850–51 in support of immediate and full termination of the trade.[5]

"Little Africas"

The arrival of African slaves to Salvador and along more remote stretches of the coast to avoid detection transformed the city into a "little Africa."[6]

Table 2.1. Estimates of Slave and
Total Population in Brazil, 1798–1890

Year	Slave Population	Total Population	Slaves as % of Total Population
1770	700,000		
1798	1,582,000	3,248,000	49
1818	1,930,000	3,817,000	51
1850	2,500,000	5,500,000	45
1864	1,715,000		
1872	1,700,000	10,112,000	17
1880	1,368,000		
1881	1,272,000		
1884	1,240,000		
1885	1,177,000		
1888	approx. 750,000		
1890		14,353,915	

Sources: Robert Conrad, *The Destruction of Brazilian Slavery, 1850–1888* (Berkeley: University of California Press, 1972), 283–85; Katia M. de Queirós Mattoso, *Bahia, século xix: Uma província no império*, trans. Yedda de Macedo Soares (Rio de Janeiro: Editora Nova Fronteira, 1992), 87, 110; James Dunkerley, *Americana: The Americas in the World, Around 1850 (Or 'Seeing the Elephant' As the Theme for an Imaginary Western)* (London: Verso, 2000), 403; Hastings Charles Dent, *A Year in Brazil* (London: Kegan Paul, Trench and Co., 1886), 294–95.

In 1835, 27,500 slaves resided in Salvador. These slaves constituted 42 percent of Salvador's population of 65,500. African-born slaves numbered 17,325, or 63 percent of the slave population. Hence, the majority of slaves in Salvador had been born in Africa and were culturally distinct foreigners in Bahia. The number of Brazilians of color, either free or manumitted, combined with freed Africans totaled about 19,500 persons. White inhabitants of Salvador composed a minority (28.8 percent) of the city's population.[7]

Similar conditions prevailed in the city of Rio de Janeiro, where slaves constituted by one estimate 38.3 percent of the population by

TABLE 2.2. ESTIMATES OF LARGEST PROVINCIAL
SLAVE POPULATIONS IN BRAZIL, 1864

Maranhão	70,000
Ceará	36,000
Alagôas	50,000
Sergipe	55,000
Pernambuco	260,000
Bahia	300,000
Minas Gerais	250,000
Rio de Janeiro	400,000 (including an estimated 100,000 in the city of Rio de Janeiro)
São Paulo	80,000
Rio Grande do Sul	40,000

Source: Robert Conrad, *The Destruction of Brazilian Slavery, 1850–1888* (Berkeley: University of California Press, 1972), 285.

1849. African-born slaves numbered 52,341, or more than 65 percent of the slave population of Brazil's capital.[8] The presence at midcentury of more than one hundred thousand slaves made Rio de Janeiro the city with the largest slave population in the Americas. Significant numbers of slaves, both African-born and Brazilian-born, resided in other coastal towns, including São Luís (Maranhão Province), Fortaleza (Ceará), Recife (Pernambuco), Maceió (Alagoas), Vitória (Espírito Santo), the city of São Paulo, and Santos (on the coast of São Paulo Province).[9]

By 1850, Brazil's slave population reached its highest number ever.

African and crioulo slaves profoundly influenced both urban and rural society in Bahia from the sixteenth to the nineteenth centuries.[10] Male slaves unloaded large ships and sailed small vessels in the harbors. They provided architectural and construction skills; many labored as artisans, tailors, and barbers. Female slaves educated their own children and raised the offspring of other Bahians while serving as domestic laborers in urban households. Slaves contributed to the creation of a rich popular culture.[11] They cultivated food on small plots both in cities and countryside. Slave labor and expertise enabled planters to produce agricultural commodities for a profit. By the early 1860s, the largest number of urban and rural slaves resided in the provinces of Bahia and Rio de Janeiro.

During the years of economic prosperity in the first half of the nineteenth century, planters large and small joined the merchant elite in paying close attention to the slave trade. On the one hand, they wanted access to cheap workers; therefore they facilitated all aspects of the slave trade between Africa and Brazil. On the other hand, their concerns over personal and public security mounted as the slave population grew through illegal importation.

The rebelliousness of African-born slaves had been demonstrated repeatedly. In Bahia, between 1807 and 1835 the combination of more than twenty rural and urban slave revolts left slave owners distraught. By the 1830s, social instability caused by economic depression, slave revolts and violence, slave flight, the existence of *quilombos* (escaped slave communities) and elite repression characterized Brazil's two largest cities (Salvador and Rio de Janeiro) and their hinterlands. Other provinces in the Brazilian empire (Pernambuco, Alagoas, Pará, Maranhão, Rio Grande do Sul) also witnessed violent conflicts in the decade of the 1830s.[12] These outbreaks have been described by historians Leslie Bethell and José Murilo de Carvalho as "the most radical and violent rebellions in Brazilian history, before or since."[13]

The maintenance of social cohesion in the empire became an issue of paramount importance. Political debates ensued over how to control rebellious slaves and what lay in store for a nation that included so many Africans and persons of color among its inhabitants.[14] Even naïve observers recognized that an expanding slave trade could have dangerous results in the future. In particular, Brazilians asked whether Brazil might succumb to an African-led revolt similar to what had occurred in the Haitian Revolution.[15]

The Malê Revolt

In the early hours of Sunday, January 24, 1835, the worst fears of Bahia's embattled elite came true. Some six hundred African slaves and freedmen,

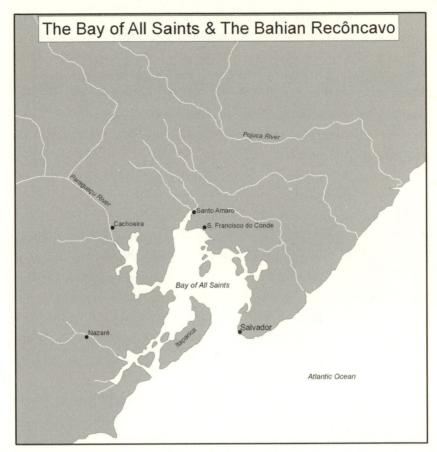

Map 2.2 The Bay of All Saints and the Bahian Recôncavo.

many dressed in white *abadás* (long frocks worn by Muslims) ran through the streets of Salvador shouting and shooting guns. For three hours they fought against at least fifteen hundred well-armed police, cavalry, National Guard soldiers, and civilians with swords, knives, clubs, and a few pistols. The uprising had been planned for months; African slaves and African freedmen from both Salvador and the neighboring region joined in the fighting.

Officials learned of the impending outbreak from two female Nagô (the term used in Bahia for the Yoruba) former slaves a few hours before the attack was launched, and they responded with great efficiency. More than seventy Africans died that night and in the tumultuous days that followed. In succeeding months, seven hundred Africans faced punishments that included execution, imprisonment, whipping, and deportation to Africa or other parts of the Brazilian empire. Nine persons who entered the battle against the Africans also died the first night. During the ensuing two decades, this failed revolt haunted slave owners and government officials throughout Brazil.

Muslim slaves played a predominant role in the 1835 uprising. Known as Malês in Bahia, African slaves who followed Islam originated from different regions and ethnic backgrounds in Africa.[16] From the late eighteenth century, ships carried thousands of slaves primarily from the Gulf of Benin in West Africa (present-day southwest Nigeria and Republic of Benin) to Bahia. Yoruba, Jeje, and Hausa composed the largest numbers of these Africans. By the 1820s Nagô slaves from the kingdom of the Yoruba made up the majority of Muslim slaves arriving to Bahia. As a result, a "Yoruba-ization" occurred by the 1830s, meaning that Yoruba Africans became the predominant ethnic group among Muslim and non-Muslim slaves and freedpersons in Bahia.[17]

The Bahian historian João José Reis emphasizes that the Malês "had a charged identity and provided a strong point of reference for Africans living there. Slaves and freedmen flocked to Islam in search of spiritual comfort and hope. They needed to establish some order and dignity in their lives."[18] These Malês had great respect for written Arabic texts; they shared their knowledge of and belief in the Koran with other Africans living in Salvador. Such intellectual skills, discipline, and determination to practice their religious beliefs left a marked impression on free Bahians, few of whom could read or write Portuguese. In the minds of many free persons, Islam became associated with subversion. From the perspective of the Bahian elite, another Malê Revolt had to be prevented by whatever means.

The 1835 revolt made clear to government officials the potential dangers tied to an expanding slave trade. One of the first letters written by the president of Bahia after the upheaval of January 24–25 alluded to the potentially "horrifying effects of similar uprisings in a province where indubitably the blacks outnumber immeasurably the whites." President Francisco de Souza Martins feared that revolts could break out in other regions of the province and emphasized the peril of allowing so many Africans to enter Bahia as part of the illegal slave trade. He wondered how this traffic could be interrupted, given the involvement of local court officials and powerful landowners.[19] The revolt of the Malês, however, did little to deter planters and merchants involved in the slave trade; importations continued to climb through 1835 and 1836, with minimal interference from local authorities along the coast.[20]

Nevertheless, concern over the outbreak of another insurrection lingered among Bahian government and police officials. Contemporary documents portray a sense of anxiety in Salvador and the outlying regions of the Recôncavo.[21] Dismay spread during the federalist uprising known as the Sabinada, in which several thousand Bahian rebels, led by radical liberals and militia and army officers, gained control of Salvador for four months, from November 1837 to March 1838. The rebels called for legal reforms, decreased taxes, an end to the privileges afforded to aristocrats, and greater autonomy for the province of Bahia from the imperial monarchy in Rio de Janeiro. To mount an effective counterattack, the provincial government-in-exile established its base in the town of Cachoeira in the Recôncavo. Composed of influential planters, it raised an estimated twenty-two hundred troops. This promonarchy faction sought to ensure that the civil war that had erupted over political differences did not lead to another slave insurrection.

In February 1838, head of the rebel government João Carneiro da Silva Rego decreed Brazilian-born slaves freed. Although personally opposed to abolition, the enlistment of several hundred slaves in the rebel army forced Carneiro's decision. In the words of the Canadian historian Hendrik Kraay, "Needless to say, these developments [the freeing of crioulo slaves] accelerated the exodus of whites from the city and caused deep concern in the diplomatic and merchant communities, not to mention the already worried provincial government."[22] A rebel army composed of Brazilian-born slaves and lower-class free persons of color heightened trepidation among planters over their capacity to maintain control over their slave property.[23] An estimated 1,091 rebels died in the fighting, with 40 dead among government soldiers during the final assault on Salvador on March 13. Local militia and imperial troops carried out fierce repression in the days that followed, including the execution of unarmed prisoners and widespread arrests. This repression of liberals ensured Bahia's inclusion in the empire and the continuation of slavery.

Several incidents reflected the continuing insecurity among the inhabitants of Salvador in the wake of the Malê and Sabinada rebellions. On April 19, 1840, an alarm was sounded at 8:00 p.m. to warn of the outbreak of a slave insurrection. This information quickly spread through the city. Families strolling in the streets immediately returned to their homes, while "considerable forces" of male citizens met at various locations to prepare for a battle with the insurgents. Police officials soon ordered these vigilante groups to disband. Dismissing the event as based on unfounded rumor and innuendo, chief of police Francisco Vigário Lobato affirmed that "given that it is well known that there is nothing to fear for the public security, in a short time tranquility returned." He could not ascertain the reason for such heightened "fears of an insurrection of Africans." In spite of widespread investigations in the days that followed, police found no evidence that slaves had plotted to rebel.[24]

This near-panic incident of April 1840 characterized the decade that followed. Thousands of African slaves arrived in Salvador and along nearby beaches. The free population often expressed their concern over the continued importation of Africans, fearing another big slave revolt. Police responded with searches and interrogations. Provincial officials assured the populace that rumors of a revolt were unfounded. They sought to demonstrate their capacity to snuff out any manifestation of organized slave resistance.

Tensions related to the African presence in Bahia continued. In 1844, police arrested an African freedman in Salvador who had been "an active participant" in the Malê Revolt. Officials accused him of conspiring with slaves and other African freedmen to incite another rebellion.[25] Police clamped down on "reunions" of Africans aboard boats in the harbor.

They emphasized the need to "maintain the greatest vigilance possible" over African freedpersons, particularly women, who traveled with minimal restrictions to sell goods in the nearby Recôncavo (*negociar para o recôncavo*).[26] The escaped slave named Lucas vexed authorities. Famous for his exploits since the early 1830s, Lucas led a group of escaped slaves and poor folk in attacks on estates near the interior town of Feira de Santana throughout 1844.[27]

The Bahian elite demanded of its police the greatest diligence in searching for African and crioulo slaves involved in suspicious activities.[28] Planters and overseers did not hesitate to punish slaves in their attempts to thwart any inclination to challenge authority or to organize a rebellion.[29] Police officials suggested that citizens who provided information about persons involved in the slave trade be paid rewards for their services, as stipulated by imperial law (Article 5 of the law of November 7, 1831). Police also called for more effective searches of quilombos suspected of harboring escaped slaves.[30]

Bahian provincial president Joaquim José Pinheiro de Vasconcelos petitioned the imperial government to take stronger measures to prohibit slave disembarkations, particularly in his province. Slave vessels had been able to leave Africans on shore at clandestine locations without interference. Vasconcelos believed that "given the huge number" of African slaves already in the province "and repeated attempts at insurrection," the arrival of more Africans would result in disastrous consequences.[31]

Another legacy of the revolt of the Malês was popular hostility toward the Muslim religion. Both the appeal of Islam and the number of its followers among Africans in Bahia were increasing at the time of the 1835 rebellion. João José Reis writes that Islam made the slaves "want not to be slaves or inferiors; it gave them dignity; and it created new personalities for its members." The Muslim leadership of the 1835 revolt (the most influential being Nagô Malês) had hoped to forge an "African front" among Africans (slave and freed) of different ethnic backgrounds and religions against mutual enemies (which included whites along with Brazilian-born crioulos of African descent without regard to their color).[32] Although seeking an immediate end to their enslavement, the Malês never spoke of an abolitionist agenda for other provinces. Nevertheless, the revolt had a profound impact on slave owners throughout the empire. To impede any further spread of Islam among slaves and freedpersons in the aftermath of the uprising, police seized objects used in Islamic ceremonies and any documents written in Arabic that they encountered.

The president of Bahia, Joaquim Marcellino de Britto, considered fear of another revolt "not without just cause." In the wake of the 1835 uprising, provincial officials called for the deportation of all freed Africans (*Africanos libertos*) from the province. Britto suggested that the imperial government negotiate with the United States over the possibility of deporting suspicious individuals to the African nation of Liberia, where former slaves from the United States had been settled.[33] Lacking resources to pay for transportation, this "most ambitious anti-African campaign" in Brazilian history failed.[34] Hostility toward African slaves and African freedpersons along with widespread distrust of Islam continued.

For the next twenty years, Bahian officials searched incessantly for Arabic documents and books, evidence of the practice of Islamic rituals, and signs of suspicious activities or meetings where rebellion might be fomented.[35] In 1849, chief of police João Mauricio Wanderley (1815–89) accused the freedman Joaquim Antônio Guimarães of carrying subversive correspondence written "in the language of the Nagô" on board a ship he frequented that sailed between Salvador and Rio de Janeiro. Wanderley suspected the African to be part of an interprovincial African communication network, which easily could have been true. Guimarães was forced to return to Africa, one of numerous deportations of suspicious African freedpersons.[36]

The arrest in Salvador in December 1850 of the African freedman Claudio for writing "Hebrew words" (most likely Arabic) reflected continuing turmoil provoked by unknown script. The arrest occurred at a turbulent moment. Africans had proven themselves capable of effective organization in the port of Salvador. The Eusébio de Queiroz Law making illegal continued importations of African slaves had been passed less than two months previous. Claiming to be a resident in the nearby province of Sergipe and carrying a legal passport, Claudio asked simply that he be allowed exit from Salvador. After an investigation, police acceded to his request and he returned to his home.[37]

British vice consul in Salvador James Wetherell wrote, "The moment the police find out the [black] man is in possession of such writing [in Arabic], they cry out plots and assassinations, rising of slaves and murders; and the poor black fellows are imprisoned and perhaps banished from the country, the greatest crime proved against them being these mystical figures."[38] Wetherell was describing events he claimed to witness in 1856, more than two decades after the revolt of the Malês.

Officials throughout the empire viewed with grave suspicion the Arabic language and Islam. In early September 1853, police in the city of Recife, Pernambuco, arrested several Africans accused of organizing "a new religious sect" under the leadership of a Muslim African freedman named Rufino. Among the materials confiscated by the police was a Koran and "many sheets of paper written in Hebraic [Hebrew, meaning in fact Arabic]."[39] News of the arrests provoked alarm that Muslims were planning a slave revolt. The city remained on edge for several days. The chief of police in Recife requested a translation of one of the pages written in Arabic by authorities in the capital of Rio de Janeiro. This precious document (found perfectly preserved at Brazil's National Archives in Rio de Janeiro) turned out to be devoted to marriage vows, not rebellion.[40] The apprehension of documents written in Arabic and other languages demonstrates that owners of slaves throughout Brazil remembered well the revolt of the Malês. To prevent the outbreak of another slave insurrection, the elite did everything in its power to impede the spread of what Carioca historians Carlos Eugênio Líbano Soares and Flávio Gomes have labeled "Malê contamination."[41]

Concern over Islamic slaves, particularly those of Nagô origin, surfaced in Rio de Janeiro.[42] In the aftermath of the 1835 revolt, owners in Salvador sold several hundred African and crioulo slaves to purchasers in Rio de Janeiro. Hundreds more Nâgo African freedpersons joined in the "exodus" from Salvador to flee persecution.[43] Some Africans who had been directly involved in the 1835 uprising in Salvador resurfaced in the city of Rio de Janeiro where their presence came to the immediate attention

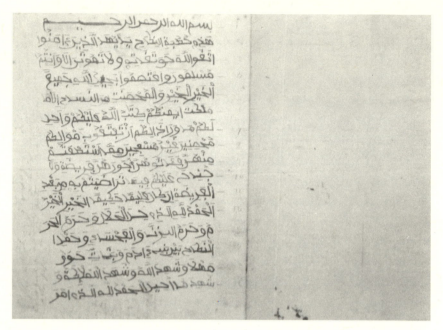

Figures 2.1 and 2.2 Arabic document sent by police of Recife, Pernambuco, to police in the city of Rio de Janeiro in October 1853, requesting translation. Courtesy of The National Archives of Brazil, located in Rio de Janeiro.

of the police. In May 1835, two of these Africans applied for permission to take up permanent residence in Rio de Janeiro. Police officials rejected the request and immediately deported the two to Africa.

Previous to the influx of the refugee slaves and freedpersons from Salvador in 1835, officials in Rio de Janeiro had never encountered materials penned by slaves. Not surprisingly, documents that surfaced written by slaves in Arabic and other languages became of utmost concern after the Malê uprising.[44] Within a month of the rebellion in Salvador, the chief of police in the city of Rio de Janeiro requested that an African Nagô (most likely a freedman) interpret a letter "in the writing of the Nagôs of Bahia." Chief of police Eusébio de Queiroz Coutinho Matoso Câmara (1812–68) learned that the document did not include letters in the language of the Nagô (Yoruba), but rather in Arabic, the "other idiom, which only the Nagôs of great education understand." The translation included homage to Allah and words that "seemed like those used by persons in the East."

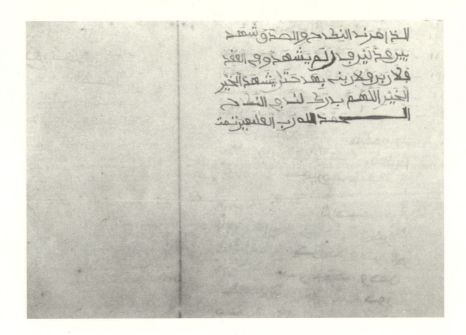

Queiroz associated the document with religious rites practiced by Nagôs to gain inspiration and spiritual fulfillment.

This letter provides a unique entrée into the far-reaching African world of urban Rio de Janeiro. Muslim slaves communicated and shared information among themselves through letters. In this case, a dialogue ensues between God and the living over whether to engage in battle. According to Soares and Gomes, the words allude to a debate among Islamic Africans on how best to resist enslavement, whether through open rebellion or nonviolent means.[45] Recently expelled Africans from Salvador offered their perspectives on the chances of a successful revolt in their new home of Rio de Janeiro to other Muslims.

Implementation of harsh imperial legislation to control slaves and African freedpersons must be considered another legacy of the 1835 revolt. An edict of February 1835 made it more difficult for slaves and freedpersons to move about in the city after 8:00 p.m. Laws passed in May and June 1835 sought to expel all African freedpersons from Salvador (one estimate for 1835 being 4,615 Africans, or 7.1 percent of the city's population) and imposed a costly annual tax of 10$ (approximately US $8.00) on all freedpersons. The provincial government deported several hundred freedpersons back to Africa, to remote provinces of the empire, or to islands off the coast. It prohibited Africans from purchasing real estate and offered a reward to slaves and freedpersons who provided information about slave conspirators.[46] Imperial Law 4 of June 10, 1835, determined that any slave who killed an owner, overseer, or members of a slaveholding family would face execution.

African freedpersons in Bahia suffered constant harassment at the hands of the police, particularly when tensions peaked over fear of a slave rebellion (in February to June 1835, April to May 1840, May to June 1844, January 1849 to January 1850, March to May 1853, and March to December 1855).[47] A perception among inhabitants of Salvador that African freedpersons incited newly arrived African slaves to rebel contributed to this hostility. Words preserved in court documents reflect the anxiety experienced by African freedpersons in Bahia at midcentury. A lawyer defending an African freedman arrested for suspicious activities pointed out that Albino Antônio d'Almeida had purchased his freedom with savings he had earned while a slave. According to the attorney, both as a slave and later as a freedman, this African had resided for many years in Bahia without any problems with the police and had gained an upstanding reputation as a hard worker. D'Almeida was married and had four children born in Brazil whom he desired to provide with an education. Why, the lawyer asked the court, would such a man who "clearly enjoys his freedom conspire against whites."[48] Unfortunately we do not know the outcome of the case.

Concern about the presence of slaves, African freedpersons, and liberated Africans in Bahia and other locales inspired discussions among antislavery proponents that focused on alternatives to the slave trade. One newspaper editor asserted that conditions in Brazil would be improved by the use of indentured African colonists as agricultural laborers rather than by the importation of African slaves. He encouraged imperial officials to promote free immigration with money from the public treasury. Fair treatment and the assurance of future freedom would provide indentured black workers personal satisfaction. By coming to Brazil, these Africans would gain "rational customs, a physical and moral education, a pure and divine religion, a political existence . . . all of this only in return for their services offered for a required time."[49]

In *The Substitution of Slave Labor by Free Workers in Brazil* (Rio de Janeiro, 1845), Henrique Velloso de Oliveira of Pernambuco claimed that laziness and idleness were the roots of all the evils in society, and that people who owned slaves manifested these indolent characteristics. By promoting free labor, "sickness, hunger, war . . . misery, the devil, slave traders . . . all would be obliterated . . . in their place would flourish well-being, abundance, peace and fortune." The author suggested a program of land reform and the recruitment of fifteen thousand young men who would be distributed throughout the nation in industrial companies. Penned originally in 1842, Oliveira held back from publishing the pamphlet for three years out of fear of retribution from a group of "refined thieves" (meaning slave owners and traders) who had harassed him for a decade.[50] The appearance of such ideas and accusations in print reflected clear disillusionment in some quarters over the continuing arrival of large numbers of African slaves.

"The Africans Are Always Scheming": The Last Months of the International Slave Trade, 1848–50

Brazilians involved in the slave trade defended themselves as responsible citizens and enlightened masters.[51] Well-informed of international events, Brazil's elite did not desire to experience what had occurred during the 1848 worker revolts in Europe or during the slave revolts in the Caribbean Basin and other nations in South America.[52] Nevertheless, their actions belied their belief that the benefits of continued slave importations outweighed potential consequences. Merchants, urban slave owners, rural planters, and influential politicians all expressed confidence that the centralized constitutional monarchy situated in Rio de Janeiro could maintain order.[53]

By the late 1840s, agitation again convulsed the Brazilian empire. Slave owners faced mounting tensions from early 1847, particularly in Salvador. This situation can be traced to slave violence, popular fears of Africans, and the appearance of organized abolitionist expression. These pressures, combined with aggressive British naval actions from mid-1850, resulted in passage of the Eusébio de Queiroz Law in September 1850, which forced an end to the transatlantic trade to Brazil.[54]

A sense of danger in Salvador can be discerned in the correspondence of Provincial President João de Moura Magalhães in February 1848.

> I am writing truthfully, providing exact information of what is happening in this province. . . . We need prompt and energetic measures to prevent insurrections by Africans. . . . Everyone still remembers what happened in 1835, [a revolt] that would have produced far greater destruction, if it had not been promptly annihilated.[55]

Magalhães lamented what he considered to be the insufficient number of police and National Guard troops stationed in the province. He argued that the security of the white minority could not be assured in Salvador and in nearby towns and townships of the Recôncavo with large slave populations (Cachoeira, Santo Amaro, and Nazaré). The president believed that an outbreak of slave revolts was likely, given the number of slaves transported into the province and "a whole population, with rare exceptions, interested in the continuation of the terrible traffic." Magalhães pondered specific battle tactics and weapons that could best be employed to put down an insurrection of slaves.[56] A citizen's patrol created at this time carried out arrests of suspicious Africans.

The chief of police emphasized the importance of maintaining strict controls over the sale of machetes, knives, and guns in the urban market of Salvador for fear that Africans, whether slave or free, might purchase or steal them. Police delegates took notice of weapons and other "objects" that could be employed in an insurrection and that might easily be concealed on beaches along the Bay of All Saints, or even underwater.[57] "There is no doubt that the Africans, regardless if they are free or slaves, are always scheming [*machinão sempre*], and they never lose sight of anything [that is happening]."[58] Awareness of "the very frequent assassinations" that had occurred fueled disquiet over the availability and low price of weapons in Salvador and the interior of the province.[59]

Echoing accusations common since 1835, Magalhães labeled African freedpersons as the "agitators behind the insurrections." He commenced a series of arrests of African freedpersons and slaves for a variety of offenses that continued unabated from early 1848 until the middle of 1850. The police commonly accused African freedpersons of violations of the edict of February 21, 1835 (decreed in the immediate aftermath of the revolt of the Malês, all slaves encountered outside after 8:00 p.m. were required to have in their possession a pass signed by their masters, and the fate of an arrested freedperson "would be appropriate to their circumstances"). Police carried out searches of houses and investigated several hundred African freedpersons. Police closely scrutinized the racial profile and geographic origins of all persons arrested at Candomblé *terreiros* (sacred meeting places for African Brazilian religious expression). Viewed as subversive foci, police emphasized the particular threat caused by African freedpersons attending such gatherings.

Police arrested the African freedman Lucio Jeronimo da Costa in early 1850, accusing him along with other African freedpersons of plotting an insurrection. Chief of police A. C. P. Chichôrro da Gama wrote:

> Everybody knows that the rumors of an insurrection reached a peak in January 1850. The head of this group of Africans was the black named Lucio; he is an African freedperson. The police carried out arrests and searches, and in some of the houses of the negros they found harpoons made from iron, rings with points and books of the occult [*livros cabalísticos*]. At the house of Lucio were found garments made of silk. [We found] his own wife carrying clothes which she planned to throw into the pond [*dique*], the same clothes worn by the barbarous ringleaders

of other insurrections [most likely the white frocks worn by Muslim African slaves and African freedpersons].

The wealth and cunning of the negro Lucio, and the way in which all of the blacks looked at him as a sort of idol, was greatly to be feared; without doubt, we hoped that Divine Justice would protect us from the bloody scenes of 1835. This negro for certain has been the leader of this movement. I did not hesitate to deport him [to Africa]. Some [freedpersons] have already departed from the province; the black Lucio has remained with my permission so that he could sell his personal possessions. Not only public security requires the deportation of this dangerous African, but also our morals demand it.

In the backyard of this African there existed a temple or meeting place for a cult to pay homage to a deity—the idol is here at police headquarters; he [Lucio] attracted superstitious persons to this location, not only Africans, but also persons born in Brazil, who deposited offerings to the owner [Lucio]. He was also able to make money by renting his house during the day or night to individuals who sought to exploit young people who went there to learn about their future or for reasons of health.[60]

On June 12, 1850, police deported Lucio and the African freedwoman Felicidade to Africa on the U.S. ship *Bridgeton* (a ship known to be involved in the slave trade). Officials legitimized their decision based on law number 9 of May 13, 1835. This law allowed for the "expulsion from the province of any African freedpersons of either sex suspected of fomenting an insurrection of slaves in any way." Chief of police Chichôrro da Gama admitted that no evidence had been found implicating the Africans in planning a revolt. Nevertheless, Bahian authorities interpreted the law as they saw fit so as to enable them to expel suspicious or disruptive African freedpersons from Bahia. Through such acts, they hoped to prevent another revolt like the one that had occurred fifteen years earlier in 1835.

Sporadic acts of violence by individual slaves or small groups of slaves inspired free residents to propose ways to protect themselves.

One "property owner" claimed that liberated Africans (taken from slave ships by the British squadron) who labored at the navy arsenal had been responsible for inciting disorder in the city.[61] These liberated Africans had "enticed slaves to practice cult rituals" and emboldened them to seek their freedom. A police delegate proposed to President Magalhães that he deport the dangerous liberated Nagô Africans to Rio de Janeiro. In return, Bahia would receive liberated Africans of other ethnicities (also rescued by the British naval squadron from slaving vessels) and disembarked in Rio de Janeiro. Such a policy would undermine the capacity of Nagôs to organize and thus would lessen popular fears.[62] Apprehension over Nagô subversion might explain why Bahian owners sent particular African slaves to Rio de Janeiro at this juncture while purchasing other slaves in Rio de Janeiro and transporting them to Salvador.[63]

Deportations from Salvador of liberated Nâgo Africans led to some remarkable outcomes. In 1849, a group of Africans petitioned for their freedom to a local judge at the town of Sorocaba in the interior of the province of São Paulo. Claiming to have been rescued from a slaving vessel by the British sometime in the mid-1830s, the slaves based their complaint on two laws. First, the group invoked the 1831 anti-slave trade law, which stated that any African transported to Brazil after that date as a slave would be free. Second, the Africans stated that they had satisfied a requirement to labor for fourteen years after having been declared "liberated" (based on a decree of João VI in January 1818). Hence, they had been transferred as prisoners against their will from the navy arsenal in Salvador to Rio de Janeiro. They were then transported to São Paulo to work at an iron factory in the town of Ipanema.[64] The Paulista historian Beatriz Gallotti Mamigonian considers the petition one of the earliest manifestations of organized protest, if not the first, by Africans in Brazil who sought their emancipation through the established legal system.

The thousand African slaves who labored in the port of Salvador added to local social tensions. In August 1848, the Municipal Council of Salvador passed a law requiring slaves who transported goods on small boats to pay a tax. As a result, fights broke out at the docks between slaves unhappy with the increased costs and free workers who did not want to compete for jobs with slave sailors. In one incident (in January 1849), police arrested a fugitive female slave, a male slave, and an African male who claimed to be a freedman, accusing them of having incited a brawl. In late 1850, the Municipal Council prohibited all slaves and freedmen from further employment in the port. Seeking to replace the slave boatmen, city merchants purchased 185 small boats and offered them at no cost to interested free Bahians. On November 1, 1850, the president of the province celebrated this transition from slave to free labor in a public ceremony. From this date until emancipation in 1888, the provincial government annually commemorated this event, portraying it as a heroic abolitionist act.[65]

In correspondence with imperial ministers, President Francisco Gonçalves Martins explained that the substitution had occurred with minimal disruption of normal port traffic. He estimated that three hundred free Brazilian males had gained immediate employment, and that in the near future another two hundred could be offered jobs. Martins asserted that the provincial government desired to act in the best interests of the subsidized sailors and their families.

The true motives of President Martins and reasons for passage of Provincial Law 344 merit close scrutiny. Martins assumed the presidency of Bahia in 1848 with a worldview shaped by slave rebellion and sedition. As chief of police in Salvador in the wake of the revolt of the Malês and long experience in Bahian political affairs, Martins had often dealt harshly with Africans residing in the city. In late 1850, Martins reacted to the perceived danger that African slaves had gained control of the harbor, a key strategic location in the city. Martins pledged to extend benefits to free Brazilians "involved in [other public] services so that we are able to be free of the present necessity of having so many slaves joined together in this city."[66] One journalist shared the president's anxiety, characterizing the slave sailors who ferried goods and persons throughout the port as "that terrible nucleus of [slave] insurrections."[67]

The Municipal Council passed and the president implemented in 1850 (with the aid of private Brazilian business interests) this so-called abolitionist legislation out of fear of the number and power of the African slaves along with African freedpersons who plied the waters of the harbor. The desire of Brazilian merchants to expel Portuguese traders (many of whom owned slaves who labored in the port) and a belief that slave sailors had hidden fugitive slaves and transported recently arrived Africans to other locations on the coast also facilitated passage of this law.[68]

Even before the 1850 decision to clear the harbor of slaves, these fears were manifest. Several events in the period between 1848 and 1850 demonstrated the unease caused by the large numbers of Africans and slaves in Salvador. In 1848, a project to improve access to drinking water by laying water pipes in Salvador pursued the secondary objective of curtailing the independence and mobility of Africans. Once the pipes were laid, slave servants would no longer carry barrels or buckets of water through the hilly streets of the city and be granted easy access to private residences.[69] Likewise, a decision in 1848 to substitute free workers for slave labor on all public works projects in Salvador should be viewed as part of a strategy to maintain security throughout the city.[70]

In 1848, the Catholic Church officially recognized for the first time two mixed-race brotherhoods (Bom Jesus da Cruz and Nossa Senhora do Boqueirão). For free persons of color who had never been allowed entry into white brotherhoods, the new policy affirmed their increasing numbers and status in the city. But the act also helped to diminish the appeal of black brotherhoods (composed of free individuals and slaves). Widening the social distance between blacks and free persons of color undermined potential alliances between the two groups.[71] One year later in 1849, the emperor's Council of State followed this initiative by declaring that "any provisions which make hateful distinctions concerning mulatto citizens of Brazil or freedmen, such as excluding them from belonging to a religious brotherhood, etc., are unconstitutional."[72]

In September 1848, the young Pedro II replaced the Liberal cabinet with a group of Conservatives. He hoped that the new ministers would prove capable of addressing problems caused by a succession of incompetent predecessors, political disagreements with England and with Argentina, and outbreaks of violence fueled by political discord in various locales in the empire. Well-known politicians joined the new cabinet, including Eusébio de Queiroz, Honório Hermeto Carneiro Leão, Joaquim José Rodrigues Torres, Paulino José Soares de Sousa, and Bernardo Pereira de Vasconcelos. All had experience with the slave trade and the institution of slavery, either as investors or critics.

As members of what was known as the Party of Order, the Conservatives sought to reinforce stability throughout the empire by whatever means and at whatever cost. To the contrary, they did not wish to lose domestic and international prestige in the face of aggressive British naval commanders enforcing the slave-trade ban. Lower-level provincial officials paid close attention to the statements by the ministers and policies passed by the cabinet. They willingly joined in the effort to end the slave trade in response to demonstrated British resolve and the obvious commitment of imperial ministries. The central government in Rio de Janeiro and officials in outlying provinces showed an increased sensitivity to the abuse and immorality associated with slave disembarkations. Most had firsthand knowledge that the arrival of more African slaves made conflicts and violence more likely.[73]

By early 1850, newly elected representatives in the Chamber of Deputies commenced the debate over ending the slave trade to Brazil. By September, the National Assembly passed the Queiroz law that made further importations illegal and established mechanisms to enforce the law. How can we explain this rapid shift in policy by a government dominated by reactionaries? British pressure certainly played an important role, but it was not the sole reason. The U.S. historian Jeffrey D. Needell suggests that "deft response of the Brazilian statesmen was crucial."[74] A third key variable can be traced to the actions of Africans residing in Salvador and Rio de Janeiro.

Public speeches in the imperial Senate demonstrate how concern about slave resistance influenced the debate over ending the slave trade. Minister of Foreign Affairs Paulino José Soares de Sousa stated:

50,000, 60,000, or 100,000 Africans had been imported each year to Brazil. Would we not be advised by all moral considerations, by civilization, in our desire to ensure our own security and that of our children, to put an end to the importation of Africans?[75]

Seeking to prevent a resurgence of the slave trade eight months after passage of the Queiroz Law, arch-Conservative Honório Hermeto Carneiro Leão inquired of his colleagues in the Senate in May 1851:

Was not the level of importations of Africans [through 1850] excessive, was it not too much, would it not have brought future dangers to the country [Brazil]? It is in our interest [to support the 1831 Brazilian law ending the slave trade], because the importation of Africans has been excessive, because the provinces from Bahia to the south found themselves overburdened with slaves; their number did not appear to be in proportion to the number of free persons. It was, then, in our interest, and to assure our future security, to take precautions in this respect, thereby halting the traffic that, while it continued, increased our [internal, domestic] dangers. I think, Mr. President, that the time has come for the government to end this dangerous situation by putting a limit on the trade in slaves; and besides, we have accepted this obligation.[76]

By signing the Queiroz bill into law in September 1850, Pedro II showed that the imperial government was determined as never before to bring Brazil's international slave trade to a rapid halt. Only a few months previous, few observers would have predicted such an outcome. Citizens from diverse social backgrounds recognized that unabated importations of African slaves posed unwanted risks. These included heightened possibility of another major slave revolt in Salvador and organized protests by African and crioulo slaves, as had occurred in response to the decree forcing slaves out of the port. In the wake of aggressive British naval tactics along the Brazilian coast and the response of the imperial government, outright popular support to terminate the slave trade coalesced quickly.[77]

Early 1850s

That police and provincial authorities suddenly acted to end the slave trade from Africa for moral and political reasons after 1850 does not provide the whole picture. It fails to explain fully why persons who benefited from slavery did not seek the resumption or continuation of the trade (as had occurred between 1830 and 1850), and it overlooks internal conditions in Brazil in the first half of the 1850s.

Slave resistance continued throughout the empire between 1851 and 1856. In no way did the tensions witnessed in the years before passage of the Queiroz law lessen; if anything, they increased. Police delegates from throughout the province wrote of their need for reinforcements to thwart slave rebellions. In 1851, police commanders sent a company of cavalry to the town of Santo Amaro in the Recôncavo to protect persons and property from "the insurrections of slaves."[78] At the same time, the provincial government doubled to four hundred the number of "pedestrian guards" patrolling the streets of Salvador.[79] These men received very low salaries and minimal training. Nevertheless, officials hoped that their presence would diminish the concerns of free inhabitants made anxious over the presence of hundreds of recently arrived African slaves.

Fear of an impending revolt in Salvador resurfaced again in May 1853. The chief of police wrote, "We had grave apprehensions that the African freedpersons and slaves were planning an insurgency." In response, police arrested "the most suspicious" African freedpersons, accusing them of plotting an insurrection. Several of these African freedpersons remained in a prison for four months. The courts deported others back to Africa.

To carry out the deportations of 1853, officials invoked Provincial Law 9 of May 13, 1835, described eighteen years after its passage as "the law that emerged from the very peculiar circumstances of this province with regards to the terrible danger of insurrection." The law stipulated that any ship (Brazilian or foreign) anchored in Salvador destined for Africa would only be issued a passport for departure if it agreed to transport African freedpersons who had been ordered deported (the number determined by the size of the crew and ship). Citing Article 5, the chief of police compelled the Dutch ship *Gouverneur Vandes El* to remain in port to await the boarding of imprisoned African freedpersons. After a four-day delay, the ship received permission to depart. For unknown reasons, Bahian officials deposited no Africans on board. The captain of the Dutch ship complained angrily that two members of his crew had died from yellow fever, which they contracted during the delay.[80]

Slave resistance created turmoil in several neighboring provinces as well. A huge slave revolt erupted in Alagoas in July 1852, causing national reverberations. An estimated thirty to one hundred slaves attacked five engenhos, killing the wife and daughter of one of the owners; setting fire to several buildings on the estates; and fleeing into nearby Jussara Forest. As the insurgents raced through the countryside attacking engenhos and farms, other slaves joined them. One official estimated that twenty-one slaves died in the fighting, and a posse sent out to pursue the slaves arrested nineteen.[81] Among those imprisoned, six were sentenced to whippings later in the year.

Perhaps seeking to assure both themselves and imperial authorities that the worst was behind them, owners of engenhos in Alagoas claimed in November that the province enjoyed "peace and tranquility." Such optimism did not linger for long. Less than fourteen months later, in January 1854, the president of Alagoas asked officials in the neighboring provinces of Pernambuco and Bahia to be vigilant that no arms or gunpowder be sent to Alagoas or other nearby provinces. Although he made no specific reference to the earlier uprising, he apparently considered it likely that these materials might end up in the hands of rebellious slaves.[82]

In the northern district of São Matheus in the province of Espírito Santo, rebellious slaves forced police delegates to request reinforcements to maintain order. One observer wrote that news of the demise of the international slave trade had convinced slaves that they had been freed. As an expression of their dissatisfaction, slaves fled from the manioc farms where they worked to join quilombos in the forests of the interior.

Planters hoped to destroy these "agglomerations of slaves" quickly by offering money to police and private slave hunters for their services. Officials involved in these searches emphasized that confiscation of weapons in the hands of the *quilombolas* (members of the quilombo) should be a priority. Slave owners demanded that all measures be taken to quash rumors accusing planters of refusing to implement the supposed imperial emancipation decrees.[83]

While scores of slaves violently resisted their condition or fled, others turned to the courts. Recognizing the potential benefits to be derived from the judicial system, African slaves appeared at courthouses and police stations to complain of bad treatment by their owners. The liberated African Sabino Francisco Muniz (most likely one of the Africans hastily disembarked on the Bahian coast from the slave ship *Ultimação* or *Relâmpago* in late 1851) challenged his status in August 1852. Aided by an unknown person versed in Brazilian and international law, Muniz invoked the law of November 7, 1831, to claim that he had been illegally transported to Brazil.[84] A legal appeal by an African seeking to remove any restrictions on his freedom as early as August 1852 is most interesting, as it compares to the legal petition submitted by the group of African liberated slaves three years previous in Sorocaba, São Paulo. Protests by slaves through the courts mounted in the years that followed. The lawyer Luís Gama in São Paulo, along with lawyers in Salvador, employed similar tactics and strategies from the 1860s to defend Africans illegally enslaved.

One last example of the turmoil that continued in the wake of the Queiroz law relates to Candomblé. While on patrol in the urban parish of Santo Antônio Alem do Carmo (one of ten parishes in Salvador), a police inspector attempted to arrest participants in a Candomblé ceremony with the help of local inhabitants. In his depiction of this episode in October 1855, the police official wrote that these religious gatherings often attracted more than two hundred persons who "practiced immoralities" that, he claimed, might result in deaths.[85] Encountering numerous slaves at hidden terreiros throughout the city, authorities viewed Candomblé with special trepidation and distrust.

That numerous inhabitants of varied class and race backgrounds found great appeal in these African ceremonies added to the unease felt by authorities and many free inhabitants alike.

Urban Slave Flight in Salvador

Table 2.3 below lists the number of slaves arrested by police in the urban parishes of Salvador from 1849 to 1885. These slaves had fled from owners and then been rounded up by police patrols in the city. Slaves arrested with origins in other provinces or the interior of Bahia were specifically noted in the records and are not included in this list.

In the year 1850, 113 African slaves fled from their masters in the city of Salvador. In no other year was that number equaled (from the available records). In that same year, a total of 173 slaves (African and crioulo) fled, and in 1851, a total of 170 slaves took off from owners, making a total of 343 slaves who fled in those two years. The number of escaped slaves in 1850–51 can be considered one of four peaks (the others being 1858–59 [447 slaves fled], 1866–68 [714 slaves fled], and 1876 [282 slaves fled]).

Table 2.3, along with Graph 2.1, offer a quantitative insight into slave resistance. They provide evidence that African and crioulo slaves responded to their historical milieu. When conditions were propitious, slaves took off. Arrest records in Salvador suggest that slaves responded to the social unrest and political agitation associated with the ending of the international slave trade in 1850 by escaping from their masters.

Conclusions

Slave resistance and the fear it instilled in the master class contributed to the rapid change of the political tide against the slave traffic between Africa and Brazil in 1850–51. Imperial ministers, political leaders in various provinces, merchants, and planters had not forgotten the 1835 Malês Revolt, even if the number of participants in that uprising had been small. With huge importations of African slaves into Bahia between 1835 and 1850, fears of instability mounted. A British consul succinctly wrote from Salvador (in April 1847), "There can hardly be a doubt,

Table 2.3. Arrests of Fugitive African and Crioulo Slaves in Salvador, 1849–85

Date	% African	% Crioulo	Total
Jan. 1849 to Dec. 1849	61.9 (88)	38.1 (54)	142
Jan. 1850 to Dec. 1850	65.3 (113)	34.7 (60)	173
Jan. 1851 to Dec. 1851	50.5 (86)	49.5 (84)	170
Jan. 1852 to Dec. 1852	57.8 (92)	42.2 (67)	159
Jan. 1853 to Sept. 15, 1853 (Inc.)	61.3 (84)	38.7 (53)	137
Jan. 1854 to Dec. 1854	50.6 (73)	49.4 (71)	144
Jan. 1855 to Dec. 1855	66.6 (62)	33.4 (31)	93
Jan. 1856 to Dec. 1856	50 (60)	50 (60)	120
Jan. 1857 to Feb. 21, 1857 and June 25 to Dec. 1857 (Inc.)	40.6 (39)	59.4 (57)	96
Jan. 1858 to Dec. 1858	48.9 (91)	51.1 (95)	186
Jan. 1859 to Nov. 19, 1859 (Inc.)	42.9 (112)	57.1 (149)	261
Apr. 30, 1861 to Dec. 1861 (Inc.)	33.7 (30)	66.3 (59)	89
Jan. 1862 and Sept. 4, 1862 to Dec. 1862 (Inc.)	29.7 (14)	70.3 (33)	47
Jan. 1863 to Dec. 1863	31.4 (33)	68.6 (72)	105
Jan. 1864 to Dec. 1864	32.2 (49)	67.8 (103)	152
Jan. 1865 to Dec. 1865	36.7 (58)	63.3 (100)	158
Jan. 1866 to Dec. 1866	38.2 (83)	61.8 (134)	217
Jan. 1867 to Dec. 1867	25.5 (65)	74.5 (189)	254
Jan. 1868 to Dec. 1868	34.1 (83)	65.9 (160)	243
Jan. 1869 to Dec. 1869	30.5 (52)	69.5 (118)	170
Jan. 1870 to Dec. 1870	39.5 (72)	60.5 (110)	182
Jan. 1871 to Dec. 1871	27.5 (22)	72.5 (58)	80
Jan. 1872 to Dec. 1872	22.7 (33)	77.3 (112)	145
Aug. 21, 1875 to Dec. 1875 (Inc.)	25.7 (9)	74.3 (26)	35
Jan. 1876 to Dec. 1876	18.7 (53)	81.3 (229)	282
Jan. 1877 to Dec. 1877	15.3 (23)	84.7 (127)	150
Jan. to Mar. 1, 1878 (Inc.)	11.7 (2)	88.3 (15)	17
Apr. 21, 1880 to Aug. 3, 1880 (Inc.)	25 (5)	75 (15)	20
Dec. 9, 1882 to Aug. 27, 1883	0 (0)	100 (31)	31
Feb. 1, 1884 to Dec. 1884	3.7 (1)	96.3 (26)	27
Jan. 1885 to Aug. 27, 1885	6.6 (1)	93.4 (14)	15

Source: Daily Correspondence from Chief of Police to president of the province, 1848–85, Maços 5702 to 5866, APEB/SACP (see endnote for the exact package numbers).[86]

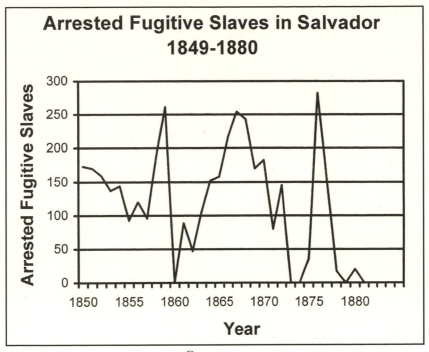

GRAPH 2.1

that should slaves be imported in still larger quantities than heretofore, the Brazilian Authorities would for their own safety, soon be compelled to adopt measures to prevent it; even as it is, the white population are ever kept in a state of alarm, by the fear of a rising of the Slaves."[87] In terminating the slave trade, imperial officials hoped to address a pressing domestic issue and at the same time to deflect international criticism.

Africans residing in Bahia—slaves, freedpersons, and the liberated Africans taken off slave ships by the British navy—also remembered well the revolt of the Malês. The 1835 rebellion demonstrated Africans' ability to organize and fight for their freedom in an urban setting within Brazil. In the subsequent fifteen years, suburban and rural quilombos proliferated both along the coast and in the interior. Subtle and more obvious manifestations of resistance and organization aided slaves. Examples included covert Islamic religious services, Candomblé ceremonies, maintenance of communication networks by slaves between city and countryside as well as along the coast, and the appearance of The Philanthropic Society of Bahia, composed of both free persons and slaves.[88] The ending of the slave trade to Bahia in 1850–51 has been attributed to the heroism of the British navy, the responses of Bahian and imperial political leaders, and the spread of transatlantic Enlightenment thought. Africans also played a significant role.[89]

The community of African freedpersons in Salvador faced a special dilemma at midcentury. Most African freedpersons endured precarious conditions in Bahian and Brazilian society; their lives differed little from those of slaves. The majority had little interest in challenging authorities on any front. Most worked long hours to earn money. Often they used their income to purchase freedom for family members who remained enslaved. Hence, African freedpersons did not wish to attract attention or to get into trouble.

In spite of conservative ways, African freedpersons bore the brunt of a concerted propaganda campaign against them in the 1840s and early 1850s. Police arrested tens of African freedpersons. After interrogations, authorities allowed most to go free, but others ended up in jail, and some were deported to other parts of the empire or back to Africa. During these years, several hundred freed Africans returned to West Africa on their own volition and with their own money. That the police in Bahia portrayed a small group of freedpersons as a major threat reflected unease about their presence and widespread distrust of freed Africans. It is but one example among many in the nineteenth century of hostility directed toward individuals (commonly dark-skinned) perceived as foreign and potentially subversive.

Elite reaction to African freedpersons offers a helpful insight into the historical moment. African freedpersons played a major role in the revolt of the Malês, and several achieved upward economic mobility during the 1840s. Once they gained their freedom, some purchased slaves. Such independence raised questions for officials. Should Africans who had attained their freedom in Bahia be allowed to live on their own without special taxes and controls over their lives? Given their experience, expertise, language skills, and historical memory, might not one or more

African freedpersons create problems, particularly after witnessing public disturbances associated with ending the international slave trade?

And what about an uninhibited African freedperson like Lucio Jeronimo da Costa, arrested in June 1850 for hosting gatherings of Africans and "persons born in Brazil"? Costa understood that he would face deportation from Bahia or a worse penalty if found out by the authorities. Nevertheless, he welcomed persons of various backgrounds to his ceremonies and festivities. Like so many other African freedpersons, Costa maintained close emotional bonds with fellow Africans who remained enslaved. He paid homage to his Islamic beliefs, remembered well the 1835 revolt, and hoped that his gatherings would provide psychological uplift and strength to all in attendance. His actions added to the alarm and sense of malaise felt by the well-to-do of Salvador. The police and president responded with policies of systematic harassment of African freedpersons and kept close observation over where such individuals resided.

The rapid shift of public opinion in favor of suppression in late 1849 and subsequent months was an outcome of myriad social tensions that had mounted during the 1840s. To assure their power, slave owners and the provincial governments took extraordinary measures to diffuse threats to the established order and impede the emergence of a viable abolitionist movement. These included the creation of large urban police forces, establishment of a citizen's patrol in Salvador, the employment of brutal slave hunters, a campaign besmirching antislavery propaganda, and close communication with officials in other parts of the large empire. Unceasing resistance by several hundreds of African and crioulo slaves, combined with devastating epidemics, made further importations of Africans an unappealing proposition after 1850 to most free Brazilians residing in the cities and the countryside. 🔲

PART TWO
1871

Two Perspectives on the

Passage of the Law of the Free Womb

CHAPTER THREE

War and Peace

A First Phase of Abolition in Bahia, 1850s–71

The year 1865 stands out as a major turning point in the history of the Americas. In the United States, the Civil War ended (1861–65), Congress passed the Thirteenth Amendment outlawing slavery and created the Freedmen's Bureau to provide aid to former slaves and refugees. In that same year, Brazil entered the Paraguayan War (1864–70). On May 1, 1865, Brazil allied with Argentina and Uruguay in a Triple Alliance to fight against Paraguay.[1] Initially viewed by many politicians as a local conflict that could be resolved through diplomacy, it escalated into a horrific conflagration of death and destruction that endured until March 1, 1870.

Debate surfaced in Brazil during the war years concerning the future of slavery. This included proemancipation statements by Emperor Pedro II in 1867 and 1868, and emancipation reforms initiated by Liberal members of the imperial government. At no time during these debates, however, did the Brazilian government threaten the right of slaveholders to determine the fate of their slave property.[2] With the cessation of hostilities, proposals for antislavery legislation became a major political issue. Finally, in September 1871, the Senate passed the Law of the Free Womb (after barely passing in the Chamber of Deputies), also known as the Rio Branco Law.

The law sought gradual emancipation by freeing the offspring of slave women. It stipulated that these children born after the law's passage (known as *ingênuos*) would remain under the care of the mother's owner until the age of eight. When the child reached eight years old, the owner had two choices. Either he could allow the child to go free and receive indemnification from the imperial government; or, the owner could decide to retain the child in a form of quasislavery until age twenty-one. The majority of owners chose the latter option. Making legal what was a common practice in Bahia, the law assured slaves the right to save money and recognized the self-purchase of manumission by slaves. It required owners to register their slaves. If an owner failed to register a slave, the slave could claim his freedom. The law also included the creation of an emancipation fund that would pay for slave emancipations throughout the empire.[3] Very few planters paid into the emancipation fund, and few slaves gained their freedom from its coffers.

Impetus to pass the Law of the Free Womb in 1871 can be traced to several sources. British antislavery policies played a decisive role, along with French condemnation of slavery, the outlawing of slavery in the United States, and the passage of Free Womb laws in Cuba and in Puerto Rico in 1870.[4] Another event that reverberated within Brazil was the decree of October 2, 1869, that ended slavery in Paraguay. Initiated by Brazilian officers, the law was imposed during the occupation of Asuncion by the armies of the Triple Alliance. Brazilian deputies and senators alluded to international opinion and antislavery legislation outside of Brazil during the months preceding passage of the Law of the Free Womb.[5]

Expanding capitalism also facilitated passage of antislavery legislation at this juncture. Brazil was changing rapidly in the late 1860s due to urbanization, immigration, and the beginnings of industrialization. Politicians and entrepreneurs sought to modernize Brazil by emulating "civilized nations," all of which used free labor.

In addition to these pressures for political reform, slave resistance continued. Although little attention has been paid to slave resistance during the war with Paraguay, the actions of slaves clearly influenced antislavery discourse in the late 1860s through late 1871. This chapter emphasizes that slave resistance combined with activism by free persons of color fueled political dissent at this juncture. It further suggests that harsh policies implemented to impress soldiers to go to the front created widespread antipathy toward the imperial and provincial officials. As a result, popular support for abolition mounted. To deal with a "profound political crisis" at war's end, in the words of historian Martha Abreu, Pedro II made passage of the Law of the Free Womb his highest priority.[6]

Reasons for the War

On October 12, 1864, long-simmering territorial disputes between Paraguay and its neighbors Argentina, Uruguay, and Brazil erupted into hostilities. Concerned over the possibility that Paraguay (450,000 inhabitants) would be absorbed as a province by Argentina (1.7 million) or Brazil (10 million), Paraguay's President Francisco Solano López demanded that Brazil not invade neighboring Uruguay (population of 250,000) in its quest to assure political influence over that country. Brazil's imperial government disregarded the ultimatum. In response, the Paraguayan navy seized a Brazilian steamer and the Paraguayan army attacked the Brazilian province of Mato Grosso. López hoped for a quick victory over more powerful opponents that had traditionally been divided. Instead, Paraguay ended up fighting a defensive war that lasted five and a half years and that caused the death of 60 percent of Paraguay's population.

Three major viewpoints prevail with regards to the reasons for the outbreak of the Paraguayan War. One posits that the aggressive actions of the dictator Francisco Solano López provoked hostilities. By increasing Paraguay's regular army to twenty-eight thousand men, thus making it the largest in South America, López upset a fragile balance of power among his neighbors. This first interpretation suggests that by supporting Uruguayan president Atanasio Cruz Aguirre, refusing to negotiate with Argentina and Brazil over territorial disputes, and in seeking to control the rivers of the region, López caused the war.

A second interpretation portrays Paraguay as a prosperous republic that had implemented a Socialist model of economic development. By means of "benevolent paternalism," in the words of the Brazilian historian Ricardo Salles, López sought to protect his nation from British imperial hegemony.[7] This view found widespread (and continuing) appeal in South America, for example in the works of the Argentine León Pomer, the Uruguayan Eduardo Galeano, the Brazilian Júlio José Chiavenato, and the U.S. historian E. Bradford Burns.[8]

A third explanation for the War of the Triple Alliance is related to the process of nation building. Instead of focusing on hostile states at war, historians have turned their attention to civil wars in the region. Argentina faced internal rebellions by regional strongmen, Uruguay failed to attain stability due to long-standing political divisions, and Brazil desired to settle festering territorial disputes. By joining in the Triple Alliance, the three member countries assured the defeat of Paraguay, which in turn weakened regional dissent and facilitated the use of nationalism to consolidate central state control.[9]

Although disagreements over the reasons and motives for the Paraguayan War continue, there is little debate that the war proved to be a cataclysmic event. As one of the first total wars, Paraguay suffered the highest rate of civilian and military casualties in any modern war. The trench warfare common during the hostilities was a precursor to the horrors witnessed in the trenches of France in World War I. Soon after the outbreak of fighting, the war with Paraguay quickly lost its appeal to soldiers at the front and potential recruits in Brazil.

"Barbarous Hunts for Men"

An estimated 90,898 Brazilian soldiers fought in the war against Paraguay. The largest contingent of troops, numbering 33,803 men, originated in the province of Rio Grande do Sul. Bahia sent the second-largest group totaling at least 15,267 soldiers. Other regions made significant contributions of men and material, including the city of Rio de Janeiro (the Corte) and the provinces of Rio de Janeiro, Pernambuco, and São Paulo.[10]

Brazil's military forces were composed of four major groups: the regular army, the National Guard, Voluntários da Pátria (Volunteers of the Fatherland), and freed slaves. Some seven thousand slaves in Brazil received their freedom to fight against Paraguay, the majority of them purchased from private owners by the imperial government. Of this total, Bahia sent 1,518 freedmen.[11]

Established in January 1865 as a way to enlist troops, the Voluntários numbered 37,438 men, which represented the largest segment of Brazil's 91,000 soldiers (two out of every five troops).[12] Voluntários made up more than half of the troops sent from Bahia (7,764 men). As a special corps created in response to the conflict, Voluntários received a financial bonus when they joined up, higher income than regular soldiers, and the promise of land grants and civil service jobs after fulfillment of their military obligation. Brazil's government also guaranteed a pension to wounded soldiers and the families of Voluntários who died at the front. It soon extended the benefits offered to Voluntários to National Guardsmen who went to war, meaning that 75 percent of Brazil's forces believed it their right to receive such benefits. Unfortunately, but not surprisingly, very few soldiers received the rewards promised by Brazil's imperial government.[13]

Patriotism flourished in Bahia in the months following the outbreak of the war. In March 1865, the first battalion of Voluntários from Bahia departed for Rio de Janeiro by ship. Schools closed in Salvador and inhabitants throughout the city placed bright cloth in the windows of their homes. Poets recited patriotic verses in the streets, music filled the air, and some fifteen thousand people lined the streets of the city to bid farewell to young soldiers.[14] The men passed through a large arch, which included a representation of an Indian, as a symbol of Brazil, crowning a volunteer soldier. The words inscribed underneath read "A Nation Aggressed Upon."[15] Expressions of patriotism also included monetary donations from the upper class and the creation of subscription funds by the residents of towns and villages to help offset the cost of the war.

But these nationalist outpourings and propaganda could not obscure dissatisfaction with the war effort. To find soldiers, the provincial government of Bahia sent representatives into the countryside. Employing tactics ranging from appeals to patriotic duty to violent arrests, these agents did whatever was necessary to satisfy troop quotas. Their appearance in a town or village often caused panic. As early as February 1865, an agent responsible for enlisting troops in Muritiba, a small village in the Recôncavo, complained that he could only find eleven volunteers in the region. He suggested more aggressive tactics be employed to his superior, for example, immediate arrests of potential recruits, given that everywhere he traveled the majority of available men fled so as not to be forced to enlist in the army.[16]

In correspondence, officials alluded to "subversives" spreading anti-war propaganda. "Fiendish preachers" warned rural inhabitants to pay no heed to the guarantees offered as incentives to join up. The testimony of angry veterans also affected recruitment. Upon their return to Bahia from Paraguay, officers and enlisted men "would not cease" in their efforts to discourage others from enlisting. Literate persons read aloud letters sent from soldiers fighting at the front to those who could not read. Stories of desperation, incompetence, and desertions at the southern front diminished the credibility of state representatives for the duration of the war. On several occasions anxious citizens confronted official recruiters when they arrived in towns of the interior looking for potential soldiers.[17]

Roused by such news, men hid in forests and outlying areas.[18] Some inflicted wounds on their bodies and a few committed suicide rather than be taken away. Armed bands roamed some areas of the interior and actively attacked recruiters in several provinces, including Maranhão, Ceará, Pernambuco, Paraíba, Rio Grande do Norte, Alagoas, Rio de Janeiro, and Paraná.[19]

In Bahia, slaves who possessed weapons joined together in one such group. Another gang composed of slaves and "criminals" attacked National Guard troops near the interior town of Camisão in December 1866, killing one and wounding eleven. Violent protests swayed several troop commanders to ally themselves with opponents of the government who sought to impede recruitment.[20]

The spread of infectious disease also undermined attempts by the provincial government to enlist soldiers. Through contact with strangers and rapid change of environments, recruits often became ill. In an attempt to protect against the spread of epidemics and sickness, medical personnel vaccinated soldiers. Carried long distances under precarious conditions, vaccines often went bad. Inhabitants of the interior commonly viewed vaccination as a source of, rather than an impediment to, outbreaks of smallpox. Similar to what Sidney Chalhoub has described in the province of Rio de Janeiro, for most persons "the vaccine was [it spread] the smallpox" [*a vacina era a varíola*].[21] Such episodes fueled mistrust among the common folk.

Under pressure to raise contingents quickly, officials commonly overlooked the requirement to vaccinate recruits. As a result, hundreds of men from the interior of Bahia traveled to Salvador without having been inoculated. Many became infected during these journeys or while waiting in Salvador to depart for the south.

One group of recruiters ventured to the "center of the province" in late 1865 searching for Voluntários. The scale of this effort is suggested by the twenty-four mules and horses used to carry supplies. During a journey that endured five months, it succeeded in rounding up one hundred forty-three men. During the return trip back to Salvador, twenty-four of these recruits became sick and could not continue, another fifteen deserted, while four more stayed behind for unknown reasons. Only one hundred men of the original group arrived at the São Pedro Fort in Salvador. Concerned about health conditions and desertion, the head of the expedition appealed to city and provincial leaders for food, clothing, and materials.[22]

Bahia gained a special reputation for its use of violence to recruit military forces. A newspaper published in Rio de Janeiro pointed to "startling events" that had occurred in the interior of the province. Official refutation did little to diminish such criticism. In the words of one observer, recruiters in Bahia had carried out "barbarous hunts for men" [*ferozes caçadas humanas*] to enlist soldiers to fight in a "war of extermination against Paraguay that devoured 800,000 *contos* [US $410 million] and 200,000 lives."[23] Thousands of lower-class Bahians did not quickly forget nor forgive the aggressions and grief inflicted by representatives of the provincial government.

Antiwar protest spread throughout Brazil. In Salvador, critics of the war discouraged soldiers and recruits camped throughout the city from embarking on ships headed to the front. Police attempted to impede these efforts.[24] In the southern port city of Paranaguá, Paraná, a municipal judge named Dr. João Antônio de Barros Jr. addressed departing troops in the public square. He shouted out that the search for soldiers had "corrupted the nation. If I were a father and my sons had been recruited, I would never hand them over without first seeing blood run and bodies fall. The people need to rise up against the authorities."[25]

Free men of color composed the bulk of the soldiers recruited in Bahia. The majority of them were poor and vulnerable to exploitation.[26] The 1872 census counted 4.25 million free blacks and persons of color in Brazil, which meant that these people composed more than two-fifths of a total population of just over ten million. At least eleven companies of black soldiers, numbering 638 men, also departed from Salvador. Known as Zuavos Baianos (Bahian *Zouaves*, a French term derived from the original Berber word *ZwAwa*, denoting a soldier who adopted the dress of the French colonial army), several mixed-race officers led these companies.[27] As part of institutional reorganization, the Zuavo battalions became part of Voluntário units after arriving at the front. Given the significant presence of blacks and dark-skinned men among Brazilian forces, Paraguayans, Argentines, and Uruguayans disparagingly labeled Brazilian soldiers as "little monkeys" (*macaquitos*).[28]

During the turbulent years of the war, conscripts faced conditions little different from those endured by slaves. Writing to the secretary of state of the United States in Washington, DC, a U.S. diplomat in Brazil penned a sobering description of recruits being transported to the front.

> One word here about the volunteers sent to the La Plata. I have known at least fifty bands of these voluntary soldiers, either passing through Petrópolis or coming on board the train at the railway station and they are invariably "brought in" as parties numbering 30 to 70 to 80. Each voluntário has an iron collar round his neck which opposite to the lock has an iron ring, about two and a half inches in diameter. Through the ring is passed a heavy chain, known as the "log chain" extending from the front to the rear files [this practice commonly employed to secure slaves], and of course, there is no possibility of escape. In this condition the volunteer soldier! goes on board the transport and sails for the River Plata![29]

Not surprisingly, Brazilian recruits became known in some circles as "roped-in volunteers" (*voluntários de corda*) or the "stick and leash volunteers" (*voluntários a pau e corda*).[30] One writer has labeled the majority of the special volunteer corps as the "Involuntary Defenders of the Fatherland" [*involuntários da Pátria*].[31]

Free men who escaped conscription faced similar treatment in the Bahian Recôncavo during the war years. Disorder at sugar engenhos in the Bahian Recôncavo demonstrates a blurring of status between free and slave. Free workers commonly *fled to* sugar estates as a way to evade government agents looking for soldiers to be sent to Paraguay. Their hope was that planters desirous of a stable workforce to ensure sugar production would protect them.[32] Many found themselves treated like slaves.

Once on these estates, free workers attempted to negotiate with owners over pay, tasks and employment schedule. Often their demands were not met. As a result, hundreds *fled from* engenhos to seek better conditions elsewhere. Few encountered job opportunities that might lift them out of poverty. Similar to slaves, the free underclass possessed few rights. They experienced precarious conditions on a daily basis. Their personal insecurity increased significantly during the war years.

The war therefore intensified a sense of shared interests and experience between slaves and free persons. Some attempted to forge alliances. One incident in the town of Cachoeira situated in the heart of the sugar-producing region of the Recôncavo demonstrates elite apprehension with these ties.

On Saturday, January 23, 1869, the ship *Lucy* embarked from Salvador, traveled across the Bay of All Saints, and docked later that evening at the town of Cachoeira. Rumor that the ship was to bring news that the war had ended preceded its arrival. An exuberant crowd estimated at one to two thousand people came to the docks to welcome the ship. They set off fireworks and rang the bells in the churches. Unfortunately, the rumor proved to be untrue, and the crowd roared its disapproval.

In writing of the episode, the head of the police force in Cachoeira affirmed that no slaves from any sugar engenho in the region had appeared in the streets that night. He emphasized that "never would the city of Cachoeira permit that slaves take part in such gatherings." The president of Bahia in turn communicated what had occurred to the minister of justice of the empire in Rio de Janeiro. He did not wish to see lower-class free persons listen to agitators and find common cause with slaves desirous of their freedom. A bond of this nature would cause disruption to planters already facing economic difficulties due to the war.[33]

Similar disquiet surfaced in other provinces. A public official in the interior of the province of Maranhão wrote:

> The demand for soldiers caused by our present involvement in the foreign war has resulted in men capable to going to the front instead hiding in the forests, in not insignificant numbers, where they resist any attempts at being recruited. Many such groups exist in this district. This Town Council has legitimate concerns that the necessities caused by their isolation might compel them to disrupt the public order; and who knows if their needs, especially with regards to hunger, will not cause them to create some alliance with the slaves.[34]

Another official lamented about conditions in the province of Minas Gerais:

> Our very backward customs allow for the abominable spectacle of joining together under one roof persons of all types, of all colors, with education, or without it [education], and even oh! What Disgrace! Slaves socializing, drinking *cachaça* [Brazilian rum], and dancing *batuques* [dance of African origin usually accompanied by drumming] with free men. There has been violence, including black slaves killing whites. For this reason I recommend to the police authorities that they make war to the death against the *batuques*, the drunks and the vagrants [*vadios*].[35]

In Rio Grande do Sul, army deserters and runaway slaves found their way to the quilombo named Pedras Brancas. Headed by a former slave named Camizão, Pedras Brancas was the largest quilombo known to have existed in the province. Based on testimony given in February 1867 by a former member of the quilombo, police learned that an estimated one hundred fifty men, women, and children resided in a well-protected village at the base of a cliff. Some fifty males were armed and prepared to defend the settlement. Groups of six men commonly ventured out in search of salt (used to preserve food), gunpowder, and shot. Other groups hunted game in the forest and fished in the rivers. Although deserters had joined quilombos in the past, provincial and imperial officials viewed with particular trepidation the fact that free men had been welcomed at a huge runaway slave community during the war years.[36]

Social and economic conditions in Brazil after midcentury undermined boundaries between slaves and free persons.[37] As the cost of slaves rose with the end of the international slave trade, fewer people could afford to purchase slaves. Hence, free persons throughout Brazil became less committed to the institution of slavery. The war years pushed forward this process. Troop mobilization brought together Brazilians from all provinces, racial backgrounds, and classes.[38] Race prejudice and class bias did not end, but different ways of looking at the world emerged. Slaveholders understood that marginalized free persons who forged ties with slaves could undermine their capacity to rule.

Social Tensions in Salvador

The long duration of hostilities forced Bahian military leaders to implement desperate measures in Salvador to satisfy the demand for soldiers. Comparable to practices in other Brazilian cities, kidnappings and violent skirmishes became commonplace in Salvador.[39] Law-abiding citizens witnessed scenes of young men being dragged to prisons to await the arrival of a transport ship.[40] Owners complained that their slaves could not step foot out into the streets of the city without being arrested and incarcerated with other war recruits. Concerned about the harsh treatment of civilians, the chief of police in Salvador expressed his displeasure. In the words of Chief C. V. de Almeida Galeão, impressments of soldiers by National Guard troops had been carried out in the most irregular manner possible. They [the National Guard] walk through the streets heavily armed and take into custody almost every person they encounter, including men known previously to have received exemptions and others with physical disabilities. The troops have even gone so far as to break into private homes. Last night at 9:00 p.m. they broke into the home of a high-ranking member of the office of the secretary of the government. There could be grave disorders or even bloodshed if there is not a stop put to this.[41]

Men who did not wish to be sent to the southern front eluded recruiters in Salvador. Slaves and free persons often hid together. To prevent being sent south, free blacks and persons of color walked around barefoot to pose as slaves or dressed up in fine clothes to appear "like the whites."[42] Families abandoned their homes and moved out of the city.[43]

Food shortages became a paramount concern. "Individuals carrying subsistence foods of the highest necessity [in Salvador] coming from the Recôncavo are being rounded up [meaning impressed as soldiers], and therefore other persons are refusing to enter the city."[44] In April 1869, Chief A. Cicero de Assis warned police throughout the province to be careful about whom they took into custody. "Do not arrest anyone who is selling or carrying cereals at fairs, open markets or in public streets, or any person who labors on the boats that are involved in this business, under the pretext of recruitment or as a replacement for someone else."[45]

The struggle for survival vexed the majority of Bahians during the war. A former Voluntário named Romão de Aquino Gomes sent at least five letters to the president of Bahia, requesting crutches and clothing so that he could continue to beg in the streets. Gomes had been badly wounded in one leg during the war, and the imperial government had failed in its promise to provide him with a pension.[46] The economic difficulties of the period contributed to the sense of malaise felt by many at war's end.[47] A witness to the desperate conditions in Salvador penned his impressions of the city in a poem entitled "Os mendigos" ("The Beggars").

Mizeria, ó Deus! O mundo ao vicio lisongêa!
ao crime banquetêa, si traz calçada a mão!
e . . . cospe seu despreso á honra, ao genio embora,
si esfarrapado chora na rua e—pede pão!!!
Such misery, O God! The world [everyone] praises vice!
[it] adulates crime [criminal acts] with banquets,
    as long as the perpetrators appear well-to-do!
and . . . [everyone] heaps their scorn on
    [individuals who possess] honor and genuine spirit,
when such a person [who is dressed] in tattered clothes cries
    on the street and—begs for bread!!!⁴⁸

Dissatisfied veterans caused numerous disturbances in Salvador during the war. One locale attractive to former solders became known as the "*republiqueta* of Paraguay" (derogatory term meaning "little republic of Paraguay"). Located near the palace of provincial government, "Paraguay" came to the attention of police as early as July 1867. Composed of an estimated one hundred forty small houses, its residents gained notoriety for their rowdy behavior. Chief of police A. Cicero de Assis wrote, "Agglomerated in a hidden place, these houses are inaccessible, constructed close to one another and unhealthy. There needs to be a police detachment stationed there, because you have no idea of the orgies and constant disorders that occur, due to the low class of people who reside there or those who rent these houses for various motives."⁴⁹

Returning soldiers believed they deserved special consideration for having fought the war. Veterans sought to displace slaves in the urban labor market. Enmity surfaced in the labor union named Union and Industry. Throughout the nineteenth century African slave porters carried goods unloaded from ships in the port to destinations in the upper city. A "captain" organized these groups (known as *cantos*) and took responsibility for clearing the steep winding alleys of objects or persons who might be in the way. With few job openings available in Salvador at war's end, Brazilian-born free men sought control over the transport of goods in the city. President Francisco Gonçalves Martins (back in office again, with interruptions from August 1868 to April 1871) intervened and called for the replacement of slave workers with veterans. This decree by the president compared to the policy he implemented in Salvador's port two decades earlier in 1850 in substituting the free boatmen for African sailors.

Martins's actions received mixed reviews in the city's newspapers. An editorial in *Diário da Bahia* affirmed that free labor ought to be encouraged by all who sought to create a strong nation. Another writer went so far as to claim that "racial prejudice has ended; men [now] distinguish themselves by their actions and intelligence."[50] Not all agreed. One journalist alleged that slaves continued to be marginalized: "Work is not a political right, and it is a cruelty to reduce them [slaves and freedmen] to the necessity of suicide and robbery."[51] Like at midcentury, free workers did not desire to compete with slaves. They looked favorably on the export of slaves out of Salvador into the interior of Bahia or the central-southern provinces.

Although production and employment of free workers rose in armament and textile enterprises in the central-southern cities of São Paulo and Rio de Janeiro, the war did little to stimulate the economy in Salvador. Corruption among politicians, poor management of resources, and the waste of war materials abounded. In the words of one observer from the Northeast, "The war is devastating our people; it has destroyed our small industries and paralyzed all of our agricultural production."[52] The urban petty bourgeoisie and the small urban middle class who sought to emulate European culture found the violent roundups of men in the cities particularly distasteful.[53] Industrialists and engineers noted with dismay the human and financial cost of the war. Among military officers of humble social origins who had risen in the ranks by means of competence and loyalty, the degrading experience of leading unprepared and poorly equipped troops into battle contributed to their unhappiness with the monarchy.

"Those Stupid Nagôs"

Disquiet fomented by the war with Paraguay contributed to a hardening of internal policy and heightened vigilance directed at Africans. Bahian officials viewed African slaves and freedpersons residing in Salvador as a significant threat to public order during and following the war with Paraguay. Within weeks of the outbreak of war, authorities lashed out at African freedpersons suspected of planning an insurrection. In January 1865, police in Salvador arrested twenty Africans during one sweep. This group included eleven freedmen and five freedwomen, along with three male slaves and one female slave. We do not know how long these Africans remained in jail or what happened to them later. Nor do we know if these Africans had been planning a revolt in Salvador.[54] What the record does portray clearly is the trepidation aroused in the elite by the presence of African freedpersons and growing fears that they might join with African slaves in an insurgency.

From the outset of the war, groups of Africans appeared before authorities en masse to protest their enslavement and working conditions. In December 1864, twenty-six African slaves walked off an estate on the island of Itaparica owned by Ignacio Dias de Andrade. Appearing before local police officials, they requested an end to abusive treatment. The police report did not mention the involvement of outside agitators or sympathetic abolitionists in promoting this protest. As in previous cases, we do not know what finally happened to these protesting slaves.[55] Nevertheless, their departure from the plantation provides evidence of African slaves probing the parameters of the slave system, trying to bring attention through the legal system to conditions on estates and to challenge the ways in which owners attempted to maintain control over their lives.

This episode and others like it marked a new and refined form of resistance. Instead of fleeing to quilombos "outside" the slave regime (*fugas para fora*), this group of slaves appealed directly to officials whom they believed might help them. The strategy has been described by the Brazilian historian Eduardo Silva as "flight [of slaves] inward [*fugas para dentro*], meaning to the interior of the slave society itself, where they [might] find, finally, the political capacity [*dimensão*] to transform the [slave] system."[56] The Africans solicited police and courts in Salvador to help them in the short term. They also hoped that other issues might be addressed, including their illegal enslavement (based on the law of

TABLE 3.1. ARRESTS OF FUGITIVE SLAVES IN SALVADOR, 1863–1870

DATE	% AFRICAN	% CRIOULO	TOTAL
Jan. 1863 to Dec. 1863	31.4 (33)	68.6 (72)	105
Jan. 1864 to Dec. 1864	32.2 (49)	67.8 (103)	152
Jan. 1865 to Dec. 1865	36.7 (58)	63.3 (100)	158
Jan. 1866 to Dec. 1866	38.2 (83)	61.8 (134)	217
Jan. 1867 to Dec. 1867	25.5 (65)	74.5 (189)	254
Jan. 1868 to Dec. 1868	34.1 (83)	65.9 (160)	243
Jan. 1869 to Dec. 1869	30.5 (52)	69.5 (118)	170
Jan. 1870 to Dec. 1870	39.5 (72)	60.5 (110)	182

Source: APEB/SACP, packages 5753, 5781, 5782, 5788, 5793, 5794, 5800, 5804, 5809, 5811.

1831). Difficult to gauge is the extent to which this group of Africans and their unknown allies believed that their actions might cause a crisis in the slave regime (as occurred subsequently from the early 1880s). African and Brazilian-born crioulo slaves paid close attention to events in the middle of the 1860s. They emulated the twenty-six courageous African slaves of Itaparica who had taken off from their estate and gone directly to the police to protest bad treatment.[57]

One of the four peaks in slave flight in Salvador (from police records covering the years 1849–85) occurred during the war years. In numbers reflecting to the two peaks in the 1850s that preceded it as well as a subsequent one in the 1870s, slaves fled when opportunities arose. Some headed to the interior of Bahia or to other provinces. This could be depicted as escaping "from" the slave system, using Silva's terminology above. Other fugitive slaves enlisted in the army. By fighting in Paraguay, they hoped to ensure their freedom. Such an action could be described as one variant of flight "into the slave regime."

A diminished police force caused by war emergency combined with slave protests and flight caused anxiety among officials in Salvador. The words of a subordinate writing to the chief of police in Salvador in June 1871 reflect the tensions of that moment:

I need specific orders from your excellency with regards to how best to carry out the nightly police patrols of the city. The men under my command pass through the streets from midnight until five in the morning. These patrols have failed to enter the [turbulent] parts of the city [meaning those locales with large numbers of slaves and freedpersons] where vigilance is most needed for the public well-being. It is similar to the situation in 1850, when my predecessor entered these districts with his patrol. If the residents did not respond to a knock at their door, the police threw rocks to force them to open the door [and respond to inquiries by the police].[58]

How should we interpret such words of alarm? Did conditions in 1871 compare to that turbulent year of 1850, when numerous inhabitants of Salvador feared the outbreak of another slave revolt?

Estimates of Salvador's population shed partial light on this question. Although unreliable, one census from 1855 reported that 15,400 slaves resided in Salvador, or 27.5 percent of a total urban population of 56,000. African freedpersons numbered 2.8 percent (1568 individuals) of the city's population. The total number of freedpersons (African and crioulo) added up to 3.62 percent (or some 2,027 individuals).

By 1870 there were 77,686 people in Salvador, including 16,469 slaves (21.2 percent) and 61,217 free persons (78.8 percent).[59] This 1870 estimate probably undercounted the urban free population. Substantial numbers of soldiers who had not yet returned from the front, inhabitants who had departed to evade recruitment and not yet returned to Salvador combined with the unwillingness by many to cooperate with census takers during a time of forced recruitment to depress the number.

The census of 1872 was more reliable. It counted 108,138 persons in Salvador. Of this total, 12,501 were slaves (11.6 percent). Of these, African-born slaves numbered 4,588 (36.7 percent of the total number of slaves), and 7,913 (63.3 percent) Brazilian-born crioulo slaves accounted for the remainder. Unfortunately, former slaves did not appear as a category in the 1872 census; therefore, we do not know their number.

These records demonstrate that significantly fewer African slaves resided in Salvador in 1872 than in 1855. There were also fewer crioulo slaves. The percentage of slaves in the total urban population had gone down from more than 25 percent in the early 1850s to less than 12 percent by 1872. Reasons for this decrease included the interprovincial slave trade that sent urban slaves to the central-southern provinces, and an intraprovincial trade that sent urban slaves to the interior of Bahia. Given this substantial decrease in the urban slave population, it is doubtful that the potential for a slave revolt in 1871 in Salvador compared to conditions in 1850. This did not mean, however, that slave resistance lessened or played a diminished role in the second half of the 1860s and first years of the 1870s.

Resistance by slaves throughout the empire created major problems during and after the war. Police stationed in the interior of Rio de Janeiro wrote from the first days of the war about the difficulties of maintaining order among the slave population. At war's end, a police delegate from the city of Campos requested extra troops to be sent to prevent an impending revolt by slaves. José Francisco de Mattos claimed that the tensions could be traced to "stupid Nagôs" (*insensatos nagôs*) who had convinced fellow slaves that they had been granted their freedom but that owners had disregarded the law.[60]

The province of São Paulo also experienced numerous incidents of slave flight. Slaves took off from plantations during the war years to join quilombos or to live on their own in forests of the interior.[61] Groups of escaped slaves appeared at court to protest their treatment. The president of São Paulo appealed to the imperial authorities that "urgent measures be taken to ensure public security" in the face of "repeated assassinations" committed by slaves. Arrested slaves demonstrated little concern about penalties for their actions, many expressing a preference for life in prison to one of captivity on an estate.[62]

In 1871 citizens residing near the city of Campinas requested the presence of an additional one hundred troops as a precaution against a potential slave insurrection. A letter signed by 238 leading persons pointed out that planters had been able to control their African-born slaves in the past, due to their "brutish character and lack of intelligence." However, the interprovincial slave trade had brought an influx of "people born in this country [Brazilian-born crioulo slaves], notably slaves from the northern provinces."

Many of the slaves who entered Campinas originated in Bahia. The petition from Campinas affirmed that Brazilian-born slaves possessed an "intellectual capacity much more developed than their primitive forbears; their spirit scarcely supports the yoke of slavery." The signers argued that slaves had begun to learn the customs of whites, thereby inspiring them to question their enslavement. Such an attitude reflected a long-standing myth held by elite observers that slaves could not organize or resist without outside help from free persons.[63] Manifestations of slave resistance occurred in several additional provinces, including Penambuco, Espírito Santo, Maranhão, Pará, and Rio Grande do Sul.[64] This was indeed a period marked by widespread turbulence.

In an analysis of the war and its relation to the "politics of abolition," the Brazilian historian José Murilo de Carvalho claims virtually no slave resistance in Brazil during the war against Paraguay.

> The rebellions and flight by groups of slaves only occurred well after [passage of] the Law of the Free Womb [in September 1871], contradicting the predictions of [Brazil's] Council of State which expected a greater number [of such incidents] and earlier [before September 1871]. Brazilian slaves remained relatively tranquil in comparison with those of the British and French colonies [from the 1820s to 1848, the years previous to slave emancipation in the British and French Caribbean islands].[65]

Surviving documents demonstrate the contrary. Slave flight, the appearance of protesting slaves before police and judges, and violence perpetrated by slaves occurred with frequency in the six years leading up to passage of the Law of the Free Womb in various provinces of Brazil.

Throughout 1870 and 1871, influential figures expressed anxiety about social conditions in the empire. Senator José Tomás Nabuco de

Araújo (Bahia) appealed to colleagues in 1870 by stating that the failure to pursue immediate reforms could result in "another Haiti [meaning a second Haitian Revolution like what had occurred in 1791–1804]."

> Gentlemen, do you want to know the results of inaction? I must speak with complete sincerity, with all the powers of my convictions. If you do not desire the consequences of a measure calmly decided by yourselves, you will have to accept the dubious results of improvidence. If you do not desire the economic inconvenience endured in the British and French Antilles, you run the risk of confronting the horrors of Santo Domingo [Haiti].[66]

During the debates in the National Assembly over the Law of the Free Womb, Theodoro Machado Freire Pereira da Silva, minister of agriculture and deputy from Pernambuco, declared that an immediate end to slavery was imperative. Reflecting on history, he pointed to British legislators who failed to respond to public opinion in England that called for abolition in the 1820s. Instead, soldiers were forced to put down slave insurrections in the colonies of Demerara (1823) and Jamaica (known as the Baptist Revolt of 1831) with "great cost and sacrifice of money and blood." Only as a result of these conflagrations did Parliament grasp what lay ahead if Britain failed to end slavery for good.[67] Senator Candido Mendes de Almeida (Maranhão) remembered well the Islamic slaves who had been brought to Brazil and their role in the revolt of the Malês.[68] In private correspondence, Baron of Cotegipe wrote that the "situation in this country is serious, if not desperate."[69] Far from being "reform-mongering," such statements were logical responses to the confrontations and challenges provoked by African and crioulo slaves and a small group of abolitionists.[70]

Abolitionists of Color

Similar to what had transpired three decades previous in the United States, an abolitionist movement composed of persons of color surfaced

Figure 3.1 Statue of Luís
Gama located at the Plaza of
Luís Gama, also known as the
Plaza of the Cistern (*Largo
do Tanque*), in Salvador.
Photograph by author.

in the 1860s in Brazil.[71] One of its major leaders was Luís Gonzaga Pinto da Gama (1830–82), born in Bahia to an African Nagô freedwoman *(Africana livre)* named Luísa Matheu Mahin.[72] Accused of involvement in the revolt of the Malês, Mahin had joined the exodus of Africans to Rio de Janeiro in the wake of the rebellion. Gama's father was a wealthy Portuguese lord *(fidalgo)* who sold his son illegally as a slave at age ten to pay off his gambling debts.

In November 1840, Gama arrived in Rio de Janeiro on board the ship *Saraiva*, one of the thousands of slaves sent out of Bahia as part of the interprovincial slave trade. One among a group of more than one hundred slaves purchased by a slave trafficker named Antônio Pereira Cardoso, Gama continued on his difficult journey, traveling by boat to the port city of Santos then walking overland to the interior towns of Campinas and Jundiaí, all in the province of São Paulo. Given the bad reputation of insurgent Bahian slaves, no coffee planter came forward to purchase Gama. As a consequence, Cardoso kept Gama as his personal slave.

For the next eight years, Gama resided on Cardoso's estate in the city of São Paulo. He learned to read and write from a student renting a room in the house. In 1848, Gama escaped and, by unknown means, obtained legal documents that confirmed that he had been born a free person. He joined the Urban Guard, a military police force, where he remained until 1854. Discharged for insubordination, Gama subsequently was able to gain employment in the São Paulo police force. Using his education and extraordinary intellectual energies, he became a lawyer. Allowed by the judicial system to practice law without a formal degree (such an individual known as a *rábula* or *curador*), Gama defended poor blacks and slaves in the courts of São Paulo.[73]

By the early 1860s, Gama gained notoriety for a collection of poems entitled *Primeiras trovas burlescas de Getuliano* (1859; The First Burlesque Ballads of Getuliano; second expanded edition published as *Novas trovas burlescas* in 1861). With satire and humor, Gama expressed his sentiments for the first time in print. A *pardo* (a person of mixed European and African ancestry) who considered himself to be a black man, Gama expressed his pride in being the son of a black African woman, praised Africa, and condemned slavery in Brazil. The Paulista historian Elciene Azevedo writes, "The tone given by Luís Gama to his poems, far from creating a lamentable image of blacks bonded to forced work and as victims of slavery, carried the reader to a black world dissociated from compulsory work and affirmed in its cultural aspects."[74] The poems exhibit an incorporation of the rich African cultures Gama experienced during his youth in Salvador into a mature worldview. Azevedo contends, "The identification of Luís Gama with Africa was linked to insubordination, to the idea that Africans could be, and in many instances had been, agents in the construction of their own history."[75] Certainly Gama's personal experience with an uncaring white father and nurturing African mother contributed to his attraction to all things African.

Gama gained notoriety in São Paulo soon after the outbreak of the Paraguayan War. Gama published a picture in the newspaper he edited that depicted black soldiers coerced into joining the army. Above the picture he printed the inflammatory words "Hunting of patriots to be involuntary volunteers."[76] Gama also asserted in speeches and in print that slaves had the right to use violence against owners. With the aid of the Paulistano Radical Club and the Masons, Gama helped many slaves to gain freedom through the court system. By the end of his career, one thousand slaves had benefited from his legal assistance. For his unceasing agitation as a lawyer and journalist, he was fired from his job in the police force of the city in 1869. Reacting to this "violent and illegal" act in newspaper editorials, Gama cynically scorned the values of the Paulista elite, incompetent judges, and the corruption of the monarchy.

> I know that some persons in this city [São Paulo], kindly taking advantage of the initiatives of the student movement [that sought reforms], sent notice to the Corte [home of the imperial government in Rio de Janeiro], and to the interior of the province, that what is going on here has resulted in enormous calamities, and is the cause of tremendous disasters and horrible desolation; all of this has been provoked by agents of the [communist] INTERNATIONAL! . . . and that I (who could not, for sure, but be part of this sinister anarchy) have been encouraging a tremendous insurrection of slaves!
>
> If some day the prestigious judges of Brazil . . . disregard their irrevocable obligations to morals and our nation corrupted by venality and the deleterious influence of power, and [decide to] abandon the sacrosanct cause of the law, and [instead] by some strange aberration, fail to uphold the norms of justice [implying injustice] with regards to those who suffer unjust enslavement, I, at my own cost, without asking for help from anyone, and under my direction only, will suggest and promote, not insurrection, which is a crime, but "resistance," which is a civic virtue, as the best way to confront the aristocratic thieves, the corrupt contrabands, the perverted justices, and all the false and impudent power-brokers.[77]

In response, politicians and judges accused him of subversion and inciting rebellion by slaves. Commenting on Gama's legal defense of African slaves illegally transported to Brazil after the 1831 law, the president of the province of São Paulo wrote that Gama had somehow "confounded philanthropy with an exaggerated *negrophilism*."[78]

Founder and editor of the newspaper *Diabo Coxo* (Lame Devil, 1864–65), the first illustrated lampoon magazine in São Paulo, Gama also founded and edited *O Cabrião* (Billy-Goat, 1865–67) and contributed to *O Iparanga, O Polichinelo,* and *O Radical Paulistano,* all in São Paulo. During the debates over the Law of the Free Womb, Gama called for an immediate end to slavery, the overthrow of the monarchy, and the establishment of democracy in Brazil. The moderate Joaquim Nabuco viewed Gama as a threat to monarchical institutions that Nabuco supported. Nabuco considered Gama irresponsible in his tactics and someone who might inspire fellow descendants of Africans to seek unacceptable positions of power.[79] Yet, numerous Bahians closely followed Luís Gama's political trajectory in São Paulo; in Salvador, activists named an abolitionist society and a "patriotic battalion" after him.

Another extraordinary figure who gained prominence during the war with Paraguay was the Bahian-born Cândido de Fonseca Galvão (1845–90), known also as Prince Obá II and "the Prince of the People." Galvão was the grandson of the powerful African prince Alafin Abiodun, who unified the Yoruba kingdom of Oyó in the late eighteenth century. Galvão's father fought in the wars that raged in that region of Africa in the early nineteenth century, was captured in battle, and sold into slavery. He was then transported to Bahia. With the help of friends among the Yoruba community in Salvador, Galvão's father quickly purchased his freedom. He then married and had children. As an offspring of freedpersons, Cândido Galvão was raised as a free black man near the town of Lençóis in the interior of Bahia.

Dom Obá II considered it his duty to fight for his country in the war against Paraguay. "As the patriotic soldier that I am, I understand that I have only been doing my duty in taking an active part in all the matters that I understand to be grave."[80] Enlisting as a Voluntário in an all-black Zuavo company that departed from Lençóis in May 1865, Galvão remained at the front until wounded in his right hand in August 1866. After his return to Bahia, where he remained through the decade of the 1870s, Galvão petitioned government officials for recognition of his service during the war and for monetary compensation. His experience in Paraguay inspired his commitment to ending slavery in Brazil and his pride in being a black man.

Galvão settled in Rio de Janeiro by 1880, where he gained renown. The wealthy considered him a "disturbed veteran" (*uma espécie de veterano resmungão*) and "folkloric aberration" due to his outspokenness and appearance in attire that included a long black morning coat, tall hat, gloves, umbrella, and walking cane. An activist of the first order, Galvão met personally with the emperor 125 times at public meetings from June 1882 to December 1884! Pedro II encouraged such encounters to discuss social and political issues with influential citizens.[81] Dom Obá II garnered great respect among "the Blacks and the Browns" (the terms commonly used by Galvão) residing in the city. Slaves, freedpersons, and free persons of color all provided financial support that enabled the prince to publish articles in newspapers. In his writings, Galvão praised the contributions of black and brown soldiers during the Paraguayan War, condemned the racism he witnessed in Brazil, and called for an end to slavery.[82] He wrote:

> The only desire that certain ungrateful [proslavery] Brazilians have is to live in laziness, and [they do] not want [care about] the well-being of the country, nor to help the blind desire of the whole nation to wash itself once and for all of the great stain of slavery. Their fate will be to end up stark raving mad in order to pay for the consciences which they owe to God and the majesties as much as to the blacks and the brown-skinned. [Such] nobles . . . [want] God for themselves and the devil for the rest . . . in that they do not want to give freedom to slavery [to the slaves] . . . as has been given in the most civilized places in Europe.[83]

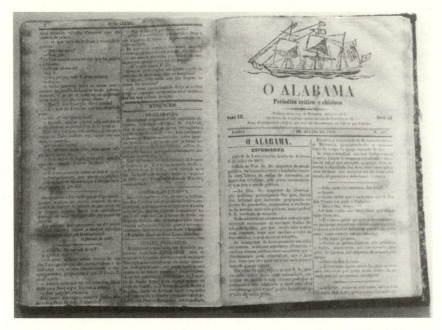

Figure 3.2 The newspaper *O Alabama: Periódico crítico e chistoso* (The Alabama: A Critical and Humorous Newspaper) was published biweekly in Salvador from 1863 to 1883 and again between 1887 and 1890. Courtesy of the Institute of Geography and History of Bahia, Salvador.

An important locus of the abolitionist movement composed of African Brazilians coalesced in Salvador. Writing for the newspaper *O Alabama*, journalists of color played a decisive role in mobilizing abolitionist protest in Bahia during and after the war. Labeled a "critical and humorous newspaper," the masthead parodied a mythical ship (named *O Alabama*) which sailed through the streets of the city "Latronopolis" (Salvador) and across the Bahian countryside.[84]

First published in December 1863, *O Alabama* covered closely the Paraguayan War and its impact on Bahia. It criticized the forced recruitment of unwilling conscripts carried out in Salvador. Police on horseback with unsheathed swords used superior force to "rope-in" soldiers. Such actions caused turmoil and bitterness. War and abolition became closely linked in the pages of *O Alabama*. In the words of one contributor, "A country cannot call itself a nation that is progressive if it has slavery; after the tremendous war with Paraguay, in which Brazil elevated itself to the highest level of splendor, it needs immediately to address this issue. The power of the [free] people is immense."[85]

O Alabama posited its abolitionist stance from early in 1866. The newspaper analyzed speeches and political debates throughout the empire and publicized the rise of abolitionist societies in several Brazilian cities. Its pages included close scrutiny of slave resistance in Salvador and the interior of Bahia. One writer appealed to delegates in Bahia's provincial assembly to ponder the impact of their words and votes: "The emancipation of workers is no longer merely an aspiration or a Christian ideal; it is a national endeavor, an obligation, a social responsibility, and no longer do forces exist today to prevent it."[86]

O Alabama questioned how Brazil's independence from Portugal (in 1822) could be celebrated while thousands of blacks remained enslaved. In subsequent years, abolitionist symbols became an integral part of Brazil's, and especially, Bahia's Independence Day festivities (September 7 and July 2).[87] Its journalists denounced abusive treatment of slaves by Bahian slave owners, racial discrimination, unhealthy working conditions, and police corruption.

O Alabama published poems with titles like "Lamentations of an African" and "Captive." These expressed sympathy with the plight of slaves and freedpersons.[88] Remarkable stories that included characters speaking a crass "street" Portuguese shed light on the sentiments of uneducated blacks. One begins with the words, "Captain [of the mythical ship *Alabama*], I am not a brute negro. I am a civilized negro. I want to have a discussion to clear up this misconception" [*Capitão, iô nan tan negro bruto. Iô tan negro civirisado; iô qué dicucão pra siclarecer idéia*].[89] Bahian president Luís Antônio Barbosa de Almeida claimed such essays fostered a "spirit of anarchy." Denouncing *O Alabama* as one of the "most contemptible" publications in the province, the president accused its writers of seeking to "create embarrassment for all parts of the government and administration."[90]

Reflecting its populist bent, the newspaper rejected the idea that leaders of the empire had a genuine interest in implementing enlightened reforms. Instead, one writer described the Law of the Free Womb as "an idea of the *povo* [people or folk] that is spreading on a large scale."[91] *O Alabama* played a major role in propagating abolitionist ideas in Bahia during and after the war with Paraguay.

Political Dissent

Disillusionment with the war and Pedro II surfaced among elite Bahians. In late 1870, a short book appeared in Salvador entitled *O Duque de Caxias e a Guerra do Paraguay: Estudo Crítico-Histórico* (1870; The Duke of Caxias and the War with Paraguay: A Critical Study). Penned by a sixth-year student at the Faculty of Medicine in Salvador who had been stationed at the front as a surgeon, Satyro de Oliveira Dias called for an open and frank discussion of what had transpired during the war. Instead of lies and distortions perpetrated by the imperial government and published in newspapers to "delude the public," he desired to "speak the truth to the nation." Dias accused the duke of Caxias as having been abominable as the commander in chief of the Brazilian army. He lamented that thousands of Brazilian soldiers had died futilely due to the duke's incompetence.

Dias meticulously analyzed Caxias's leadership from his arrival in Paraguay in October 1866 until his hasty desertion and return to Rio de Janeiro in February 1869. Dias accused Caxias of being a traitor to the nation motivated solely by a desire to be judged favorably in history.[92] Besides failing as a military strategist and leader, Caxias had committed "administrative errors," proved incapable of supplying troops adequately, paid soldiers inequitably, and "scandalously" handed out "medals of merit" to his friends back in Rio de Janeiro.[93] In the author's opinion, the real heroes had been the citizen-soldiers who had fought heroically and steadily during the war.

Politicians also expressed their unhappiness with the war effort. Liberal representatives in Bahia's provincial assembly questioned war policies and made plain their distrust of Pedro II and his allies in Bahia. Accused by Conservatives of being "anarchists" and "enemies of order and social prosperity," these reformers aligned themselves with a radical bloc that became known as the Republican Party. At the close of the 1869 session (which met from April 11 to June 11), some one hundred people waited in the streets to commend Liberal delegates. The crowd included students from the Faculty of Medicine and well-known political figures. A parade ensued that wound its way to the offices of the *Diário da Bahia*, where the multitude applauded calls to support a Republican Party and "the people."[94]

Conclusions

The War of the Triple Alliance cost dearly in terms of lost men and wasted financial resources. An estimated 300,000 died in the war, out of a total population of 12.2 million in the four countries involved (2.4 percent). In comparison, 620,000 men died during the U.S. Civil War, out of a total population of 31 million (2 percent).[95] Paraguayans made up more than three-quarters of the total who perished in the conflict (or an estimated 225,000 men), the majority from starvation and disease. Paraguay began the war with a population of 450,000 inhabitants, and ended with 220,000, of whom 28,000 were men. Perhaps as many as 60,000 Brazilian soldiers died, or more than two-thirds of the total Allied losses. Difficult, if not impossible, is to measure the total cost of the war. Certainly the estimate of 400 million U.S. dollars cited above (from 1885) suggests a staggering loss of treasure.[96]

Slaves responded to opportunities created by the war. They fled from owners to enlist in the army, to join quilombos in the interior, hide in Salvador, or travel to other provinces. Groups of slaves appeared before police and judges to appeal for protection from abusive owners. They paid close attention to articles published in *O Alabama*. They made contact with newly formed upper-class abolitionist societies that emerged in Salvador in the late 1860s.

Pomp and pageantry at war's beginning and end could not hide the disillusionment felt by a large segment of Brazil's lower class and Bahians in particular. This underclass had minimal confidence in the policies or promises of political and military leaders. Soldiers and their families in Brazil suffered due to harsh recruitment practices and failed promises of reimbursement for their efforts. Such treatment caused them to be receptive to the spread of antislavery ideas in the Bahian Recôncavo. Slave owners squelched attempts by the free underclass to join with slaves in shared endeavors.

In response to domestic pressures (slave resistance, an abolitionist movement composed of blacks and persons of color, the appearance of abolitionist societies in several provinces, widespread disillusionment with the war effort, the emergence of a Republican movement opposed to Pedro II and monarchical institutions), and international pressures (the end of the U.S. Civil War, British and French condemnation, abolition of slavery in Paraguay in 1869, passage of a Law of the Free Womb in Cuba and Puerto Rico in 1870), Pedro II chose a Bahian to push through emancipation legislation. José Maria da Silva Paranhos (1819–80), better known as the Viscount of Rio Branco, understood the dire impact of the war on Bahia and the nation. He had witnessed the violent protests directed at recruiters, the outright hostility of war veterans, and the disruptions caused by slave resistance. Only a measure that appeared to be a viable step toward final emancipation in a distant future, but one that did not infringe on planter-merchant rights in the present, resolved the impasse.[97] In the words of a Bahian, "It was necessary for the government to play a role in this difficult endeavor, and this occurred, thanks to the spirit of the epoch. Yes, Brazil finally embraces those great words—*equality, fraternity, and liberty.*"[98]

The reality was something different. The Law of the Free Womb did little to weaken the resolve of many owners to retain their slaves. It would take another seventeen years of struggle before the imperial government gave official sanction to the end of slavery. ▣

CHAPTER FOUR

Castro Alves

While the war raged against Paraguay, a radical abolitionist gained a national following in Brazil. Born in the interior of Bahia, Antônio Frederico de Castro Alves (1847–71) lived an intense and short life. He wrote his first poems critical of slavery at age fourteen. At age sixteen, he showed early symptoms of tuberculosis. By the time he had reached twenty, both of his parents had died from tuberculosis and his older brother had committed suicide. In the face of extraordinary personal adversity, Castro Alves demonstrated impressive resolve and strength. At the time of his death in July 1871, at age twenty-four, Castro Alves had gained widespread fame as a critic of slavery and the imperial government. Influenced by African Bahian culture and resistance, Castro Alves recited his poems in settings ranging from public street gatherings to the private homes of the planter elite. Without a doubt, the writings and political actions of Castro Alves facilitated passage of the Law of the Free Womb, a critical initiative in bringing an end to Brazilian slavery, two months after his death.

From his earliest youth, Castro Alves showed remarkable intellectual abilities. His father was a physician and his mother a member of the Bahian aristocracy. The family resided for short periods in interior Bahian towns of Muritiba and São Félix before moving to Salvador in 1854. Raised and educated in Salvador, Alves attended a private Bahian middle school (Ginásio Baiano) the first year it opened in 1858. Founded by the educational reformer Abílio César Borges (1824–91), the Ginásio Baiano attracted elite students from Salvador, smaller towns in Bahia, as well as from other provinces. Borges implemented innovative approaches to learning. Influenced by progressive ideas about education, for example, those espoused by José Pedro Varela in Uruguay and Horace Mann in the United States, teachers rejected physical punishment of students for misbehavior or failing to perform adequately in the classroom.[1] While a student, Castro Alves read prolifically, including the works of Virgil, Homer, Camões, Byron, and Hugo. He studied the French language in school, and it is likely that he learned to read English on his own.[2] Impressed by the bourgeois democratic ideas that framed his intellectual formation, Alves praised the French Revolution in his poems.

The urban milieu of Salvador also helped shape the life and writings of Castro Alves. When he entered the Ginásio Baiano in the late 1850s, Africans and their Brazilian-born descendants resided and labored across the city. Alves drank deeply of the black world that surrounded him. In the words of Bahian novelist Jorge Amado, "The sounds of the *atabaques* [meaning the narrow conical drums used to summon the gods in Candomblé ceremonies] traversed all the city and came to resonate in the soul of Castro Alves."[3] He witnessed firsthand the brutalities inflicted on slaves and the discrimination universally experienced by persons of color. And, at his father's private clinic located on the first floor of their home, Alves observed the physical sufferings endured by sick and injured slaves.[4]

From 1862 to 1867 he resided in the coastal city of Recife in Pernambuco while attending classes at the Recife Law School. In subsequent years, Alves continued his legal studies in the city of São Paulo and visited the city of Rio de Janeiro. He returned to Bahia in late 1869 where he remained until his death in 1871.[5] While in São Paulo, he met and communicated with a rising generation of Brazilian intellectuals and political leaders, including Luís Gama, Joaquim Nabuco, Rui Barbosa, future governor of Bahia Luís Vianna, and the future presidents of Brazil Rodrigues Alves and Afonso Penna. Through his writings and recitations Alves gained the admiring attention of these talented, well-connected individuals.

Castro Alves played a decisive role in forcing the abolitionist debate to the forefront of Brazilian politics. At a time (the middle of the 1860s) when Liberals spoke vaguely about gradual emancipation at some undefined date in the future, Alves called for immediate abolition. An astute observer of the Brazilian political scene, he specialized in a genre of poetry know as *condoreirismo* ("condorism," meaning a poetry of liberation that is inspired by the flight of condor in its natural habitat of the Andes mountains). In spite of his own experiences with suffering and tragedy, Alves sought to uplift audiences with a message of hope, exhilaration, and empowerment. The final stanza from one of his early poems entitled "O século" (1865; "The Century,") displays his passion:

> Enough! . . . I know that youth
> is Moses on Mount Sinai
> reaching out his hands
> for the tablets of the law.
> March on! For he who falls
> in the [abolitionist] fight with honor
> falls in the arms of history,
> into the heart of Brazil.
> From the peaks of the Andes—
> those high wide pyramids—
> a million centuries are watching you.[6]

The Bahian intellectual Edison Carneiro (1912–72) praised Alves's writings as "poetry of combat, always seeking popular vindication. No other Brazilian poet aligned himself so fully on the side of the [common] people as Castro Alves."[7]

This chapter places the poetry and worldview of Castro Alves into an historical context. It emphasizes the poet's determination to bring about reform in his country. Furthermore, it points to the close ties between Alves's poetry and the first phase of the abolitionist movement in Bahia.

"Poet of the Slaves"

Soon after his arrival in Recife in January 1862, Castro Alves began composing a series of poems that called for the immediate abolition of slavery throughout the empire. Such an uncompromising stance made him one of the first and most visible advocates demanding an end to an institution that had been integral to Brazil's economy and society for more than three centuries. Several factors led Alves in this direction. He was influenced by the abolitionist movement in the northern United

States (1830–60) and by Lincoln's Emancipation Proclamation (1863) that formally initiated an end to slavery. Alves judged the Union victory over the South (1865) to be a symbol of divine justice. In the poem "The Century," he asked, "Don't you hear a cry in the North?"[8]

The outbreak of hostilities against Paraguay also influenced Alves's political views. Witness to harsh recruitment tactics in Recife, he denounced police violence. Although he wrote a couple of patriotic poems in support of the war effort, Alves questioned the motives for the conflict and appealed to imperial leaders to care for the orphans of soldiers who did not return home.[9] His enlistment in the Academic Battalion of Volunteers (Batalhão Acadêmico de Voluntários) in August 1865 had more to do with the poet's desire to show fraternal solidarity with soldiers who went off to war rather than any personal interest in fighting. One year later, he disregarded a letter he received from the police in Bahia requesting that he enlist as a soldier.[10]

Alienated by the emperor's conservative stance on emancipation during the war years, Alves criticized the government's plan to wait until the cessation of hostilities with Paraguay to implement emancipation reform. With the hope of garnering support for immediate abolition, he focused on the degradation and immorality of slavery as central themes in his poetry. Alves quickly gained renown as the "poet of the slaves" (*poeta dos escravos*).[11]

During a six-month period in mid-1865, Alves wrote at least sixteen abolitionist poems. These writings reflected Alves's desire to force abolition on to the national political scene. He hoped to raise the awareness of common Brazilians about the injustices that prevailed throughout the nation. Alves recited his verses at public gatherings, where his words reached a large audience.[12] With rhetorical and emotional flourishes, Castro Alves presented his poetry to interested listeners at antislavery and literary meetings. Public recitations offered a way to communicate information and ideas. Gatherings of common folk fostered a sense of community and shared interest. In the words of one Bahian journalist, "We lack the means to analyze [Alves's] literary productions: [instead] we judge him, like the majority of readers, by our ear, with our souls, by means of impressions received and emotions experienced."[13] Very few of these early poems were published in student or academic journals.[14] In fact, a complete collection of his work remained unpublished until 1883 when they appeared under the title *Os escravos* (1883; The Slaves).[15]

Alves's personal intensity and capacity to incite a live audience are evident in the poem "América" (1865; "America"):

> Wake up, mother country. Don't bow your head.
> The tropic sun will dry up all your tears.
> Look on the edge of the wide horizon:
> the dawn moon of better years.
> It won't take much. Shake off the chain
> that you call wealth. It mars what could be good.
> Don't stain the page of the nation's story
> with foul displays of slave's blood.
> If you'll be poor, so what? Be free,
> as noble as the condor of the high lands.
> Remove the weight of Atlas's shoulders.
> Lift the cross from God's hands.[16]

In "America," as in other poems penned during these months, Castro Alves addressed a wide range of issues. He hoped that individuals would act responsibly, expressing his dismay over wealth attained through exploitation and condemning the reactionary position of the Catholic Church with regard to abolition.

The poem "Bandido negro" ("Black Bandit") was most likely also written in 1865.[17] In it, Alves described an escaped slave who called on fellow slaves to resist their masters. Symbolic of Castro Alves's politics, it demonstrated his support of activists such as Luís Gama in São Paulo.[18] The poem invoked disturbing images of black men spreading terror across the countryside. It conveyed the unmistakable message that those who abused slaves would face retribution for their acts.

The earth quakes from the sudden shock
My horse is swift, black, sweating—
she flies on to hidden caves.
The sky shakes out a danger cry,
for the black bandit rides by
and the black bandit calls out:

Drip down, dewdrops, slave's blood,
drip down, dewdrops on the hangman's face.
Grow tall, cornfields, ripe red.
Grow, rough wild revenge.[19]

Castro Alves composed the poems "Vozes d'Africa" ("Voices of Africa") and "O navio negreiro e tragédia do mar" ("The Slave Ship and Tragedy at Sea") soon after his arrival to the city of São Paulo in March 1868. In the former, Alves asks:

God! Where are you? Why don't you answer me?
For two thousand years I have called on you,
With a plea echoing in vain through space . . .
Have I not had enough grief, oh cruel God?
For then your eternal breast knows no bounds
Of vengeance and malice?
And what have I done, Lord? What heinous crime
Have I ever committed that your vengeful
Sword should oppress me so?[20]

In "The Slave Ship" (first published in 1869), Castro Alves wrote of conditions on a slaving vessel transporting African slaves from their homelands in Africa to the Brazilian coast. He provoked audiences by depicting the horrors witnessed on board. The first five stanzas begin with the phrase "We are on the high seas," which set a tone of remoteness and vulnerability. In the third section of the poem, Alves exclaimed:

Swoop down from the heavens, eagle of the oceans!
Descend more, yet more . . . look where human eyes cannot
And sound the depths of this wandering hell!
Yet I will turn my eyes upon this well of grief! . . .
Listen to the death-songs, gaze into their deadened eyes! . . .
This theater of evil . . . My God, My God, what horror!²¹

"The Slave Ship" has been criticized as an "anachronism," given that the international slave trade to Brazil had ended eighteen years previously.²² But this criticism fails to consider the relationship of the poem to the historical moment, and it does not appreciate the poet's strategies as a political organizer on behalf of abolition. There is little doubt that Castro Alves understood that the Eusébio de Queiroz Law of 1850 resulted in a precipitous decline of the number of ships plying the Atlantic Ocean to bring African slaves to Brazil. His intention, rather, was to render in detail one horrific voyage of that terrible trade as a way to force slavery, the living legacy of the slave trade, to the center of political discourse. Alves sought to mobilize an abolitionist movement capable of seeking an immediate end of slavery in Brazil.

Furthermore, despite the end of the African slave trade in the early 1850s, trafficking in slaves in 1868 remained a topic of controversy among activists and intellectuals. Ships still continued to transport African slaves to Cuba. Brazilians expressed fear of a resumption of the international slave trade at this juncture to satisfy the demand for slave labor in Brazil.²³ *O Alabama* reminded its readers that Bahian president Francisco Gonçalves Martins had participated in a slave-smuggling ring earlier in his career. The newspaper also condemned the interprovincial slave trade responsible for the transport of an estimated 5,000 to 7,500 slaves each year (which rose to 10,000 per year from 1872 until the internal trade ended in 1881) from the North-Northeast to the Center-South of Brazil.²⁴ The trauma of separation and conditions endured by slaves during these journeys compared to those experienced during the international slave trade from Africa to Brazil.

The *Correio Paulistano* of São Paulo (1869) and the *Jornal da Tarde* of Rio de Janeiro (1870) both printed "The Slave Ship."[25] By reciting in public and later publishing this provocative poem, Castro Alves desired to bring notice to the few committed radicals in Brazil at that moment. Several journalists, like the poet himself, hoped to generate hostility toward slaveholders. The motive for writing "The Slave Ship" had as much to do with political struggles of the late 1860s as with one poet's philosophical reminiscence of a commerce responsible for carrying 4.5 million Africans to Brazil. More than any other contribution, the verses from "The Slave Ship" helped make Castro Alves a figure of national prominence.

In early November 1868 the poet was seriously injured while out hunting when his gun misfired into his left foot. For the next six and a half months, he attempted to recover from the wound at his residence in São Paulo. In spite of visits from friends, Alves experienced depression, intensified due to the end of a love affair with the actress Eugênia Câmara. In mid-May 1869, Alves traveled by boat to Rio de Janeiro, where two prestigious surgeons attempted to repair his damaged foot. Their efforts failed and led to the amputation of his left leg below the knee. For the remainder of his life, Alves used a wooden leg and crutches to move about.

On November 25 of that year, Castro Alves returned to Bahia. Suffering from tuberculosis and seeking to regain his strength from the loss of his leg, Alves traveled west to the interior towns of Curralinho (today the city of Castro Alves) and then to the Fazenda Santa Isabel located near the town of Itaberaba. The estate was located near Orobó, a region famous as home to some of the largest quilombos in Bahia in the eighteenth century. Alves encountered local residents who remembered well the destruction of those quilombos in 1797.[26] He took horseback rides to experience the countryside and to forget about the physical and emotional problems that plagued him. During these outings, Alves also witnessed public slave auctions and saw posted fugitive slave notices, learning firsthand about slave flight.[27]

His experiences in the countryside of Bahia inspired Castro Alves to compose a short poem of seven verses entitled "Saudação a Palmares" (1870; "Salute to Palmares"). The poem paid homage to the seventeenth-century quilombo located in the interior of the provinces of Alagoas and

Pernambuco.[28] With more than twenty thousand residents, Palmares had flourished for a century (1590s–1694), controlling an area the size of Portugal. Given that "Salute to Palmares" ranks as one of his most radical poems, its timing and message represented a clear political statement.

"Salute to Palmares"
Among the high climbing cliffs,
a bold eagle's nest.
Hail, land of the bandit!
Hail, home of the jaguar,
green hills where the palm groves
unfurl Indian feathers
in the pigeon-blue air
and struggle to wave free.

Hail this place of courage
where the echo's loud reply
sends the cry of the hunter
across the trembling plains.
You can hear the dogs bark
and the trumpets sound out
while black crows fly back
across the burning fields.

Palmares! I salute you,
Hard stone boat
in the endless shipwreck.
You've unveiled the thunder,
set loose the gust of wind
and released the flapping banner
to the sound of sailors' howls
on the waves of slavery.

Great place of bravery,
fortress of liberty,
you grab the handle of your sword
and laugh across the valley:
"I come from each horizon.
Master! Look me in the face."
You laugh the laugh of a mountain
and you smile a jackal's smile.

Immoral eunuchs sing to kings
in their marble palaces
and kiss the iron chains
which they dare not break.
I sing about your beauty,
half-naked huntress.
Your legs wear the red skin
of a tapir.

Half-breed! Your dark breast
never felt an unclean kiss.
Smooth, bright, hard, firm
you save yourself for noble love.
Black Diana, wild one,
you listen underneath the trees
to voices that the breezes bring
from your hard strong hunters.

Hail the fighting Amazon.
Among the rocks of open ground,
the loud roar of the waterfall,
you know how to drink and fight.
Hail, up high in the climbing cliffs
the nest of daring dreams
of the condor and the bandit—
freedom and the jaguar.[29]

Despite its importance to modern Brazilians, little was known about the quilombo Palmares in the 1870s. In spite of a long tradition of slave resistance in Bahia and throughout the Northeast, few intellectuals had spoken of, much less written about, Palmares. Members of the Brazilian Institute of History and Geography (in Rio de Janeiro) carried on "lively discussions" about Palmares at their meetings in 1840, but only around 1851 did they begin to search for materials that might provide evidence about what happened at Palmares.[30] In 1870, a twenty-one-year-old law student named Joaquim Nabuco (1849–1910) dedicated three pages of an essay entitled "A escravidão" (Slavery) to the *"quilombo dos Palmares."*[31] The man who would later become Brazil's most famous abolitionist showed a remarkable ignorance of slave resistance when he referred to Palmares as the "only attempt of the negroes among us to emancipate themselves."[32]

"Salute to Palmares" has received mixed reviews from scholars. Among those critical of the piece was the Bahian anthropologist Edison Carneiro. In his book *Castro Alves (1847–71): Uma interpretação política* (1947; Castro Alves [1847–71]: A Political Interpretation), Carneiro derided Castro Alves's "Salute to Palmares" as a creation of "pure imagination."[33] He believed that, given his lack of knowledge of what happened at Palmares, Alves should never have attempted to write about this seventeenth-century quilombo. Conscious of the fact that Alves had planned to write a longer "epic poem" about the quilombo Palmares, Carneiro stated dismissively that both poet and public had been spared a disastrous outcome. In Carneiro's opinion, "Salute to Palmares" had "no roots [or relationship] in time or space" [*sem raizes no tempo e no espaço*].[34]

Such a critique should not deter our effort to evaluate the literary and political merits of the poem. A close reading demonstrates that Castro Alves understood the broad outline of what had occurred at Palmares. "High climbing cliffs" described the mountainous areas where Palmarinos constructed villages for defensive purposes. The sound of the barking dogs alluded to vicious dogs used by *capitães-do-mato* (slave hunters) in their search for fugitive slaves. "Burning fields" symbolized the sugarcane set on fire by soldiers from Palmares during their incursions into the plantation zone. Other descriptive terms such as "fortress of liberty," "half-naked huntress," and "daring demons," particularly when spoken with passion by Castro Alves, left listeners moved with clear, concise words and ideas to ponder.

The poem "Salute to Palmares" encouraged listeners to reflect on a past in which slaves had fought for their rights. The verses applauded heroic blacks determined to gain their freedom. The poet desired that his message of flight and liberation extol the courage exhibited by African and Brazilian-born crioulo slaves for centuries throughout Brazil. Castro Alves hoped "Salute to Palmares" might inspire listeners to join in the effort to end slavery.

Two other important political poems by Castro Alves appeared in 1870. In "Deusa Incruenta" ("Bloodless Goddess"), Alves alluded to a free press as decisive in bringing about political and social reform in a civilized society. He believed that war, tyranny, crime, and slavery could all be eradicated. It is an eloquent poem, as exemplified by the following lines:

> The cave addressed the sky: What prodigious Goddess is this?
> Space responded: "It is the Diva of the West!
> The conscience of the world! The Me of Creation!"
> When the vile Bastille trembled uprooted
> And the hammer-blow sounded from top to bottom,
> The human catapult, the voice of Mirabeau! . . .
> When that ideal Quasimodo stirred up from the abyss
> And the kings howled in the cataclysm
> The Bellringer sounded the alarm through the centuries![35]

Alves believed it was the responsibility of the artist-propagandist to bring attention to desperate lives of the poor and marginalized. "Bloodless Goddess" has been described as a "flagrantly social" poem in which Alves applauded the capacity of newspapers to spread ideas.[36]

"Estrophes do solitário" ("Solitary Stanzas") called for action. He begins with the words "Enough of the cowardice! The hour has struck [to end slavery]" and proclaims that "a new generation tears through the earth; the revolution [abolition] thunders." A later verse affirms:

> Meanwhile, this century has deemed it fair
> To unfurl the flag of equality,
> To be Byron's brother . . .
> And prodigal to will in testament
> To this Brazilian Greece, a new free flag,
> To the world, a nation.[37]

In mid-1870, "Solitary Stanzas" appeared in Salvador in the pages of *Diário da Bahia*.[38] Alves's childhood friend Rui Barbosa was a source of inspiration for these verses.[39] Barbosa joined the editorial board of the recently founded newspaper *O Radical Paulistano* in São Paulo a year earlier. In an editorial, Barbosa called for reforms while berating Pedro II.

> Dom Pedro II, who in 1867 and 1868 solemnly declaimed about the urgency of abolitionist reform, who made a great display of his negotiations in our country and abroad, who used every means to show off his humanitarian tendencies—now, in front of all our eyes, the one thing that he could justifiably brag about is ripped to shreds by his despotic demonstration of authority, his silent retreat from all of his promises, his mysterious and unjustifiable withdrawal.

Barbosa concluded, "Abolition, whether the government wants it or not, is going to come soon. That's just the way it is."[40] An influential politician and trusted confidante, Barbosa's unyielding stance stimulated Castro Alves to continue writing and speaking.

Shortly before his death in 1871, Alves published his "Carta ás senhoras bahianas" (Letter to the Women of Bahia) in the newspaper *O abolicionista*.[41] As was common in the United States, Castro Alves linked abolition with female emancipation. In this eloquent essay, the poet appealed to female readers to consider their role as reformers. "[Giving a modest sum of money to an abolitionist group] is truly in the spirit of Christianity, [an act] fully associated with the future of women in modern societies." The letter showed a profound optimism: "You are the daughters of this magnificent land of America—nation of utopias—[composed of] regions created so that everyone can realize their dreams for liberty, an end to all prejudice [and] the attainment of true morality." He wrote that heroic women appeared throughout history "above the tumult of indecisive souls," citing Joan of Arc, Cassandra, and Harriet Beecher Stowe. Alves did not want the rights of women to be overlooked: "The nation which attains the emancipation of men needs also to ensure the emancipation of women. The land which creates universal suffrage does not have the right to refuse the vote to half of America." Unfortunately, the women of Bahia had to wait several decades before gaining the right to vote in Brazil (in 1932).[42]

Castro Alves believed that his poetry could inspire political action among his listeners. Alves traveled throughout Brazil reciting his poems. He published one collection of his verses before his untimely death, with another ready for publication. Alves called for a free press and the legal right to unrestricted assembly. He condemned any infringement of those freedoms by imperial authorities. Previous to the appearance of Castro Alves, few Brazilians spoke the word abolition or considered in a serious manner how such a reformist agenda might be implemented.

Cognizant of the potential benefits of organized protest, Alves helped establish one of the first abolitionist societies in Brazil while studying in Recife in 1866; later he joined in founding the Seventh of September Abolitionist Society in Salvador in 1869. These groups, predominantly composed of the bourgeoisie, had repercussions within the imperial government. For example, during the debates over the Free Womb Law in 1871, the antislavery deputy from Bahia Dr. João José de Oliveira Junqueira pointed to the contributions of the Seventh of September Abolitionist Society. Among its prestigious members, he noted, "questions of major importance" had been addressed. Junqueira pointed out that other abolitionist societies had been established in Salvador along with the interior towns of Cachoeira and Lençois, thus confirming "that the idea of emancipation of [the] slaves exists among a great part of the population [of Bahia]." Fellow representatives, including Dr. Theodoro Machado Freire Pereira da Silva, deputy from Pernambuco and minister of agriculture, acknowledged the significant "public spirit" witnessed in the province of Bahia concerning the "slavery question."[43]

Opinions vary widely on the role and impact of Castro Alves. In his study of the Bahian poet, the literary scholar David Haberly has written that "despite his [Castro Alves's] sincerity and his identification with the captives, his abolitionist verses were not calls to action, but appeals for pity and paeans to resignation," and that he was "unable to see abolitionism as a political cause."[44] Such a view echoes earlier Brazilian authors who wrote disparagingly about Castro Alves over the course of the twentieth century. Euclides da Cunha, who gained fame for his description of the expeditions that destroyed Canudos in *Os sertões* (1902; translated into English as *Rebellion in the Backlands*, 1944), commented on the career and influence of Alves in a speech at the Law Faculty of São Paulo (December 1907). Da Cunha depicted Alves's poetry as an "exaggeration of words" and the product of "impulsiveness." "The appearance [or glorification] of Castro Alves is, in great part, inexplicable," he said. Subsequent Brazilian authors berated the poems and minimized the influence of Castro Alves, including Arthur Ramos, Edison Carneiro, and Mário de Andrade.[45] Others, however, have presented Castro Alves in a markedly different light. In dedicating his *O Brasil nação: Realidade da soberania brasileira* (1931; 2d ed., 1996; The Brazilian Nation: Reality of Brazilian Sovereignty) to "the glory of Castro Alves," the Brazilian historian Manoel Bomfim (1868–1932) wrote:

Castro Alves raised his voice of revolutionary fervor to a level that completely dominated the environment [*Castro Alves alteou a sua voz de apóstolo revolucionário a ponto de dominar completamente a ambiência*]. He sought to struggle against injustice, to attack grotesque militarism, to pay homage to the glory of [critical] thought, and the benefits of employment. Such an animated poetry was absolutely new in Brazil; it was eminently social, and at the same time a literature of combat; [it was a poetry] entirely outside of [political] parties, and it appealed directly to the souls [of the people]. The great merit of Castro Alves was that his poetry was the exact expression of the essential sentiments of the nation. Exact expression, but so new, so sincere, and so potent, that it appeared as a revelation."[46]

Novelist Jorge Amado echoed this accolade. In *ABC de Castro Alves* (no date), Amado affirmed that the revolt of the Malês in 1835 remained fresh in the memory of Bahians when Alves wrote his poetry three decades after the event. Amado viewed Castro Alves above all else as a poet who encouraged slave insurgency. Alves "did not seek only to lament the conditions of black men, he wanted to liberate them. His song is not a lament, it is a hymn."[47]

Castro Alves's poetry left an important legacy. The Law of the Free Womb passed two months after his death, the culmination of the first phase of the abolitionist movement in Brazil. Alves reminded senators and deputies and common folk alike of the abuse and injustice associated with the enslavement of fellow human beings. Castroalvinian verses inspired hundreds of activists during the subsequent seventeen years leading up to liberation in May 1888. In spite of being denounced as "Communists" and "subversives," poets recited Alves's verses by memory in salons, at abolitionist meetings, and on the streets of cities and villages throughout the nation.[48] Publishers printed several collections of his poetry between 1871 and 1888, including six editions of "The Slaves" (or parts of it).[49] To mark the tenth anniversary of his death in 1881, multitudes of people gathered in Salvador, Rio de Janeiro, and São Paulo to pay homage to the life and work of this bard from Bahia.[50] As an abolitionist poet, Castro Alves challenged his fellow Brazilians to look critically and with open minds to their past so as to give them the tools to forge a better nation in the future: one shorn of slavery. It is no wonder that Castro Alves is heralded as an accomplished poet and political activist extraordinaire.[51]

A Final Reflection

In his response to both domestic and international politics of the 1860s, Castro Alves grappled with complex philosophical and psychological questions. A committed democrat, he supported the Republican Party that had coalesced in 1869. Alves scoffed at the reactionary stance of imperial officials and the Catholic Church. He condemned the use of violence by police and all forms of warfare. Although he sometimes moved in elite circles, he penned verses of social protest readily understood by people with little formal education. In the opinion of Edison Carneiro, "Never has a Brazilian poet felt more inclined [been more sympathetic] toward struggle, toward revolution, toward mass movements."[52] Alves respected the strong sense of regional pride often exhibited by Brazilians yet encouraged his listeners to view themselves as part of a great nation. He believed that shared Pan-American values could help to overcome racial and class antagonism. Alves brought Enlightenment thought associated with international abolition into the hearts and minds of his fellow Brazilians.

One of a handful of radicals speaking out in Brazil in the late 1860s, he exhibited a genuine appreciation of African culture and expression. Aware of the widespread appeal of Candomblé from his travels in the streets of Salvador and interior of Bahia, he understood the power and subtleties of African resistance. Alves's background distinguished him from the majority of abolitionists in Brazil. As the historian Celia M. Azevedo has noted, "Although Brazil did not have institutional segregation of free black people at the time of the rise of abolitionism, the white elite and black people—free and slave—lived in two worlds apart." This separation impeded "intellectual communication between white abolitionists and the black inhabitants of Brazil."[53] Intimate with African Salvador and sensitive to the suffering around him, Alves spoke and wrote in an attempt to break down those barriers. ▨

PART THREE
1888

Three Perspectives on

Abolition in Bahia

CHAPTER FIVE

Candomblé

The word Candomblé has its origins in a Bantu verbal form *ku-bon-da* or *ku-lomba*, meaning to praise, pray, worship, invoke, and "by extension, the place where these ceremonies are performed."[1] In Bahia, Candomblé was the name given to African Bahian religious ceremonies that paid homage to *orixás* (Yoruba word meaning male and female divinities).[2] Houses of Candomblé provided locales for the preservation of the rich cultures brought by African slaves transported to Brazil since the sixteenth century. Descendants from several African ethnicities (including Yoruba, Jeje, Kongo, and Angola) paid homage to their deities at terreiros in Bahia. Candomblé ceremonies often occurred at night in the homes of African freedpersons in Salvador or at more remote locations in the suburbs of the city and in the countryside.[3] Representatives of the Catholic Church along with influential Bahians considered Candomblé a cult practice that should be extinguished.[4] Appearing in official correspondence in Bahia for the first time in 1807, the word Candomblé came into popular use by the 1850s. Police documents, court cases, and newspaper accounts from midcentury to 1888 suggest that Candomblé was a form of resistance to the slave regime with ties to the abolitionist movement.[5]

"These Gatherings Are Attracting Brazilians of All Colors and Classes"

Africans practiced Candomblé in regions of West and South-Central Africa that include the modern nation-states of Nigeria and the Republic of Benin (Sudanese culture), and Angola, Congo, Gabon, Zaire, and Mozambique (Bantu culture). After arriving in Bahia, Africans continued to meet to pay homage to their gods and goddesses and to celebrate an annual cycle of religious festivities. For much of the Bahian elite, Candomblé represented "uncivilized" and dangerous behavior.

When included in police reports, the word Candomblé implied that untrustworthy Africans had met to carry out their ceremonies and indulge in lascivious acts. Contemporary descriptions of Candomblé revealed the racist attitudes prevalent in Europe and in Brazil that judged African "fetish" (*feitiço*) worship as inferior to Catholic religious thought and expression. After the arrest of a male leader (*curandeiro*, translated as witch doctor or charlatan) of a Candomblé ceremony in the Santo Antônio parish of Salvador, a police official wrote that he entered a house

> in which [the participants] performed superstitious and revolting scenes that not only offended our Sacred [Catholic] Religion but also the morals of inexperienced families. [Those who lead such ceremonies] are able to worm their way [*insinuar-se*] into the spirit of skeptics and non-believers, proclaiming to be [the embodiment of] a mysterious force. In this way, they are able to attract a huge crowd of [persons of] both sexes. Like parasites sucking sweat [from one's skin] they extort from each participant a payment of five thousand reis for the night. At these sinister gatherings, [the leaders] abuse our beneficent God. Young persons along with other participants at these bacchanals [are] always out of control, of bad backgrounds, accustomed to defamation. Aided by supposed religious leaders [they] commit all types of immoralities, [seeking] the libidinous fulfillment that induced them [to attend the Candomblé ceremony].[6]

Police scribes along with journalists alluded to Candomblé as a "focal point" of agitation and deprivation that appealed to persons of little income, minimal formal education, and who seemingly did not understand with what they were getting involved.[7]

After the failed revolt of the Malês, Candomblé remained a potent symbol of African subversion of the Brazilian nation. Descriptions of police sweeps (*invasões*, translated as invasions) of terreiros shed light on such attitudes.

In one of the houses we arrested an African named José, slave of Antônio Cypriano da Cunha Bettencourt, in whose possession was a found a box painted red, with contents inside that included three books written in unknown letters [most likely Arabic] along with other books. . . . In another house we arrested another African who says that he is the slave of the Cardosos. . . . Although the house is in terrible condition it is without doubt a front for huge gatherings [*reuniões* of Africans] . . . the second African has a house at his disposal and resides separate from his owners. . . . It was [also] necessary for us to close this second house, and I have the keys which I am sending to Your Excellency.[8]

The word *reunião* (reunion or meeting) as used by police in the report quoted above might be interpreted in different ways with regard to this document from 1853. It could have been employed simply to describe a gathering of Africans for whatever reason. Or it could imply that literate African Muslim slaves had been meeting and possibly plotting another rebellion. More likely, however, the word suggested Candomblé, similar to the way in which the term commonly appeared in documents to denote gatherings at terreiros in Salvador.

Candomblé and Islam became linked in the minds of the police. In the letter above, the search of one house turned up unknown red boxes and books written in an unintelligible language. The individuals who carried out the investigation were obviously perplexed over the source of these materials. Officials typically placed a high priority on the seizure of goods and on the translation of documents written in any language other than Portuguese (particularly Arabic, Yoruba, and Hebrew) as a means of surveillance.

The communiqué noted two African slaves had been arrested. In naming their owners, the police raised questions about whether the owners took their responsibilities seriously. Furthermore, the slaves had access to private houses. The message was that in the protected space of two homes (even one in "terrible condition"), slaves had proved capable of acting independently of their masters and of the authorities. To impede future meetings, the police confiscated the door key, signaling higher ups that they had done their job efficiently by gaining effective control over a place of African subversion.

Provincial authorities viewed African freedpersons with particular trepidation. After the Malê Revolt of 1835, African freedpersons suffered persecution and harassment by police. The latter recognized both their close ties to enslaved Africans and the impressive capacity of African freedpersons to organize.[9] The freed Africans who remained in Salvador after the suppression of the 1835 revolt and the deportations that followed represented a direct link to earlier rebellions. Police accounts often included the names and number of African freedpersons arrested during nighttime sweeps of the terreiros, as if to emphasize that freedpersons more than slaves posed a special threat.

In November 1855, during the height of a devastating cholera epidemic, police searched all the houses owned by African freedpersons in the urban parish of Sé in Salvador. One police officer concluded:

> We found nothing that would indicate an impending revolt, but I did take all of the objects associated with their [Africans'] religious beliefs, such as figures, symbols, dead and dried toads, bells, some clothes which I plan to burn. . . . I sent the owners of the houses where we found the objects to the Aljube prison, where I plan to leave them for three days, including Valeriana Maria Gertrudes, a freedwoman [*liberta*]; Luisa, her slave; two women named Esperança, both slaves of Alexandre, an African freedman who earns his income cutting meat; Constança da S. Horta, freedwoman; and Felicidade, African slave of Maria Luisa, freedwoman. The African [named] Amaro I plan to leave in prison for several days . . . because in his house I found most of the confiscated objects, which leads me to believe that he is a major priest among the Africans. One black freedman named Rufo seems to me to have encouraged insubordination among his followers; this Rufo already was imprisoned in the past and

was to be deported, but was not [deported] because of the many grandiose promises he made.[10]

Given the presence of figurines, toads, and bells, it is likely the house had been used for Candomblé ceremonies. By listing the material items confiscated, the arresting officers sought to assure their superiors that they had deterred the spread of African influence and culture. In spite. of police surveillance and harassment, however, houses of Candomblé continued to offer a locale where slaves and freedpersons could interact with less fear and inhibition than in more public environments.

After interrupting festivities and closing down houses of Candomblé, police typically arrested participants. They used laws that made it illegal for slaves and freedpersons to travel at night without a passport and prohibited public gatherings that included drumming that disrupted the public tranquility.[11] Police sweeps commonly provoked the wrath of those in attendance at ceremonies. As one police official recounted:

> Today at 6:00 a.m. [October 21, 1855] on Resgate Hill a group of male and female crioulos [Brazilian-born blacks] departed from the city, and without doubt they were headed to one of those houses of debauchery that exist in this district known as *candoblés* [sic]; one of them shouted out obscene words and I responded that such words could not be permitted. Far from accepting my advice, I received harsh insults, and therefore ordered him arrested. . . . I was unable to carry out the arrest because many of the group disobeyed my orders and impeded our actions. Such gatherings [of Candomblé] can lead to death. . . . They are often attended by vagrants. . . . At times there are more than two hundred people gathering to practice immoralities at such *candoblés*.[12]

In another episode, police encountered seventeen men and twenty-five women "joined together in sacred drumming." Those arrested included four "dark" persons of mixed race (*pardos escuros*), eight crioulos, and thirty Africans. Among the group of Africans, seven were slaves. One of the African slaves was a runaways[13]

The presence of Bahian-born crioulos at terreiros raised suspicions among provincial authorities that Africans and Crioulos might find common ground. Earlier, these relationships had been tenuous at best. Criuolos most often considered fellow Brazilians of diverse backgrounds more trustworthy allies than Africans. This could be clearly seen in Bahia where no crioulo slave had joined with Africans in the more than twenty slave revolts and conspiracies recorded between 1807 and 1835. In fact, Bahian-born crioulos commonly aided police in their quest to repress Candomblé.[14] Police documents after midcentury that depicted crioulo participation almost always conveyed the important political message that Africans had forged bonds with crioulos in Bahia. Without disrupting such encounters, police could not assure their capacity to maintain public security and effective control over the urban slave population.

In the turbulent months at the end of 1855 (in the wake of the outbreak of the cholera epidemic and with the presence of thousands of recently arrived Africans in the province), a terreiro that attracted so many crioulo blacks led to close scrutiny by provincial officials. The police inspector emphasized that this Candomblé presented a special danger because of its capacity to overcome traditional ethnic and racial divisions that historically had impeded alliances between Africans and crioulos.

In the wake of this event, one high-ranking police official alluded to the problems caused by allowing Bahians of diverse racial and class backgrounds to attend Candomblé ceremonies and revel in festive batuques and dances.

> On October 29, 1858, I described to you [secretary of the police] the actions taken to disperse and impede the frequent gatherings of Africans, which under the pretext of the [Catholic] mass of the seventh day for their fellow countrymen, are becoming huge [and] are attracting persons of the nation [born in Brazil]

of all colors and conditions [social or class] [*os frequentes ajuntamentos de Africanos . . . são tomando dimensões grandes, notando-se n'esses ajuntamentos pessoas do Paiz de todas as cores e condições*]. The majority of slaves who flee [from their owners] do so because of these batuque*s*, where they remain for several days. . . . Finally I note that persons of a certain class take part in these barbarous and dangerous diversions, and that they are introducing superstitions and inflammatory and violent attitudes, the consequences of which will be terrible, contrary to civilization and with the passage of time prejudicial to the public's well being.

Such tendencies are not only seen in the capital [Salvador]—in small towns along the coast and in the interior they find an echo and the proof of this can be seen in the results of an investigation carried out by a police delegate in the town of Barra do Rio de Contas, where in an attempt to destroy a huge quilombo (which these gatherings evolve into) there were four deaths, one being a soldier from the National Guard and three among those who resisted arrest, one of whom was an African woman.[15]

Within the space of a terreiro and at larger festivities, observers claimed that Africans made contact with and subverted Brazilian-born crioulos. These gatherings attracted fugitive slaves. Evidence from several sources affirms that whites and light-skinned Bahians frequented houses of Candomblé.[16] Motives for participation varied; they included a strong sense of community found at the terreiro and the pleasure experienced at sacred festivities. Journalists lamented that such "reunions" with their "drumming, horrible sounds and shouts" [*tabaques, congùs, algazarras e gritos*] had transpired within the "illustrious city" of Salvador and in outlying towns.[17]

Gatherings at terreiros provided an ideal locale for liberated Africans (*Africanos livres*) to share their experiences and perspectives. In spite of being removed from slaving vessels by the British or freed soon after being landed, liberated Africans remained under the "protection" of the

Bahian provincial government or private individuals (until an imperial decree that provided their freedom on September 24, 1864). Lamentably, little distinguished liberated Africans from enslaved Africans in terms of laboring conditions and personal rights. Nevertheless, many demonstrated a fierce determination to be immediately freed unconditionally. Having witnessed firsthand British commitment to terminate the slave trade, liberated Africans sought freedom for all slaves.

Liberated Africans came to be viewed as key figures in Bahian terreiros. Many possessed skills learned at terreiros in Africa. One official lamented, "Many times the liberated Africans have created disturbances in the city because other Africans have refused to be seduced by their religious ceremonies [*fazerem feitiço*, implying Candomblé or other forms of African religious expression] and their desire [the liberated Africans] to be free [from enslavement; *tratarem de liberdade*]."[18]

This sentence raises several questions. What sort of "disturbances" had been caused by the liberated Africans? Was it merely loud drumming, singing, and chanting? Or was it something more? And why would other Africans "refuse to be seduced by their religious ceremonies?" Perhaps refusal reflected ethnic division among Africans over decisions concerning participation in specific Candomblé terreiros. Another intriguing question is related to the perception by the scribe that the liberated Africans "desired to be free."

Candomblé Viewed as Inefficient Economics

Affluent Bahians accused terreiros of inculcating values antithetical to rational economic pursuits. They believed that Africans who stayed up late into the night at a terreiro did not perform their tasks efficiently the next day (which might have been true!). African slaves and freedpersons played a key role in the cultivation of food crops on small plots in and around Salvador. In the view of many, more time spent at Candomblé festivities meant less food would be available to the city's inhabitants. In Salvador, police officer João de Azevedo Piapitinga touched on these themes in a note written in April 1862:

It has been seven or eight years since I took over the responsibility for this parish, and one of the first things which I did was to go to all of the locations where there existed *condonblés* [*sic*] of the Africans, and finished them off. Then I forced the participants to labor on their agricultural plots. I allowed for dances [*batuques*] to occur outside their houses and in public view, which began in the morning and lasted until five at night. In this way the Africans lived happily and the output from the plots increased.[19]

Police delegate Piapitinga extolled the fact that men under his command had moved quickly to arrest participants in a nearby Candomblé. Officials acquiesced to African Bahian cultural expression but only within defined parameters. For example, Piapitinga disregarded provincial law of August 2, 1860, which prohibited dances and batuques by slaves "at whatever hour."[20] Instead, he allowed for dance and drumming on certain days at selected locations that could easily be watched by police. He believed that such a strategy of accommodation would help to ensure minimal disruption in the availability of food supplies. In seeking to comprehend Candomblé through the prism of economics, other variables entered into Piapitinga's calculations. He subsequently wrote that such gatherings were "not as simple as I wanted to believe."[21] Such a phrase suggests that "finishing off" the terreiros located in the Santo Antônio parish of Salvador did little to influence the daily customs of African and Bahian-born black inhabitants of the city.

Police concern about Candomblé impeding the efficient cultivation and availability of food crops in the early 1860s merits scrutiny. A drought in the Recôncavo lasting from 1857 to 1862 created a "catastrophic situation" in Salvador.[22] Urban slave flight in Salvador rose to a peak in late 1857 and early 1858 (as noted in Chapter 2, Table 2.3). Inhabitants of the city faced severe shortages of meat, manioc, and foods grown on small plots and farms in and around the city; prices of primary necessities rose to unprecedented levels.

As a response to food shortages, municipal representatives (*vereadores*) at the Town Hall published a by-law on January 16, 1858.

Figure 5.1 The orixá Omolu wears African straw to protect righteous persons against pestilence and to spread illness among those who have committed immoral acts. This picture is taken at the terreiro São Jorge in Salvador. Courtesy of Phyllis Galembo.

The new rules put price controls on manioc flour and limited the locations where it could be sold in the city. President of the province João Lins Cansação de Sinimbú reacted by revoking the law. As a proponent of unimpeded capitalism, he believed that the price of manioc flour should be determined by demand and availability. Aligned with commercial interests in the city, Sinimbú criticized local officials who had sought to intervene in the workings of the urban market. Unfortunately, Portuguese merchants who controlled the distribution of manioc flour demonstrated minimal concern for the urban poor who could not afford to pay for the flour. A public uproar predictably ensued. On February 28, hundreds of persons appeared in front of the palace of the president. The protest turned into a riot when many of those present threw rocks and smashed windows. Only the arrival of a large contingent of soldiers wielding bayonets and swords restored order. Ultimately, the municipal vereadores had their way, instituting price controls on manioc flour.

The 1858 food riot has been traced to antiforeign sentiment among the free poor inhabitants of Salvador. This hostility was directed toward three groups: President Sinimbú (an outsider originally from the province of Alagoas) and his political supporters; Portuguese merchants who traded in manioc flour in Bahia; and African slaves and freedpersons owned or employed by the Portuguese who transported and sold the manioc flour to consumers.[23]

In the aftermath of these popular protests over food prices, Candomblé terreiros faced a severe backlash. Police carried out five sweeps of houses of Candomblé in Salvador in the twelve months that followed (April 1858 to March 1859). This represented the largest number of invasions registered officially since police began keeping daily records in October 1848.[24] Other acts of aggression directed at terreiros, for example, hostile threats and covert destruction of property at night, most likely occurred during these months as a way to intimidate participants. In this manner, authorities could diminish the appeal of Candomblé without the publicity and difficulties associated with breaking into a house during a ceremony and carrying out arrests. Responses by officials also included the whipping of slaves accused of involvement in the protest and arrests of freedmen under the pretext of "planning an insurrection [of slaves]."[25]

At the same time, owners of rural estates in the province of Rio de Janeiro expressed similar misgivings about the negative economic effects of African religious gatherings. Just before Christmas in 1857, slaves from several estates in the coffee region of São João do Principe rebelled. The slaves had "spoken of liberty" and claimed that they would become the new "owners of the land." Police arrested two former slaves for fomenting "insubordination." One owner wrote that the freedmen had taught the slaves at his estate and others how to "make and apply poisons which they call *feitiço*" (which in this context is interpreted as a magical potion derived from Candomblé practices).[26] A year later planters from the same locale requested police to intervene to prevent another uprising. One police delegate left behind an extraordinary description of what he saw.

> The slaves of the estates meet together at night in reunions which include *tables* [*mesas*, meaning altars] in hidden places, and there they carry out gross and mysterious practices, in which they learn how to use certain poisonous herbs, and where they meet with their chiefs, known as *sorcerers* [*feitiçeiros*, translated as witch doctors or leaders of Candomblé], and share ornaments of different sorts, which appear to be talismans to be used against their owners. . . . It is important to note that in recent time not one slave on the estates drink [alcohol], when such a practice used to be a constant habit, which means that slaves learn at those meetings not to indulge in drink. . . . Also the slaves have stopped working on Sundays on their small plots. . . . The *feitiçeiros*, or *curandeiros* [healers] have gained immense prestige, by means of their character or with money, presenting themselves as a saint, and the stupid folk pay homage to them.[27]

The author associated late-night meetings of Africans with practices inimical to the interests of slave owners. Such nocturnal gatherings could easily have been a form of Bahian Candomblé, given the transport of African slaves from Salvador to Rio de Janeiro as part of the interprovincial slave trade from the 1830s through 1857 (when the document was written).[28] Another possibility could be that this was a *macumba* ceremony, African religious expression that compared closely to Bahian Candomblé brought to Brazil by Bantu slaves. The belief that African rites had enabled slaves to be more discerning with regards to alcohol consumption and caused them to devote less time to their food gardens fueled anti-African sentiment in the provinces of Rio de Janeiro and Bahia.

"Those 'Africanas' Are Harmful and Prejudicial to Our Nation"

The presence of women as participants and even leaders at houses of Candomblé aroused a special wrath among provincial authorities. Given that Candomblé represented an African religious universe distinct from Brazil's European-oriented society, women often played a predominant role.[29] Believers in Candomblé viewed the female priestess of a terreiro (*mãe-de-santo*) who led rites as a spiritual leader both inside the sacred space of a terreiro and in the larger community. In the place of individual aggrandizement or privilege common in the day-to-day secular world, communal sharing characterized all relations within a terreiro. Followers of Candomblé paid close attention to the directives of females who held positions of responsibility in a terreiro.

This inversion of gender and racial hierarchy resulted in harsh reactions in Salvador and in the countryside. Police commonly intervened in Candomblé ceremonies to arrest participants and confiscate or destroy religious objects. The threat of deportation remained a tactic employed by police in their attempts to coerce Africans through the 1860s. In one incident in March 1861, an owner of a sugar engenho accused the African freedwoman Constança of "criminal activities." Police arrested the woman and sent her to the Aljube prison in Salvador. An official involved described the incarcerated woman as

one of those Africans [female *Africanas*] who is harmful and prejudicial to our nation. . . . She goes to what are called '*candonblez*' [*sic*], never leaving evidence behind to prove her involvement. . . . Such practices abuse the good faith of some followers and the ignorance of others. . . . They [Candomblé ceremonies] inculcate superstition among the less educated members of society. . . . I have resolved to request her deportation as the only solution, as a means of purifying the nation . . . and as an example to others.[30]

Journalists writing in the decade of the 1860s characterized Candomblé as a spreading cancer within Bahian society. Symptoms they suggested included the capacity of Candomblé to appeal to persons of diverse racial and class backgrounds. According to one journalist, a terreiro in the Barris neighborhood of Salvador brought together a remarkably varied clientele: "Married women seeking remedies to ensure their husbands remain sexually attracted to them, slaves requesting ingredients [for a potion] to lessen the wrath of their owners, women seeking advice on the ways to attain happiness, and even businessmen desiring success in their endeavors!" Such interactions threatened the social order, "creating problems for the [male] heads of families, who on many occasions partake of these pernicious drugs provided by a charlatan [of Candomblé]."[31]

The writer considered the rituals and potions little more than worthless quackery. Furthermore, he claimed the ideas and belief system perpetrated through such meetings undermined the ability of fathers and husbands to maintain their nuclear families intact. As a result, wives and daughters had become lost, imprisoned against their will, deprived, drunk, infected by witchcraft, and entrusted to "brute and vicious negros."[32] The journalist claimed that in allowing their female partners to attend houses of Candomblé, injudicious males contributed to their own ruination. The message was that naïve and vulnerable women had become the conduit for transmitting unwanted African practices into Bahian homes.

Another newspaper article alluded to "devilish tricks" carried out at Candomblé terreiros in a locale known as Barreiras on the outskirts of Salvador. With what was described as a "*red feijoada*" (*uma feijoada vermelha*; feijoada was a popular dish among Africans and crioulos in the nineteenth century composed of rice, beans, and meat, and now one of Brazil's famed culinary delights), "Conservative" politicians had offered a free meal to supporters. The majority of those who partook of the meal were blacks and people of color who resided in *favelas* (shanties often constructed on the hillsides around Salvador) and frequented nearby terreiros.

The phrase "red feijoada" raises several possibilities of interpretation. On a simple level, red might have been the actual color of the beans used to prepare the dish. However, invoking the color red more likely had other connotations related to local politics. Red was likely an allusion to the blood shed by animals when sacrificed at Candomblé ceremonies. The essayist alluded to a "red feijoada" to suggest that Conservatives desired to "conserve Candomblé." In other words, he sought to demean politicians who cultivated ties to Candomblé as a means of gaining the endorsement of voters.

Another way to interpret the phrase "red feijoada" emerges through the prism of international affairs. The color red was linked to Communist ideals in the wake of the February 1848 publication of the *Communist Manifesto* in London. The book was viewed as an evil doctrine by many in Brazil. Communism was considered as a threat to the right to own private property and to entrepreneurship in a free market. Not surprisingly, conservative defenders of the status quo in Brazil used the word to besmirch antislavery proponents from the late 1860s on. By including the descriptive adjective red, the author equated the diplomacy of Bahian politicians toward participants in Candomblé with sympathy toward Communism. Using modern terminology, the politicians had been "soft" in their response to Communist subversion. Within Brazil's male-dominated secular society, such political ties also implied that male politicians had demonstrated weakness in relations with the women leaders of Candomblé terreiros.

In his depiction of the event, the journalist noted the presence of followers of *Ogam*. In writing "Ogam," the author perhaps meant an *Ogá*, which translates as an influential person who dispenses financial, social or political support to the Candomblé. Or (more likely) the word implied

Ogum, the Yoruba god of iron and war. One of several powerful orixás worshipped in Bahian houses of Candomblé, Ogum provides sustenance to farmers, hunters, warriors, and blacksmiths. Obviously distrustful of everything and everyone associated with Candomblé festivities, the author exclaimed in closing, "My man, I am a devoted follower of Saint Anthony," meaning the holy saint of the established Catholic Church. Given that Ogum is the African orixá associated with the Catholic figure St. Anthony among believers in Candomblé, the journalist sought to emphasize that in no way had he wavered in his Catholic beliefs.[33]

The influence of African and Bahian-born crioula women in terreiros created a dilemma for provincial authorities. In the protected space of terreiros, female leaders and participants perpetrated a value system and rituals more oriented to Africa than to western thought embodied in Roman Catholic norms or secular ideologies. In their response, provincial officials followed patterns visible since the early nineteenth century.[34] On the one hand, police commonly disrupted Candomblé ceremonies. Based on a series of provincial laws (*posturas*) after midcentury that outlawed "dances" and "gatherings of slaves at whatever place and whatever hour," police searched houses, invaded terreiros, confiscated materials and arrested participants.[35] With such tactics, police sought to undermine the influence of female priestesses of terreiros.

On the other hand, negotiation rather than conflict determined relations between state representatives and members of terreiros. Many provincial officials recognized the benefits to be gained from quiet diplomacy. By the 1860s, police were granting permits that allowed for specific gatherings for modest fees. Such procedures assured that the police would not "invade" the terreiro or arrest those present.[36] For larger festivals, police commonly turned a blind eye, if only because it was obvious that they lacked the manpower and resources to stop these gatherings. Such a nonaggressive response caused a furor among numerous wary residents of Salvador. A dismayed journalist for *O Alabama* wrote, "What about our police! They allow the most ignorant part of our population, particularly those of the African race, to participate in Candomblés, where they take part in foolish ventures, become full of themselves, [and participate] in other bizarre practices."[37] In spite of public criticism, tact proved beneficial. Such initiatives created useful linkages at the local level and allowed for the diffusion of pent-up social tensions.

Leaders of Candomblé also had much to gain from quiet negotiation. In place of confrontation, heads of terreiros sought recognition from established authorities. Dialogue helped to co-opt individuals hostile to the existence of terreiros. Negotiation created shared interests between participants in terreiros and the police. It facilitated communication that in turn allowed for flexibility and accommodation. Certainly not all discussions succeeded in resolving tensions. Instances abounded of disgruntled residents demanding that a terreiro be removed from their neighborhood. And police showed little interest in dialogue during times of high insecurity, such as the late 1860s during the war with Paraguay and the mid-1880s on the eve of abolition. Nevertheless, negotiation proved to be a strategy of utmost importance in allowing terreiros to exist with lessened concern about police sweeps or closure.

At least twenty-four terreiros of Candomblé existed in Salvador and its suburbs in the decade of the 1870s, this estimate based on newspaper accounts and historical documents. Most likely the actual number was at least double, given that many terreiros never came to the notice of the police. When the North American sociologist Donald Pierson carried out his research in Salvador from 1935 to 1937, he heard estimates of between two and three hundred terreiros in existence.[38] With an increase in the number of terreiros, opportunities increased for greater numbers of individuals to participate and for more women to play a leading role in the terreiros.

"An Infinite Number of Men and Women Are Making Stupid Sacrifices to Crude Idols"

The Catholic Church protested the way in which Candomblé eroded its influence. In the eighteenth and early nineteenth centuries, Africans and crioulo blacks commonly joined Catholic brotherhoods. Black lay sodalities often included among their members both male and female slaves, along with a few wealthy whites and free pardos. Black

Figure 5.2 Created by the sculptor Tati Moreno, these spectacular orixás stand above the *dique* (a dike or dam; more commonly understood as a small lake) of Tororó (word of Tupi origin, meaning sudden downpour of rain) near the soccer stadium in Salvador. Photograph by author.

brotherhoods followed Catholic rituals, for example, paying homage to Christian saints and in burial ceremonies. But these practices often disguised a spirituality centered on African orixás.

With the increasing secularization of Brazilian society in the first half of the nineteenth century, the appeal of brotherhoods diminished.[39] To retain its influence, the Catholic hierarchy encouraged Africans and their descendants to attend masses and participate as members of the brotherhoods, but they did not demand that the ties to terreiros be severed. After the middle of the nineteenth century, the Catholic hierarchy reassessed this position.

The conservative Catholic leadership took offense that so many left Catholic mass to head directly to their terreiro to participate in its activities and ceremonies. It also became public knowledge that some houses of Candomblé included Catholic priests among their members. A journalist accused one priest named Manuel Vieira of "being the absolute antithesis of the famed Vieira of past glory [Padre Antônio Vieira, Portugal's famed seventeenth-century intellectual who lived and preached in Bahia]; he is more and more an infamous hypocrite . . . a consummate *candomblezeiro* [participant in Candomblé], a lively *sambista* [participant in samba dance and drumming], an assassin who has killed many."[40] Although likely that the accused Vieira thoroughly enjoyed his visits to terreiros, it was difficult to believe that the priest had ever taken the life of anyone. Obviously, observers (in this case, a journalist at the newspaper *O Alabama*) relished the opportunity to exaggerate the threat posed by those who attended Candomblé rites.

The annual cycle of Candomblé festivities unhinged elite inhabitants of Salvador. One big event was the New Yam Festival (*Festa do Inhame Novo*) celebrated each November. Participants expressed gratitude to the orixás and the deceased for the first fruits of the new harvest. They cooked yams and the meat of sacrificed goat and then shared the stew with everyone present. This act had great symbolic meaning as an offering of thanks to higher spirits and respect for the natural world.[41] The first celebration in the annual cycle of Candomblé rituals, the festival attracted "an immense number of Africans" and Bahians to terreiros in Salvador.[42] These commemorations included hundreds of people dancing and loud drumming.

Popular views of the New Yam Festival as a "heathen" practice surfaced in newspaper accounts.

—Don't tell me that it [the New Yam Festival] is becoming an annual event?

—It is an African custom, introduced and then adapted by the ignorant masses among us. It consists of the sanctification of the first fruits from the harvest of each year by African gods. Before the celebration of the ceremony it is prohibited by the followers of the African sects to eat it. That which was a religious custom observed by the Africans is now accepted and practiced among the majority of the Brazilians.

—"The Mill" [locale of the festivities] is a *candomblé*, whose "mother of the *terreiro*" is an African woman known as Aunt Julia.

—To describe the range of licentiousness, the scenes of extravagance and debauchery that occur inside closed doors, in that infernal bacchanal, is something impossible to do. Semi-nude women covering themselves only with a short serge and a piece of cloth over their breasts, dancing with seductive movements and lewd appearances. Women and men joined together create the most indecent part of this perverted orgy. Acts of wicked sacrilege, scenes of barbarous fanaticism, the disregard of the Ten Commandments, the reverence and blind adoration of cult figures [*buxigangas*], and ridiculous figures of wood, smallpox adored like a divine object, and to complete this multitude of insolent acts, many of the female participants falling down unconscious, affected perhaps by some drug, to finish off the party to the delight of impure satiation.

—What people! Stupidly intoxicated in a state of barbarous superstition, putting themselves at the disposition of expert connivers. They do not reflect on the possibility of a time to believe in a true God, fulfilling the rules of Catholic religion, and instead adore the gods of the heathens.[43]

Several interpretations can be gleaned from this newspaper article. Similar to biases encountered in other documents, the author character-ized Candomblé as contrary to established Catholic doctrines. Men and women carried out immoral acts in the darkened recesses of the terreiro. Women danced without inhibition and in some instances entered a trance-like state with the arrival of an orixá. Words and phrases highlight the sense that Africans could not be trusted. In spite of such disturbing ac-counts, terreiros nevertheless succeeded in attracting huge numbers of fol-lowers, particularly to the major events such as the New Yam Festival.

Another festivity that attracted hundreds, if not thousands, of people to Candomblé terreiros was the Closing of the Basket (Fechar o Balaio). Occurring during the eleven days prior to Easter Holy Week, its origins can be traced to the preparation among Africans for the *entrudo* (popular street celebrations that later became known as Carnaval). During the Closing of the Basket, leaders of terreiros prepared the orixás for their journey back to Africa, from where they returned after the conclusion of Christian Easter celebration. One journalist lamented that the Closing of the Basket celebrations attracted the "most ignorant of our population, and principally Africans." Furthermore, the police of Salvador had descended into "black spiritism" by doing little to impede such "grotesque" gatherings.[44]

In one remarkable episode described in the newspaper *O Alabama*, a man from the town of Valença (on the coast south of Salvador) noted that an African *pai-de-santo* (male leader of a Candomblé) in Salvador named Miguel Augusto had gained "fame" in the region. As a result, he transported his wife to Salvador to meet with Augusto. The woman claimed to Augusto that "occult powers" had entered her body impeding her ability to participate fully in Catholic mass. After disrupting the long-awaited encounter at the terreiro, police sent the woman to a priest at the Catholic Church located at Piety Square in the hope that the demons could be "exorcised."[45]

Such episodes provoked the wrath of those who hoped to extirpate Candomblé from Bahia. One journalist wrote in October 1868 that a "seditious candomblé" had been "seething" (*está fervendo um amotinado batucagé*). According to him, African and Brazilian men and women present had offered "stupid sacrifices to crude idols" [*estúpidos sacrifícios a ídolos grosseiros*].[46] Reflecting on the widespread appeal of Candomblé, another writer alerted his readers to the fact that "here [in Bahia] persons [meaning observant Catholics] pay money to [Catholic] missionaries to aid them in the conversion [to Catholicism] of Indians [present in the interior of the province], when in our midst [in Salvador] there are so many people who need to open their eyes [to the existence of numerous terreiros]."[47]

Figure 5.3 A *Baiana* "cleansing" the spirit of a believer in the orixás with popcorn in front of the Catholic Church of Saint Lazarus in Salvador. Every Monday hundreds of Bahians arrive here dressed in white to pay homage to the Catholic saint Lazarus and African spirits. Photograph by author.

Why did so many Africans and their Bahian descendants participate in Candomblé ceremonies during the nineteenth century, in spite of police harassment, political persecution, and ridicule? The sociologist Reginaldo Prandi offers helpful insights in this regard. Marginalized blacks and persons of color found a sense of community and even attained limited upward mobility within houses of Candomblé, for example, by becoming a *pai-* or *mãe-de-santo* (male or female head of the Candomblé). Leaders of Candomblé in Bahia invoked some twelve orixás to intervene in the present world through the use of sacred forces. Given its African roots, Candomblé focused on immediate material needs associated with sickness, unemployment, and poverty faced by the majority of Africans and their descendants in Bahia.[48]

Through a wide array of rituals and practices, Africans and their descendants sought self-affirmation and individual justice within terreiros not readily available in the Catholic Church or through other religions. This special appeal of Candomblé continued through the nineteenth and twentieth centuries. In the words of a twenty-first-century devotee describing the nineteen houses of Candomblé existent in the Federation district of Salvador (in 2000):

> Candomblé is not folklore, nor is it only a religion or ideology. A terreiro of Candomblé has its followers, its piece of land and its traditional techniques of work, its system of distribution and consumption of material goods. [It is] a social organization that represents another manner of looking at [or understanding] the world.[49]

Candomblé as a Dilemma for Intellectuals of Color

Given the scarcity of written or published sources from the nineteenth century that describe Candomblé, the Bahian newspaper *O Alabama* offers a unique source for analyzing attitudes toward Candomblé. Numerous articles included in its pages told of "barbarous and repugnant scenes" witnessed at terreiros in Salvador.[50]

As an upwardly mobile bourgeoisie of color, editor Arístides de

Santana depicted Candomblé in the harshest terms. He and fellow journalists writing for the newspaper painted Candomblé as an African practice, which propagated "uncivilized" and "lascivious" behavior. They lamented that the ceremonies, which in the past took place in remote suburban or rural locales (roças), had become increasingly visible in the center of the "capital city" of Salvador.[51] "An infinite number of houses [of Candomblé]" had been constructed by Africans in particular parishes of the city. Making a clear connection between Candomblé and slave resistance, O Alabama lamented that authorities had done little to impede the creation of "true quilombos," while owners had allowed for "dances" at all hours of the night. "Nauseating smells" from animal sacrifices outraged citizens residing nearby.[52] O Alabama pointed to the many ways in which male and female leaders of the houses of Candomblé corrupted naïve initiates in the darkened recesses of terreiros. One writer criticized police for failing to act: "In another country, it [the Candomblé terreiro] would have been found and made to disappear."[53] Police ineptitude received common notice. Contributors emphasized that police participation in Candomblé festivities was one reason why terreiros flourished in and around Salvador.[54]

Journalists from O Alabama often included the word feitiço when writing about Candomblé. Feitiço is defined as "sorcery, witchcraft, black art; bewitchment; fetish; magic."[55] For many Bahians, feitiço meant African "customs."[56] The term provoked images of bestial acts performed by Africans and deluded crioulos within terreiros. Although often associated with female practitioners, contributors to O Alabama did not hesitate to accuse male feitiçeiros of malicious deeds. Observers viewed feitiço as related in some unknown way to the worship of demons and a pantheon of African gods and goddesses. Feitiço resulted in perversions of all sorts, including sacrifice of living animals and the coercion and detainment of young women at terreiros. Its forces enabled leaders of terreiros to sway persons of all classes and races.

Feitiço implied uninhibited sexuality. Essays accused men and women of dancing with minimal garb and engaging in sexual orgies. Feitiço symbolized the "other," the unknown, a seductive African spiritual force that boded evil for everyone involved. As scientific inquiry and Enlightenment ideals from Europe gained vogue among middle- and upper-class Bahians, the obvious popular appeal of feitiço and Candomblé presented a dilemma, particularly to better off free blacks and persons of color. As a result, journalists of color at *O Alabama* did not hesitate to label feitiço as "scandalous" behavior contrary to "the morality of our land."[57]

Such views about culture translated into political discourse. *O Alabama* vacillated between monarchist and Republican sympathies. During the Paraguayan War, its journalists wrote about the costs and human suffering in Bahia caused by the conflict. Nevertheless, several articles supported policies pursued by the imperial government. During the same period of the late 1860s, *O Alabama* advocated Republican ideals. It called for the protection of human rights, particularly those of slaves, published information about antislavery initiatives in other parts of the empire, upheld the right to a free press and educational reform, and claimed that race discrimination had diminished as individual freedoms had increased.[58] In calling for abolition, the journalists at *O Alabama* desired to see emancipation legislation passed and implemented by established authorities.

In spite of the political division evident at *O Alabama*, its contributors agreed on the devious nature of Candomblé. As provincial agents representing the monarchy struggled to fulfill troop quotas to fight against the Paraguayan enemy, terreiros gained a reputation for hiding men who did not wish to go to the front. After returning from Paraguay, numerous veterans settled at the "little republic [*republiqueta*] of Paraguay."[59] The locale known as "Paraguay" gained renown in Salvador. Described as an "urban quilombo" due to its appeal to numerous black folk and frequent run-ins between residents and the police, an influential terreiro flourished in its midst. The Paraguay terreiro often hosted festivities every night for several days.[60]

Editors at *O Alabama* refused to accept the possibility that the black and mixed-race underclass, meaning all those persons who attended secret Candomblé ceremonies, could be agents of their own liberation. These journalists showed their class and racial bias by denigrating the legacies of Africa in Bahia and commending ideas associated with the West. The liberal faction writing for the newspaper judged terreiros founded on African cultural values as boding ill for an emerging Republican ideology which subscribed to Christian thought and capitalist relations of production based on free labor. Arístides and his fellow journalists sought to forget an African past embodied in Candomblé to prepare for a future oriented toward Europe and the United States.

Candomblé and Abolition

The evidence suggests that Candomblé propelled participants into the abolitionist movement. Terreiros provided an intricate network of communication that spread information throughout the city and countryside. They commonly provided shelter and sustenance to fugitive slaves. Candomblé inspired devotion and spirituality among its followers; ceremonies inculcated a sense of personal affirmation among Africans and their descendants in a hostile and racist milieu. Members of terreiros learned from one another about their history and culture in Africa, in Brazil, and in the Americas. Candomblé contributed to the forging of political consciousness; terreiros helped to overcome ethnic and religious divisions among Africans and Brazilian-born crioulos.[61] Candomblé rejected the exploitation and abuses associated with slavery and strategies, practices, and values associated with Candomblé undermined the interests of Bahian slave masters. Provincial officials were correct when they viewed terreiros as places that spread an ideology of liberation.

Few sources survive to help a modern-day observer to interpret precisely the views of members of terreiros with regard to the abolitionist movement. A few insights can be gleaned from newspaper accounts. In October 1866, the newspaper *O Oculo Mágico* (The Magic Lantern) published the following:

> There exists in Saint Michael [the plaza of St. Michael located in the parish of Santana in Salvador] two or three houses where constantly a large number of negros are meeting. Even on Sundays they are getting together, and in such numbers that they do not

stay inside the house, but also sit out in the front of the house and on the street. It has been noted to us that there exist similar locations in [the parish of] Brotas and [neighborhood of] Cabula, where every Sunday they [blacks] are gathering and dancing. It . is necessary to take all precautions, particularly these days when the idea of liberty is in the air! [*principalmente hoje com a idéia que corre de liberdade*!] Besides this the meetings here in the city are disruptive, and unless we are mistaken, such reunions are prohibited by a city ordinance or police regulations.[62]

In the view of many observers, Candomblé had direct ties to the abolitionist movement. Leaders of terreiros knew well of the ideas of liberty that were "in the air" at midcentury and particularly from the second half of the 1860s. They had paid close attention to shifting political winds throughout the nineteenth century, and they had provided locations for Africans and Bahian-born alike to meet and discuss their situation. Committed members and periodic visitors alike absorbed and responded to such messages and information furnished at houses of Candomblé.

A second episode offers a glimpse into links between Candomblé and abolitionist debates in Bahia. On August 8, 1877, sixteen Africans arrived into the port of Salvador on board the ship *Paraguassú*. These Africans had left Salvador either voluntarily or had been deported in years previous; most likely all had been slaves and purchased their freedom before leaving from Bahia. All the Africans except one possessed passports granted by the British colonial government in Lagos, Nigeria. The one exception retained his original Bahian passport. Officials stationed in the port of Salvador would not allow the Africans to disembark on that August day; the chief of police wrote an urgent message to the president of Bahia requesting advice on how to proceed.[63] Why would the arrival of sixteen Africans cause such consternation?

From the 1820s to 1899, approximately eight thousand Africans and Brazilian-born crioulos returned to West Africa. Some had been deported by Bahian authorities; the majority departed at their own expense voluntarily.[64] A large upsurge of Africans returning to Africa occurred in the seven years following the revolt of the Malês in 1835. Hundreds of Africans frequently traveled from Lagos to Salvador and back from the 1850s. The anthropologist Randy Matory writes that "theirs was a truly transnational identity configuration and commercial endeavor, long before transnationalism and globalization became the catchwords of our present era."[65] One of the principal business activities of these entrepreneurial Africans was trading in items used in Candomblé ceremonies. Several inhabitants of Salvador made the journey to West Africa and back for the specific purpose of learning the African rituals of Candomblé.

The Africans who appeared on board the ship in the port of Salvador had been residing in Lagos. A "commercial and cultural Mecca," in the words of Dr. Matory, Lagos provided a rich cultural milieu that "embraced multiple ethnic groups and cross-cut continents."[66] These former slaves from Brazil interacted with British officials and missionaries present in Lagos from 1830s (Lagos was declared a British protectorate in 1861). They became acquainted with westernized former slaves from Cuba and Sierra Leone. Urbane and educated, they had firsthand knowledge of events on the West African coast, in Brazil, and throughout the Atlantic Basin.

The arrival of sixteen Africans aware of the currents of international abolition surely made a striking impression on Salvador's slave community. By 1877, the number of slaves in Salvador had diminished significantly. This occurred primarily due to the sale of slaves to the central-southern provinces and the transport of urban slaves to the interior of Bahia. The environment in Salvador was one, in the words of U.S. anthropologist Rachel Harding, where the "presence [of Africans and their descendants] was increasingly questioned and marginalized."[67] In such a milieu, the arrival of an entourage from Lagos had "transformative effects."[68]

By carrying goods and information to terreiros, the Lagos entourage enhanced the reputation of houses of Candomblé as dynamic meeting places closely in touch with West Africa and the outside world. African contacts inspired activities that affirmed the independence of Africans and Brazilian-born crioulos alike. For this reason and others, port officials in Salvador warily pondered what to do about sixteen cosmopolitan Africans in their midst.

An unanswered question is the role of Candomblé in fostering slave resistance and aiding the abolitionist movement in the interior of Bahia. Partial light is shed by events in the interior of São Paulo province, a locale where hundreds of African and crioulo slaves arrived via the interprovincial slave trade. From the 1850s, influential planters accused individuals associated with Candomblé of being responsible for poisonings and crimes. During the tumultuous period of 1882–1885, slaves on several estates revolted. Police also found evidence of planned insurrections. Historian Maria Helena Machado demonstrates that leaders of Candomblé helped mobilize and encourage plantation slaves to rebel. Among these was one Felipe Santiago, a crioulo freedman, born in the province of Maranhão, son of an African Mina woman, most likely of Jeje or Nagô descent. Having resided in Campinas, São Paulo, for at least twelve years, he gained a reputation for his skills as a curandeiro and maintained close contacts with numerous Africans and crioulos. With the goal of sparking a widespread slave revolt on several estates, Felipe Santiago organized gatherings of slaves. As a result of his activities, one hundred twenty slaves on one estate fought with troops and fled. This was but one episode among many where activities associated with Candomblé helped to destabilize the slave regime and gave impetus to abolitionists.[69]

In the period between 1850 and 1888, Candomblé quietly (and sometimes not so quietly!) encouraged its followers to undermine and subvert the capacity of slave owners in Bahia, particularly in Salvador. The fact that police search and seizure operations directed at Candomblé increased in terms of number of invasions and level of repression during periods of popular protest and heightened antislavery activity supports this interpretation. Candomblé provided a place for Africans and others to discuss their social conditions and plans for the future. Participants of Candomblé in Salvador and the interior of Bahia responded in positive ways to the changing political milieu of these years. They sought an end to the slave regime at the earliest moment possible and personal fulfillment in all segments of their lives without intrusion.

CHAPTER SIX

A Second Phase of Abolition, 1871–79

An interprovincial slave trade that sent slaves from Salvador to the central-southern provinces gave impetus to the second phase of abolition in Bahia. Commencing after 1831 and reaching its highest levels in the 1870s, this internal slave trade fueled debates over the future of slavery in Bahia. The export of slaves from Bahia pitted planters who desired slaves to produce agricultural goods against an emerging urban middle class committed to modernization and free labor. The internal slave trade provoked abolitionist critics of the slave regime into action. Causing turmoil throughout the province, it sent unwilling slaves to alien locales. Slaves from Bahia proved to be hugely disruptive to their new masters. Slave resistance in the central-southern provinces and in Bahia played a decisive role in the abolitionist struggles of the 1870s and after.

The Internal Slave Trade from Bahia, 1831–81

In the wake of Brazil's 1831 law prohibiting further slave importations from Africa, Bahian owners sold their slaves to purchasers from the central-southern provinces. In the immediate aftermath of the revolt of the Malês, Bahian owners sent ninety-eight slaves to Rio de Janeiro. Within two months of the revolt, another three hundred eighty slaves were sent out of Bahia.[1] In 1840, Bahian-born Luís Gama was sold as a slave in Bahia and transported to Rio de Janeiro as part of the organized interprovincial trade. With thousands of African slaves arriving directly from Africa into the ports of Salvador, Rio de Janeiro, and Santos during the 1830s and 1840s, slave price differentials between Brazil's North-Northeast and Center-South were minimal. As a result, the interprovincial slave trade remained small (the number transferred is not known) and secondary to the international slave trade as a source of slave labor for the central-southern provinces. This changed in 1850.

The ending of the international slave trade, combined with increasing sugar and coffee prices, caused slave prices to rise throughout Brazil from midcentury until 1860. In the 1860s and 1870s, the market value of slaves diverged in the two major slaveholding regions. In Bahia and other provinces in the Northeast, slave prices steadily decreased, a reflection of the fall in the price of sugar. In the central-southern provinces, the cost of a slave steadily rose, this caused by higher prices of coffee. Driven by the increase in coffee prices and exports, the price differential in the cost of slaves between the Center-South and the North-Northeast widened significantly. Slave sales and prices in all regions dropped off precipitously in the period 1881–83 with the halt of the interprovincial slave trade and as eventual abolition became clear.[2]

Demand in Brazil's central-southern provinces for slaves to work in cities, towns and countryside partially drove the increasing cost of slaves in that region after midcentury. One outcome was the rapid expansion of the interprovincial slave trade that sent at least 222,500 slaves from the North-Northeast and the province of Rio Grande do Sul to the Center-South from 1850 to 1881.[3] Several factors caused planters in the North-Northeast to sell their slaves, including a downturn in exports and prices of Brazilian cotton when U.S. cotton production rose after the U.S. Civil War ended, droughts (1857–62, 1877–80), and problems in the sugar sector (lack of investment, competition from Cuba and European beet sugar producers, and decreased sugar prices in international markets). Slave owners in Brazil's southernmost province of Rio Grande do Sul sold their slaves to the Center-South due to an influx of European immigrants more than willing to work as cheap labor and difficulties in the beef jerky industry that traditionally had employed slaves.

Salvador became a major entrepôt in the internal slave trade. Slaves transported from the interior of Bahia to the city were embarked on ships destined for Rio de Janeiro. Urban owners also sold hundreds of their slaves and sent them away from the port of Salvador. Ships originating in provinces north of Bahia stopped in Salvador to pick up slaves.

TABLE 6.1. POLICE RECORDS OF SLAVES TRANSPORTED
FROM SALVADOR, 1853–78

1853	1368
1854	1884
1855	1010
1856	1756
1857	1262
1858	879
1859	554
1860	1907
1861	1750
1862	380
1863	385
1864	531
1865	247
1866	264
1867	233
1868	386
1869	911
1870	784
1871	521
1872	453
1873	547
1874	2479
1875	1840
1876	1318
1877	——
1878	——
1879	282
total:	23,931

Source: "Mappa dos escravos despachados por esta repartição de Agosto 1853 até Novembro 1873," Salvador, November 18, 1873, APEB/SACP, m. 5820; and *Relatórios do presidente da província* (Bahia, 1876), 106–7; 1877, 60; and 1879, annex; as cited in Robert Wayne Slenes, "The Demography and Economics of Brazilian Slavery, 1850–1888" (PhD dissertation, Stanford University, 1975), 603, 661.

Official police records(as shown in Table 6.1) demonstrate the following numbers of slaves transported from Salvador to the Center-South (most commonly the port of Rio de Janeiro) from 1853 to 1878. Between these years, a total of 23,931 slaves were sent out of Salvador via the port according to police registers. This number does not include the hundreds of slaves sent before 1853, nor those dispatched clandestinely on ships and overland.[4]

Four periods stand out with regard to slave exports depicted in Table 6.1 above. Between 1853 and 1861, more than one thousand slaves were transported annually out of Bahia, except for the years 1858 and 1859. The cause of this can be traced to the calculations of owners of small properties (foodstuffs, coffee, tobacco) responding to the halt of the international slave trade to Brazil. Such individuals no longer had easy access to slaves at a low price, and hence sold the few slaves they owned to purchasers from the Center-South. Seeking to reduce this high number of slave departures, the Bahian provincial assembly instituted an export tax of 65$ in 1853 (US $37.70) on every slave sold. Concern among large planters about the future of slavery in the province caused a Bahian representative in the national Parliament to call for an end of the internal trade in 1854.[5]

An annual average of 347 slaves exited Salvador between 1862 and 1868. A rise in cotton cultivation in Bahia during the U.S. Civil War and the disruptions caused by the war with Paraguay brought about this downturn in slave transfers. Small farmers who might have sold their slaves to the Center-South before the outbreak of the Paraguayan war did all they could to hold on to them during the conflict. Responding to opportunities created by the scarcity of foodstuffs in local and regional markets during the war, small farmers desired to use their slaves to cultivate crops. Small farmers also acted on the assumption that a slave might be needed as a substitute military recruit in their stead.

Between 1874 and 1876, a total of 5,637 slaves exited Salvador. This peak in slave transfers was related to the significant decline in the prices of cotton and sugar cultivated in the North-Northeast, and a spike in demand and prices of coffee produced in the Center-South. Another reason

Map 6.1 Provinces and Regions of Nineteenth-Century Brazil. Courtesy of Walter Johnson, ed., *The Chattel Principle: Internal Slave Trades in the Americas* (New Haven, CT: Yale University Press, 2004), 326.

for the upsurge related to concern that the interprovincial slave trade might be halted. Like traffickers and planters who reacted to attempts to suppress the international slave trade to Brazil in the late 1820s and late 1840s, central-southern buyers and Bahian sellers responded quickly to the shifting domestic demand for slaves between 1850 and 1880.

Although official records do not provide the exact numbers of slaves dispatched out of Bahia from 1877 to the end of 1880, it is evident that the number fell off rapidly, as evidenced in 1879 when police officially registered 282 slaves exiting from Bahia. The fact that fewer slaves were sold to the central-southern provinces was partially related to the sugar sector. In the late 1870s, sugar planters in Bahia hoped that their fortunes might improve. The result was a rise in demand and purchase of slaves.

Who were the slaves sent to the Center-South in the interprovincial traffic? The majority were males between the ages of eleven and forty years old.[6] Approximately 35 percent were female.[7] A list of 218 slaves departing Bahia in 1877 based on the port records of the provincial government supports these estimates. The sample of slaves transported from Salvador south on board ships from June 28, 1877, to October 2, 1877, shows 74 of 218 (40 percent) as female.[8] Planters in the provinces of Rio de Janeiro, Minas Gerais, and São Paulo purchased the majority of males arriving from the North-Northeast to cultivate and process coffee. Some female slaves continued as domestic laborers after arrival in the port city of Rio de Janeiro, others turned to prostitution as a way to earn money, while many ended up toiling in homes and on the land of agricultural estates in the Center-South.[9]

When analyzing Bahia's involvement in the interprovincial slave trade, historians have paid much attention to the export of slaves from Bahia to the Center-South. This focus overlooks transfers of slaves within the province of Bahia. Large sugar planters in Bahia sought to hold on to their slave property in spite of the downward trend in sugar prices and output from the late 1850s. The wealthiest planters, for example owners of sugar engenhos, proved most able to weather the hard times. It was they who had the financial means or had access to capital to enable them to retain slaves or purchase others. Demand for slaves to cut and process sugar in the Recôncavo played a decisive role in determining the price and placement of slaves in Bahia. While thousands of slaves were transported to the Center-South in the 1870s, an *intraprovincial* trade moved hundreds of slaves from one locale to another in the interior of Bahia or from Salvador to the interior of the province.

The End of the Internal Slave Trade in 1881

Numerous slave owners in Bahia reacted negatively to the steady drain of slaves out of Bahia after 1850. These individuals believed that selling slaves to the Center-South was detrimental to both their economic interests and their political power. In response to antislavery critics and proponents of the internal slave trade, they claimed to be enlightened masters. Their supporters in Bahia's provincial assembly vigorously supported this argument. In the words of the Conservative representative Vigário Rocha Vianna, "The slaves of Bahia are perfectly treated. [Bahian] owners have humanity [have shown themselves to be humane]."[10] Fellow legislator Moreira do Castro echoed this sentiment when he stated that "exportation [of slaves from Bahia] will never improve their [slaves'] luck [treatment], [it will only] worsen it [under new masters in the central-southern provinces]."[11]

The construction of the first modern sugar refinery in Bahia in 1880, a rise in the provincial output and value of coffee and tobacco, and the spread of cocoa farms in the south of Bahia combined to galvanize political opposition to the continued outflow of slaves.[12] Authorities in Bahia maintained the tax on each slave sent out of the province to stifle the export of slaves to the Center-South. The tax ranged from 65$ in 1853 (US $37.70) to 200$ (approx. US $100.00) throughout the 1870s, except in 1876, when the export tax reached its highest level at 240$ (US $122.40). This effort was opposed by antislavery advocates in Bahia.

Antitax proponents preferred to see slave sales and transfers to the Center-South unimpeded by provincial or imperial fees of any sort. They believed that allowing the interprovincial slave trade to function without interference (what might be called the "free market") would help to erode the institution of slavery in Bahia. In the words of one proponent, the transfer of slaves out of Bahia sustained "an abolitionist ideology that will force agriculture to enter a new [phase of] existence founded on free labor."[13] By this the journalist suggested the export of slaves out of Bahia would help to bring about the demise of slavery in the province. This in turn, he believed, would contribute to the eventual destruction of slavery throughout Brazil.

In the late 1870s, Bahian slave owners and their allies in the provincial government sought a complete halt to the internal slave trade.[14] This decision related to future prospects in Bahia's economy. Simply put, planters hoped for an agricultural renaissance. For this to happen, they needed cheap labor. Free immigrant laborers never arrived in Bahia as they did in other parts of Brazil and the Americas. Dry climate, minimal access to private landholding, and a lack of subsidies offered by the provincial government (as had been provided in the province of São Paulo) discouraged free immigration. Hence, Bahian planters emphasized continued access to slave workers for the short term. They realized the likelihood of slave emancipation in the not-too-distant future and believed that in a postemancipation environment, former slaves would represent a potential free labor pool.

By 1880–81, these issues were moot because the interprovincial slave trade had been ended by prohibitive import taxes imposed in the central-southern provinces.[15] Planters and politicians in that region believed that halting the interprovincial slave trade would prove beneficial to slaveholder interests throughout the empire.[16] They did not wish to create disequilibrium within the empire by moving a majority or all slaves to the central-southern provinces. Slave owners sought to prevent geographic and political discord, as had occurred between the South and the North in the antebellum United States.

Another motive for imposing excessive taxes on slave imports to slow the growth of the slave population in the Center-South related to immigration. Planters in the expanding coffee frontiers of São Paulo Province believed their future success would be maximized with free workers, not slaves. It was increasingly clear to coffee planters and politicians in the Center-South that the presence of slaves discouraged free European immigrants from coming to southern Brazil. Free laborers, they learned, considered it demeaning to work side-by-side with slaves. Immigrants believed that their upward mobility was impeded when forced to compete with slave workers. Hence, coffee planters sought an immediate end to the interprovincial slave trade to promote free immigration.[17]

Slave owners in the central-southern provinces desired to halt the internal slave trade in 1880–81 can also be traced to slave resistance. The Brazilian historian Celia Maria Marinho de Azevedo points out that many of the slaves, men and women, who arrived from the North-Northeast proved particularly difficult for owners to control. These slaves had been torn from their houses and associations to which they had adapted and forced south by the trade. New owners in the central-southern provinces often imposed harsh demands on the recently displaced slaves, viewing coercion and violence as ways to assure a docile workforce. Their strategies often proved wrong. Many of the newly arrived slaves reacted with work slowdowns, protests, flight, and rebellions.[18]

Examples abound. On orders from the president of Rio de Janeiro in March 1876, a local judge researched slave crimes in the Barra Mansa region of the province in the years following passage of the Law of the Free Womb in 1871. Among the thirty-two slaves who had committed violent crimes from September 1871 to May 1876 (such as the assassination of owners and administrators), thirteen of the perpetrators had been transported to Rio de Janeiro from provinces of the Northeast.[19] The numbers demonstrate that recently arrived slaves transported to Rio de Janeiro via the interprovincial slave trade reacted violently in their new environments.

In a striking petition sent from four rural townships to the president of Rio de Janeiro in late 1877, more then eight hundred landowners expressed dismay over their inability to control the slave population. "Conditions on rural establishments have been profoundly shaken and disturbed, the chains of discipline ruptured, and the moral force and prestige of owners of slaves have been completely destroyed." The letter alluded to "hordes" of slaves "without principles." Unenforceable laws and insufficient numbers of police had aggravated the situation.[20] Although not stated explicitly in the letter, we know that the interprovincial trade had brought numerous slaves from Bahia and the Northeast into the region.

Bahian slaves were visible in the upheavals that unsettled the interior of Rio de Janeiro and São Paulo in the 1870s and up to 1888.[21] They had been sold to the Center-South because their sale brought high returns to Bahian owners. In other words, a strong "pull factor" influenced owners in Bahia to sell their slaves. Yet this response to the demand for slaves in the coffee region by Bahian slave owners should not cause one to overlook "push factors" involved in their decision to sell slaves. Similar to military recruitment practices that "cleansed" Bahia of disruptive free men and slaves during the war with Paraguay, slaves selected by their owners for sale from Bahia in numerous instances were the most difficult to coerce and control.[22]

Overland caravans departing from Bahia destined for Minas Gerais often included hostile slaves who killed the drivers in order to escape.[23] In spite of the large-scale transfer of "difficult" slaves out of Bahia, slave resistance in no way diminished in the province.

The U.S. historian Richard Graham posits that the slaves sent from Bahia and the North-Northeast played a major role in forcing the abolition of slavery in the empire. "If cause and effect runs from internal slave trade to slave discontent to slave action in fleeing the plantations [in 1887–88 in the provinces of São Paulo and Rio de Janeiro] to abolition of slavery [in 1888] to the declaration of the republic [1889]—then, the political importance of that trade was great indeed."[24] In focusing on the Center-South, Graham overlooks the disruptions in Bahia caused by slaves and the nationwide repercussions of the abolitionist movement in Bahia. It is to this story that we return.[25]

Urban Slave Resistance in Salvador in the 1870s

The internal slave trade tore slaves from their families, friends, and environments to which they had adapted. Its toll on the personal lives of slaves sent south and loved ones left behind in Bahia was incalculable.[26] The horrors of the trade fueled slave resistance and the abolitionist movement in Bahia.

As seen below, the number of escaped slaves arrested in Salvador fluctuated between 1870 and 1878, but it is likely that the actual number of runaways remained high throughout the period.

In the year 1870, police apprehended 182 slaves. Many believed that inadequate police patrols contributed to the large numbers of slaves taking off. Arrests decreased from 182 to 80 (a decrease of 44 percent) in the year 1871. Awareness among slaves of the impending decision of the Law of the Free Womb clearly contributed to this downturn. Slaves and

TABLE 6.2. ARRESTS OF FUGITIVE SLAVES IN SALVADOR, 1870 TO 1878

DATE	% AFRICAN	% CRIOULO	TOTAL
Jan. 1870 to Dec. 1870	39.5 (72)	60.5 (110)	182
Jan. 1871 to Dec. 1871	27.5 (22)	72.5 (58)	80
Jan. 1872 to Dec. 1872	22.7 (33)	77.3 (112)	145
Aug. 21, 1875 to Dec. 1875 (Inc.)	25.7 (9)	74.3 (26)	35
Jan. 1876 to Dec. 1876	18.7 (53)	81.3 (229)	282
Jan. 1877 to Dec. 1877	15.3 (23)	84.7 (127)	150
Jan. to Mar. 1, 1878 (Inc.)	11.7 (2)	88.3 (15)	17

Source: APEB/SACP, packages 5809, 5811, 5818, 5828, 5832, 5836.

their allies hoped that provisions in that law might offer slaves improved legal standing and greater possibilities to attain freedom through the courts in Salvador (which in fact it did). Hence, many remained patient in the short term.

In the period between 1848 and 1885, the largest number of slaves apprehended (282) in Salvador occurred in 1876 (based on available records). The upsurge of slave flight in the city of Salvador in 1876 can be linked to the peak in slave transfers, averaging more than one hundred each month at this juncture, to the Center-South and to the interior of Bahia. As in other parts of the Americas, slaves often reacted to being sold by running away from their owner.[27]

Authorities registered numerous episodes where slaves fled in groups. On April 6, 1876, for example, police arrested seven male crioulo slaves and two female crioula slaves who had taken off together. On September 21, 1876, police arrested another group of nine male crioulo slaves and four female crioula slaves who had joined another mass escape. In June 1877, fourteen African slaves, of whom four were women, fled from an affluent family in Salvador.[28] As these selected, but representative, cases suggest, during this turbulent era crioulo slaves were now highly visible in resistance to the slave regime. After years of African and crioulo slaves residing and laboring in close proximity to one another in Salvador, shared strategic interests and overcame differences that previously divided them.

Although we need to be cautious of reading too much into police lists and descriptions of fugitive slaves, they nevertheless offer direct testimony into the responses of African and Brazilian-born crioulo slaves to what they witnessed in Salvador in the mid-1870s. Slaves understood that they had a better chance of gaining a hearing with police and judges as a group, rather than individually, to protest bad treatment and questions related to illegal enslavement. Slaves and abolitionist supporters sought to ensure that the question of the future of slavery remained in the public eye and a major political issue.

In his study of abolition in Brazil, the Brazilian historian Jacob Gorender suggests that slave resistance in the 1870s was characterized by individual initiatives and later in the 1880s by organized collective acts by groups of slaves. He writes that this shift in strategies and tactics "demonstrates an evolution in slave consciousness across this period, an evolution intimately associated with the abolitionist movement of free men. Such phenomena permit one to speak of slaves as an *autonomous force* in the process of abolition."[29] Gorender underestimates the organized, collective acts of slaves that proliferated from the late 1860s and continued steadily thereafter. Nevertheless, he insightfully suggests that an evaluation of the complex and ever-changing dynamics of abolition needs to situate slaves and their multifaceted strategies of resistance at the center of the story.

Along with individual and mass escapes, slaves also sought to protect their personal rights through the courts. In one instance, a former slave and soldier named Luís Antônio dos Santos faced off against his former owner Ambrosio Alba da Silva. Previously known by the name Romaldo, Santos had changed his name to hide his identity. Silva argued that his slave Romaldo (a.k.a. Luís Santos) had escaped and enlisted in a battalion of Voluntários from the town of Santo Amaro. Soon after Santos's return from the Paraguayan front, Silva called on the police to arrest the returned veteran. Silva requested reimbursement for the cost of what he would have received if he had sold the slave to the army. This followed the practice in place since December 1866 when the War Ministry, following the lead of Pedro II, decided to compensate owners who freed their slaves to fight in the war (an offer to which few owners responded). Silva also desired government indemnity for lost labor service during the years Santos served at the front. Although we do not know the outcome of the case, it is clear that the chief of police had little sympathy for the former owner's demands. He rejected the suggestion that Silva merited payment for lost services. He also stated that an individual like Luís Santos, "who had shed his blood for a nation aggressed upon," should not be returned to captivity.[30]

The festering discontent among the urban poor in Salvador during the 1870s promoted restlessness among slaves. Similar to events two decades earlier in 1858, some two thousand free persons gathered outside the presidential palace in Salvador to protest the scarcity and high cost of manioc flour and other subsistence goods in late March 1878.[31] In response to drought conditions in provinces north of Bahia (five hundred thousand people perished in Ceará alone), entrepreneurs in Salvador sold large quantities of manioc flour to commercial agents willing to pay high prices. President Baron Homem de Mello estimated that five thousand sacks of manioc flour had been shipped out of Bahia from June 1877 to March 1878. As merchants and farmers harvested profits by satisfying this external demand, local prices rose steeply and left thousands of Bahians unable to purchase basic foodstuffs.[32] The effects were disproportionately borne by the nonwhite masses of the city.

Although the public demonstrations of March ended without bloodshed, anxiety continued throughout the province for several months. In response, *vereadores* (city council members) at the Town Hall discussed ways to increase the availability manioc flour in the city. They called on the president to act. On April 11, 1878, the president issued a circular aimed at increasing grain supplies by prohibiting farmers in outlying townships of Nazareth, Jaguaripe, Maragogipe, Cachoeira, and Santo Amaro from impeding sale and distribution of their crops to the urban market of Salvador. Gangs roamed Salvador at night complaining about the lack of food, one group shouting threats to set fire to houses owned by merchants who exported the manioc flour. To deal with this tense situation, the chief of police sent out patrols to protect citizens and property.[33]

Urban slaves viewed these protests by angry free persons as beneficial to their interests. Different from the hostility directed at African slaves and freedpersons in the wake of the 1858 food riots, the protesters of 1878 did not unleash their fury at slaves. In the intervening two decades, the sale and distribution of food had been transformed. With far fewer Africans in an expanding city of free people, no longer did Africans have influence over this key sector of the urban economy. Disaffection among the urban poor with corrupt merchants and their allies in the provincial government enhanced the possibility that the free persons might act on common class interests with the city's slave population.

Abolitionist Strategies

Two distinct abolitionist vectors coalesced from the late 1860s. The first was composed predominantly of individuals from the Bahian urban bourgeoisie who joined abolitionist societies. These organizations tended to be conservative in their worldview as well as in their strategies for reform. A second vector recruited more from black sectors, including the lower classes, emphasized confrontation. Following tactics employed from the late 1850s, blacks and persons of color played a major role in this latter group. Closely attuned to regional and national political debates related to slave emancipation, a small cadre of activists spread their ideas in the streets of Salvador and throughout the province.

The moderates in abolitionist societies called for slave emancipation at some time in the future. These societies collected funds to purchase manumission for individual slaves, published articles in several newspapers in support of emancipation, and met to discuss politics. In Salvador, these entities included (among others) the Seventh of September Liberating Society (1869–76), the Humanitarian Abolitionist Society (1869–70), and the Commercial Abolitionist Society (1870–72). The Twenty-Fifth of June Liberating Society was founded in the Recôncavo town of Cachoeira in September 1870. Within a year, it included 117 members, all males. Abolitionist societies also sprang up in the towns of Lençois and Camisão (present-day Ipirá in the dry *sertão* backlands of Bahia).[34]

What all these early "abolitionist" societies had in common was a desire to see the imperial government direct the process of emancipation. Members supported legislation that ensured freedom to all slave offspring. They desired minimal disruption in the transition to free labor. With passage of the Law of the Free Womb in late 1871, abolitionist societies throughout the province disappeared (the Seventh of September Society continued until 1876, but played a minimal role after 1871). The reduced activism of moderate abolitionists did little to change the outlook of radicals who continued to press for immediate emancipation.

Radical demands continued unabated after 1871. These people were more radical in both worldview and strategies. Intellectuals tied to the newspaper *O Alabama*, for example, played a leading role among this more aggressive force. They criticized the demise of Bahian abolitionist societies after 1871 and even questioned Pedro II's capacity to rule and his commitment to the cause of liberty after passage of the Law of the Free Womb.

O Alabama often published with fanfare provocative abolitionist articles. These articles condemned the trauma caused by the interprovincial slave trade. Paying close attention to history, writers from *O Alabama* analyzed earlier failed attempts to raise the abolitionist banner in Bahia. Journalists also covered regional, national, and international action and opinion related to emancipation.

Read closely by provincial authorities who noted with disdain the newspaper in their correspondence, *O Alabama* often raised the specter of slave abuse. To make its case, the newspaper included stories based on the scantiest of evidence or rumors to embarrass local officials and provoke the police into checking out the veracity of the accusations. On July 28, 1876, *O Alabama* claimed a woman who lived in the Sé parish of Salvador had beaten her slave for an hour, affirming that neighbors had reported hearing the screams of the slave. Another story published in that same edition denounced an owner named Angelo for shackling his slave to a wooden stockade for several days in spite of the slave having suffered serious wounds from his owner. In its edition of April 4, 1877, *O*

Alabama claimed that a female slave had been tortured at the Convent of Carmo. The police immediately visited the convent to look into the matter. They learned that the slave had injured her foot in a personal mishap and had been receiving treatment from a doctor. Police investigated all of these episodes and found no evidence to confirm the accusations. Not all claims published in *O Alabama* proved fictitious, however. Police also discovered episodes of "excessive castigation" of slaves described by the paper and then took steps to halt this treatment.[35]

Enemies of *O Alabama* did not sit by peacefully. Some were so angered by *O Alabama*'s assault that they took direct action. In a well-publicized court appearance, editor Arístides Ricardo de Santa Anna accused a medical doctor and his son of assaulting him on the street in Salvador. The attack occurred as retribution for an article published in *O Alabama* in which Arístides described the doctor's son as an unemployed, spoiled hooligan well known in the city for taunting others with racial epithets. The two assailants inflicted a head wound that left Arístides lying on the ground bleeding profusely. Seeking justice, Arístides took his assailants to court. During the proceedings, Arístides explained that at the scene of the crime the doctor had yelled out "Negro!! You have been writing against white men!"[36] Although the suit failed due to insufficient evidence, Arístides's statements demonstrated his determination not to back down from controversial topics related to race and abolition.

By the use of astute propaganda and by reporting all known cases of abuse, intellectuals associated with *O Alabama* refused to allow the abolitionist cause to weaken after 1871. One result was that vociferous abolitionist "meetings" (the English word often appeared in official records and newspapers) became commonplace in Salvador during those years.[37] Groups that traditionally had stayed out of politics now lent support to the cause of abolition. For example, the Eutherpe Philharmonic Society (a prominent group of musicians in Salvador) and even the police bands used monies made from their public concerts to pay for letters of emancipation for individual slaves.[38]

Coverage of these events published in *O Alabama* did much to enhance the appeal of the abolitionist cause. As the number of slaves present in Salvador dwindled during the course of the 1870s, abolitionist agitators in Salvador shifted their attention outside the city.

Slave Resistance in the Interior

In spite of traffickers having sent 25,000 to 30,000 slaves southward as part of the interprovincial slave trade from the 1830s, Bahia remained a province with a substantial number of slaves up to the end of slavery in 1888. In the early 1870s, the Bahian slave population remained between 165,403 and 200,000 slaves. The higher number seems the best estimate because owners commonly hid the number of slaves in their possession so as to shirk tax payments and legal obligations imposed by the Law of the Free Womb. This made Bahia the third-largest slaveholding province in Brazil, behind only Minas Gerais and Rio de Janeiro and ahead of São Paulo. By 1886–87, Bahia had fallen behind São Paulo Province, but trailed closely. At this late date, Bahians still owned at least 76,838 slaves, or some 10 percent of the total slave population of Brazil.[39]

During the decade of the 1870s, slaves who traveled back and forth between countryside and city disseminated information and fresh ideas to fellow slaves. Slaves from the interior commonly traveled to Salvador to transport food and goods to urban markets. There they made contact, in the words of one slave, with "diverse common folk" [*diversas pessoas do povo*].[40] After returning to plantations and farms, they shared their knowledge of urban abolitionist protests and news of slave resistance weakening support for slavery in the streets. Travel and communication stimulated resistance.

Many slaves fled to recently formed quilombos during the decade. In response, officials in Salvador sent out police and troops to search for and destroy these communities. One police patrol traveled to Ilheus in the south of the province in 1874. In the interior near the town of Lagoa they came upon the remnants of two abandoned quilombos, but found no runaways. The second-lieutenant in command noted that it was beyond his capacities to capture fugitive slaves because they are "hidden, protected and advised" by slaves who resided on nearby estates.[41] Using quilombos as a base of operation, roving gangs of

fugitive slaves often raided sugar engenhos, other rural residences in the
Recôncavo, and slave caravans. As a result, travel on roads in the interior
was precarious.

In the Recôncavo, a small number of overseers of estates were killed
by slaves angered by poor treatment.[42] In an episode in June 1876, nine
slaves appeared one morning at the office of the police delegate in the town
of Nazareth to inform him that they had beaten to death the administrator
at the engenho where they labored. Two of these slaves were only thirteen
and seventeen years old. Everyone in the group admitted participating in
the beating and stated their belief that they would all be found guilty.[43]
But the slaves also stated they preferred prison to being returned to the
estate. There is evidence that on numerous occasions during these years
slaves willingly accepted jail terms rather than remain with their masters
across slaveholding regions of the empire.[44]

At times, slave resistance had a more obvious political content.
During the decade of the 1870s, slave revolts threatened the old order. In
June 1872 in the town of Taperoá (just outside Valença), slaves encircled
the home of Anna Maria de Jesus Oliva, the owner of an engenho. They
made several attempts to break into the house. Although their efforts
ultimately proved unsuccessful, the terrified family was forced to huddle
inside behind locked doors and shutters. When reinforcements arrived
from a nearby engenho to aid the besieged owners, the slaves put up a
fight rather than flee. Testimony provided to the authorities revealed that
two free men had joined with the rebellious slaves in the attack. When
soldiers finally arrived on the scene, they arrested six male slaves and four
female slaves. Newspapers in Bahia published accounts of the uprising
and the news even traveled to Rio de Janeiro.[45] In Salvador, provincial
officials inquired about the circumstances that provoked the uprising,
deciding that "outside influences," implying abolitionist agitators, had
been a factor.[46]

In September 1878, slaves assassinated Alexandre Gomes Argolo,
prominent owner of the sugar engenho Itatingui located near the town
of São Francisco do Conde in the Bahian Recôncavo. News of the
assassination sent shock waves through the province of Bahia. The local

judge investigating the case claimed to have no knowledge of anyone who might want to kill Argolo. It did not appear that theft had been a motivation, given that money and jewels in the house had not been touched. The investigating judge accused the plantation's slaves with the murder.[47] In the ensuing interrogations, twelve slaves admitted to having been involved in the successful plot. One slave had entered through a window in the main house of the estate at dawn and the rest followed. Encountering Argolo asleep in his bed, the slaves beat the man to death. The local police delegate requested reinforcements to ensure that those who had committed such a "monstrous episode" would not escape.[48]

The case received extensive coverage across the region, given the nature of the crime and prominence of the victim. Although we do not know the specific motive for the assassination, it most likely occurred as retribution for abusive treatment inflicted on the slaves of the engenho.

Two months later on November 23, the jury found the twelve slaves guilty of the assassination of the planter. Nine of the slaves were condemned to death, one was sentenced to twenty years in prison, and another two were sentenced to four hundred strokes of the whip. Officials carried out imprisonment and whippings, but we do not know from surviving records about the fate of the nine slaves who faced the death penalty. The deceased planter's wife attended all of the proceedings and punishments.

In an attempt to minimize the bad news of Argolo's death, Bahia's president Baron Homem de Mello appeared at a well-publicized ceremony three weeks later in the Recôncavo near the site of the murder. Along with the president and his wife, ten dignitaries from Bahia attended, including the two delegates of the provincial assembly, Dr. Arístides César Zama and Arístides de Sousa Spinola. Lieutenant Colonel Francisco Sodre Pereira, owner of the engenho Campina, presided. Seven female and male slaves, ranging in age from nine to fifty-five years old, were given letters of manumission. President Mello praised this act of beneficence in a laudatory letter sent to the Interior Ministry in Rio de Janeiro, assuring imperial officials of the capacity of Bahian planters to implement emancipation reforms without provoking violence.[49]

The high-ranking officials who attended the festivities had full knowledge of the slave uprising in São Francisco do Conde from newspapers. They had witnessed the destabilizing effects of the interprovincial slave trade on Salvador and the interior of the province. Furthermore, these same politicians had endured scathing commentary by a small group of abolitionists for over a decade. The pressures exerted by activists of color proved relentless. We must suspect that these letters of manumission offered a way to appear as the enlightened arbiters of the destiny of slaves and to mute the critics in their midst.

Capitalism and Antislavery in Bahia

Rational economic decisions and antislavery initiatives proved compatible and mutually reinforcing in the Atlantic world of the nineteenth century.[50] As a result, the culture and ideals associated with capitalism played an important role in the spread of abolitionist ideals. Numerous Bahians drank deeply of these new currents of thought.

Since the turn of the nineteenth century, international and Brazilian capital had a major impact on Bahia.[51] Evidence of this included Bahian involvement in the international slave trade, the export of agricultural commodities from the province, the expansion of local markets, the entrepreneurial activities of the urban merchant elite, and the ever-widening ties of the port city of Salvador to cities throughout the Atlantic Basin.

After 1850, interest mounted to attract investments that might enable Bahia to move into a more advanced phase of industrial capitalism. In the 1850s, sugar planters purchased steam engines in an attempt to remain competitive in increasingly competitive world markets. A small middle class that sought to emulate European example and to modernize emerged in Salvador. Several banks were founded in the 1850s, including the Bank of Bahia in 1858. In December 1861, seventy-eight expositors showed 419 items at the first Exposition of Products and Manufactures of the Province in Salvador. The following year this event included 154 exhibitors and 852 products. The first railroad line in Bahia linked the interior town of Alagoinhas with Salvador in 1863, and other lines became operable in the Recôncavo in the 1870s. To make the lower and upper city of Salvador more accessible, the city constructed the Lacerda elevator in 1874. The 1870s was a decade of technological change, new ideas, and social transformation.[52] By 1880, Bahia produced nearly one-half of all industrial output in Brazil (which included refined sugar output).[53]

Several Bahians reflected on the changing international economy and the labor question in their writings in the 1870s. The medical doctor Satyro de Oliveira Dias in his book *The Duke of Caxias and the War with Paraguay: A Critical-Historical Study* (1870) encouraged readers not to overlook positive benefits associated with Brazil's involvement in the war with Paraguay. "The war [with Paraguay was] the fertile beginning of inappreciable future benefits."[54] Dias believed that one of those benefits was that slavery would soon disappear in Brazil. In the same year, Dr. Polycarpo Lopes de Leão published an antislavery tract entitled *Como pensa sobre o elemento servil* (1870; How to Think About the Servile Element). Lopes condemned slavery as contrary to the natural rights of all persons and the ideals of Christianity. He believed that free workers pursued all activities with greater diligence and intelligence than slaves.[55] Both authors looked favorably on changes in the international political economy. They viewed the entrée of capital into Bahia as a beneficent force that would bring the demise of slavery in its wake.

An extraordinary figure of the period, Luís Tarquínio (1844–1903), was described by a biographer as the "journeyman of hope" [*o garimpeiro da esperança*].[56] Born into poverty, grandson of a slave, Tarquínio was drawn to money and economics. After attending a public primary school in Salvador for three years between ages seven and ten, Tarquínio found work to help support his mother who earned her income by washing clothes. At age fifteen he came to the attention of the Bruderer family, owners of a commercial house in Salvador. So began one of the most remarkable business careers in the history of Bahia and Brazil.

A capitalist entrepreneur par excellence, Tarquínio published anonymously a tract entitled *O elemento escravo e as questões econômicas do Brazil* (1885; The Slave Element and the Economic Questions of Brazil). Desirous of an end to slavery in his country, Tarquínio nevertheless pondered with skepticism the economic consequences of immediate abolition. To ease the transition to free labor in Brazil, he proposed the creation of a lottery that would free eighty thousand slaves each year regardless of sex or age by reimbursing owners with lottery proceeds. Tarquínio's plan required that former slaves sign a compulsory contract. Based on this legal agreement, freedpersons would receive a salary for labor performed during four years under the direction of their former owners. Tarquínio also called for the distribution of plots of fertile land to former slaves to facilitate the transition to freedom.[57] None of his ideas bore fruition.

His interest in social reforms was not limited to ending slavery. Like another famous Brazilian entrepreneur named Baron of Mauá, Luís Tarquínio helped to bring British business practices and industrial methods to Brazil.[58] In 1891, two years after abolition, he founded the Cloth Factory of Boa Viagem in Salvador. With plans to employ sixteen hundred workers, Tarquínio constructed a workers' community alongside the cloth factory composed of 258 houses, a school, and a theater. An avid reader influenced by diverse writers (John Burns, Charles Fourier, Robert Owen, Claude Henri de Saint-Simon, James Lowell, Henry George, Upham Williams, Annie Bellingstey), Tarquínio pursued a wide range of progressive policies to benefit former slaves. The social programs he implemented on behalf of the workers at Boa Viagem (healthcare, education, cultural opportunities, affordable housing, rights of women in the workplace) had few precedents within or outside of Brazil.[59]

The spread of international capitalism helped to disseminate an antislavery message in Bahia, particularly among the small bourgeoisie residing in the port city of Salvador. The ever-inquisitive Luís Tarquínio visited Europe *twenty-three times* from 1864 to 1900 to observe factory production techniques and labor practices. Tarquínio's colleague medical doctor Manoel Victorino traveled to hospitals in Paris, Vienna, Berlin, and London to learn about the most advanced medical practices. Victorino's thesis *Moléstias parasitárias intertropicais* (1876; Intertropical Parasitic Diseases) mixed science with an abolitionist message.[60] Improved communication among Brazil's cities and with foreign countries

Figure 6.1 Statue of Luiz Tarquínio next to the Cloth Factory of Boa Viagem. Photograph by author.

stimulated antislavery discourse. Concerned citizens discussed the impact of emancipations in other parts of the Americas. Intellectuals probed how best to assure a smooth transition from slave labor to free labor.

Along with these changes propelled by expanding capatalism, the cultural values associated with the industrialized countries of Europe and the United States seeped into Bahia. From the 1850s through emancipation in 1888, a segment of the urban bourgeoisie in Salvador optimistically evaluated conditions in their province through a prism of what might be labeled a "culture of capitalism." In this environment, slavery lost its credibility and legitimacy. Modernizers considered slavery an institution inherited from a past that ought to be eradicated as soon as possible.

In spite of a greater sensitivity to the abuses associated with slavery, few Bahians showed much interest in the future well-being of former slaves after emancipation. Polycarpo Lopes de Leão is a good example. After studying law in Olinda, Portugal, and traveling in Europe, he returned to Bahia. In his book *How to Think About the Servile Element*, he called for an end to slavery based on economic (capitalist) analysis. Lopes estimated that the cost of maintaining a European domestic servant (20$ or US $9.00) would be less than the cost to rent an unskilled slave each month (30$ or US $13.50).[61] No longer would slave owners be responsible for slaves who fell ill. There would be no loss of capital investment with the death of a slave. The danger of property destruction and violence related to the presence of slaves would be ended. Children would benefit with improved education, in that they would no longer be in contact with "persons of more or less bad customs, like slaves."[62] Antislavery sentiment did not necessarily translate into humanitarian concern.

A reactionary and racially biased posture characterized an influential strain among a majority of abolitionists in Bahia and in other regions of the empire. Such persons desired to transform Brazil into a modern nation. To accomplish this goal, slavery needed to be ended. Of equal importance, however, was the necessity of maintaining controls over free workers in the future. Conservative "emancipationists" (those who supported an antislavery position) had little confidence that former slaves could be trusted to act responsibly. Proponents of immediate abolition commonly shared such a bias. Maintenance of the status quo, meaning the preservation of elite influence and protection of private property, underlay most gestures of humanitarian concern. In Bahia, Antônio Carneiro Rocha and Jeronymo Sodre subscribed to this worldview.[63] On the national scene, Joaquim Nabuco expressed similar perspectives. Such attitudes have been depicted by David Haberly as a mix of "anti-slavery and anti-slave."[64] For many the outcome was, in the words of Celia Maria Marinho de Azevedo, a "struggle for reforms [the abolitionist movement], so that in the end all would continue as before."[65]

Conclusions

An interprovincial slave trade that sent slaves from Bahia to the central-southern provinces combined with the intraprovincial transport of slaves had a significant impact on the interior of the province as well as Salvador in the 1870s. The number of slaves residing in the city declined precipitously. Slaves reacted with hostility when torn from families and environments to which they had adapted. Observers decried the abuses associated with the internal slave trade and the treatment of slaves. Increasing involvement of Bahians in the national and international economy prompted discussions on a wide range of issues, including how slavery degraded all persons associated with the institution and the benefits of free labor.

Progressives faced two major dilemmas. First, numerous planters both large and small had little interest in giving up their slaves. Modernization of sugar production along with hopes of an agricultural renaissance fueled this sentiment.[66] And second, immediate abolition loomed as a decision that might lead to "anarchy" (the term seldom defined). Many feared the wrath of former slave owners who would not receive reimbursement for their slave property if slaves were declared free overnight as well as possible retribution from former slaves.

A growing political polarization around the issue of emancipation characterized the 1870s. Influential delegates to Bahia's Provincial Assembly clamored that the Law of the Free Womb of 1871 would resolve all issues related to a gradual emancipation. Radicals did not sit idly by. In the words of a Bahian writing in September 1875, "The law of September [the Law of the Free Womb] is miserable legislation, [it] is a fallacy [*sophisma*], a mockery [*zombaria*] for the slave, an immense harm done to the nation. Who is it that the law freed? No one."[67]

Political activists caused significant repercussions in the 1870s. With slaves playing a leading role, they helped transform abolition into a national issue of the highest priority. Such pressures made it impossible for politicians to shirk the topic. In an oft-cited speech by Jeronymo Sodré before the Chamber of Deputies in Rio de Janeiro in March 1879, the Bahian delegate alluded to a "volcano" to describe the social climate in several Brazilian provinces.[68] An advocate of immediate abolition since midcentury, Sodré condemned the Law of the Free Womb as a flawed and inadequate reform. He claimed that all inhabitants of the empire merited their freedom.[69]

Sodré's appeal found an audience. Within eighteen months, the question of what was to be done became a central debate in provincial assemblies and among imperial ministers in Rio de Janeiro.[70] Subsequently, a third and final phase of the abolitionist movement coalesced after 1880. 🔲

CHAPTER SEVEN

Liberation, 1880–88

In his book *A escravidão, o clero e o abolicionismo* (1887; Slavery, the Church, and Abolition), the Bahian of color Luís Anselmo da Fonseca (1848–1929) wrote, "What is certain, not counting Maranhão—the most reactionary of all [of the provinces]—in no other province has abolitionism encountered greater obstacles in attaining its goals, nor been so small a movement [as in Bahia]."[1] Several factors influenced Fonseca's negative evaluation. Owners of sugar engenhos in the Recôncavo freed few slaves before 1884 for whatever motive, whether economic, political, or humanitarian. European immigrants never arrived in sufficient numbers to take the place of slaves in the rural labor force. Few outspoken abolitionists appeared on the scene and those who did encountered a great deal of hostility. Writing only one year before Princess Isabel signed the decree ending slavery in Brazil, Fonseca still wondered what it would take to end slavery in his home province of Bahia.

"We Demand that All Workers No Matter What Race Have a Right to a Salary!"

Black and mixed-race activists mobilized a vociferous and combative movement among common folk in the third phase of abolition that commenced in 1880. Intellectuals and politicians also joined in. This group raised their voices in the streets of Salvador and in the provincial legislature. Becoming more aggressive in their tactics, abolitionists organized an Underground Railroad that enabled fugitive slaves to travel clandestinely to Salvador. Their subversive activities provoked the wrath of slaveholders and resonated throughout the province and the empire. As had occurred during the earlier two phases of abolition in Bahia (1850s–79), slaves played a key role in the third and last stage of the abolitionist movement in Bahia.

Upheaval caused by recalcitrant slaves in the interior of Bahia continued from 1880 until abolition in May 1888. As in other regions of Brazil, slaves continued to challenge owners' control over their lives.[2] Hundreds of slaves fled, either individually or in groups, from plantations and farms. Reasons for flight varied. Some slaves reacted to harsh treatment by masters and administrators.[3] Some sought the aid of abolitionists. Others arrived at the doorsteps of judges hoping to gain legal protection from illegal enslavement (based on the 1831 and 1871 legislation).[4]

Several episodes of slave violence in 1882 had a marked impact on provincial politicians. In September, slaves resident at a sugar estate owned by the Carmelite order of Bahia in the parish of São Sebastião de Passé assassinated the Carmelite priest João Lucas do Monte Carmelo Vasconcelos. This act resulted from the failure of a series of negotiations at the engenho of Carmo over several years between the slaves and the priest. Administering the property since (approximately) 1866, João Lucas became increasingly harsh in his treatment of the slaves by the early 1880s, as a result of an upsurge in slave runaways. The slaves on the engenho appealed directly to João Lucas to moderate his punishments and protested to police officials as well, but to no avail. The priest's decision to end the longstanding right granted to the slaves to cultivate food on small plots during free time on Sundays and other issues caused disquiet among the slaves on the estate.

The day following the murder of the priest, soldiers aided by inhabitants of the region captured eleven slaves suspected of the crime. The slaves remained in jail for two years. Senator and soon-to-be imperial prime minister Baron of Cotegipe (João Maurício Wanderley) called for harsh penalties to be imposed.[5] During the trial in March 1884, a fifth-year student from the Faculty of Medicine named Rafael José Jambeiro defended the slaves. Although not having a degree in law, Jumbeiro was allowed to act as a legal representative before the court (known as a *rábula* or *curador*) due to his ability to read, write, and debate. Jambeiro was one of numerous students from the Faculty of Medicine who brought attention to the abolitionist cause by speaking in the courts, writing in newspapers, and organizing public protests. The convicted slaves received prison sentences ranging from twenty years to life. One account penned by the Bahian writer João da Silva Campos based on urban legend and oral interviews taken in the late 1920s claims, however, that the convicted slaves were released from prison soon after the signing of the emancipation law four years later in May 1888.[6]

In a meticulous analysis of the events leading up to the murder, the Bahian historian Walter Fraga Filho has written that the slaves of the engenho Carmo carried out a "rebellion of rupture." By this term he suggests that the slaves involved in the execution of the priest João Lucas had responded to a "crisis of legitimacy." Even members of the Carmelite convent in Salvador, which owned the engenho Carmo, had criticized João Lucas for his abusive acts and some discussed ending slavery on the engenho. The slaves knew of the dissent among the priests in Salvador both from stories told by slaves who had traveled to Salvador and from abolitionists who made contact with them near their estate. The testimony of the slaves arrested after the murder demonstrated that slaves on the estate sensed that police officials and judges in Salvador might prove sympathetic to their plight. Therefore, the slaves accepted the likely consequences of murdering the abusive priest-administrator.

Certainly the slaves had heard of the murders of other overseers and masters on other estates in the Recôncavo. For example, three months earlier slaves had assassinated the manager of a nearby sugar plantation after he forced them to work on Sundays. In this context João Lucas's refusal to negotiate or compromise over the work routines of the slaves was certainly dangerous.[7] With this "rebellion of rupture," the slaves not only desired to end their bad treatment and abuse but also believed that this act might aid them in their quest for freedom.

Similarly, the town of Leopoldina located near the port town of Viçosa in southern Bahia also experienced the wrath of its slaves. Swiss and German immigrants founded it early in the century. By 1850 some fifty-four foreigners and their families had settled in the area along with their sixteen hundred slaves.[8] The foreign-born residents often fought bitterly with neighboring Brazilian settlers who had also been attracted to the fertile coastal lands. One result of this contention was both sides stirred up the slaves owned by their rivals. Local officials accused the Swiss and Germans of abusing their slaves. Rumor had it that in retaliation the foreign settlers had passed information to slaves employed at estates owned by Brazilians that legislation had been passed guaranteeing them their freedom.[9] The intention of both sides was to undermine the authority of their enemies.

On various occasions in September 1882, a group of slaves threatened to kill Brazilians who had recently purchased the coffee estate Matum. The slaves were aware of the abusive treatment inflicted on slaves on other properties of the new owners. In the wake of the initial confrontations, the slaves refused to return to work. Owners of nearby farms feared that news of the uprising would spread and provoke violence throughout the region. In appeals to provincial authorities, the planters pleaded for immediate action. With the aid of forty settlers from the region, police surrounded the property and arrested ten slaves involved in the protest.[10] But the region was not pacified. In December, slaves resident on a nearby estate named Monte Cristo shot to death the administrator. Nine slaves were arrested.[11] Then, in May 1884, slaves on the estate Matum where the confrontations began, succeeded in assassinating José Antônio Vinerote, administrator of the estate.[12] As violence by slaves mounted in the first half of the 1880s, Bahian abolitionists adjusted their strategies.

To aid their efforts to end slavery, activists sought out the support of freed slaves and fellow free people of color.[13] The pardo historian, engineer, and linguist Teodoro Sampaio (1855–1937) was the son of a slave woman and Catholic priest. He condemned slavery in speeches and articles and joined with fellow radicals at public "meetings" aimed at spreading abolitionist ideas. The black artist Manoel Raímundo Querino (1851–1923) was among many young Bahians to join abolitionist societies in Salvador. Querino signed a Republican manifesto in 1870 and wrote proabolition articles in two little-known labor newspapers in Salvador entitled *A Província* (The Province) and *O Trabalho* (Work). The first black Brazilian to write Brazilian history, Querino emphasized to his readers the necessity of providing skills to the Bahian underclass.[14]

He helped found the Lyceum of Arts and Trades (Liceu de Artes e Ofícios) in 1872. The Lyceum offered much needed training to slaves and their children and continues today, providing educational opportunities and apprenticeships to the young people of Salvador. The black medical doctor Francisco Alvares dos Santos championed immediate abolition in Bahia in his university lectures and at public forums. These protests by intellectuals were reinforced by mass action. Lower-class black workers also organized abolitionist protests. Roque Jacinto da Cruz and Manoel Benício dos Passos were among the most visible.

The medical doctor Luís Anselmo da Fonseca received much attention during these years for his efforts to end slavery. Not only did he publish the first history of abolition in Bahia in 1887, but he also worked clandestinely with fellow organizer Eduardo Carigé. Fonseca often attended and spoke at public gatherings in Salvador. A man of color, Fonseca's education and upper-class status did not deter him from his political efforts on behalf of the lower classes of Bahia. After slaves officially received their freedom in 1888, Fonseca and Querino continued to fight racism in Salvador and offer aid to the marginalized.

Drawn by the mounting strength of abolitionism, activists of color from other parts of Brazil traveled to Bahia to lend support to the cause of abolition. One of the most important was the pardo José Carlos do Patrocínio (1853–1905). The offspring of a thirteen-year-old slave girl and a Catholic priest, Patrocínio understood from an early age the harsh reality faced by blacks and persons of color in Brazil. Patrocínio initially became well known for his writings and skills of organizing in Rio de Janeiro.[15] He twice ventured to Bahia, once in 1879 on the way to cover a drought in Ceará as a newspaper writer and then in 1882 en route to the cities of Maceió (Alagaos) and Recife (Pernambuco) as an abolitionist organizer. During the second visit, Patrocínio disembarked to the cheers of a large crowd that had gathered for his arrival. As the invited speaker and guest of honor, he addressed an overflow audience in the auditorium at the Lyceum of Arts and Trades about the abolitionist cause elsewhere in Brazil. He emphasized to his audience that everyone could aid the abolitionist cause through collective endeavors and effective use of the press.

Between December 1882 and early February 1883 Patrocínio returned to Ceará and journeyed to the interior of the province. There he made contact with several women who were influential in abolitionist societies.[16] Employing tactics that had been successful in Rio de Janeiro, Patrocínio mobilized urban protesters, port workers, and sailors. His activities helped Ceará to become the first province to end slavery in Brazil in March 1884.[17] This declaration of abolition of slavery in Ceará had immediate reverberations, particularly in the cities of Salvador and Rio de Janeiro.[18] Ceará became known as the "second Canada." This phrase implied that similar to the beacon of freedom that Canada had earlier represented to slaves fleeing from the U.S. South via the Underground Railroad, slaves from all over Brazil could be assured of a safe haven in this small northeastern province.[19]

Bahians of middle- and upper-class backgrounds also joined in the abolitionist movement in Bahia. Eduardo Carigé Barauna (1851–1905) was one such individual. Unhappy with the slow pace of reform in Bahia, Carigé aligned himself with the radical vector of the abolitionist movement. One of very few members of the Bahian bourgeoisie to demand immediate abolition from the late 1860s, he gained renown as a public speaker. The son of a medical doctor, Carigé enrolled for a short period at the Faculty of Medicine in Salvador. After deciding against a career in medicine, he became a respected journalist and playwright.[20] During the Paraguayan War, Carigé criticized the treatment of slaves by owners in Bahia and also helped establish one of the early abolitionist societies in Salvador. His unceasing efforts and critical commentary made him a controversial figure in Bahia.

Carigé sought to inform Bahians about political events and abolitionist initiatives elsewhere in Brazil. From the early 1870s until 1888, he organized numerous public meetings that focused on abolition. At these gatherings, he invited poets and orators to speak out against the evils of slavery. In July 1881, Carigé joined with colleagues to commemorate the tenth anniversary of the death of the abolitionist poet Castro Alves. At the end of the month, these festivities culminated in a huge demonstration to promote abolition. Well-known figures who participated included medical doctor and journalist Frederico Lisbôa, the medical doctor and philosophy professor Arthur Americano, and the Paris-trained epidemiologist from Pernambuco named Joaquim de Aquino Fonseca. Bahia's delegate to the imperial Chamber of Deputies Rui Barbosa spoke in praise of Castro Alves.[21] Coinciding with the protest, the newspaper *O Monitor* published a special issue devoted to abolitionist articles, local actors performed Castro Alves's abolitionist play *Gonzaga,* and Salvador's municipal officials renamed a beautiful public square in the upper city that overlooks the bay in honor of the poet.[22] One participant wrote:

> The province continues in peace, having passed tranquilly through the patriotic festivities that concluded in a splendid session at the [Polytheama] theater in honor of Castro Alves. The cause of abolition is gaining ground; it is moving forward at a rapid pace! There is no doubt. The wave increases, and it would be best to create an opening [in a dam] to prevent a flood that could cause great devastation in its passage.[23]

In the wake of these events, Carigé joined with some thirty individuals to found the Bahian Liberating Society in 1883. The Bahian Liberating Society would gain attention more through the deeds of individual members than from the initiatives of the organization itself. Its members demonstrated an uncanny capacity to create disturbances in Salvador and the Recôncavo. They contributed editorials to local newspapers and gained attention as a result of their audacious acts, which included nighttime visits to slaves on plantations and harsh criticism of reactionary Bahian planters. They used the offices of the *Gazeta da Tarde* for meetings and hid fugitive slaves in the building that housed the newspaper.

Similar to groups organized in the city of Rio de Janeiro after 1880 like the Central Emancipation Society and the Abolitionist Confederation founded in 1883, the Bahian Liberating Society directed much of its energies toward generating abolitionist sentiment among the urban lower class of Salvador.[24] Roque Jacinto Cruz, treasurer of the Bahian

Liberating Society, was devoted to this end in particular. A black artist and shoe cobbler, Cruz built a large following through public speeches across the city. He was effective in part because his direct, uncomplicated language was easily understood by persons with little formal education. Cruz recited verses of Castro Alves and emphasized the contributions of Africans and their descendants in Brazilian history, including Luís Gama and José do Patrocínio. Cruz also praised his colleague in the movement, Eduardo Carigé, as a hero who ranked among the greatest personalities in Brazilian history.[25]

Carigé and his allies carried out several daring acts to bring national attention to the injustice of slavery. On April 11, 1883, a group led by Carigé used several small boats to intercept a launch in the harbor of Salvador headed toward the English steamship *Trent*. On board the boat was Lino Caboto, the personal slave of the Baron of Cotegipe. Cotegipe was an inflammatory Bahian politician who had condemned abolitionists as dangerous anarchists on a number of occasions. Removing Lino from the launch, Carigé and his entourage transported the slave to shore. With Lino at their side, a waiting crowd then proceeded through the streets to the offices of the *Gazeta da Tarde*. Their goal was to prevent Cotegipe from departing from the port with the slave.

When the police arrived, they faced an angry crowd estimated at thirty to forty persons that included a belligerent Carigé, Pamphilo da Santa Cruz, owner of the *Gazeta da Tarde,* and Bahian writer and abolitionist activist Sergio Cardoso. The protesters agreed to hand over Lino Coboto to the police, but demanded that the police not allow the slave to be returned to his master on board the *Trent*. Carigé understood well the publicity to be gained from an audacious act like this, which disputed directly the authority of a prominent slave owner like Cotegipe.

Shortly after these events, the *Trent* prepared to embark on its voyage for Rio de Janeiro. But the abolitionist protestors were not finished. Inspired by their successful abduction of Lino Coboto, a contingent arrived alongside the *Trent* in small boats and tried to board the vessel. Struggling to gain access to the ship, they shouted that they wanted to speak directly with Cotegipe about the political situation in Bahia and

Brazil, but the attempt ultimately failed. Cotegipe had no interest in a public confrontation over his slave or over the topic of abolition. The chief of police wrote of the episode: "I continue to employ the means at my disposal to guarantee the right of prosperity and [the capacity] to repress such illegal aggressions that, from one instant to the next, without energetic measures taken, could put at risk the public order."[26]

In the wake of the declaration of abolition in Ceará in March 1884, Carigé and his allies immediately organized a meeting at the headquarters of the Bahian Liberating Society to push their advantage. Representatives from several towns in Bahia were invited and attended. Elder statesman and former journalist Dr. Arístides Spinola read a speech he had presented earlier in the Bahian Provincial Assembly. Spinola accused reactionaries of constant attempts to besmirch individual abolitionists and stifle public debate in Bahia.

> [They are] claiming it [abolition] to be a transplant of communist doctrines that have convulsed the whole continent [of Europe]; this is a false conception. We demand that all workers no matter what race have a right to a salary. We fight against the institution of slavery in the name of humankind, in the name of the laws of progress and civilization.[27]

After the meeting adjourned, a huge procession passed through the streets of the upper city to the Polytheama Theater. Salvador's largest auditorium, its four thousand seats were filled. After speeches and poetry readings that advocated abolition, Carigé handed letters of manumission paid for by the Bahian Liberating Society to a group of slaves seated in the front row. The standing audience erupted in applause and cheers. Later that year, the Liberating Society organized another parade and an Abolitionist Festival at the same theater to celebrate the emancipation decree passed in the province of Amazonas, the second Brazilian province to grant freedom to its slaves.[28]

Eduardo Carigé and his colleagues from the Bahian Liberating Society were also willing to break the law on behalf of their objectives. Carigé traveled clandestinely to rural areas of the Recôncavo to interview slaves about mistreatment. Among his companions on these often harrowing journeys were Luís Anselmo da Fonseca, Pamphilo da Santa Cruz, Frederico Lisbôa, and Francisco Pires de Carvalho. In some instances, these abolitionists helped slaves escape, creating in effect an Underground Railroad in imitation of the U.S. experience. Often fugitive slaves made their way to the offices of the Liberating Society in Salvador. Some were then transported by ships to other provinces by the group. Other slaves were taken by the group's members to locales outside of Salvador where they were protected by sympathizers.[29] How effective were these efforts? Carigé's own assessment is suggestive. Soon after the May 1888 decree ending slavery in Brazil, Carigé estimated that he personally had helped to liberate more than three thousand slaves, and that he had helped to hide or had sent out of the province another four thousand slaves.[30]

Abolitionist activists encouraged slaves residing in rural areas to take complaints against abusive masters to the police. In one incident, two slaves named Justino and Placido fled from the engenho Cabaças and walked to the offices of the police in the town of Alagoinhas, claiming that their owner had beaten them. In describing this episode, an observer wrote that slaves from other nearby estates had often appeared in "identical conditions," suffering from similar "acts of barbarism."[31] Although we do not know what happened with Justino and Placido, it is obvious that the two slaves believed that they might encounter persons in the town who could offer succor.[32] Since one of the main lines of Bahia's Underground Railroad led from Alagoinhas to Salvador, fugitive slaves who were able to make contact with the right people in Alagoinhas had a good chance of escaping the region and gaining their freedom.

In a remarkable incident of slave flight in February 1885, fifty-one slaves including adults and children fled from an engenho in the Recôncavo and traveled to Salvador. Appearing at the local police barrack, the slaves complained that their owner had failed to provide them with adequate rations. The chief of police ordered the arrest of the group and then requested that the owner appear to discuss the situation.[33] Deserting an estate carried with it potentially dire consequences for the slaves, for example, beatings once they were returned to the master's control. Mass escapes by slaves from rural estates who then showed up in the city provided useful evidence to Carigé and fellow protesters intent on besmirching Bahian slave owners. The escapes also demonstrated a mounting sense of confidence among slaves and abolitionists that their protests would gain the attention of provincial and imperial officials.

During one of his many journeys in the Recôncavo, Carigé met with a free black woman named Pureina who informed him of brutalities inflicted on her brother Sabino. She claimed that Sabino had been "barbarously beaten" by the owner of a nearby estate. Carigé confirmed the woman's description of events by interviewing witnesses to the beatings. He then requested that the president of the province intervene, accusing the slave owner of having "disregarded all the principles of humanity."[34] Descriptions of the abusive use of holding stocks and brutal whippings helped undermine the authority of slave owners.[35]

As the struggle over slavery developed, planters residing in the Recôncavo fulminated over worsening conditions. In one letter, seventy-seven inhabitants from the township of Muritiba (in 1885) lamented that they did not deserve "confrontations" with slaves or abolitionists they experienced. They had treated their slaves in a benevolent and fair manner, they claimed, because they viewed their slaves as investments to be protected. They complained that abolitionists had recently arrived in the area and incited slaves to flee from the engenhos. According to these planters, slave fugitives ended up enduring worse conditions once under the control of such agitators. They also claimed that numerous fugitive slaves had traveled to nearby cities to join urban quilombos. The petitioner complained in particular of a dangerous character identified as Cesário Ribeiro Mendes, a lawyer who resided in the town of Cachoeira. Mendes, they asserted, had called for "slave insurrection" in his public statements and newspaper articles. The signers of the letter attributed their mounting difficulties to "pseudo-abolitionists" who roamed the countryside without hindrance.[36] By this term, they suggested that individuals involved in the abolitionist movement had no humanitarian interest in the well-being of slaves. Instead, abolitionists sought personal gain by encouraging slaves to flee and then absconding with these fugitive slaves for personal gain, for example, by selling them to planters in other regions of Bahia or the empire.

Illegal activities carried out by Carigé and his followers apparently included the theft of mail. In a court case from early 1880, a prosecutor representing the provincial government inquired about mail pouches stolen from the public post office in mid-1879. The prosecutor accused Carigé of having stolen private correspondence and documents. One witness at the trial, Silvestre José da Costa, stated that Carigé had admitted to him that he had opened the mail pouches. Although this case was dropped, prosecutors later decided to reopen the case.[37]

The second trial in 1887 opened with the defendant Eduardo Carigé notably absent. It became clear that the stolen items had included registries of slaves from the township of Maragogipe. With the help of an African freedman named Emygdio, Carigé had removed mail pouches from the ship *Iberia* before it departed Bahia bound for Rio de Janeiro. The culprits were attempting to obscure claims of ownership to make slave sales more difficult, thereby disrupting the internal slave trade out of Bahia to the Center-South (that still continued in 1880).[38] By returning to a court case in 1887 that had been closed seven years previous, prosecutors desired to send a clear message to Eduardo Carigé and anyone else who aided abolitionists that they would face harsh reprisals for their subversive activities.

An astute strategist, Carigé allied himself with politicians and with fellow journalists like the abolitionist Rui Barbosa (1849–1923). Barbosa had a national reputation and maintained close ties with well-known figures such as Joaquim Nabuco. An unceasing advocate of educational reform, Barbosa taught evening classes to former slaves during his years in São Paulo. Through such courses he sought not only to provide basic literacy but also to draw lower-class Brazilians into the abolitionist movement. A prolific writer, Barbosa penned radical critiques of the slave regime using famous pseudonyms—Salisbury, Grey, Lincoln—for several newspapers, including *O Ipiranga*, *A Independência*, and *O Radical Paulistano* (all in São Paulo). Taking over editorial direction of the *Diário da Bahia* (in Salvador) from Manoel Pinto de Souza Dantas in the late 1860s, Barbosa pressed his Liberal agenda and often denounced in print the illegality of slavery in his home province of Bahia.[39]

Elected as representative from the second district of Bahia to the Chamber of Deputies, he won respect among abolitionists for his diplomacy, intellect, and speaking skills during his tenure in office (1878–85). On several occasions (1874, 1875, 1881, 1888), Barbosa made public speeches in Bahia with regard to imperial politics and emancipation.[40] Barbosa criticized fellow Liberals for a lack of political will and false posturing with regard to abolition. He supported the political reform proposed by his colleague Manuel Pinto de Sousa Dantas in 1884 (known as the Dantas project for emancipation). Rui Barbosa's unyielding stance against slavery at the highest levels of the imperial government did much to force the question of abolition to the center of political discourse in Bahia and at Rio de Janeiro, the capital of the empire.

The determination and political successes of a small group of organizers that included Castro Alves, Eduardo Carigé, Roque Jacinto Cruz, and members of the Bahian Liberating Society caused disquiet in Bahia. Looking ahead, planters and merchants and others of the urban bourgeoisie had no desire to encounter charismatic black leaders or an organized labor movement forged by struggle over emancipation.[41] The "great obstacles" to social mobilization noted by Luís Anselmo da Fonseca included a concerted propaganda campaign instigated by Bahian slaveholders opposed to immediate abolition and the use of the courts as a form of intimidation. Within this hostile environment, individuals surfaced whose contributions proved indispensable. These included representatives of the Catholic Church and feminists.

Unwanted Priests and the Women of Bahia

In his book *Slavery, the Church, and Abolition* (1887), Luís Fonseca castigated the Catholic clergy for its unwillingness to speak out on behalf of slaves. Fonseca contrasted the reactionary stance of the Catholic Church in support of slavery in Bahia with a more secular proabolition environment evident in Pernambuco and Rio Grande do Sul. In these latter provinces "clericalism never was able to establish firm roots." Instead, "public spirit, liberalism, personal initiative and independence" flourished."[42] In spite of the church hierarchy's conservative position in Bahia, individual Catholic priests did come to the aid of the abolitionist movement.

Father Romualdo Maria de Seixas Barroso led the fight against slavery and racism in Bahia. "The negro is not an inferior member of humanity; he is, like a woman, a distinct type, who, like her, ought to [be able] to play a role in the general harmony [of society]." Barroso praised Thomas Jefferson's writings in support of civil liberties and Harriet Beecher Stowe's famous abolitionist book *Uncle Tom's Cabin* (1852).[43] He helped found the Association for the Friends of Slaves in Salvador and contributed articles to the *Diário da Bahia* that called for immediate abolition.[44] At the first gathering of the Abolitionist Society of Cachoeira in May 1884, Father Guillherme Pinto da Salles spoke out on behalf of the enslaved. He stated that Jesus Christ had not distinguished between slaves and free persons. Salles encouraged all listeners to fulfill their Christian duty by publicly proclaiming their support for the organization.

Government representatives expressed dismay over the actions of these radical priests. Judge Pedreira in the town of Viçosa complained about the controversial topics addressed in sermons preached by Father Geraldo Xavier de Santa Anna. The latter in turn accused the judge of having refused to bring public attention to emancipation decrees because he was "against [a declaration of] freedom." At one mass with an audience composed mostly of slaves, Santa Anna condemned slavery, the Brazilian monarchy, Bahian landowners, and the reactionary posture of the provincial government. When shouts erupted from the audience in response to his statements, Santa Anna stressed that he had a right as a citizen and a responsibility as a Christian to speak his mind. Judge Pedreira asserted that "no one could shut him up; [Santa Anna's words had caused] great [meaning harmful] effects on ignorant people." The well-known fact that priests met with slaves at clandestine meetings at night added to the anxieties of local officials. In this instance, Judge Pedreira requested advice from the president of the province on what to do with a

Figure 7.1 "The Monster of 28 September 1885" (referring to the Law of the Sixty Year Olds), suggesting that the law prevented slaves sixty years and older from gaining their freedom. *O Faisca*, November 1, 1885.

priest who had refused to abide by his oath to "teach and practice good will and nothing more" [*ensinar e praticar o bem e só o bem*].[45]

A short eight months previous to Santa Anna's run-in with Judge Pedreira, the imperial Chamber of Deputies passed the Law of the Sixty Year Olds (Lei dos Sexagenários). This 1885 law stated that slaves sixty years old or more would be free after providing unpaid labor to their masters for another three years, or until they reached age sixty-five. As with the Law of the Free Womb in 1871, resistance by slaves and by abolitionists had helped cause passage of imperial legislation. U.S. historian Robert Conrad judged that political support for the Law of the Sixty Year Olds was related to the "growing social and economic disintegration" in Brazil at that juncture.[46] Conditions in Bahia support this interpretation.

In his letter of May 1886 complaining of Father Santa Anna's actions, Judge Pedreira noted that letters of manumission had already been granted to ninety-five slaves older than sixty-five years old at a local plantation.

Pedreira asserted that local slaveholders knew best how to implement gradual emancipation following imperial laws. The planter who granted these manumissions explained to the newly freed their rights and legal obligations as slave owners and merchants from nearby estates witnessed the ceremony. Judge Pedreira endorsed public ceremonies such as this as a way to promote mutual understanding and to prevent "disagreeable incidents." In spite of his optimism, Pedreira did not feel at ease with the local situation. Distrustful of his critics, the judge kept in touch with authorities in Salvador by letter sent by boat rather than by telegram because he feared telegrams might be intercepted. Pedreira knew well that telegraphed messages could easily fall into the hands of abolitionist sympathizers.

Many women had joined the movement. Women abolitionists participated in public gatherings at theaters as well as in public demonstrations in Bahia. During a parade on Sunday afternoon September 14, 1884, twenty-one women walked through the streets of the city on behalf of a group calling themselves the Symbol of Liberty Club. The marchers carried a sign paying homage to Joaquim Nabuco. The twenty-one women were recruited to symbolize each of the twenty provinces of Brazil along with the national capital of Rio de Janeiro.[47] Other Bahian female abolitionists appeared in large numbers at the annual July 2 independence festivities, using the event as a forum to denounce slavery.[48] Women were active in abolitionist societies, and some wrote anonymous tracts published in newspapers and journals.[49] In early March 1888, two sisters of the agitator Cesário Ribeiro Mendes along with Maria da Paixão Gomes Faria, head of a secondary school, appeared at the courthouse in the Recôncavo town of Cachoeira where Mendes was being tried for his abolitionist activities. In an attempt to disrupt the high-profile court proceedings, the women threw flowers and commenced chanting "Long Live Abolition! Down with the slave owners!"[50]

Despite their importance, female abolitionists in Bahia received minimal attention in the press, official correspondence, or historical accounts. Reasons for this lack of recognition include the dominant influence of males in the public life of nineteenth-century Bahia and the fact that few women rose to leadership positions in the abolitionist movement. Yet, this in no ways means that women played a minimal role. Castro Alves clearly appreciated the contributions of women, penning his famous "Letter to the Women of Bahia" in 1871 shortly before his death. Appearing in the newspaper O *Abolicionista*, the letter claimed that women could and should take a leading role in the abolitionist movement.[51] Castro Alves's public statement and others written by other abolitionists appeared in the press on numerous occasions in subsequent years.[52] Because of this connection, Rui Barbosa often invoked the memory of Castro Alves in his quest to garner political support among females. He entitled one article "For the Slaves! To the Women of Bahia."[53]

Advocates of immediate abolition in Bahia contended with several groups who impeded successful mobilization. Some paid lip service to abolitionist societies and even published articles supportive of emancipation but viewed freedom for slaves as best achieved through a gradual process. The number of educated urban bourgeoisie who for reasons of education and class might have lent needed support remained small.[54] Most important of all, planters and merchants supportive of the monarchy and the prime beneficiaries of slavery continued to have much influence. Hence, activists looked to the courts and the press for aid in their quest to end slavery in Bahia.

Justice

During the final phase of abolition, slaves, abolitionists, and sympathetic lawyers appeared often in the courts of Salvador and in interior towns of the province to confront slaveholders. Even as planters debated how best to deflect criticism and retain control over their slaves, abolitionists continued to press their case. A key part of their strategy was to seek out judges supportive of the movement. Although it is impossible to know how many slaves gained their freedom as a result of judicial rulings, in early 1887 one journalist estimated that 930 slaves had received letters of manumission through the decisions of courts during the preceding months. Of this number, 534 were Africans and 406 "nationals" (meaning crioulo slaves born in Brazil).[55]

It is clear that the courts in Bahia became a forum of utmost importance to supporters of abolition. Several judges responded positively to petitions presented on behalf of slaves.[56] In Salvador, Judge Amphilophio Botelho Freire de Carvalho freed some two hundred slaves based on Brazil's law of 1831, which guaranteed freedom to slaves who could prove that they had been transported illegally into Brazil after that date.[57] Lawyers, including Raimundo Mendes Martins, Otacílio dos Santos, Isaias Guedes de Melo Matos, and Passos Cardos, also contributed their expertise to the cause.[58] In his 1887 book *Africanos livres* (Free Africans), the lawyer Elpidio de Mesquita derisively inquired:

> Is it possible that that still today, after fifty-six years of the enslavement of free Africans [*Africanos livres*], [a practice] that is contrary to the law of the nation [of 1831], that the atmosphere of justice in our country remains so irrespirable that these unfortunate ones [free Africans] who have resisted death on farms and under the whip even [still] now are not able to protect themselves from the effects of unjust condemnation before the tribunals of the empire?[59]

During one famous court case in Cachoeira, Bahia, in 1887, a well-known landowner named Colonel Joaquim Ignacio de Siqueira Bulcão accused the activist Cesário Mendes of hiding slaves in his home. Bulcão claimed that a slave named Caliscto and an *ingênuo* (meaning a child born after the Law of the Free Womb in September 1871) named Adriano had fled from his estate with the help of Mendes in May 1885. Bulcão stated to the court that the two remained under Mendes's protection. Denouncing Mendes as "the scourge" of the Recôncavo, Bulcão demanded that his slave and ingênuo be returned to him and that Mendes be imprisoned.

Colonel Bulcão had a clear motive for accusing Cesário Mendes of helping slaves to escape. As editor of the liberal newspaper *Jornal da Tarde* (published in Cachoeira), Mendes had written several articles calling for an immediate end of slavery in the province. After residing in Cachoeira for several years, Mendes had firsthand knowledge of conditions on local sugar engenhos and relentlessly criticized mistreatment and injustice. Bulcão hoped that the imprisonment of Mendes would put a halt to the disturbances caused by his articles and by the actions of other abolitionist agitators in the region.

In the court proceedings that followed, members of the Bahian Liberating Society entered the fray. Eduardo Carigé requested that the court decide on the guilt or innocence of the slave Caliscto and the ingênuo who had escaped from Bulcão's estate. Carigé sought to derail any debate over Cesário Mendes's involvement so as to prevent Mendes from going to jail. This strategy failed. In the end, the judge found Mendes guilty and sentenced him to a prison term on July 23, 1887. The judge also affirmed the colonel's ownership of the male slave and ingênuo, ordering that they both be returned immediately to the estate.[60]

This outcome led to public protests in Cachoeira and Salvador. Lawyers associated with abolitionists immediately prepared an appeal while a flurry of newspaper articles used the case to publicize abusive acts perpetrated by Bahian planters.[61] In a lengthy analysis of the legal doctrine on which the original decision had been based, the public defender from Cachoeira criticized the judge for gross legal errors. The defender noted that six of the eight witnesses who claimed knowledge about the escaped slave and young ingênuo failed to provide any specific evidence to support their statements. Further, he cited the Law of the Free Womb to confirm that the ingênuo Adriano possessed rights equal to any free Brazilian citizen. Although required by the law to remain under the authority of his owner until at least the age of eight years, an ingênuo could not be defined as "an object to be dominated, or property, or a thing." Therefore, according to the public defender, Adriano should not be considered a fugitive slave. The defense also pointed to the lack of proof to show that Mendes in fact had hidden the slaves or that he maintained any contact with them at present.[62]

In spite of widespread public sympathy, Mendes languished in jail in Cachoeira for more than eight months. In January 1888, jury selection began in preparation for the appeal. Finally, on March 2, 1888, the court absolved Mendes of guilt in the affair.[63] That an abolitionist agitator ended up in jail for eight months on the eve of abolition confirms that planters in the sugar regions of the Recôncavo had little intention of giving up their right to own and control their slaves even as the courts turned against them and public protests mounted. The fact that Mendes was ultimately found innocent and allowed to go free shows at the same time that the courts played a pivotal role in protecting individual rights and bringing publicity to the abolitionist cause.

It is clear that Eduardo Carigé and the Bahian Liberating Society made astute use of the courts to gain publicity. Emulating sensationalist tactics employed earlier by journalists at the newspaper O *Alabama*, Carigé accused in court an influential planter from the Recôncavo in 1887 of having assassinated a slave twelve years earlier. Carigé based his accusation on information provided to him by an escaped slave named Silvestre. In reaction to a terrible beating by João Argolo, Silvestre fled from the engenho Agua Comprida to Salvador. He sought out Carigé and informed him of these terrible events. Silvestre claimed he had seen Argolo kill the slave named Damião with a blow to the head. But he could not provide corroboration since the only other witness to the episode was dead. Silvestre complained that Argolo had a pattern of whipping and brutalizing his slaves and that the matriarch of the family, Dona Anna Argolo, often observed the beatings of slaves.

During the resulting court case, five slaves and one freedman testified about Argolo and conditions on the engenho. None of the witnesses, however, knew or had heard anything about the alleged murder of Damião. All claimed that Damião had died from an affliction described as "fatigue" (*cansaço*). The slave Romana agreed that Damião had been sick just before his death and that a doctor had treated him. Romana contradicted Silvestre by telling the court that her owner, João Argolo, seldom physically punished his slaves. When a whipping did occur, she said, the slaves had access to an infirmary for treatment. Not surprisingly, none of the slaves owned by Argolo made statements to the court implicating their owner.

Eduardo Carigé and Pamphílo da Santa Cruz both offered testimony. Carigé introduced himself as an official representative of the Bahian

Liberating Society. He characterized Silvestre as a credible witness who, he believed, had told the truth about the murder twelve years before. Carigé's friend and colleague Santa Cruz supported this assessment in his testimony. As owner and editor of the newspaper *Gazeta da Tarde*, Santa Cruz also published articles covering the trial. He informed the court that soon after the appearance of one article detailing the accusations, an unidentified black male had arrived at his office and stated that the slave Silvestre spoke the truth about the murder of Damião. Santa Cruz explained that unfortunately he had no knowledge about this visitor who had shared this information with him.

Several other witnesses spoke at the trial, including the accused João Argolo and his neighbors who owned estates near his engenho. Argolo alleged that he had never abused his slaves and claimed that Silvestre had lied about the events. Neighbors of Argolo could not recall the alleged episode and stated that they regarded the Argolo family as responsible citizens of the Recôncavo. It does not appear that Argolo was asked directly by the judge or the lawyers about the recently inflicted wounds clearly visible on the body of Silvestre. In the end, the judge dropped the case on June 8, 1887, finding the evidence insufficient to find Argolo guilty of crimes committed twelve years earlier. Nevertheless, coverage of the trial in the newspapers of Salvador helped build support for the abolitionist cause. Testimony by participants at the trial along with newspaper editorials reacting to the testimony forced one well-known Argolo family to face harsh accusations and to defend itself with statements of dubious credibility.[64]

Legal action continued to cause problems for planters and for provincial authorities right up until the signing of the emancipation decree in 1888. Baron of Cotegipe, a Bahian who served as prime minister of Brazil (in office from 1885 to March 1888), referred to the tactics pursued by abolitionists in the courts as "illegal and anarchic."[65] Bahia's chief of police Domingos Guimarães labeled "Carigé et al. fake *humanitarians.*"[66] Accusing the courts of having succumbed to the influence of a band of agitators who had caused upheaval in Salvador and the interior of the province, he wrote:

I am certain the [imperial] government does not want *anarchy*; by the simple request of Carigé, the judge [unnamed] offers him the legal right to protect escaped slaves. He has done even more; when Carigé knows that a slave is at the police headquarters waiting to be sent back to an owner, Carigé goes to the judge and receives papers that enable the slave to leave under the auspices of the court! The situation is intolerable. As soon as abolition arrives we are going to witness the *end of an epoch* [*venha logo a abolição e vermos em que param as modas*].[67]

Eduardo Carigé's confrontational tactics eventually caused friction with his more conservative colleagues. To counter Carigé's prestige and well-earned reputation as a troublemaker, the moderate members who controlled the Bahian Liberating Society renamed it the Bahian Abolition Society in June 1887. Later that year they sent a manifesto to delegates of the provincial legislature calling for the end of slavery. Among the fifteen men who signed were four medical doctors whose political views had been shaped by their experience at the Faculty of Medicine in Bahia. Attempting both to support abolition and distinguish themselves from radicals like Carigé, the petition emphasized that the signatories were "neither *crazed* [*loucos*] nor agents of a *revolutionary party*." Instead, the Bahian Abolition Society desired for concerned citizens to face up to the fact that slavery had "perverted the habits" and "polluted the morals" of all Brazilians. Abolitionists deserved respect for their role in a "holy crusade" as "*liberators of the* [national] *territory*." The manifesto suggested that a failure to respond with a political solution in the near term could lead to revolutionary upheaval in the future.[68]

Newspapers

Several Bahian newspapers played a major role in spreading abolitionist ideas after 1880. Bahian editors paid close attention to the activists who edited and published newspapers in Rio de Janeiro, including José do Patrócinio, Joaquim Nabuco, and André Rebouças. Patrocínio wrote:

The critical source for [creating] political discourse among a people is newspapers. Newspapers unite [opposing] opinions into parties; it disciplines parties to participate in government; it is newspapers that strengthen or weaken governments. The part of society [including the urban bourgeoisie] to whom politics is of interest do not have the capacity to maintain a newspaper to the degree of perfection of [required by] a modern newspaper. [The large landowners] forged laws that destroyed small property, made it impossible for Brazilians to learn about industry and business, and thereby placed the nation in the hands of foreigners and owners of slaves.[69]

Bahian journalists echoed Patrocínio's views. In the words of one who witnessed the attempts of slave owners to stifle popular protests and intimidate activists in the Bahian Recôncavo, "Long Live Abolition! Long live the abolitionist press! Live! Power to ideas! Long live the freedom to think!!" [*Viva a abolição! Viva a imprensa abolicionista! Viva! O poder da idéia! Viva a liberdade de pensar!!*].[70]

The preeminent activist of his era, Eduardo Carigé, joined with Bahian colleagues in founding the *Gazeta da Tarde* (The Afternoon Gazette) in Salvador in 1880. He recruited medical doctors, lawyers, professors, and schoolteachers to write articles and provide financial contributions to support the paper. *Gazeta da Tarde* helped spread abolitionist ideas to Bahians of diverse backgrounds.

Gazeta da Tarde took on controversial topics. In one instance, the newspaper published an account of a group of slaves who burned to death in a fire. The slaves had been hidden by traffickers on the top floor of a building in the lower city waiting to be embarked illegally to the coffee regions of the Center-South as part of the interprovincial slave trade. In response to the coverage of this tragic episode, an antislavery group known as the Sailors Club forced their way into several private homes and commercial buildings located next to the port to rescue slaves held in similar circumstances.[71]

Plagued by limited circulation and numerous business failures, several small newspapers were started after 1880 to provide coverage of local and national antislavery initiatives. *A Gargalhada* (Burst of Laughter), *Renascimento* (Rebirth), *O Balão* (The Balloon), *Illustração Bahiana* (Bahian Illustrations), *O Socialista* (The Socialist), and *A Lanterna* (1882–1907; The Lantern) appeared in Salvador. These periodicals included discussions of race, labor relations, and debate over the future of the monarchy. *O Lábaro* (The Standard), originating in the town of Maragogipe, suggested a nine-point plan for ending slavery as early as 1882. *Actualidade* (Actuality) of Santo Amaro echoed this support for abolition.

One of the most radical newspapers was *O Asteróide* (September 1887–May 1889; The Asteroid). Published in the interior town of Cachoeira, its editors provided in-depth coverage of abolitionist activities in Bahia and in other provinces of the empire during its run. The complete title on the masthead concluded with the phrase "An Organ of Abolitionist Propaganda" (*Orgam da Propaganda Abolicionista*). Disdainful toward Pedro II and the imperial government, the newspaper accused Prime Minister Baron of Cotegipe of having established a "dictatorship." [72] Alluding to the sugar region of Santo Amaro as "one big holding stock" [*todo Santo Amaro é um só tronco*], the newspaper incited slaves to flee from their masters. [73] Pointing with pride to fearless citizens and the local abolitionist group named *Club Carigé* (founded in 1887 and named after Eduardo Carigé), *O Asteróide* covered dramatic events in the last days of the slave regime in Bahia. The newspaper opposed European immigration and promoted instead the idea of creating employment for former slaves and Brazilian-born workers. [74]

O Asteróide demonstrated a keen sensitivity to Bahian and Brazilian history. One writer asked, "The nation! Who is it that proclaimed the nation!? In 1822—[it was] Independence or Death—today, my sons, we want in [this year of] 1888—Liberty and life. Long live free labor!" [75] The war with Paraguay remained a vivid memory for the writer.

What is going on here, Bahia? During the war with Paraguay, our province sent 8,000 Bahians marching to the "slaughterhouse"

of López, and yet we refuse to give a bit of money to purchase
freedom for the slaves. How is that we spent so much money
during that thankless and shameful war to purchase slaves who
were sent to the "theater of death," and yet now we refuse to
spend an equal amount so that they can partake of life?! Where
has your conscience gone? [and] your discretion, your Christian
sentiments—your coherence, your sense of justice?[76]

In discussing the recent history of the sugar region of Santo Amaro
published in January 1888, a journalist for O *Asteróide* denounced the
African Bahian owner of a local newspaper named O *Popular* (The
Popular).

The press there is a disgrace; it could not be more subservient [to
the interests of slave owners in Santo Amaro], and particularly
[this is evident] with the newspaper O *Popular*, whose owner,
being himself a recent descendent of Africans, opens his newspaper
to all of the infamies of the slaveocrats [for example accusations
of acts of communist subversion perpetrated by abolitionists]; it
appears that he himself [due to his refusal to condemn slavery]
would be interested in traveling to Angola, Porto Novo, Onni
etc. [locations on the west coast of Africa where slave ships had
picked up slaves and then transported them to Bahia] to search
for his own parents who remain there as potential captives.

The same author pointed to similar biases among common folk residing
the Recôncavo.

Any slave who dreams of his liberty, even if his owner is assured
of payment, gives up, because very quickly the [free] people
conspire against him with indomitable ferocity. [Santo Amaro]
was the first city to conspire against the abolitionist platform of
Counselor Dantas [the 1884 plan for emancipation submitted
by Prime Minister Manoel Pinto de Souza Dantas from Bahia];

its inhabitants called for a gathering of what they called the "farmers" but at which appeared persons from all of the social classes—whites, mixed race, blacks, freedmen [*brancos, pardos, pretos, libertos*], rich and poor—to give support [to this proslavery position]. Not one of them reflected on the conditions of the poor slaves, even those who were descendants of them![77]

The animosity evident among free descendants of Africans toward ending slavery offended this author. In spite of the fact that they shared racial characteristics with slaves, many such persons residing in the Recôncavo of Bahia showed no support for emancipation. Such antipathy added to the difficulties faced by abolitionist organizers in the region. It is a good example of the corrupting influence of the slave regime on individuals, regardless of their racial or class background.

The newspaper *O Faisca* (October 1885–May 1887; The Spark) published in Salvador proved relentless in its support for immediate abolition. It castigated Baron of Cotegipe for leading "this nation of slave traders" [*este paiz negreiro*] and applauded abolitionists like Carigé, Barbosa, Luiz Alvares dos Santos, and José Mariano.[78] *O Faisca* called for responsible political leaders to implement viable reforms. In seeking to make public festivities relevant, it emphasized that "the holidays of our time need to have a character that is eminently social."[79] By this statement the writer implied that the celebrations associated with major holidays, such as Bahia's independence day on July 2, could play an important role in spreading the abolitionist message to the Bahian public. *O Faisca* also published a series of large sketches that depicted abusive Bahian owners and slaves defending themselves. For the majority of Bahians who could not read, such images offered commentary about current events.

Newspapers of Bahia played a key role in spreading abolitionist ideas in Salvador and throughout the province. These publications celebrated abolitionist activists past and present. Journalists often wrote eloquently about abolitionist "meetings" and closely covered the speeches of prestigious personages at public gatherings, parades, and poetry readings. Helpful analyses of political debates in Bahia and among

Figure 7.2 A shackled slave observing the rise of the "Sun of Liberty." The short poem that follows affirms that all Brazilians have a responsibility to free their brothers who remain enslaved. *O Faisca*, July 4, 1886.

imperial officials in Rio de Janeiro were also covered. Contributors often displayed an impressive historical memory, alluding to the past to defend their opposition to slavery. The press, therefore, provided a unique forum for blacks and persons of color to offer their opinions and mobilize support.[80] By the mid-1880s, newspaper coverage and editorial opinion in Bahia and across the nation made the question of emancipation a daily and vexing issue for slave owners and their allies.

Reaction and Acquiescence

In response to the increasingly effective abolitionist mobilization after 1880, an influential segment of the Bahian slavocracy organized their allies and spread their own propaganda. At their urging, police harassed organizers and participants at abolitionist gatherings in Salvador and other towns of the province.[81] Provincial authorities reacting to these pressures attempted to shut down the Underground Railroad that linked interior towns to Salvador and tried also to halt the movement of agitators

TABLE 7.1. SLAVE POPULATIONS (ROUGH ESTIMATES) IN BAHIA,
PERNAMBUCO, RIO DE JANEIRO, AND SÃO PAULO PROVINCES, 1864–87

YEAR	BAHIA	PERNAMBUCO	RIO DE JANEIRO	SÃO PAULO
1864	300,000	260,000	300,000	80,000
1874	165,403	106,236	301,352	174,622
1884	132,822	72,709	258,238	167,493
1887	76,838	41,122	162,421	107,329

Source: Robert Conrad, *The Destruction of Brazilian Slavery, 1850–1888*
(Berkeley: University of California Press, 1972), 285, table 3.

in the countryside. Slave owners also sought with little effect to discredit abolitionist activists in court hearings and in sympathetic newspapers.

Despite the growing effectiveness of abolitionist groups, Bahians continued to own a substantial number of slaves in the early 1880s. Estimates of the slave population in four provinces shed light on the way in which Bahian slave owners viewed their world in the late 1870s and early 1880s.

As noted earlier, a more realistic estimate for the slave population in Bahia in 1874 would be closer to two hundred thousand slaves. The steady export of slaves out of Bahia from the 1840s though the late 1870s came to halt by 1881 with passage of provincial laws in the central-southern provinces that restrained the internal trade. Unsure in the early 1880s of what the future held, many Bahian planters still held on to their slaves. One motive for such intransigence can be attributed to the hope of an increase in agricultural production. Another reason can be traced to the desire to resist abolition to force indemnification from the imperial government if slavery was ultimately surrendered. Slave owners believed that the imperial government had an obligation to provide a fair reimbursement for their investment in slaves, which they considered to be their property.

Proslavery elements had their own newspapers and denounced those calling for reforms. The newspapers *O Guarany* (The Guarani) and *O Tempo* (Time), both published in the Recôncavo town of Cachoeira, printed articles sympathetic to the interests of planters. From their perspective, abolitionists posed an immediate danger to the nation as well as to themselves.

> The Socialist movement is unmistakable in the abolition [abolitionist movement seen] among us. Today abolition is the flag which is hoisted in the public square. Tomorrow communism will be the symbol sprung forth to the four winds; there will be a struggle between capital and work, like that in Europe which led the proletariat into the greatest insanity [*loucuras*] [including] assassination and the destruction of public and private buildings by dynamite [perhaps alluding to the 1848 worker revolts that erupted in several European cities or the civil war in France and siege of Paris 1870–71].[82]

Proslavery writers called for measures to prevent a resurgence of "new Lucases" (alluding to Lucas da Feira, famed fugitive slave leader of a band of fellow fugitives who was captured and executed in 1849) who surely would bring chaos once again to the interior of Bahia. "Prepare the people for free labor and then end slavery." This could be best accomplished by forging a coherent plan for immigration, rules that forced laborers to work, and laws to impede vagabondage.[83] Another writer warned, "We are not in Africa." By this phrase he implied that without strict controls, workers in Bahia would descend to undisciplined ways popularly associated with Africa.[84] Such bias reflected anti-African attitudes prevalent in Bahia and Brazil throughout the nineteenth century.[85]

In the face of slave resistance and abolitionist agitators, most Bahian planters recognized that their days as slave owners were numbered. This realism is suggested by the steep decrease in Bahia's slave population (down almost half between 1884 and 1887; see Table 7.1 above). From 1884 the provision of letters of manumission to groups of slaves had gained vogue in Bahia. In some cases these were efforts by Bahian planters to portray themselves to imperial authorities and the Bahian public as capable of managing the volatile world around them. Public displays of slaves receiving their freedom provided a convenient opportunity for planters and their allies to appear sympathetic to emancipation while resisting comprehensive abolition.

At one such gathering at the end of 1884, the slave owner Francisco Muniz Barretto de Aragão of Cachoeira presented a letter of manumission to his slave Luís in return for a payment from the slave. By requiring an indemnity, Muniz wanted to show that Luís had commenced his life as a free man with an appreciation of work, thrift, and personal responsibility. In his comments before a small audience who attended the "modest and simple festivity," Muniz spoke directly to Luís:

> Today you can take more pride in yourself than many whites and rich [persons], because you have shown yourself to be a man of integrity and honor, qualities which are lacking among many who, looking to fish in troubled waters, spend their time inciting slaves to commit crimes and to rebel against society, without themselves making the smallest sacrifice to assure the freedom of just one slave.[86]

In these remarks, Muniz gave voice to a complaint heard throughout Bahia and across the nation that abolitionists should keep to their own business and stop inciting slaves to escape. A planned and orderly program of emancipation was best left in the hands of slave owners themselves. One sympathetic journalist present that day concurred: "It is in this manner that Brazilian and particularly Bahian society responds without condescension to the attacks of critics who are without conscience or integrity [meaning those who demanded immediate abolition]."[87] The article noted that the newly freed Luís cried as an expression of gratitude for receiving his "gift."

Planters in São Paulo pursued a similar strategy. In March 1888, the Paulista politician and landowner Paula Souza communicated with the prominent Bahian politician Arístides César Zama. Souza suggested that providing letters of manumission a wise course to follow by planters who had shown themselves incapable of preventing slaves from fleeing from their estates. By granting freedom, the planter could appear to be motivated by kindness and humanitarian concern instead of having succumbed to intractable slaves and their abolitionist allies. Souza suggested that such an act would help to create good relations between former owners and freedpersons. In so doing, newly freed former slaves would think more positively about remaining as free workers on the estates where they had labored as slaves.

Souza desired to send a message to the slave owners of Bahia, Minas Gerais, and Rio de Janeiro. He believed that sooner or later these provinces would witness an upheaval caused by slave flight similar to what had already occurred in São Paulo. Souza's plan provided an alternative future with a controlled transition to free labor that would minimize conflict and violence. Within weeks newspapers in the interior of the province of São Paulo published his plan.[88] Souza's manifesto also appeared on the front page of newspapers in the heart of the Recôncavo, one of the last bastions of slaveholding in Bahia.[89]

Paula Souza's letter gave confidence to those Bahian slave owners who remained undecided on how to react to the mounting crisis in the first months of 1888. In one episode, the planter Colonel Temistocles publicly dispensed letters of manumission to the fifty-four slaves he owned. Witnesses of this event included a priest, other landowners from the township of Cachoeira, and some free black inhabitants from the region. Temistocles also agreed to hire all his former slaves as wage laborers and provide them with all the material goods that they might need in this new role. Temistocles and his wife were seen to shed tears while handing out the letters of manumission, as did many of the slaves who were freed. Reports state that the audience expressed their delight with applause and cheers. The owner then ate lunch with his former slaves. Three of the freedmen were selected to make short speeches in which they praised Temistocles and vowed in the name of their compatriots that they would never abandon the estate. This spectacle impressed the other planters in attendance, and within days twenty-four owners of neighboring estates provided letters of manumission to an additional 121 slaves.[90]

Not all slaves responded to these staged rituals of master generosity with the humility and submission desired by the slave owners. After receiving manumission, very few freedpersons worked the hours desired by former owners. Others requested compensation beyond that offered by their employers. Many simply picked up and departed from the estates to try their luck elsewhere. Certainly a desire to leave the places where they had lived as slaves, suffering whippings or worse, was predictable. One administrator writing in early 1888 from the engenho Mataripe in the Bahian Recôncavo insisted that he had treated the free workers (who had been slaves and then gained their emancipation) under his direction with fairness during the previous three years. Now the administrator lamented that he himself had received "ungrateful compensation." Once freed, the slaves had become "absolute vagrants, [the result of] an impossible situation created by the liberals."

The administrator admitted that some freedpersons had settled near the estate and planned to work there in the future. Nevertheless, he was convinced that if he made further concessions, freedpersons would be unwilling to cut sugarcane or maintain the equipment of the engenho. "I have already given them two-thirds of the income derived from the sugar production, which in spite of low wages is in the range of more than 4$ [US $2.04; most likely for a week's labor] They receive what I consider to be a magnificent income; but instead [of being satisfied] they prefer to wander as vagabonds, and they desire to create total chaos."[91]

Bahian planters who acquiesced to the strategy of handing out letters of manumission to groups of slaves from the middle of the 1880s did so because they had little choice. Slave flight, disruptions caused by activists, and negative newspaper coverage of slavery made it necessary for planters and their allies in Salvador to reevaluate their strategies. Acquiescence did not mean that proslavery elements suddenly accepted recently freed slaves as citizens possessing rights and civil liberties. Instead, providing letters of manumission to slaves might best be interpreted as a tactic that allowed traditional patterns of exploitation to be maintained under a cloak of paternalistic good will.

Final Months

In the months preceding final liberation, bad weather added to the social tensions in Bahia. In 1886, a destructive drought similar to those experienced in 1857–62 and the late 1870s affected the sertão of Bahia and regions to the north. The drought had a devastating impact on agriculture, forcing thousands of freedpersons to seek relief in the towns of the Recôncavo or Salvador itself.[92] From late 1886 to 1890, numerous petitions for aid depicted the desperation of the region. Little employment was available and food became scarce, particularly the local staples of corn and manioc flour. Officials throughout Bahia urged the president to offer food relief and provide aid to settlers heading to the south away from the ravages of the drought.

Chief of police for the province Domingos Guimarães complained of a breakdown of order. Fearful that abolitionist agitation during the drought might provoke violence, he prohibited a "meeting" of abolitionists that had been planned for a public square in Salvador (in mid-1887).[93] In spite of an estimated three to four thousand slaves remaining in Salvador out of an urban population of 140,000 to 150,000 inhabitants, slave owners in the city "tenaciously" defended their slave property.[94] In early 1888, Guimarães again vented his dismay: "The city [of Salvador] is in abnormal conditions. Since the first day of the month [of January 1888], thugs [*desordeiros*] have caused disturbances and attacked police in the streets." One member of the police force was killed, and civilians wounded in street skirmishes were taken to a hospital. Given the insufficient number of officers at his disposal, Guimarães considered further outbreaks of gang violence likely a few days later when thousands of Bahians would celebrate the annual Bonfim festival that paid homage to Salvador's patron saint. His ability to maintain order was further weakened because soldiers had been ordered out of Salvador into the sertão to meet the challenge caused by the drought.[95]

Throughout 1887 and early 1888, abolitionist activists traveled to the engenhos, farms and towns across the Recôncavo, informing slaves that if they fled from their masters freedom would be ensured.[96] One sign posted by these militants in the towns of Cachoeira and São Felix proclaimed:

> Slavery is robbery . . . the good citizens of these towns will NEVER allow you to be re-enslaved. The slave who escapes from his engenho fulfills his Christian obligations, similar to the way in which God demanded that his people flee from captivity in Egypt. Flee, Flee and you will be Free.[97]

Although their actions were dangerous, abolitionists carried their message throughout the province. This activism in the countryside was similar to that of abolitionists in several other provinces, including São Paulo, Rio de Janeiro, and Pernambuco. The breadth of this campaign contrasted with the earlier experience in the United States, where one author has described the U.S. South as a "police state" committed to protect against the infiltration of unwanted persons and abolitionist tracts.[98]

The mounting collapse of the slave regime in Bahia was obvious in the Recôncavo. On March 25, 1888, at 5:30 in the afternoon, three hundred angry inhabitants from the parish of Pirajá appeared before a police delegate demanding protection for three male slaves and one female slave whose owners were preparing to transport them back to their estates. In the words of the police delegate, "the crowd was immense and they wanted to finish off [kill] the two men [who claimed to be the masters]" [*a massa do povo era immensa e queria acabar com esses dois homens*]. When asked for proof of ownership, neither was able to show documents to confirm that they owned the slaves. To deal with this explosive confrontation, the delegate put the slaves in the local jail under his care and escorted the two men out of town. The next day, the police delegate sent a representative of the planters to the nearby town of São Sebastião to discuss with a superior what ought to be done. Although we do not know the outcome of this episode, it does show vividly popular revulsion with the arrogance and intransigence of slave owners in the region.[99]

Five weeks later, on May 2, six slave hunters entered the town of Cachoeira in search of eighteen escaped slaves. In its reports, the abolitionist newspaper O *Asteróide* described the slaves as "Brazilians," implying that the editors saw these descendants of Africans as fellow citizens and not "fugitive slaves." Nevertheless, three of the slaves fell into the hands of the hunters who deposited them in the local jail until they could be transported back to their owners.

Upon the return of these "human wolves," the people of Cachoeira disarmed the slave hunters and then forced them out of town. This success was followed by a parade through Cachoeira that included the three slaves detained earlier who had been released by the protesters. Reminiscing about this dramatic scene, one observer wrote, "Flight is a consequence of slavery, and only flight will bring liberation to our beloved nation. Long live the people of Cachoeira! Long live the abolitionist idea! Death to the slave hunters and the hypocrites" [*A fuga é a consequencia da escravidão, e somente a fuga fará a libertação de nossa tão cára pátria! Viva o povo Capueirussuense! . . . viva a idéia abolicionista! morra os capitães do matto e os tartufos*].[100]

What motivated these activists and protesters of Cachoeira? Surely some had been moved by the inflammatory words of abolitionists and newspaper articles in the preceding months and years. Others had witnessed or heard of owners signing letters of manumission that suggested the end of slavery was near. Perhaps, however, their acts of courage were tied to events from the more distant past. If educated journalists and officials evoked the war with Paraguay in their writing in the late 1880s, certainly the common folk remembered that crisis with equal or greater immediacy.[101] Slave hunters (*capitães-do-mato*) searching for escaped slaves bore a striking resemblance to the hated military recruiters who had combed the region looking for recruits in the late 1860s.

Powerful emotions combined with a growing sense of moral outrage. But could mounting examples of direct action be traced to economic variables? Tobacco production had expanded rapidly in Cachoeira in the 1880s, creating a group of prosperous small farmers. Perhaps this growing class of small farmers and a newfound economic stability influenced the decisions of protestors who confronted slave hunters. And what about the racial characteristics and class of these people? Did the crowd include "whites, mixed race, blacks, freedmen, rich and poor" [*brancos, pardos, pretos, libertos, ricos e pobres*], all joined together in a mutual quest to derail a slave hunter? With free blacks composing a large segment of the upwardly mobile class of farmers growing tobacco, these individuals surely played a role in challenging rural planters and their allies.

In the wake of the declaration of final liberation on Sunday May 13, festivities broke out throughout the province. In Cachoeira, inhabitants paraded through the streets shouting *Vivas* for Eduardo Carigé, Luís Anselmo da Fonseca, and Joaquim Nabuco. Women and young girls placed candles on the steps of the municipal court building, the scene of past debates and confrontations over slavery.[102] On a Saturday in early June, Carigé arrived with his wife and fellow activists from Salvador. Joining up with a large contingent from Cachoeira, the entourage visited the Carigé Club of Cachoeira and the offices of the newspaper *O Asteróide*. The following evening the choral "P. Regente" (named after Princess Isabel who had signed the imperial decree ending slavery) sang the "abolitionist hymn." The revelry continued until 3:00 a.m., and Carigé embarked from Cachoeira for Salvador the following day.[103]

In Salvador, celebrations spontaneously erupted on May 13 and lasted for a week. On the steps of the São João Theater before a jubilant crowd, long-time abolitionist and medical professor Dr. Manoel Victoriano spoke of the significance of the law ending slavery. The archbishop of Bahia drafted a pastoral letter in which he called on former abolitionists to begin a new crusade to aid former slaves in their search for employment, food, and clothing.[104] Crowds paraded through the main thoroughfares of the upper city. Orators recited the poetry of Alexandre Fernandes, Torquato Bahia, and Constância Alves, the verses later published in the newspaper *Diário da Bahia*.

On the Friday night of May 18, hundreds of persons attended a mass in front of the Church of Bonfim to celebrate liberation. The priests Arsênio Pereira and João Nepomuceno, both provincial deputies, celebrated a mass. After the service, a large group walked to the home of

Frederico Marinho to pay homage to this jurist who had been a tireless advocate of abolition since 1872.[105]

Commemorations also took place in Lagos, Nigeria, during that week following May 13. African and crioulo former slaves from Bahia walked through the streets of the African city and attended a high mass at the Roman Catholic Church. Thirty members of the Brazilian Emancipation Committee sent a letter to the British governor, expressing thanks for the aid that he had provided. Another committee composed of Africans heralded the British government for its role in forcing an end to the international slave trade earlier in the century. The head of the Brazilian Emancipation Committee stated that abolition in Brazil marked "a new Era for the Negro race," that would result in "the addition of valuable civilizing Centres in our midst, by the emigration of repatriates [Africans in Brazil] now longing to return to the bosom of their fatherland; and no one, here present, I venture to say is more alive to the importance to the Colony of such valuable Civilizing Centres than your excellency [the British governor]."[106] Given Great Britain's imperial agenda in West Africa, such words found a special resonance among British administrators and governors.[107]

Conclusions

Aware of the seizure of slave vessels by the British squadron at midcentury and subsequent arrest of several slave traders, African and crioulo slaves responded with acts of resistance. Slave flight created lots of problems for slaveholders in Bahia. Estimates of the volume of slave flight in Salvador from 1848 to the early 1880s suggest that hundreds of slaves seized the day and pursued opportunities when they arose. Slaves appeared at police stations throughout the province seeking protection or a day in court to vent their grievances. One such moment occurred at a police station in Salvador in May 1883. Carolina took no flack from her owner Dona Anna Francisca da Rocha Martins as they stood before a police delegate in Salvador. After a short and heated discussion, Martins suffered a heart attack. In spite of prompt medical attention, she expired shortly after.[108] Whether it was a single confrontation, like what happened between Carolina and

Dona Martins, or more publicized events like groups of slaves taking off together from an estate, all such manifestations of slave resistance helped to throw the slave regime of Bahia into convulsions by the mid-1880s.

People of color played a decisive role all three phases of the abolitionist movement of Bahia from the early 1850s to 1888. They wrote in newspapers and sent letters to officials. They organized public meetings to discuss what was happening in Bahia and other parts of the empire. A predominantly urban movement, organizers faced off against powerful enemies in Salvador. They proved capable of working effectively with Bahians of varied backgrounds who shared their ideals.

For a province often portrayed as backward and marginal in the second half of the nineteenth century, it is striking the rich intellectual discourse contained in the newspapers of Bahia. Journalists wrote with insight about events in their province, in other parts of Brazil, and internationally. Newspapers created bad publicity for the planters and for merchants who owned slaves. Articles provided useful descriptions of historical events and the political economy of Brazil. Individuals like Luís Gama and Eduardo Carigé, who risked their lives to end slavery in Bahia and other parts of Brazil, gained prominence through such publications.

Thousands of slaves throughout the empire attained their freedom during the last phase of the movement, whether through escape, letters of manumission, or the Golden Law of May 1888. This final decade marked the end of four and a half centuries of Portuguese and then Brazilian involvement in the transport and enslavement of Africans and their descendants. Racial biases intimately related to the uninhibited exploitation of Africans did not suddenly evaporate. In the wake of liberation, former slaves entered a world that cared little about their well-being.[109] ▦

PART FOUR
1888–1900

Freedom

CHAPTER EIGHT

The Aftermath

Exactly five years after liberation, at noon on May 13, 1893, Bahian government officials joined with former abolitionists Eduardo Carigé, Frederico Lisbôa (appointed director of the state archive of Bahia), and others to set fire to the documents that had recorded the history of the slave regime in Bahia. This act came in response to a central government directive of January 25, 1891, calling for the destruction of all documents related to slavery. After a fire that lasted for several hours and consumed numerous bundles of papers, two large wagons carted away the ashes while the city's police band played patriotic music.[1] Although precious documents perished in the flames, slavery and the struggle for emancipation remained indelible memories for Bahians.

In hopes of aiding former slaves, one contingent of former abolitionists convened in Salvador after emancipation. Founded on May 16, 1888, the May 13th Society took as its name the date that slavery officially ended in the Brazilian empire. The May 13th Society continued to meet until after the turn of the century. Its membership included Luís Anselmo da Fonseca, Eduardo Carigé, and Pamphilo de Santa Cruz, among other former abolitionists. In spite of the involvement of such well-known persons, the secretary recorded that the society could have accomplished more for the former slaves if there had not been "the absolute absence of many of our compatriots from the abolitionist campaign."[2]

On several occasions during the 1890s the society paid homage to abolitionists from Bahia, other parts of Brazil, and abroad. For example, its members placed a small statue of Harriet Beecher Stowe in the main office of the society. Goals of the society included the establishment of primary and mechanical arts schools for former slaves throughout the state and the presentation of lectures open to the public.[3] Carigé and others widely proclaimed it more legitimate and just to indemnify former slaves than to indemnify former masters. They also worked to derail all plans aimed at facilitating the immigration of foreign workers, believing that immigrant labor would retard full integration of former slaves in the economy.

As a component of this expanded postemancipation agenda, the May 13th Society opened the Machado Portella School, which offered day and night classes to freedpersons and their children. The school was named after Manoel do Nascimento Machado Portella, president of Bahia (1888–89), founding member of the May 13th Society and an ardent advocate of making public education accessible to all Bahians, regardless of race or class background. It received support from private donations along with a small subsidy from the state. Its directorate lamented the difficulties in maintaining the school's facilities due to the "enormous economic crisis which for many years has affected the nation." Female and male teachers taught classes to both adults and children. By 1896, 178 Bahians had attended the school; 20 specialized in art. A list of 67 students who enrolled in evening classes in 1899 shows that the ages of the students (all male) ranged from eleven to thirty. These boys and men labored during the day in a wide range of urban professions.[4] The former slaves who attended the society's school in Salvador demonstrated their determination to attain a basic education and beyond.

Labor Organizations and Labor Strikes in Salvador

Former slaves as members of the broad urban underclass in Bahia endured difficult times from the late 1880s to 1900. During the drought of 1887–90, inhabitants of the city suffered through food shortages as the cost of manioc flour, "the principal food of the negroes of this city," doubled. In one report from mid-1889, U.S. consul David Burke described an "organized collecting procession [meaning a disciplined crowd seeking cash donations]." Young boys who participated held up black banners on which appeared large letters spelling the word FOME (Hunger) and asked for monetary donations from observers.[5] Lack of fresh water, waste in the streets, outbreaks of yellow fever and smallpox, along with the sale of bad meat plagued the urban population.[6] One way in which workers responded to these difficulties was to join labor organizations and strike actions.

Supporters of abolition and numerous freedpersons became active in the emerging labor movement in Bahia. In 1876, workers founded the League of Bahian Workers (Sociedade Liga Operária Bahiana). Their demands included fair wages and decent working conditions. One of its members was the black historian Manoel Querino. Commonly alluding to workers as the "oppressed classes," Querino supported Socialist programs as a way to aid urban workers of Salvador. A relentless defender of workers' rights, he argued that organized labor needed to remain separate from government. In 1889, Querino was elected to a seat on the city council as a representative of labor. He later ran unsuccessfully for a seat in the federal assembly.[7]

Labor strikes became an important form of labor protest in Bahia. Free port workers and employees of the urban transport system in Salvador walked off the job to demand higher wages in 1881. The strike ended only with the intervention of the police. Between 1889 and 1896, at least thirty-one strikes occurred in Bahia, which included ten in the interior of the state and twenty-one in Salvador.[8] As in port cities throughout the Americas and the Caribbean, former slaves in Salvador supported strike actions as a way to express dissatisfaction with low wages and labor conditions.[9]

Foreign observers at the time described a vibrant urban labor movement in Salvador. Commenting on a confrontation between management and labor during a two-week period in March 1891, U.S. diplomat David Burke wrote, "Working men and women in public employment, such as coal, stevedores, firemen, engineers, lightermen, in fact nearly all the labor skilled and unskilled, went out on a 'strike.'"

> The cause of the strike is the extraordinary increase in the cost of living on account of the low rate of exchange. Prices of many of the necessaries of life have more than doubled. So therefore there was a very good reason for those workmen, who under a higher rate of exchange and lower living prices received but little

to exact an increase in wages. [In the past] an increase [in wages] whenever asked was granted. When the entire increase demanded was not granted such a compromise was made with the striking party as to be satisfactory to them. This climate is very favorable for "strikers." [The weather] being so mild and the workmen being chiefly negroes who can pick up from the fruits of the earth sufficient to support them for many weeks, they can, if united, compel their employers to grant any advance they may demand, though, they may, as in the strike just finished, accept what they might deem a fair compromise.[10]

The establishment of the Workers Protective Association of Bahia (Centro Operário da Bahia) in 1894 with the support of the state government reflected the desire of the region's merchant-agricultural elite to influence the direction taken by organized labor in Bahia.[11] Concerned about the influx of anarchist and Socialist ideas from Europe, business interests sought to co-opt labor leaders like Manoel Querino. Minutes from the proceedings of the association confirm the close ties between this organization and state officials. At the second meeting of members in the Polytheama Theater, the president of the Workers' Protective Association called out several times "Long Live the Republic!" In response, Governor Joaquim Manoel Roiz Lima hailed the urban workers as an important "component in assuring the order and progress of the Brazilian Republic."[12] Representatives of labor organizations from towns in the interior of the state attended this second meeting. The goals of the Workers Protective association included classes for workers, fair wages, the encouragement of women to join the association, publication of a worker newspaper, and passage of legislation ensuring an eight-hour day. One debate within the group centered on how the association might distance itself from the influence of the state government.[13]

In spite of the engaged posture of state representatives, a "lock-out" in the first week of September 1897 pitted sailors and port workers, in alliance with the foreign import houses, against the state government of Bahia. State officials called for stricter controls on all goods transported

Figure 8.1 "Long Live Carnaval."
O Faisca, March 7, 1886.

through the port of Salvador so as to raise extra income from taxes. After a week of hostile confrontations, the inspector of the port met with a lawyer representing the workers and negotiated a settlement. Government leaders did not want goods to rot on the docks in the short term or an extended stand-off with well-organized port workers. This episode and others inspired a heightened confidence among Salvador's laboring classes and led to the creation of a workers' syndicate in the early part of the twentieth century.[14]

Carnival and Candomblé

Organized political expression by Bahians of color was a staple of Carnival celebrations in the late nineteenth century. Parades, music, floats, and dancing associated with this annual affair had their origins in the *entrudo* (pre-Lenten festivities). During the entrudo, inhabitants of the city played pranks and pushed against the normal rules that governed relations between classes and sexes. One common feature was that the pranksters sprayed water on passerbys on the streets. Even normally reticent women often joined in the festivities. Upper-class Bahians made fun of slaves and free persons of color in these "street fights" by throwing dirty water or urine at them as they passed, followed by handfuls of flour. In response, lower-class revelers paraded in front of the houses of the elite wearing masks and mocking the customs of well-to-do Bahians. By the late 1870s and early 1880s, public officials demanded an end to the malicious acts increasingly associated with the entrudo. One reason for this crackdown had to do with politics. Unruly behavior provoked displeasure among affluent Bahians already offended by the rising tide of abolition and Republicanism. Because the entrudo allowed the underclass of the city to flaunt openly the traditional rules of hierarchy that the wealthy held dear, these "pranks" seemed to become more self-consciously political as slavery and monarchy came under pressure.[15]

Out of entrudo evolved the modern phenomenon of Carnival (Carnaval), festivities related to the ostentatious parades that have brought widespread international attention to Brazil during one week in late February or early March. Even in the late 1880s, Carnival processions were marked by their splendor, attracting an estimated eighty thousand people to Salvador. Two types of floats dominated the parades between 1884 and 1888. One group focused on a theme or idea, while the other group poked fun at society and politics. The former offered observers an attractive European façade with bright decorations. Such floats reflected the desire of the Bahian elite to emulate European culture and norms. The more overtly political floats emphasized political messages conveyed by words, gestures, and small skits rather than appearance. These floats stirred the passions more directly of the thousands of lower-class persons who lined the streets of the city.

During the 1890s, political debate over what constituted accepted Carnival behavior coincided with debates about appropriate social hierarchy and race relations in postemancipation Bahia. Bahians of color joined newly formed Carnival clubs such as African Embassy and the African Merrymakers. These clubs paid homage to African culture and the African contributions to Bahian society in their performances. Although their themes were different, they followed the example of lavish elite Carnival groups by passing through the streets in a refined manner. As a result the clubs received praise from city officials and positive coverage in the conservative press for their restraint and decorum. One journalist from the *Jornal de Notícias* affirmed that the artful participation of the African Embassy "gave zing to the Carnival of '96, and their presence in the future is not merely anticipated—it is indispensable."[16]

By the end of the decade, the number of Carnival clubs composed of people of color grew. The more recently founded entities were distinct from the traditional Carnival clubs oriented toward Africa. The newer groups tended to be more boisterous and less organized than the larger, more restrained middle-class clubs, often employing symbols and terms derived from Candomblé ceremonies.

While the earlier black groups were praised, residents of the city castigated the unruly blacks and persons of color who joined the new clubs. The *Jornal de Notícias* lamented:

> Once again, we remind the police of the necessity, in the name of civilization and to the credit of Bahia, to put a stop to these degrading parades of an entirely African character and people outside the bounds of taste and respect, who organized so that during Carnival they may traverse our streets. The majority of these groups carry instruments of *candomblé* and wear immoral costumes. They often do not allow one to hear the music or jokes of the clubs and independent masqueraders, such is the infernal racket they make.[17]

Affluent Bahians found it possible to praise the floats and forms of popular cultural expression that portrayed a civilized and disciplined African society as a way to sustain the myth of a peaceful and racially integrated Bahia. At the same time, they viewed more spontaneous processions of the dark-skinned urban underclass as uncivilized, vulgar, and threatening. The wealthy accused participants of the new Carnival clubs of being bent on returning to provocative practices and occasional outbreaks of violence associated with entrudo.[18] That is, praise for "safe" and useful blacks was a tactic to control "dangerous" blacks.

As they had during the nineteenth century before emancipation, leaders of Candomblé terreiros helped to articulate the concerns and aspirations of many Bahians after 1888. In spite of attempts at diplomacy and negotiation with state authorities, repression of Candomblé groups by the police continued through the 1890s. The anthropologist Raimundo Nina Rodrigues (1862–1906) complained about police invasions of houses of Candomblé during this period in his book *Os africanos no Brasil* (1905; *The Africans in Brazil*). Rodrigues visited numerous terreiros inspired by a desire to understand the legacies of African cultural expression in Salvador. He wrote that "cults" had played an important and beneficial role in Africa. Unfortunately, in Bahia officials viewed such practices as a form of witchcraft. Rodrigues described how the slave regime persecuted Africans for their religious devotion. He considered it outrageous that in the years following emancipation police looked to extinguish Candomblé ceremonies with no sympathy for what they meant to adherents.[19]

The aggressive actions carried out by authorities directed at terreiros reflected the insecurity of the Bahian elite who sought reassurance that their influence would not be diminished by abolition. For them the vibrant African Bahian culture that flourished throughout the city seemed to challenge actual authority as well as elite cultural values.[20]

Conflict and Negotiation in the Countryside

In the immediate aftermath of liberation and well into the years that followed, former masters and former slaves struggled over the definition of property rights and individual freedoms. These struggles were the continuation of all sorts of negotiations between slaves and masters that preceded by several decades formal abolition in 1888, including access to a plot of land, time allotted to cultivate food and crops, and the purchase of emancipation.[21] Bahian society reflected a racial hierarchy with blacks and people of color at the bottom. Discrimination and coercion abounded. One former Confederate general's observation that "nothing but freedom" had been gained by the four million freedpersons in the U.S.

South aptly described conditions in Bahia after May 1888.[22] In spite of these bleak realities, the few remaining Africans in Bahia and their many Brazilian-born descendants defended their interests as best they could.

Former slaves rejoiced alongside abolitionists during the first days after liberation. Freedom offered former slaves immediate and unimpeded physical mobility. Although this might seem a limited benefit in a place with so little opportunity, it represented the essence of freedom to many former slaves. One landowner observed that abolition had not come as a surprise to him or his neighbors; *"everything had become anarchy before this time [May] and everything continues in the greatest of confusion. On those properties with less turbulence, there is what I would describe as a 'respectful inertia.'"*[23]

For those who had been enslaved, the decree of May 13 took away the legal right of planters to hold them against their will. Three days after the declaration of abolition at least three thousand former slaves traveled into Salvador from the countryside to join in festivities.[24] Watching this movement, anxious landowners and provincial officials hoped that these freedpersons would return to their engenhos later to labor. Those who had gained their freedom desired to experience their newfound liberty to the utmost and at the conclusion of the festivities, some former slaves remained in Salvador.

In the town of Viçosa, the abolitionist priest Geraldo Xavier de Santa Anna stood before, in the words of a police official, a "great reunion" of blacks and "ignorant people" on May 19 to prophesize about the future. Chastised by landowners as "the source of all bad things around here," the crowd praised Father Santa Anna for all he had done in the struggle for emancipation. People shouted "Viva" in support of the Liberal Party and the hoped-for end of the monarchy, joining in revelry that continued into the night. On May 20, "a huge samba" took place, with a crowd of dark-skinned men dancing with knives, clubs, and bows and arrows. They shouted, "Long live the liberals!" and "Death to the conservatives!" They eventually appeared in front of the house of a municipal judge, threatening him and his family. Although dispersing soon after, such confrontations caused alarm among residents of the town. Planters accused their former slaves of partaking in sexual "orgies" for days after learning of their freedom. One police delegate concluded his description of what he saw as chaos with a plea to the president of the province to send more police forces to the interior.[25] Clearly many former slave owners saw the joy of their former servants as the crumbling of civilization.

During the first months after May 13, many former slaves reunited with family members who had been separated by sales.[26] Slaves previously sold to the coffee planters of the central-southern provinces now returned to Bahia to search for loved ones they had been forced to leave behind. Many former slaves left the large estates to settle on small plots of land throughout the Recôncavo, struggling to maintain families intact. In the words of the elderly black artist Licídio Lopes (reminiscing in 1969 at age eighty-two), "After the end of slavery, the Africans, who labored with great diligence, began to work for themselves, and they saved a lot of money and became owners of land, where they lived and performed Candomblés and raised their families."[27]

The mostly illiterate freedpersons were forced to rely on sympathetic literates to aid them in negotiating with provincial officials over personal rights in the face of efforts by former owners to control them. In November 1888, Eduardo Carigé petitioned the president of the province on behalf of a former female slave:

> Victoria, crioula, mother of Victorina who is twelve years old, Eutropio who is six years old and Porcina who is ten years old, in wishing to give an education to her children, claims that her former owner, the citizen Marcos Leão Velloso, owner of the engenho Coité in the region of Inhambupe, refuses to give up these children, preferring to have them work in the sugarcane as if they were slaves and subject to punishments. The African Felicidade of the Nagô nation also requests that her grandchildren be freed from the control of the same Marcos Leão Velloso. Since this reality is an attack upon the natural right of liberty of the 13th of May that ended slavery in the empire, the supplicants request the help of your excellency, certain that he will

help, if only because they wish to educate their children to the benefit of the nation.[28]

Although we do not know how Victoria had made contact with Carigé, the fact that she confided in him reflects her sense of trust and her sense of political rights. The letter indicates that Victoria fully understood the meaning of freedom as well as the motives and coercive intentions of the landowner Velloso. The letter also makes clear her ardent desire to provide an education to her children.[29]

The courts provided an important forum where former slaves could protest continued experience of injustice and abusive treatment. During one court proceeding, which took place in late 1888, the freedman José da Silva enlisted the aid of a lawyer to seek the money owed to him by his former master. Silva, who gained his freedom on May 13, 1888, declared that his mother had actually purchased his emancipation two years earlier. The owner who received the payment had then refused to allow Silva to go free as promised. Instead, he took the mother's 100$ (US $38.00) and registered both mother and son as slaves in his possession. Not surprisingly, the judge decided against the destitute José da Silva and his mother.[30]

In spite of setbacks and a lack of funds, freedpersons commonly appealed to the courts in their quest for fair treatment in the decade following emancipation. In March 1895, the African Torquato Teixeira Gomes shot the planter Antônio de Araújo near the town of São Francisco do Conde. Gomes, who resided on the engenho Nazareth, had a reputation in the area for special healing abilities (described as a *feiticeiro*, or curer). In this case, Araújo had demanded that the African use his healing skills on him. Gomes refused, saying he had no special expertise in curing the ills of others. When he attempted to leave the scene, Araújo impeded him and had his mounted followers encircle the African in a threatening manner. They called Gomes a "negro" and struck him. Gomes reacted to this bullying by shooting Araújo. At his trial following the homicide, seven witnesses described the incident.[31] Although the outcome of the proceedings is lost, the fact that Gomes ended up in a courtroom instead of being abused or tortured by Araújo's followers implies altered legal and cultural norms after abolition.

Slaves had acquired a sophisticated knowledge of the courts and law from abolitionists and from each other. After abolition, freedwomen often believed that the courts would intervene on their behalf. As a result, numerous freedwomen challenged planters over the control of their children. When it became obvious by late 1888 and 1889 that corruption in small town courts led to decisions that favored landowners rather than freedpersons, women of color directed their appeals to the president of the province (or subsequently governor of the state of Bahia after November 15, 1889). For example, Maria Antônia de Jesus from the village of Palmeiras complained that a local judge had allowed a planter to take away her two children "by force and with threats to [her] life." Unable to articulate her feelings of outrage with written words, Jesus found a curador to pursue her complaint. She claimed that her two boys had been born free, yet now were forced to live like slaves. The judge's order that led her to appeal had prevented her sons from even visiting Maria's house, obviously convinced by the planter that she would attempt to hide them. Through her curador, Maria pleaded that the president intervene on her behalf and return her children.[32] This and numerous other cases describe the hostility and cruelty of landowners and the biases of rural judges during the period immediately following emancipation. At the same time they also show the determined response of newly emancipated women to unwanted encroachments in their private lives by planters and other powerful figures.

At the same time, former slaves struggled to defend their legal rights to land. In a court hearing in the township of Santo Amaro, the former slave Manoel Casemiro de Jesus accused Manoel Emílio dos Santos of ruining his property. Having purchased the land (from whom is not noted in the court record), Jesus planted manioc, coffee, tobacco, and hay and protected his cultivated plots with wire fence. He had also built a small hut to store his crops. Santos claimed that Jesus had settled illegally on land that Santos owned. With the aid of two state officials, Santos destroyed Jesus's house and furniture. The former slave desired restitution to rebuild the house and replace damaged furniture and household goods.

Comments by witnesses during the trial portrayed Jesus as a hardworking man who diligently maintained his property. Santos rejected this depiction, accusing Jesus of having murdered his own (Jesus's) wife a few years previously and reminding the court that Jesus had been a lowly slave in the not distant past on the engenho Boa Sorte (Good Luck Plantation). After listening to these accusations and slanderous comments about his character, Jesus stood before the judge and asked, "Is not an ex-slave able to defend his rights in court? Am I to be prevented from protecting my personal rights?"

In the end, the freedman Manoel Casemiro de Jesus lost this appeal due his failure to demonstrate legal title to the land. The disputed property remained in the hands of Santos who showed that he had inherited the property. Jesus had been deceived when he paid for the land, and then thrown off after much painstaking care of the property.[33]

In the months preceding and following emancipation, planters debated what the future held with regard to labor contracts and relations with former slaves. Landowners, many of them in debt, sought to minimize any disruption of production so as to assure that their incomes would not be interrupted. Negotiated settlements with former slaves and the resulting complex of employer-employee relations had a profound impact on subsequent social interactions and racial attitudes. Eric Foner writes, "It is the on-going struggle over the definition of freedom and the control of labor that unites the experience of the American South with that of other postemancipation societies. The rise of the peasantry was as much a response to the conditions of emancipation as a legacy of slavery."[34] Bahia confirms his judgment.

Freedpersons defended individual and group interests by bargaining over contracts and acceptable workloads. From the first days after liberation, freedmen who settled in the Recôncavo commonly refused to labor more than three or four days of each week on sugar estates.[35] One owner of a Bahian engenho lamented that freedpersons failed to appear for work during the critical period of the harvest, "even though they are paid punctually!!!" Those freedpersons who accepted employment on plantations often refused to work after 3:00 p.m. in the afternoon, informing estate administrators that their services would not be available in the evening.[36] Such a demand reflected the terrible memory of a past when planters forced slaves to boil sugarcane well into the night. Wages paid to freedpersons by landowners rose rapidly during the first few months after May from an average below 500 réis (US 26 cents) per day to more than 800 réis (US 40 cents).[37] Workers negotiated with employers over income and labor conditions without hesitation and with surprising success.

In one of the most detailed descriptions of the first days of freedom in Brazil, an administrator for two engenhos in the township of Rio Fundo in the Recôncavo related how he prepared to negotiate labor agreements with twenty-seven former slaves. Anfilófio Carvalho observed that in the week after emancipation the estates seemed like cemeteries due to the silence that prevailed day and night. Not even the sounds of drumming (*sambinha*) or laughter could be heard among the huts of the recently freed slaves. Carvalho affirmed that the "tranquility" of the engenhos had not been affected, and those recently emancipated had remained nearby. Carvalho considered it his obligation to prepare the freedpersons and their children for responsible lives, but he did not hide his cynicism. Previous to emancipation, whenever a slave had a headache or ailment, he could miss work for three or four days and not lose his ration of food on Sunday (enough to provide for the following week). In the uncertain transition to free labor former slaves sought the continuation of food allotments along with wages. After May 13, "the free persons want me to guarantee their sustenance, even when I am receiving so little income? What is this?!! What refined thieves!!"

This administrator believed that anyone who dealt with former slaves needed to protect themselves from what he saw as unscrupulousness. Planters and politicians would be the victims of "a thousand speculations." All responsible persons ought never to believe "for one instant" in the integrity or honor of the freedpersons. "A woman without experience in negotiations and with unlimited good faith will embarrass herself and be completely misled without taking great caution." The writer suggested that a new system of record keeping would be necessary, particularly on those lands where absentee owners could do little to impede the movement of former slaves from one location to another.

Nevertheless, Carvalho exuded a sense of confidence in the first days after emancipation. He felt capable of determining the terms of negotiations with former slaves. "I did not immediately contract their [former slaves'] services, without which they will be without daily bread! In spite of this, on the 17 and 18 [of May], many of the freedpersons did not wish to contemplate the gilded sun of liberty and demanded to work, which they did happily." During the negotiations that took place on Sunday, May 20, Carvalho met with the freedpersons to establish a labor schedule and "other measures which circumstances required." Carvalho planned to pay 500 réis (US 26 cents) in daily wages to the freedpersons. "In light of unanimous agreement," the freedpersons would be permitted to cultivate sugarcane on their own plots "on the two days not reserved for their service at the engenho." The former slaves "who desired" would also be allowed to cultivate tobacco and manioc on their own plots. One senses that the situation was not quite as settled and calm as Carvalho's portrayal. Carvalho observed that "it has not been possible to resolve everything; the meetings will continue until the complete reestablishment of work [is effected]."[38]

Certainly not all negotiations between masters and their former slaves proceeded smoothly and many planters found it difficult to accept the realities of the new era. In São Paulo Province, even with immigrants pouring in to work on coffee estates at the time of emancipation, owners attempted to retain former slaves on lands planted with sugarcane. At the *usina* (steam-powered sugar factory) Esther, sons of the owner Artur Nogueira desired to show off their beneficence. To create an air of solemnity around the occasion of the first wages paid to freedpersons, the sons requested Nogueira to preside over the affair. Father and sons sat at a table while their former slaves dressed in Sunday clothes approached when called by name. Nogueira then handed the wages to the newly freed laborers. As the event progressed, Nogueira showed signs of increasing strain. Finally he stood up, looked around, and stated, "No, no. I am not able to pay a negro."[39]

In the Recôncavo and interior of Bahia, the three-year drought that commenced in 1887 caused an influx of poor folk into towns. Recently freed slaves walked away from the estates to nearby villages in the hope of finding food and some modicum of protection. Not all freedpersons were destitute. Some skillfully navigated the new conditions. During the drought, recently freed farmers did not hesitate to hold back from the market manioc flour cultivated on their plots in an attempt to earn the higher profits occasioned by crop failures. In the middle of 1889 (reminiscent of events in Salvador in 1858 and 1878), the provincial government attempted to keep the price of manioc flour down by storing crops and setting price controls, but freedpersons and the longer-established farmers resisted. In the town of Maragogipe former slaves disregarded government directives and increased their prices above the official rate of 200 réis (US 10 cents) per liter. Angered by what they saw as price gouging, inhabitants of the town broke into the houses of those involved. One police delegate claimed that the populace would have killed these freedpersons if he had not intervened.[40]

Throughout the state, expansion of subsistence agriculture by former slaves represented an important social transformation in the aftermath of emancipation. Within a few days of emancipation, freedpersons sought access to land previously inaccessible on which to cultivate food and other crops. One shocked inhabitant noted that "armed freedmen have returned [to the engenhos] demanding to remain on the property, without employment and without renting the land, not interested in any arrangement with the owner, only desirous of the promised abolition of private property to the exclusive benefit of the freedman."[41]

The rural underclass made it a priority to cultivate both food for household consumption and crops that could be sold in local markets during the 1890s. Besides bargaining over wages, former slaves negotiated at length with landowners over the right to grow sugar, manioc, coffee, and tobacco on private plots. Such initiatives reflected not only a response to market conditions but also a means to assure food on the table, individual independence from landowners, and protection of families.[42] As access to land expanded, freedpersons and lower-class free folk generally played a leading role in the cultivation and distribution of foodstuffs.[43]

The more than 130,000 slaves who gained their freedom after 1885 in Bahia looked to exert their independence from the control of landowners in the countryside. They followed the example of hundreds of slaves who had gained their emancipation before comprehensive abolition. What distinguished the weeks and months after 1885 was that the slave regime of Bahia faced its disintegration. Slaves understood this. They sought legal protection, access to land, and educational opportunities for themselves and their families.

As with former masters, the psychological importance of abolition cannot be understood merely in a quantitative sense. In so many subtle ways freedom brought profound changes and new opportunities for those who had suffered enslavement. Personal relationships and physical space that had long been negotiated with owners of sugar engenhos or farms were now further transformed. Freedpersons understood that returning to estates without their rights clearly delineated could mean the resumption of unwanted labor obligations like those they had experienced before emancipation. For that reason alone, written contracts and the ability to make independent personal decisions became of utmost importance.[44]

Inhabitants of the Bahian countryside commonly depicted recently freed slaves as unfit for life without masters. The head of the City Council of Victoria wrote:

The unfortunate agricultural class of our nation has long endured a deplorable state of decline. Our situation turned quickly and profoundly desperate, after the extremely violent shock [*violentissimo abalo*] caused by the unconstitutional, antieconomic, anarchic, and pseudo-humanitarian "law" of May 13th. We hope that earlier examples on the American continent have not been forgotten, and consideration taken of the lamentable [*triste*] moral education of the slaves, so as to prevent transgressions of the laws and the outbreak of social upheaval by hundreds of thousands of ignorant persons who will be invading a society for which they are not prepared. The small farmers are abandoned without the means to continue with their work. The people who have little faith in the present, look to the future and plead: Give us a *new abolition*. Only as such will things improve.[45]

In another letter from Nazareth, the head of the city council emphasized that after the "hallucinations of the moment life in the countryside must return to its inevitable relations, with public respect for the ideas of liberty and property. It was a necessity in this century to destroy the terrible institution [of slavery], but an outcome which sacrifices the life of the owner merely to free him of an impertinent insect [is unacceptable]."[46] In the face of "the chaos of labor, the ruin of sugar production, public poverty, popular distrust and an imminent conflagration," the Bahian planter Moniz Barreto de Aragão deemed the wisest response to be "prudence."[47]

Canudos: The Last Quilombo

From November 12, 1896, until October 5, 1897, Bahians witnessed a devastating war of aggression carried out by state and federal military forces against a town known as Canudos. Located in the northeastern interior of Bahia, Canudos was founded in 1893 by the religious leader Antônio Vicente Mendes Maciel (1830–97), also known as Antônio Conselheiro, or Anthony the Counselor. Under his charismatic direction, it grew rapidly to become the second-largest city in Bahia, with an estimated population of eighteen thousand to twenty-five thousand inhabitants and with fifty-two hundred houses and two churches.[48] Canudos served as a magnet to poor inhabitants of the sertão in Bahia and other provinces of the Brazilian Northeast.

Born in the town Quixeramobim in the interior of the province of Ceará, Antônio endured several traumas during his youth and as a young adult. His mother died when he was four, and he was raised by an alcoholic father who beat him. In spite of these difficulties, Antônio

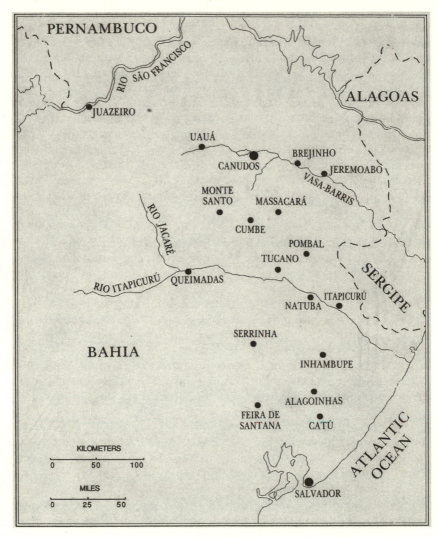

Map 8.1 Canudos Region, 1893-97. Robert M. Levine, *Vale of Tears: Revisiting the Canudos Massacre in Northeastern Brazil, 1893-1897* (Berkeley: University of California Press, 1992), 69. Courtesy of University of California Press.

became a proficient student. In 1857, he married Brasilina Laurentina de Lima and had two children. The marriage ended when Brasilina became romantically involved with a local police official. Distraught by this event, Antônio lived with another woman for a short period, fathering another child. Having learned to read and write, he was employed at various times in small businesses, as a professor and as a type of public defender, also described as a "lawyer for the poor." Antônio found it unsatisfactory to remain in one place and began to travel throughout the provinces of the Northeast.

Antônio Conselheiro arrived in the north of Bahia in 1874 after having journeyed through the provinces of Pernambuco, Alagoas, and Sergipe. He immediately attracted a following of "whites, blacks, mestizos, wealthy people and the miserably poor."[49] His followers included Kaimbé and Kiriri Indians as well. Antônio Conselheiro became a sort of wandering evangelist who made the sign of the cross and other Christian gestures and who spoke phrases in Latin. Many considered Conselheiro to be a Christ figure. He rejected that idea. Nevertheless, Antônio did not hesitate to offer spiritual ministrations to his flock of followers.

His entourage seldom numbered more than one thousand persons in the first years of his wanderings. They constructed and repaired chapels (ten in Bahia), built walls around cemeteries (six in Bahia), dug small wells to provide water for inhabitants of the dry backlands, and provided aid and advice to those who requested it.[50] On June 6, 1876, police in the town of Itapicuru, Bahia, arrested Antônio, claiming that he had murdered his wife and stepmother. Transported to Salvador, the chief of police in Salvador sent Antônio to Fortaleza, Ceará, to face criminal charges. On August 1, police in Fortaleza released Antônio due to a lack of evidence. He then returned to Bahia and assembled his followers.

A local judge from the town of Inhambupe writing in October 1886 described the commotion Antônio caused in the region.

The followers and associates of Antônio Conselheiro call him the Son of God, the new Christ or Messiah. He promulgates ideas

TABLE 8.1. FREE AND SLAVE POPULATION IN THE
MUNICIPALITIES INFLUENCED BY THE PRESENCE OF
ANTÔNIO CONSELHEIRO (BASED ON THE 1872 CENSUS)

PLACE	FREE POPULATION	SLAVE POPULATION
Conde	10,300	1,178
Inhambupe	18,940	2,663
Entre Rio	8,386	2,611
Alagoinhas	17,755	3,763
Itapicuru	14,058	1,152
Soure	5,329	358
Pombal	6,728	624
Tucano	6,434	764
Monte Santo	9,907	1,438
Geremoabo	35,324	1,460
Total	133,161 (89.25 %)	16,038 (10.75 %)

Source: Yara Dulce Bandeira de Ataide, "Origens do povo do Bom Jesus Conselheiro," *Revista USP* 20 (December–February 1993–94), 95.

that are subversive of the true religion, morals and order. In this artificial manner he instills in the spirit of the masses and lower and ignorant classes sentiments of fanaticism and superstition and [encourages] attacks on legal precepts and social rights.[51]

The northeastern region of Bahia where Antônio traveled included a substantial slave population, and in the two years preceding abolition, Antônio Conselheiro's ideas spread among slaves. Fugitive slaves sought refuge in his entourage.

The Bahian historian José Calasans has written that one observer described a gathering of "2,000 persons, all slaves" who desired to hear an evening sermon of Antônio's. This occurred near the town of Conde. The listeners lingered until midnight. Antônio distributed "significant quantities" of food obtained from well-to-do landowners and businessmen who desired to help out the poor followers of Antônio. Such depictions inspired the Bahian historian Edmundo Ferrão Moniz de Aragão (1911–97) to label Antônio Conselheiro an abolitionist.

> Antônio Conselheiro, in his peregrination through the sertão, before the Law of May 13th, spoke to the slaves to console them, promising liberation and a better life. From the beginning of his career, he struggled for abolition. He could not comprehend how a nation that called itself Christian and civilized could maintain a regime so barbarous as slavery. He went from slave quarters to slave quarters to carry his message of hope, faith and consolation. It was not without reason that he received the dedicated cooperation of a great number of former slaves during the battle at Canudos.[52]

In the aftermath of emancipation, former slaves joined up with the Conselheiristas and gained renown as the "dreaded [ones of the] 13th of May" (*os temíveis treze-de-maio*). Inhabitants in the sertão also employed the term *carijés* when alluding to former slaves who joined in the Conselheiro's entourage (most likely a reference to the Bahian abolitionist Eduardo Carigé).[53] Professor Calasans has described Canudos as "the last quilombo," by this phrase suggesting that the settlement included a significant number of freedpersons.[54]

Landowners generally condemned the rapid growth of Canudos after its founding in June 1893. For them, migrants who ventured to Canudos meant fewer workers available to labor on estates. Hundreds, if not thousands, of former slaves settled at Canudos. In fact, one of the streets at Canudos was named Street of the Negroes. Writing on February 28, 1894, landowner José Américo to Cícero Dantas Martins bemoaned that

> today things aren't what they used to be. . . . [We have to contend with] that damned "Conselheiro Antônio," who is exercising more power now than the first Napoleon. I no longer feel Brazilian: the

worst offense a man can commit is to call me a Brazilian subject. I am thinking about naturalizing myself African. We will soon see this sertão confiscated by [the Conselheiro] and his people, who now number more than 16,000, all miserable ex-slaves and criminals from every province, without a single one who is a human being; [the Conselheiro is] imposing his own laws, raising an army of soldiers, and doing anything he wishes.[55]

Governor Luís Vianna of Bahia and the Republican administration in Rio de Janeiro refused to sit by as Canudos grew and Antônio Conselheiro became more powerful. As had occurred two centuries previous at the quilombo Palmares (in existence from the 1590s to 1694), the central government determined to send a military expedition to destroy the settlement. Republican leaders in Rio de Janeiro believed that they could put an end to Canudos with minimal difficulty. This proved to be a grave miscalculation.

From late 1896 to September 1897, four different military expeditions waged war against Canudos. The first small force set out under the leadership of a lieutenant on November 12, 1896, with three junior officers and 104 soldiers. Suffering a quick defeat at the hands of the Conselheiristas, the expedition returned to the town of Juazeiro. A second expedition was organized in Monte Santo (located southwest of Canudos) and launched against the Conselheiro on January 12, 1897, numbering 561 men. This larger expedition was defeated as well. The third contingent departed on February 21, led by Colonel Moreira César and including 1,281 soldiers. It too failed in its mission to destroy Canudos, with enormous loss of soldiers and the death of Colonel César.

A fourth expedition was finally successful. The force was divided into two columns and marched from their bases in Jeremoabo and Monte Santo on June 16 and July 19. The expedition, demonstrating the growing embarrassment of the federal government, included three generals, several colonels, majors, captains, lieutenants, and 4,500 enlisted soldiers. The expedition was supported by a second force (what some have called the fifth expedition) led by the Brazilian minister of war Marechal Carlos Machado Bittencourt. It included another 2,614 soldiers and 300 officers.

On October 5, 1897, the last defenders of Canudos perished or were captured after fierce hand-to-hand combat. Antônio Conselheiro had died in the struggle more than two weeks earlier. The victorious army burned the remaining houses and dynamited the ruins. Victorious troops carried out atrocities, including rape, executions with guns, and beheadings.[56] The victors handed over surviving children from the settlement to local farmers, soldiers, and shopkeepers. Some of the young females were sent to houses of prostitution. Soldiers then transported small groups of survivors to the town of Alagoinhas and to Salvador.[57] One writer estimates that thirty thousand people died, including twenty-five thousand defenders of Canudos and five thousand military troops. So ended, in the words of the Bahian anthropologist Antônio Olavo, "one of the most dramatic and emotional moments in all of the history of Brazil" and the Americas.[58]

Why did the Bahian state government and the Republican government in Rio de Janeiro unleash such violence to destroy this town of twenty-five thousand mostly destitute inhabitants? Various reasons have been posited, including the government's perception that Antônio Conselheiro was a dangerous religious fanatic and a bandit. The hierarchy of the Catholic Church had also condemned Antônio as "an impostor priest whose appeal threatened its political power."[59] Republican sympathizers of the government claimed that the Conselheiro desired a return to rule by the monarchy as had existed before 1889.

Placing Canudos in the context of Bahian history, however, suggests emphasizing the presence of blacks and persons of mixed race at Canudos is essential to understanding the cruelty and violence. Effective resistance by the Conselheiristas provoked government officials and the rural oligarchy at a time when these groups were threatened by the end of slavery. Much like the numerous quilombos that existed in Bahia during the nineteenth century and earlier, the inhabitants at Canudos used the environment astutely. They traded with local inhabitants and gained the trust of marginalized persons in the countryside by building

Figure 8.2 Photo of children who survived the destruction of Canudos. Courtesy of Antônio Olavo.

broad coalitions of the poor and oppressed. The Conselheiristas fought tenaciously and with extraordinary skill against the troops sent to destroy them, employing guerrilla tactics against an enemy with superior weapons (including eighteen canons) and technology. For powerful Brazilians, this was a struggle for the nation's future. Would Brazil be modern and civilized, or as they feared, would it be overrun by the brutal and brutalized underclass? The elite of Bahia had demonstrated for centuries its distrust of an underclass composed of diverse racial and ethnic backgrounds. Such attitudes contributed to the refusal by influential leaders in Salvador and Rio de Janeiro to allow former slaves and the people of the sertão to reside independent of established Republican and Catholic authorities.

Conclusions

Africans and their descendants responded to their freedom with vigor and creativity. In the countryside, former slaves negotiated over labor conditions and wages on estates where they resided. Some settled at or near the 115 quilombos (created previous to the emancipation decree of 1888) scattered throughout the province.[60] Hundreds traveled to Salvador in search of opportunity. Others journeyed to Canudos seeking to improve their situation. Education for their children and themselves was of highest priority. Their desire to learn to read and write bursts forth from the documents. As in other regions of a huge nation, a popular culture oriented toward Africa flourished.

Numerous slaveholders throughout Bahia were not equally prepared for liberation on May 13. Landowners denounced the "anarchy" that had been unleashed in the months previous to and immediately after the emancipation decree. Planters sought to retain control over workers by offering salaries and other inducements. Physical and psychological coercion was common. The rural and urban elite impeded reforms. Exclusion and marginalization of the underclass, predominantly composed of persons with dark skin, characterized most sectors of Bahian society in the century that followed. ▨

Conclusion

T he abolition of slavery in Bahia suggests the importance of international (or external) pressures for reform. The British played the most important role in ending the African slave trade to Brazil. English cruisers on the high sea intercepted slave ships bound for Bahia and made their presence visible all along the Bahian coast. U.S. diplomats resident in Bahia also exerted pressures that contributed to halting the slave trade by harassing slave traders and reporting their activities to Brazilian officials and the U.S. government. Subsequent condemnation of slavery itself by England (after ending the institution throughout its empire in 1833), France (after 1848) and the United States (after 1865) fueled the abolitionist movement in Bahia.

Expanding industrial capitalism in the nineteenth century (another external force) also influenced the way abolition played out in Bahia. On the one hand, owners of sugar engenhos looked to investments and improved technology in the form of steam engines to enhance output and profits during a time of decreasing sugar prices and increasing competition in the 1870s and 1880s. Similar to Bahian farmers who cultivated coffee, cocoa, and tobacco, sugar planters hoped to adapt to international and domestic demand for their products. In spite of the high prices paid for slaves by coffee planters from the central-southern provinces, many Bahian planters held on to their slaves. With few immigrants from Europe entering Bahia, slaves remained an important source of labor. Individuals who held on to their slaves in the 1870s and until 1888 had little sympathy for abolitionist ideas.

On the other hand, cultural values associated with capitalism inspired antislavery protest in Bahia as they did throughout the Atlantic Basin. Free labor became closely linked to the ideal of free trade. Urban entrepreneurs and intellectuals in Salvador drank deeply of such ideas.

They sought to emulate countries in West Europe and the United States that had ended slavery and moved forward with industrialization.

Domestic (internal) pressures also played a major role in ending slavery in Bahia. The most important was slave resistance. Salvador witnessed the largest urban slave revolt in the Americas in 1835. Few Bahians forgot this revolt in the two decades that followed. Organized protests and resistance by African slaves, African freedpersons, and liberated Africans caused Bahian owners to reevaluate the continuation of slave importations at midcentury. This could be seen in the decision by the Town Council of Salvador in 1850 no longer to allow slaves and freedpersons (African and crioulo) to labor in the port. That same year the Eusébio de Queiroz law brought a permanent halt to the international slave trade to Brazil. Both laws were seen by many observers as abolitionist legislation that would inevitably lead to the demise of slavery in Bahia and Brazil.

Slave flight and protests during the war with Paraguay contributed to pressures to pass further antislavery legislation. This occurred in 1871 in the form of the Law of the Free Womb, a law that guaranteed the emancipation of all children of slave women born after this date. Resistance by slaves from midcentury through the 1880s also contributed to passage of the emancipation decree of 1888.

A small group of abolitionists worked synchronically with slaves in Bahia in their quest to end slavery. In certain instances, slaves inspired allies to mobilize on their behalf. This often occurred when slaves turned themselves into the police after taking off from owners or committing violent acts such as the assassination of an estate administrator. Such incidents created opportunities for activists to publicize the abuses of slaveholders. In other circumstances, abolitionist agitators took the initiative, going to the countryside, for example, to help slaves flee from their owners and then leading them to freedom via the Brazil version of the Underground Railroad.

People of color played a critical role in the abolitionist movement in Bahia. Few of these individuals entered politics. Instead, much of what they did happened in the streets of cities and more remote locales of the interior. Hence, unearthing information and clear descriptions about such activities has not been an easy task for historians and other scholars. Their initiatives have only recently gained close attention. Names like Rui Barbosa and Joaquim Nabuco have come down through the decades as the big players in this drama. This book focuses on the lives and activities of lesser-known participants.

The presence of women in the abolitionist struggle has also received little attention. African women and women of color tied to Candomblé terreiros helped to weaken the slave regime of Bahia. Women of the bourgeoisie joined abolitionist societies and made their opinions known in public. Indeed, Salvador was, in the words of the anthropologist Ruth Landes, as much a "City of Women" in the nineteenth century as in the century that followed.[1] The involvement of Bahian women in the overthrow of slavery in the province of Bahia is one of many hidden histories that merits future study.

Numerous comparisons can be made between abolition in Bahia and other provinces of the empire. Black and colored activists and intellectuals in urban areas acted courageously from the 1850s, including the cities of São Paulo, Rio de Janeiro, Salvador and Fortaleza. Urban reformers organized "meetings" in cities and journeyed into the countryside to provide information and direct aid to slaves from the 1860s. Episodes of this nature (the ones that we know about) occurred in several provinces, including Rio Grande do Sul, São Paulo, Rio de Janeiro, Bahia, Pernambuco, and Ceará.

Tensions in the late 1860s during the war with Paraguay inspired the formation of abolitionist societies throughout the empire. These early societies proved to be short-lived and of secondary influence. All those established in Bahia disappeared soon after 1871. Nevertheless, individuals associated with these first abolitionist societies, including Castro Alves and Eduardo Carigé, made major contributions. Aware of the failures of the abolitionist societies of the late 1860s, Carigé helped found the Bahian Liberating Society of 1883. By means of this entity, Carigé hoped to maintain ties with the upper classes as well as to relate to the common folk of Bahia. Dissatisfaction among elite members with

Carigé's militancy resulted in a moderate faction of the Bahian Liberating Society breaking away to form the Bahian Abolition Society in 1887.

Comparable to the indomitable activists Antônio Bento in São Paulo or João Clapp in Rio de Janeiro, individual Bahians often took enormous risks in their public and private endeavors to end slavery. Bahian newspapers like O *Alabama*, *Gazeta da Tarde*, and *Diário da Bahia* all aided in the struggle, similar to newspapers in other cities and towns of the empire. And exactly as they did in other cities and all over the Brazilian countryside, the slaves of Bahia pushed forward the process of abolition at every turn.

The war with Paraguay (1864–70) cannot be underestimated for its impact on political attitudes and worldview of the Bahian underclass. The modern Brazilian nation as we know it today commenced during the war years.[2] Numerous provinces in the empire sent men of diverse class and racial backgrounds to the front and the contributions and abilities of black and mixed race soldiers did not go unnoticed. Like in the independence wars in Spanish America (1810–25), Cuba's Ten-Year War against Spain (1868–78), and the Civil War in the United States (1861–65), the participation of slaves and free men of color from Bahia in the Paraguayan War had a direct impact on abolitionist discourse and legislation during and after the conflict.[3]

The often-brutal recruitment of soldiers for the war effort caused upheaval throughout the empire. Hundreds of free inhabitants in cities and countryside reacted with hostility when forced to enlist. They protested in public squares, scorned Pedro II, lambasted provincial officials, and hid from recruiters. Living in a patriarchal society ruled by influential families and small elite, they felt their marginalization and lack of power. The insecurities of the war years corroded differences that separated the free underclass from slaves. The abuses of recruitment enhanced ties between lower-class free persons and slaves. As a result, support for the slave regime weakened and interest in abolition widened.

Like the revolt of the Malês in 1835, the war with Paraguay influenced subsequent events long after it had ended. Disenchantment with provincial politicians and the slow pace of social reform had

long-term consequences. During the last phase of the abolitionist struggle of the 1880s, free folk of the interior willingly gave aid to activists
and slaves alike. At Canudos (1893–97), folk of different racial and geographic origins forged a community in the interior of Bahia. Numerous Conselheiristas remembered well or heard about the dark days of
recruitment during the war with Paraguay. They understood the dangers
inherent in pursuing their goals independent of the dictates of the Bahian
elite and hierarchy of the Catholic Church.

Officers and soldiers learned harsh lessons about guerrilla warfare
while fighting in the war with Paraguay. Minister of War Carlos Machado
Bittencourt (1840–97) and Julião Augusto da Serra Martins (1841–1906)
were both veterans of the Paraguayan conflict and played key roles in the
final military expeditions launched against Canudos.[4] To do battle with
the Conselheiristas, the federal government ultimately brought together
soldiers from seventeen Brazilian states. Like the violence unleashed on the
"savage Republicans" of Paraguay, Brazil's republican army annihilated
the followers of the "dangerous monarchist" Antônio Conselheiro.

In her book entitled *O Império do divino: Festas religiosas e cultura
popular no Rio de Janeiro, 1830–1900* (1999; The Divine Empire:
Religious Festivities and Popular Culture in Rio de Janeiro, 1830–1900),
historian Martha Abreu writes:

> [One] cannot fail to reflect on the persistent force of African
> legacies [*heranças*] and the exuberant manifestations of popular
> faith [in the second half of the nineteenth century]. In spite of
> persecution, criticism and strange surprises, in some form both
> were accepted and incorporated into the life of the city, in spite
> of facing a political strategy and forms of control more efficient
> than simple repression.[5]

Abreu's comments aptly depict Salvador and Bahia after emancipation
in 1888. Manifestations of Bahia's rich African cultures that endured
through the nineteenth century continued to flourish. In spite of police
persecution until late in the twentieth century, members of Candomblé

terreiros throughout Bahia have never weakened in their collective quest to uphold African traditions and keep African Bahian culture alive.

Carnival celebrations have evolved over time, yet still today address themes evident from the late 1800s. The cultural association Ilê Aiyê (Yoruba term meaning House of Life) is a good example. Founded in 1974, members of Ilê Aiyê established a Carnival *bloco* (Carnival group or club) a year later. They did so in reaction to the pervasive discrimination faced by Bahians of color who desired to participate in Carnival blocos in Salvador. Ilê Aiyê became the first African Brazilian bloco to parade in modern Carnival celebrations. Involved in a wide range of cultural and educational activities oriented toward Bahians of color, Ilê Aiyê's success testifies to the extraordinary strength and determination of the descendants of those Africans who survived the middle passage to Bahia.

This book on abolition in Bahia places slaves and freedpersons at the center of the story. At each critical juncture, in 1835 during the revolt of the Malês, in 1850 with the demise of the international slave trade, in 1871 with passage of the Law of the Free Womb, and in 1888 with passage of the law that officially ended slavery in the Brazilian empire, slaves and freedpersons played a key role. Celia M. Azevedo has written that the study of abolition—and I would add its aftermath—in Brazil "is still in its infancy."[6] Certainly these opinions apply to Bahia. ▣

Glossary

Abadá long white frock worn by Muslims

Africano/a liberto/a African-born former male or female slave, also known as an African freedman or freedwoman

Africano/a livre most commonly denotes a "liberated African" removed from a slave ship by the British or taken into protective custody soon after arrival in Brazil by Brazilian officials aiding in antislave trade suppression efforts.

Antislavery squadron England outlawed the international slave trade in its empire in 1807; from 1808 to 1864, the British Antislavery Squadron patrolled along the African coast, in the Caribbean Basin, and along the coast of South America seeking to capture vessels and arrest crews transporting slaves.

Batuque dance of African origins commonly accompanied by drumming; descendants of Africans partook of this diversion during free time, and it remains a popular pastime in Bahia

Caboclo a person of mixed European and indigenous ancestry

Cabra mulatto

Candomblé Bahian term denoting an African Brazilian religion that combines Yoruba beliefs with Catholicism

Canto this word translates as a "corner"; it is the term used to denote a group of African slaves and freedmen who carry goods, for example from the lower to the upper city of Salvador

Canudos the town known as Canudos was created in northeast Bahia by the followers of a charismatic leader named Antônio Conselheiro (Anthony the Counselor); attracting common folk of the interior and former slaves, within four years its population grew to twenty-five thousand inhabitants, making it the second-largest city in the state of Bahia; viewed as a threat to the new

Republic and the planter elite of Bahia, military troops destroyed the city and killed most of its inhabitants in September and October 1897

Capitão-do-mato exact translation is captain of the forest; commonly used to denote a man employed to hunt for fugitive slaves

Carnaval Portuguese term denoting the annual festivities that attracts thousands of revelers. Carnival (in English) formally begins on a Saturday and concludes four days later on Fat Tuesday; it commonly lasts seven days; the Sunday of Carnival is always seven weeks before Easter; its origins can be traced to pagan festivals in ancient Greece or Rome

Crioulo/a a person born in Brazil; the word carries a pejorative meaning when used in modern-day Brazilian Portuguese

Curador an educated person who represented a slave before a court; such an individual was allowed to defend a slave without having received formal training as a lawyer; the Eusébio de Queiroz law that ended the slave trade to Brazil in 1850 created the position "special *curador* for Africans"; this "special curador" represented Africans who claimed to have been illegally transported to Brazil after an 1831 law that freed any African who arrived after that date

Curandeiro a healer viewed as possessing special abilities derived from African spirits

Engenho sugar mill; sugar plantation

Entrudo annual pre-Lenten festivities in nineteenth-century Brazil; it is the precursor to Carnaval

Escravo/a male or female slave

Escravo/a crioulo/a a slave born in Brazil

Fazenda a farm, ranch, estate, or plantation

Feitiço a derogatory term denoting witchcraft associated with African spiritism and remedies

Liberto/a a male or female former slave who has been freed

Livre free

Malês Revolt Revolt of the Muslims in Salvador in 1835, the largest urban slave revolt in the history of the Americas

Mulato/a a person of mixed white and black ancestry; the origins of the word mulatto can be traced to the Latin word *mulus*, meaning mule; it is sometimes used in Brazil to demean another person

Nagô an ethnic group in West Africa who are known as the Yoruba and who represent 21 percent of the ethnic composition of present day Nigeria and 12 percent of the Republic of Benin; traffickers transported thousands of Nagô slaves to Bahia in the first half of the nineteenth century

Negro/a a black person; in the nineteenth century, the term was commonly associated with being a slave; it continued to be employed as a pejorative description through the twentieth century; the word has gained positive use in recent years as a word affirming Afro-Brazilian pride

Negro/a livre free black

Orixá Yoruba word for divinities; in Bahia, followers of Candomblé pay homage to a pantheon of some twelve *orixás*; each *orixá* is associated with a particular color, metal, animal, and natural event (such as lightening or fire), and play a special role in human relationships or experiences (such a love, war, and justice)

Pardo/a a person of mixed white and African ancestry; the term commonly suggests a brown or mulatto person; a term used in the nineteenth century, the word *pardo* or *parda* is seldom employed outside of official documents in the twentieth and twenty-first centuries

Preto/a a black person, or person of African ancestry; in nineteenth-century Bahia, it commonly was used to describe an African-born black person

Quilombo escaped slave community

Rábula an educated person who represented a slave before a court; such an individual was allowed to defend a slave without having received formal training as a lawyer

Recôncavo fertile region outside of the city of Salvador, approximately sixty miles long and varying in breadth of up to thirty miles; on its land planters large and small cultivated sugar, coffee, and tobacco with slave labor

Samba dance and music of African origins commonly practiced in Brazil

Terreiro a house or site where followers of *Candomblé* practice their religion

Voluntário da Pátria Volunteers of the Fatherland; these were Brazilian males recruited to fight in the war against Paraguay, also known as the War of the Triple Alliance (1864–70)

Yoruba an ethnic group from West Africa known in Bahia as the Nagô

Sources for Glossary:

Hendrik Kraay, ed., *Afro-Brazilian Culture and Politics: Bahia, 1790s-1990s* (Armonk, NY, and London, England: M. E. Sharpe, 1998), 177–80; Mieko Nishida, *Slavery and Identity: Ethnicity, Gender, and Race in Salvador, Brazil, 1808–1888* (Bloomington and Indianapolis: Indiana University Press, 2003), 167–68; George Reid Andrews, *Afro-Latin America, 1800–2000* (New York: Oxford University Press, 2004), 209–11. Thanks to Professor Robert Krueger for help with the words *rábula* and *curador*.

Archives

Arquivo Nacional, Rio de Janeiro:
  Secção do Poder Executivo (ANRJ/SPE)
  Secretaria de Polícia da Côrte, Ofícios com anexos (ANRJ/Polícia)
Arquivo do Instituto Histórico e Geográfico Brasileiro (AIHGB), Rio de Janeiro
Arquivo do Museu Histórico Nacional (AMHN), Rio de Janeiro
Biblioteca Nacional, Secção de Manuscritos (BNRJ/SM), Rio de Janeiro
Arquivo Histórico de Itamaraty, Notas recebidas do governo do Brasil (AHI/Notas), Rio de Janeiro
Arquivo Público do Estado do Rio de Janeiro (APERJ), Rio de Janeiro
Arquivo Público do Estado da Bahia, Salvador:
  Secção do Arquivo Colonial e Provincial (APEB/SACP)
Arquivo do Instituto Geográfico e Histórico da Bahia (AIGHB), Salvador
Arquivo do Centro Opérario do Estado da Bahia, Salvador
Arquivo Histórico do Museu Imperial, Petrópolis
Arquivo Público do Estado de São Paulo (APESP/Polícia), São Paulo
Great Britain, Public Record Office, Foreign Office (FO), "General Correspondence Before 1906: Brazil," FO 13
U.S. National Archives (USNA), Dept. of State, Record Group 59, Dispatches from Bahia, T:331 and Dispatches from Brazil, M:121

Notes

Introduction

1. Seeking compromise when writing the U.S. Constitution in 1787, opponents of slavery in the U.S. North and proslavery advocates in the U.S. South agreed to allow the continuation of slave importations to the United States for two more decades. Article 1, Section 9 of the U.S. Constitution affirmed, "The Migration or Importation [of African slaves] shall not be prohibited by the Congress prior to the Year one thousand eight hundred and eight, but a Tax or duty may be imposed on such Importation, not exceeding ten dollars for each Person." See W. E. B. Du Bois, *The Suppression of the African Slave-Trade to the United States of America, 1638–1870* (1896; reprint, New York: The Library of America, 1986). For a helpful description of the political debates in Great Britain associated with ending the international slave trade, see Hugh Thomas, *The Slave Trade: The Story of the Atlantic Slave Trade, 1440–1870* (New York: Simon and Schuster, 1997); and Adam Hochschild, *Bury the Chains: Prophets and Rebels in the Fight to Free an Empire's Slaves* (Boston and New York: Houghton Mifflin Company, 2005).

2. Personal correspondence from David Eltis, May 18, 2006.

3. Seymour Drescher, *Econocide: British Slavery in the Age of Abolition* (Pittsburgh, PA: University of Pittsburgh Press, 1977). Other scholars support Drescher's views with regards to the "economic irrationality" of British abolition, including David Eltis, *Economic Growth and the Ending of the Transatlantic Slave Trade* (New York: Oxford University Press, 1987); and Robert W. Fogel et al., *Without Consent or Contract*, 4 vols. (New York: W. W. Norton, 1989–92).

4. Seymour Drescher, *Capitalism and Antislavery: British Mobilization in Comparative Perspective* (New York: Oxford University Press, 1987); Seymour Drescher, *The Mighty Experiment: Free Labor versus Slavery in British Emancipation* (New York: Oxford University Press, 2002); Barbara L. Solow and Stanley L. Engerman, eds., *British Capitalism and Caribbean Slavery: The Legacy of Eric Williams* (Cambridge: Cambridge University Press, 1987).

5. David Brion Davis, "Capitalism, Abolitionism, and Hegemony," in Solow and Engerman, *British Capitalism and Caribbean Slavery*, 209.

6. David Brion Davis, *The Problem of Slavery in Western Culture* (Ithaca, NY: Cornell University Press, 1966); David Brion Davis, *The Problem of Slavery in the Age of Revolution, 1770–1823* (Ithaca, NY: Cornell University Press, 1973); David Brion Davis, *Slavery and Human Progress* (New York: Oxford University Press, 1984). Scholars who might be included in the "Davis School" include Roger Anstey, *The Atlantic Slave Trade and British Abolition, 1760–1810* (Atlantic Highlands, NJ: Humanities Press, 1975); Roger Anstey, "The Pattern of British Abolitionism in the Eighteenth and Nineteenth Centuries," in *Anti-Slavery, Religion, and Reform: Essays in Memory of Roger Anstey*, ed. Christine Bolt and Seymour Drescher (Kent, England: W. Dawson and Sons, 1980), 20–42; James Walvin, "The Rise of British Popular Sentiment for Abolition, 1787–1832," in Bolt and Drescher, *Anti-Slavery, Religion, and Reform*, 149–62; Walvin, *Questioning Slavery* (New York: Routledge, 1996); Howard Temperley, "Anti-Slavery as a Form of Cultural Imperialism," in Bolt and Drescher, *Anti-Slavery, Religion, and Reform*, 335–50; Clare Midgley, *Women Against Slavery: The British Campaigns, 1780–1870* (New York: Routledge, 1995). See also Robert J. Allison, "Introduction: Equiano's Worlds," in *The Interesting Narrative of the Life of Olaudah Equiano, Written by Himself*, ed. Robert J. Allison (Boston: St. Martin's Press, 1995), 1–17.

7. For an overview of the rich historiography of the Haitian revolution, see Franklin W. Knight, "The Haitian Revolution," *American Historical Review* 105, no. 1 (February 2000): 103–15. See also Carolyn E. Fick, *The Making of Haiti: The Saint Domingue Revolution from Below* (Knoxville: University of Tennessee Press, 1990), 15–75; Robin Blackburn, *The Overthrow of Colonial Slavery, 1776–1848* (London: Verso, 1988); David Geggus, "British Opinion and the Emergence of Haiti, 1791–1805," in *Slavery and British Society 1776–1846*, ed. James Walvin (Baton Rouge: Louisiana State University Press, 1982), 123–49; David Geggus, "Haiti and the Abolitionists: Opinion, Propaganda and International Politics in Britain and France, 1804–1838," in *Abolition and Its Aftermath: The Historical Context, 1790–1916*, ed. David Richardson (London: Frank Cass and Company, 1985), 113–40; David Geggus, ed., *The Impact of the Haitian Revolution in the Atlantic World* (Columbia: University of South Carolina Press, 2001). Helpful studies of slave resistance in the Caribbean include Michael Craton, *Testing the Chains: Resistance to Slavery in the British West Indies* (Ithaca, NY: Cornell University Press, 1982); Craton, "Slave Culture, Resistance and the Achievement of Emancipation in the British West Indies, 1783–1838," in Walvin, *Slavery and British Society*, 100–22; Robert Kent Richardson, *Moral Imperium: Afro-Caribbeans and the Transformation of British Rule, 1776–1838* (Westport, CT: Greenwood Press, 1987); Hilary Beckles,

"Caribbean Anti-Slavery: The Self-Liberation Ethos of Enslaved Blacks," *Journal of Caribbean History* 22, nos. 1–2 (1990): 1–19.

8. For the United States, see Sterling Stuckey, *Nationalist Theory and the Foundations of Black America* (Oxford: Oxford University Press, 1987); Herbert Aptheker, *Abolitionism: A Revolutionary Movement* (Boston: Twayne, 1989); John Ashworth, *Slavery, Capitalism, and Politics in the Antebellum Republic* (Cambridge: Cambridge University Press, 1995). For Brazil, João José Reis and Eduardo Silva, *Negociação e conflito: A resistência negra no Brasil escravista* (São Paulo: Companhia das Letras, 1989); João José Reis and Flávio dos Santos Gomes, orgs., *Liberdade por um fio: História dos quilombos no Brasil* (São Paulo: Companhia das Letras, 1996); Warren Dean, *Rio Claro: A Brazilian Plantation System* (Stanford, CA: Stanford University Press, 1976); Ronaldo Marcos dos Santos, *Resistência e superação do escravismo na província de São Paulo, 1885–1888* (São Paulo: Instituto de Pesquisas Econômicas, 1980); Hebe Maria Mattos de Castro, *Das cores do silêncio: Os significados da liberdade no sudeste escravista-Brasil, século xix* (Rio de Janeiro: Arquivo Nacional, 1995); Maria Helena Machado, *O plano e o pânico: Os movimentos sociais na década da abolição* (Rio de Janeiro: UFRJ/EDUSP, 1994); Maria Helena Machado, *Crime e escravidão: Trabalho, luta e resistência nas lavouras paulistas, 1830–1888* (São Paulo: Editora Brasiliense, 1987); Lilia Moritz Schwarcz, *Retrato em branco e negro: Jornais, escravos e cidadãos em São Paulo no final do século xix* (São Paulo: Companhia das Letras, 1987); Celia Maria Marinho de Azevedo, *Onda negra, medo branco: O negro no imaginário das elites—século xix* (Rio de Janeiro: Paz e Terra, 1987); Lana Lage da Gama Lima, *Rebeldia negra e abolicionismo* (Rio de Janeiro: Achiamé, 1981); Sidney Chalhoub, *Visões da liberdade: Uma história das últimas décadas da escravidão na corte* (São Paulo: Companhia das Letras, 1990); Flávio dos Santos Gomes, *Histórias de quilombolas: Mocambos e comunidades de senzalas no Rio de Janeiro, século xix* (Rio de Janeiro: Arquivo Nacional, 1995). An insightful analysis of the historiography of slave studies in Brazil that focuses on slave resistance is João José Reis, "Slaves as Agents of History: A Note on the New Historiography of Slavery in Brazil," *Society and History* 51, nos. 5/6 (September/December 1999): 437–45.

9. E. Bradford Burns, *A History of Brazil*, 3d ed. (New York: Columbia University Press, 1993), 99–196; Emilia Viotti da Costa, *The Brazilian Empire: Myths and Histories*, rev. ed. (Chapel Hill: University of North Carolina Press, 2000); Lilia Moritz Schwarcz, *As barbas do imperador: D. Pedro II, um monarca nos trópicos* (São Paulo: Companhia das Letras, 1998).

10. Ubiratan Castro de Araújo, "1846: Um ano na rota Bahia-Lagos: Negócios, negociantes e outros parceiros," *Afro-Ásia* 21–22 (1998–99): 85, 102.

11. Robert Conrad, *The Destruction of Brazilian Slavery, 1850–1888* (Berkeley: University of California Press, 1972); Katia M. de Queirós Mattoso, *Bahia, século xix: Uma província no império*, trans. Yeda de Macedo Soares (Rio de Janeiro: Editora Nova Fronteira, 1992).

12. B. J. Barickman, *A Bahian Counterpoint: Sugar, Tobacco, Cassava and Slavery in the Recôncavo, 1780–1860* (Stanford, CA: Stanford University Press, 1998); B. J. Barickman, "Até a véspera: O trabalho escravo e a produção de açúcar nos engenhos do Recôncavo baiano (1850–1881)," *Afro-Ásia* 21–22 (1998–99): 186–91. An earlier version of this article appeared as "Persistence and Decline: Slave Labour and Sugar Production in the Bahian Recôncavo, 1850–1888," *Journal of Latin American Studies* 28, no. 3 (1996): 581–633. See also Waldir Freitas Oliveira, *A crise da economia açucareira do Recôncavo na segunda metade do século xix* (Salvador: FCJA; UFBA-Centro de Estudos Baianos, 1999); Mary Ann Mahoney, "The World Cacao Made: Society, Politics, and History in Southern Bahia, Brazil, 1822–1919" (PhD dissertation, Yale University, 1996).

13. Jacob Gorender, *A escravidão reabilitada* (São Paulo: Editora Ática, 1990), 158.

14. There are at least four definitions of an Africano livre, which can be translated as Liberated African or Free African. One is that an African has been "liberated" from a slave ship by the British squadron and then brought to a Brazilian port and placed under the responsibility of Brazilian officials. A second meaning denotes African slaves who were taken into custody by Brazilian officials soon after being landed on the Brazilian coast by a slave ship and hence "liberated." A third definition implies an African transported to Brazil illegally after passage of the 1831 law. And a fourth definition suggests that an African previously enslaved has gained his freedom (more commonly known as an *Africano liberto*). When a document or book offers a clear meaning of the term Africano livre, I note it.

15. Gorender, *A escravidão reabilitada*, 158; Machado, *O plano e o pânico*, 78, 190, 220–21.

16. Antônio de Castro Alves, *The Major Abolitionist Poems: Antônio de Castro Alves*, ed. and trans. Amy A. Peterson (New York: Garland Publishing, 1990), 23.

17. Celia M. Azevedo, *Abolitionism in the United States and Brazil: A Comparative Perspective* (New York: Garland Publishing, 1995), xxiv.

18. Herbert S. Klein and Francisco Vidal Luna, "Free Colored in a Slave Society: São Paulo and Minas Gerais in the Early Nineteenth Century," *Hispanic American Historical Review* 80, no. 4 (November 2000): 917–18.

19. Richard Graham, "Free African Brazilians and the State in Slavery Times," in *Racial Politics in Contemporary Brazil*, ed. Michael Hanchard (Durham, NC: Duke University Press, 1999), 30–58; Hendrik Kraay, ed., *Afro-Brazilian Culture and Politics: Bahia, 1790s to 1990s* (Armonk, NY, and London England: M. E. Sharpe, 1998), 3–29.

20. João José Reis, *Slave Rebellion in Brazil: The Muslim Uprising of 1835 in Bahia*, trans. Arthur Brakel (Baltimore, MD: Johns Hopkins University Press, 1993), 225.

21. Mieko Nishida, *Slavery and Identity: Ethnicity, Gender, and Race in Salvador, Brazil, 1808–1888* (Bloomington and Indianapolis: Indiana University Press, 2003), 20, 85.

22. Rebecca Baird Bergstrasser, "The Movement for the Abolition of Slavery in Rio de Janeiro, Brazil, 1880–1889" (PhD dissertation, Stanford University, 1973), 19.

23. Eugene Ridings, *Business Interest Groups in Nineteenth-Century Brazil* (Cambridge: Cambridge University Press, 1994), xiii–xiv.

Chapter One

1. Robert Edgar Conrad, *World of Sorrow: The African Slave Trade to Brazil* (Baton Rouge: Louisiana State University Press, 1986), 192. Other studies of the international slave trade to Brazil include Leslie Bethell, *The Abolition of the Brazilian Slave Trade: Britain, Brazil and the Slave Trade Question, 1807–1869* (Cambridge: Cambridge University Press, 1970); Philip D. Curtin, *The Atlantic Slave Trade: A Census* (Madison: University of Wisconsin Press, 1969); and Pierre Verger, *Fluxo e refluxo do tráfico de escravos entre o golfo do Benin e a Bahia de Todos os Santos: Dos séculos xvii a xix*, trans. Tasso Gadzanis (São Paulo: Corrupio, 1987). The English translation of Verger's classic work is entitled *Trade Relations Between the Bight of Benin and Bahia from the 17th to 19th Century*, trans. Evelyn Crawford (Ibadan, Nigeria: Ibadan University Press, 1976). See also Jeffrey D. Needell, "The Abolition of the Brazilian Slave Trade in 1850: Historiography, Slave Agency and Statesmanship," *Journal of Latin American Studies* 33, no. 4 (November 2001): 681–711; Herbert S. Klein, *The Atlantic Slave Trade* (Cambridge: Cambridge University Press, 1999); Joseph C. Miller, *Way of Death: Merchant Capitalism and the Angolan Slave Trade, 1730–1830* (Madison: University of Wisconsin Press, 1988); Manolo Florentino, *Em costas negras: Uma história do tráfico Atlântico de escravos entre África e o Rio de Janeiro (séculos xviii e xix)* (São Paulo: Companhia das Letras, 1997); Luís Henrique Dias Tavares, *Comércio proibido de escravos* (São Paulo: Editora Ática, 1988); Roquinaldo Amaral Ferriera, "Dos sertões

ao Atlântico: Tráfico ilegal e comércio lícito em Angola, 1830–1860" (MA thesis, Federal University of Rio de Janeiro, 1996); Jaime Rodrigues, *O infame comércio: Propostas e experiências no final do tráfico dos Africanos para o Brasil (1800–1850)* (Campinas: Editora da Unicamp, 2000); Selma Pantoja and José Flávio Sombra Saraiva, orgs., *Angola e Brasil nas rotas do Atlântico sul* (Rio de Janeiro: Bertrand Brasil, 1999); Dale T. Graden, "'An Act Even of Public Security': Slave Resistance, Social Tensions and the End of the International Slave Trade to Brazil, 1835–1856," *Hispanic American Historical Review* 76, no. 2 (May 1996): 249–82; David Eltis, Stephen D. Behrendt, David Richardson, and Herbert S. Klein, *The Transatlantic Slave Trade: A Database on CD-ROM* (New York: Cambridge University Press, 1999).

2. David Eltis, *Economic Growth and the Ending of the Transatlantic Slave Trade* (New York: Oxford University Press, 1987), 195. Robin Blackburn estimates that the total slave population of the Americas increased from 330,000 in 1700 to nearly three million in 1800 and peaked in the 1850s at more than six million (*The Making of New World Slavery: From the Baroque to the Modern 1492–1800* [London: Verso, 1997], 3).

3. Richard Graham, "Another Middle Passage?: The Internal Slave Trade in Brazil," in *The Chattel Principle: Internal Slave Trades in the Americas*, ed. Walter Johnson (New Haven, CT: Yale University Press, 2004), 294.

4. Conrad, *World of Sorrow*, 68, 126–53; Tavares, *Comércio proibido*; Ubiratan Castro de Araújo, "1846: Um ano na rota Bahia-Lagos: Negócios, negociantes e outros parceiros," *Afro-Asia* 21–22 (1998–99): 85, 102. See also Louise H. Guenther, "The British Community of Bahia, Brazil, 1808–1850" (PhD dissertation, University of Minnesota, 1998), 66–74.

5. Verger, *Flux e refluxo*, 431.

6. Ibid., 431–32.

7. Cited in Hugh Thomas, *The Slave Trade: The Story of the Atlantic Slave Trade, 1440–1870* (New York: Simon and Schuster, 1997), 576.

8. Eltis et al., *The Transatlantic Slave Trade*. A partial list of Bahian ships can be found in appendix 1 of Verger, *Fluxo e refluxo*, 637–47. Other ships intercepted most likely had links to Bahia, but captains and crews denied it. Some of the intercepted ships had no slaves on board. Thanks to David Eltis for help in interpreting the *The Transatlantic Slave Trade* CD-ROM database.

9. Cited in Guenther, "The British Community of Bahia," 59–65, 72. See also U.S. Consul Woodbridge Odlin to Secretary of State Forsyth, Salvador, April 3, 1835, USNA, T 432:3; J. J. da Silva to police delegate of first district, Salvador, May 1, 1848, APEB/SACP, m. 5699.

10. Vice-Consul of Great Britain James Wetherell to vice president Alvaro Tibério de Moncorvo e Lima, Salvador, August 22, 1851, APEB/SACP, m. 1188.

11. Warren Howard, *American Slavers and the Federal Law, 1837–1862* (Berkeley: University of California Press, 1963), 11–12; Charles Davis to Secretary of State William Marcy, Havana, May 22, 1854, USNA, T 20:29.

12. John Gilmer to Secretary of State Buchanan, Salvador, May 10, 1845, USNA, T 432:4. This document substitutes the name Darling for Duling. Thomas Duling was brought to trial in the United States in October 1845 for slave trading and acquitted.

13. U.S. Consul George Gordon to Secretary of State Calhoun, Rio de Janeiro, April 22, 1845, USNA, T 172:10.

14. Cited in Eltis, *Economic Growth,* 114.

15. U.S. diplomat J. Watson Webb observed that Great Britain had made great strides after opening up the steam trade between Liverpool and Rio de Janeiro in 1850, "doubling the importations of Britain and France in three years." This cut into U.S. exports to Brazil (Webb estimated a decrease of 20 percent per year), which had been rapidly expanding in the 1840s, partially due to the use of clipper ships. Webb to Carlos Carneiro de Campos, Rio de Janeiro, September 23, 1864, AHI/Notas, 280/1/8. See also Henry R. Wise to Ferreira Franca, Rio de Janeiro, September 24, 1844, AHI/Notas, 280/1/1. For descriptions of the expansion of the British empire in the name of antislavery, see John Gallagher and Ronald Robinson, "The Imperialism of Free Trade," *The Economic History Review* 6, no. 1 (1953): 11; Richard Graham, *Britain and the Onset of Modernization in Brazil, 1850–1914* (Cambridge: Cambridge University Press, 1968); Howard Temperley, *White Dreams, Black Africa: The Antislavery Expedition of the River Niger, 1841–1842* (New Haven, CT: Yale University Press, 1991); Howard Temperley, "Anti-Slavery as a Form of Cultural Imperialism," in *Anti-Slavery, Religion, and Reform: Essays in Memory of Roger Anstey,* ed. Christine Bolt and Seymour Drescher (Kent, England: W. Dawson and Sons, 1980), 335–50; Suzanne Miers, *Britain and the Ending of the Slave Trade* (London: Longman, 1975); Richard Roberts and Suzanne Miers, "The End of Slavery in Africa," in *The End of Slavery in Africa,* ed. Miers and Roberts (Madison: University of Wisconsin Press, 1988), 3–68; and Robin Law, "The Transition from the Slave Trade to 'Legitimate' Commerce," *Studies in the World History of Slavery, Abolition and Emancipation,* I, no. 1 (1996): 1–13 (published on the Web at http://www.hnet.msu.edu/~slavery).

16. Eltis, *Economic Growth,* 115.

17. Chief of Police Wanderley to president, Salvador, October 16, 1851, APEB/SACP, m. 5708; Verger, *Flux e refluxo,* 433–34.

18. Chief of Police Wanderley to president, Salvador, November 18, 1851, APEB/SACP, m. 5709; Verger, *Flux e refluxo*, 434–38; Ubiratan Castro de Araújo, "Viagem à escravidão," *Revista Nossa História: Publicação da Biblioteca Nacional* 1, no. 3 (January 2004): 74–80.

19. Deposition of Gilbert Smith to U.S. Consul George Gordon, Rio de Janeiro, May 9, 1845, in Gordon to Buchanan, Rio de Janeiro, June 2, 1845, USNA, T 172:11.

20. A. Oaksmith to U.S. Consul John S. Gillmer, Salvador, July 26, 1852, USNA, T 331:1. See Winston McGowan, "African Resistance to the Atlantic Slave Trade in West Africa," *Slavery and Abolition* 11, no. 1 (May 1990): 5–29.

21. R. Roddman to H. Chamberlain, Salvador, January 12, 1825, AHI/Notas, 284/2/15.

22. Tindal to British Consul Porter, May 2, 1848, Salvador, APEB/SACP, 1193.

23. Perceptions among slaves of British good will and support for emancipation in and near the city of Rio de Janeiro is noted in Carlos Eugênio Líbano Soares and Flávio Gomes, "'Com o pé sobre um vulcão': Africanos Minas, identidades e a repressão antiafricana no Rio de Janeiro (1830–1840)," *Estudos Afro-Asiáticos* 23, no. 2 (2001): 360–61. See also Chief of Police Vanancio José Lisboa to president of the Province of Rio de Janeiro, Rio de Janeiro, November 22, 1850, APERJ, collection 96, maço 1, pasta 1.

24. British Consul Edmund Porter to Lord Palmerston, Salvador, December 21, 1849, Foreign Office of Great Britain, General Correspondence, FO 13, vol. 268, fols. 371–77.

25. Salustiano Ferreira Santos to Minister of the Empire (Interior), Salvador, June 30, 1853 (originally written on December 23, 1849), ANRJ/SPE IJJ 9 339.

26. President Martins to Minister of the Empire, Salvador, January 1, 1850, ANRJ/SPE, IJJ 9 339; Member of the Câmara of Salvador to president, Salvador, October 25, 1853, ANRJ/SPE, IJJ 9 339. See also Verger, *Trade Relations*, 348.

27. *Falla que recitou o prezidente da província da Bahia, o Conselheiro Desembargador Francisco Gonçalves Martins, n'abertura da assembléia legislativa da mesma província em 1. de Março de 1850* (Bahia: Typographia Constitucional, 1850), 10–20.

28. Director of Public Health Dr. José Vieira de Faria Aragão e Ataliba et al. to president, Salvador, February 12, 1853, ANRJ/SPE, IJJ 9 339; Ataliba to president, Salvador, April 5, 1853, ANRJ/SPE, IJJ 9 339. For helpful perspectives on sickness and disease, see Donald B. Cooper, "The New 'Black Death': Cholera in Brazil, 1855–1856," in *The African Exchange: Toward a Biological History of Black People*, ed. Kenneth F. Kiple (Durham, NC: Duke University Press, 1987),

235–56; Sidney Chalhoub, *Cidade febril: Cortiços e epidemias na corte imperial* (São Paulo: Companhia das Letras, 1996), 60–78; Daurel Alden and Joseph C. Miller, "Unwanted Cargoes: The Origins and Dissemination of Smallpox via the Slave Trade from Africa to Brazil, c. 1560–1830," in Kiple, *The African Exchange*, 35–109; Richard Evans, "Epidemics and Revolutions: Cholera in 19th Century Europe," *Past and Present* 120 (August 1988): 123–46.

29. Sidney Chalhoub, "The Politics of Disease Control: Yellow Fever and Race in Nineteenth-Century Rio de Janeiro," *Journal of Latin American Studies* 25, no. 3 (October 1993): 449–53; Chalhoub, *Cidade febril*, 74–75.

30. "Sessão em 9 de Setembro de 1850," *Anais do senado do império do Brasil* (Rio de Janeiro: Senado Federal, 1978) (hereafter cited as ASIB), 518–19.

31. Chalhoub, "Politics of Disease Control," 448, n. 14.

32. Interim Chief of Police Chichôrro da Gama to vice president, Salvador, August 8, 1850, ANRJ/SPE, IJ 1 405.

33. Police delegate Antônio Pinto da Silva Valle to president, Rio de Janeiro, April 22, 1855, APERJ, collection 96, m. 2, pasta 1.

34. Cooper, "New Black Death," 239–50. For a description of cholera outbreaks in the United States, see Charles E. Rosenberg, *The Cholera Years: The United States in 1832, 1849, and 1866* (Chicago: University of Chicago Press, 1987).

35. Cooper, "New Black Death," 242.

36. Anna Amélia Vieira Nascimento, *Dez freguesias da cidade do Salvador* (Salvador: FCEBa/EGBa, 1986), 160–63; Johildo Lopes de Athayde, *Salvador e a grande epidemia de 1855* (Salvador: Centro de Estudos Baianos da Universidade Federal da Bahia, 1985); Onildo Reis David, *O inimigo invisível: Epidemia na Bahia no século xix* (Salvador: EDUFBA/Sarah Letras, 1996).

37. Eric Anderson, "Yankee Blackbirds: Northern Entrepreneurs and the Illegal International Slave Trade, 1808–1865" (MA thesis, University of Idaho, 2000), 281.

38. British Consul Earl of Clarendon to British Consul John Morgan, Bahia, September 15, 1855, APEB/SACP, m. 1190; Howard, *American Slavers*, 124–26.

39. Bethell, *Abolition of the Brazilian Slave Trade*, 374; U.S. Consul John S. Gillmer to Secretary of State Marcy, Salvador, February 1, 1856, USNA, T 331:1; Secretary of Police in Bahia to minister of justice José Thomaz Nabuco, February 14, 1856, ANRJ/Polícia IJ6 472; Chief of Police Mattos to president, Salvador, February 23, 1856, APEB/SACP, m. 5718. For descriptions of U.S. involvement in the international slave trade after 1808, see W. E. B. Du Bois, *The Suppression of the African Slave-Trade to the United States of America* (1896; reprint, New

York: The Library of America, 1986), 163–92; Howard, *American Slavers*; Peter Duignan and Clarence Clendenen, *The United States and the African Slave Trade, 1619–1862* (Stanford, CA: Stanford University Press, 1963); Anderson, "Yankee Blackbirds."

40. Bethell, *Abolition of the Brazilian Slave Trade*, 374; President of the Province Moncorvo e Lima to Minister of Empire, Salvador, March 4, 1856, ANRJ/SPE, IJJ 9 340.

41. *Estatutos da sociedade philantropica estabellecida no capital da Bahia em benefício dos Brazileiros que tiverão a infelicidade de nascer escravos* (n.d., n.p.); Chief of Police Chichôrro da Gama to police delegates and subdelegates, Salvador, May 1, 1850, ANRJ/SPE, IJ 1 405.

42. Jailton Lima Brito, *A abolição na Bahia, 1870–1888* (Salvador: Centro de Estudos Baianos, 2003), 70.

43. Luís Anselmo da Fonseca, *A escravidão, o clero e o abolicionismo*, edição fac-similar de 1887 (Recife: Editora Massangana, 1988), 244.

44. Peter Linebaugh and Marcus Rediker, *The Many-Headed Hydra: Sailors, Slaves, Commoners, and the Hidden History of the Revolutionary Atlantic* (Boston: Beacon Press, 2000), 213, 242–47.

45. *Representação que AS.M Imperial diregem os negociantes da Praça da Bahia quixando-se das violências que soffrem os navios Brasileiros dos cruzadores inglezes na costa d'Africa* (Bahia: Typographia do Correio Mercantil de Reis Lessa E Ca., 1845).

46. Linebaugh and Rediker, *Many-Headed Hydra*, 311.

Chapter Two

1. Great Britain, Sessional Papers, 1850, Volume IX, *African Slave Trade*, Report no. 590, "Report from the Select Committee of the House of Lords on the African Slave Trade," 28–29. This is cited in Jane Elizabeth Adams, "The Abolition of the Brazilian Slave Trade," *The Journal of Negro History* 10, no. 4 (October 1925): 634.

2. Minister of Justice José Ildefonso de Sousa Ramos to president of Rio de Janeiro, Rio de Janeiro, June 17, 1852, APERJ, PP2, collection 2, maço 1.

3. U.S. diplomat Henry A. Wise wrote, "It is the most anxious desire of the United States to see them [the countries of the western hemisphere] . . . *free from all interference from any quarter in the regulation and management of their domestic concerns. .. . .* Brazil has the deepest interest in establishing the same policy, especially in reference to the important relation between the European and African races as it exists here and in the southern portion of our Union. That under no other [circumstances] can the two races live together in

peace and prosperity in either country. That the avowed policy of Great Britain is to destroy that relationship in both countries and throughout the world." Wise to Minister of Interior Ernesto Ferreira França, Rio de Janeiro, September 24, 1844, AHI/Notas, 280/1/1. See also David Eltis, *Economic Growth and the Ending of the Transatlantic Slave Trade* (New York: Oxford University Press, 1987), 114.

4. Leslie Bethell, *The Abolition of the Brazilian Slave Trade: Britain, Brazil and the Slave Trade Question, 1807–1869* (Cambridge: Cambridge University Press, 1970); Robert Edgar Conrad, *World of Sorrow: The African Slave Trade to Brazil* (Baton Rouge: Louisiana State University Press, 1986); Eltis, *Economic Growth*; Hugh Thomas, *The Slave Trade: The Story of the Atlantic Slave Trade, 1440–1870* (New York: Simon and Schuster, 1997).

5. For one description of the shift in political opinion against continuation of the slave trade to Brazil in 1850–51, see Eltis, *Economic Growth*, 210–17.

6. João José Reis, "Quilombos e revoltas escravas no Brasil," *Revista USP* 28 (December 1995–February 1996): 24.

7. João José Reis, *Slave Rebellion in Brazil: The Muslim Uprising of 1835 in Bahia*, trans. Arthur Brakel (Baltimore, MD: Johns Hopkins University Press, 1993), 6. A revised and expanded edition of this book is *Rebelião escrava no Brasil: A história do levante dos malês em 1835* (São Paulo: Companhia das Letras, 2003). See also Maria José de Souza Andrade, *A mão-de-obra escrava em Salvador, 1811–1860* (São Paulo: Corrupio, 1988).

8. Mary C. Karasch, *Slave Life in Rio de Janeiro, 1808–1850* (Princeton, NJ: Princeton University Press, 1987), 65–66.

9. Maria Odila Leite da Silva Dias, *Quotidiano e poder em São Paulo no século xix* (São Paulo: Brasiliense, 1984); Lilia Moritz Schwarcz, *Retrato em branco e negro: Jornais, escravos e cidadãos em São Paulo no final do século xix* (São Paulo: Companhia das Letras, 1987); Maria Cristina Cortez Wissenbach, *Sonhos africanos, vivências ladinas: Escravos e forros em São Paulo, 1850–1880* (São Paulo: Editora Hucitec, 1998); Marilene Rosa Nogueira da Silva, *Negro na rua: A nova face da escravidão* (São Paulo: Editora Hucitec, 1988); Marcus J. M. de Carvalho, *Liberdade: Rotinas e rupturas do escravismo no Recife, 1822–1850* (Recife: Editora Universitária da UFPE, 1998). African slaves and their descendants labored in cities across the Americas. See George Reid Andrews, *Afro-Latin America, 1800–2000* (New York: Oxford University Press, 2004), 15–42.

10. Gilberto Freyre, *The Masters and the Slaves: A Study in the Development of Brazilian Civilization*, trans. Samuel Putnam (Berkeley: University of California Press, 1986); Gilberto Freyre, *Order and Progress: Brazil from*

Monarchy to Republic, trans. Rod W. Horton (Berkeley: University of California Press, 1986).

11. The literature on African Brazilian history and culture in Salvador and the province of Bahia is extensive. See Stuart B. Schwartz, *Sugar Plantations in the Formation of Brazilian Society: Bahia, 1550–1835* (Cambridge: Cambridge University Press, 1985); Kátia M. de Queirós Mattoso, *To Be a Slave in Brazil, 1550–1888*, trans. Arthur Goldhammer (New Brunswick, NJ: Rutgers University Press, 1986); João José Reis, *A morte é uma festa: Ritos, fúnebres e revolta popular no Brasil do século xix* (São Paulo: Companhia das Letras, 1991); João José Reis, *Slave Rebellion in Brazil*; Nina Rodrigues, *Os africanos no Brasil*, 5th ed. (São Paulo: Nacional, 1977). For Rio de Janeiro, see Karasch, *Slave Life*; Jacob Gorender, *O escravismo colonial*, 4th ed. (São Paulo: Ática, 1985); Sidney Chalhoub, *Visões da liberdade: Uma história das últimas décadas da escravidão na corte* (São Paulo: Companhia das Letras, 1990).

12. Reis, *Slave Rebellion*, 14–20; Karasch, *Slave Life*, 311–16; João José Reis and Flávio dos Santos Gomes, orgs., *Liberdade por um fio: História dos quilombos no Brasil* (São Paulo: Companhia das Letras, 1996).

13. Leslie Bethell and José Murilo de Carvalho, "Empire, 1822–1850," in *Brazil: Empire and Republic, 1822–1930*, ed. Leslie Bethell (Cambridge: Cambridge University Press, 1989), 68.

14. Reis, *Slave Rebellion*, 40–69; Ofício do Marques de Aguiar a o Conde do Arcos, Salvador, June 6, 1814, ANRJ/SM, II-33,24,29; Alexandre Gomes Ferrão Castelbranco to Pedro I, Salvador, March 15, 1816, BNRJ/SM, Documentos biográficos, C,9,5; Resolução do conselho interino do governo da Bahia, Salvador, November 28, 1822, BNRJ/SM, II-34,10,23; João Severiano Maciel da Costa, *Memória sobre a necessidade de abolir a introdução dos escravos no Brasil* (Coimbra: Imprensa da Universidade, 1821).

15. For the legacies of the Haitian revolution in Brazil, see Carlos Eugênio Líbano Soares Flávio Gomes, "Sedições, *Haitianismo* e conexões no Brasil: Outras margens do Atlântico negro," *Novos Estudos CEBRAP* 63 (July 2002): 131–44.

16. Reis, *Slave Rebellion*, 93–97; Maria Inês Côrtes de Oliveira, "Quem era os 'negros de Guiné'?: A origem dos Africanos na Bahia," *Afro-Ásia* 19–20 (1997): 37–73.

17. Paul E. Lovejoy, "Background to Rebellion: The Origins of Muslim Slaves in Bahia," *Slavery and Abolition* 15, no. 2 (August 1994): 156–57, 170.

18. Reis, *Slave Rebellion*, 110.

19. President Francisco de Souza Martins to minister of justice, Salvador, February 14, 1835, ANRJ/SPE, IJ 1 707.

20. Bethell, *Abolition of the Brazilian Slave Trade*, 78–79.

21. Chief of Police Antônio Simões da Silva to president, Salvador, March 28 and October 16, 1835, APEB/SACP, m. 2949; Chief of Police Francisco Gonçalves Martins to vice president, Salvador, March 27, 1835, APEB/SACP, m. 2949.

22. Hendrik Kraay, "'As Terrifying as Unexpected': The Bahian Sabinada, 1837–1838," *Hispanic American Historical Review* 72, no. 4 (November 1992): 518.

23. President of the Province Antônio Ferreira Barretto Pedrosos to Minister of War, written from outside Salvador, January 11 and February 4, 1838, ANRJ/SPE, IG 1 116; Police Commander Manuel Ignacio de Luna to president, Salvador, March 19, 1838, APEB/SACP, m. 3113. See Kraay, "'As Terrifying as Unexpected'"; and Paulo Cezar Sousa, *A Sabinada: A revolta separatista da Bahia, 1837* (São Paulo: Brasiliense, 1987).

24. Chief of Police Francisco Vigário Lobato to president, Salvador, April 22, 1840, APEB/SACP, m. 2429.

25. Clovis Moura, *Rebeliões da senzala: Quilombos, insurreições, guerrilhas*, 3d ed. (São Paulo: Livraria Ciências Humanas, 1981), 101–2, 118–20; Police delegate José Ponce de Leão to chief of police, Salvador, June 11, 1844, APEB/SACP, m. 6182; Police delegate Pedro Cerqueria e Lima to chief of police, Salvador, June 26, 1844, APEB/SACP, m. 6182.

26. Chief of Police M. M. de Leão to delegates, Salvador, July 12, 1844, APEB/SACP, m. 5693.

27. Sélia Jesus de Lima, "Lucas Evangelista: O Lucas da Feira; Estudo sobre a rebeldia escrava em Feira de Santana, 1807–1849" (MA thesis, Federal University of Bahia, 1990). See also Francisco Maria Pessôa to president, Salvador, May 13, 1846, ANRJ/SPE, IJ 1 402; João Joaquim da Silva to president, Feira de Santana, Bahia, September 10, 1846, APEB/SACP, m. 3114.

28. Chief of Police João Joaquim da Silva to president, Salvador, December 12, 1845, ANRJ/SPE, IG 1 118.

29. President Soares de Andréa to minister of justice, Salvador, June 10, 1845, ANRJ/SPE, IJ 1 400.

30. Chief of Police Simões da Silva to president, Salvador, April 3, 1839, APEB/SACP, m. 2951; Chief of Police Evaristo Fernando d'Argollo to president, Salvador, July 26, 1839, APEB/SACP, m. 2949; Chief of Police Andre Pereira Lima to president, Salvador, February 13, 1841, APEB/SACP, m. 3109.

31. President Joaquim José Pinheiro Vasconcelos to minister of justice, Salvador, December 14, 1841, ANRJ/SPE, IJ 1 399.

32. Reis, *Slave Rebellion*, 112–24, 123, 129–36.

33. President Britto to minister of justice, Salvador, October 17, 1835, ANRJ/SPE, IJ 1 707.

34. Hendrik Kraay, "Introduction: Afro-Bahia, 1790s-1990s," in *Afro-Brazilian Culture and Politics: Bahia, 1790s–1990s*, ed. Hendrik Kraay (Armonk, NY: M. E. Sharpe, 1998), 15.

35. Chief of Police d'Argollo to president, Salvador, July 26, 1839, APEB/SACP, m. 2949; Judge Francisco de Paulo de Vigário Sayao Lobato to president, Salvador, April 22, 1840, APEB/SACP, m. 2949; police delegate Ponce de Leão to chief of police, Salvador, June 11, 1844, APEB/SACP, m. 6182; Chief of Police da Silva to president, Salvador, December 12, 1845, ANRJ/SPE, IG 1 118.

36. Chief of Police Wanderley to president, Salvador, August 18, 1849 and October 10, 1849, APEB/SACP, m. 5704.

37. J. M. Wanderley to chief of police of Sergipe, Salvador, February 10, 1851, APEB/SACP 5707.

38. James Wetherell, *Brazil. Stray Notes from Bahia: Being Extracts from Letters, &c. during a Residence of Fifteen Years* (Liverpool: W. Hadfield, 1860), 138.

39. Alberto da Costa e Silva, "Buying and Selling Korans in Nineteenth-Century Rio de Janeiro," *Slavery and Abolition* 22, no. 1 (April 2001): 85–86; *Correio Mercantil* (Rio de Janeiro), October 28, 1853.

40. Alexander Joaquim [illegible] to minister of justice, Recife, Pernambuco, October 5, 1853, ANRJ/Polícia, IJ 6 216. Thanks to Khaled Fustok for the translation.

41. Carlos Eugênio Líbano Soares and Flávio Gomes, "'Com o pé sobre um vulcão': Africanos Minas, identidades e a repressão antiafricana no Rio de Janeiro (1830–1840)," *Estudos Afro-Asiáticos* 23, no. 2 (2001): 346.

42. Chalhoub, *Visões da liberdade*, 187–88; Reis, *Slave Rebellion*, 229–30.

43. Mina-Nâgo implies Yoruba Africans with origins along the Mina coast of West Africa, which includes present-day southwest Nigeria and the Republics of Benin, Togo, and Ghana.

44. Soares and Gomes, "Com o pé sobre um vulcão," 345–51.

45. Chief of Police Queiroz to minister of justice, Rio de Janeiro, February 27, 1835, ANRJ/Polícia, IJ 6 170; Soares and Gomes, "Com o pé sobre um vulcão," 344–45.

46. Reis, *Slave Rebellion*, 6, 207, 223–30; Fundação Cultural do Estado da Bahia, *Legislação da província da Bahia sobre o negro: 1835–1888* (Salvador: FCEB, 1996), 17–23. Hendrik Kraay considers an estimate of 7 percent high in *Race, State and Armed Forces in Independence-Era Brazil* (Stanford, CA: Stanford University Press, 2001), 19.

47. Chief of Police d'Argollo to president, Salvador, July 26, 1839, APEB/SACP, m. 2949; Police delegate Ponce de Leão to chief of police, Salvador, June 11, 1844, APEB/SACP, m. 6182; President João José de Moura Magalhães to minister of justice, Salvador, February 9, 1848, ANRJ/SPE, IJ 1 710; Anna Amélia Vieira Nascimento, *Dez freguesias da cidade do Salvador* (Salvador: FCEB, 1986), 98–99; Minister of Justice Pimento Bueno to president, Rio de Janeiro, March 15, 1848, APERJ, collection 5, m. 6.

48. G. J. [illegible] to vice president, Salvador, July 27, 1853, APEB/SACP, m. 3119. See also Maria Inês Côrtes de Oliveira, *O liberto: O seu mundo e os outros; Salvador, 1790–1860* (São Paulo: Corrupio, 1988); Mattoso, *To Be a Slave*, 153–212; Manuela Carneiro da Cunha, *Negros, estrangeiros: Os escravos libertos e sua volta à África* (São Paulo: Brasiliense, 1985); Mieko Nishida, *Slavery and Identity: Ethnicity, Gender, and Race in Salvador, Brazil, 1808–1888* (Bloomington and Indianapolis: Indiana University Press, 2003).

49. *O Censor: Periódico mensal político, histórico, e literário* (Salvador), 3 (November 1837): 176–85. The "required time" was ten years.

50. Henrique Velloso de Oliveira, *A substituição do trabalho dos escravos pelo trabalho livre no Brasil* (Rio de Janeiro: Laemmert, 1845).

51. Robert Edgar Conrad, ed., *Children of God's Fire: A Documentary History of Black Slavery in Brazil* (Princeton, NJ: Princeton University Press, 1983), xx–xxi. For the long-term implications of the myth of benevolent Brazilian slave owners both within and outside of Brazil, see Michael George Hanchard, *Orpheus and Power: The "Movimento Negro" of Rio de Janeiro and São Paulo, Brazil, 1945–1988* (Princeton, NJ: Princeton University Press, 1994), 47–56.

52. Robin Blackburn, *The Overthrow of Colonial Slavery, 1776–1848* (London: Verso, 1988), 473–515; Seymour Drescher, "British Way, French Way: Opinion Building and Revolution in the Second French Slave Emancipation," *American Historical Review* 96, no. 3 (June 1991): 709–34; Neville A. T. Hall, *Slave Society in the Danish West Indies: St. Thomas, St. John and St. Croix*, ed. B. W. Higman (Baltimore, MD: Johns Hopkins University Press, 1992), 30–33, 191–227. For descriptions of concern about an impending "civil war" in Cuba at this juncture, see U.S. Consul Robert B. Campbell to Secretary of State Buchanan, Havana, July 17, 1848, USNA, Dept. of State, Record Group 59, Dispatches from Cuba, T 20:22; and Campbell to Secretary of State Clayton, Havana, August 28, 1849, T 20:22. See also Gabino La Rosa Corzo, *Runaway Slave Settlements in Cuba: Resistance and Repression*, trans. Mary Todd (Chapel Hill: University of North Carolina Press, 2003), 200. E. Bradford Burns wrote, "Visions of the successful slave revolt in Haiti haunted the elites just as it inspired slaves. Unrelenting black pressure through guerrilla warfare helped to persuade

the Colombian government to manumit the remaining slaves in 1852. Major slave threats to established order occurred in Venezuela in 1835 and Peru in 1848." (*The Poverty of Progress: Latin America in the Nineteenth Century* [Berkeley: University of California Press, 1980], 114–15).

53. See Jeffrey D. Needell, "Party Formation and State-Making: The Conservative Party and the Reconstruction of the Brazilian State, 1831–1840," *Hispanic American Historical Review* 81, no. 2 (May 2001): 288; and José Murilo de Carvalho, *A construção da ordem: A elite política imperial*, 2d ed. (Rio de Janeiro: Editora UFRJ, Relume-Dumará, 1996).

54. Chalhoub, *Visões da liberdade*, 196–97.

55. President Magalhães to minister of justice, Salvador, February 9, 1848, ANRJ/SPE, IJ 1 710.

56. See also President Francisco Gonçalves Martins to minister of war, Salvador, October 24, 1848, ANRJ/SPE, IG 1 119; Commander Coelho to president, Salvador, October 4, 1848, ANRJ/SPE, IG 1 119.

57. Police delegate Bernardino Ferreira Peres to president, Salvador, December 12, 1845, APEB/SACP, m. 3001-1.

58. Chief of Police J. M. d'Argolo Gois to subdelegates, Salvador, January 26, 1850, APEB/SACP, m. 5705.

59. Antônio Rodrigues Navarro to president, Maragogipe, Bahia, May 19, 1848, ANRJ/SPE, IJ 1 710; Chief of Police Gama to president, Salvador, July 23, 1853, APEB/SACP, m. 5712.

60. Chief of Police Gama to president, Salvador, June 22, 1850, APEB/SACP, m. 5707-01.

61. For descriptions of Africanos livres (liberated Africans), see Conrad, *World of Sorrow*, 154–70; Alfonso Bandeira Florence, "Nem escravos, nem libertos: Os 'africanos livres' na Bahia," *Cadernos do CEAS* (Salvador) 121 (May–June 1989): 58–69; Alfonso Bandeira Florence, "Entre o cativeiro e a emancipação: A liberdade dos Africanos livres no Brasil (1818–1864)" (MA thesis, Federal University of Bahia, 2002); Beatriz Galloti Mamigonian, "Do que 'o preto mina' é capaz: Etnia e resistência entre Africanos livres," *Afro-Ásia* 24 (2000): 71–95.

62. Police delegate in Salvador João Joaquim da Silva to president, Salvador, March 27, 1848, APEB/SACP, m. 3113. See also Soares and Gomes, "Com o pé sobre um vulcão." For British concerns about sending Yoruba slaves from Bahia to Rio de Janeiro, as expressed by the British chargé d'affaires in Brazil, see Luís Henrique Dias Tavares, *Comércio proibido de escravos* (São Paulo: Editora Ática, 1988), 133.

63. Herbert S. Klein, *The Middle Passage: Comparative Studies in the Atlantic Slave Trade* (Princeton, NJ: Princeton University Press, 1978), 97, n. 5; Dale T. Graden, "From Slavery to Freedom in Bahia, Brazil, 1791–1900" (PhD dissertation, University of Connecticut, 1991), 151–54. For descriptions of Brazil's internal slave trade, see Conrad, *World of Sorrow*, 171–91; Gorender, *O escravismo colonial*, 323–31; and Richard Graham, "Nos tumbeiros mais uma vez? O comércio interprovincial de escravos no Brasil," *Afro-Ásia* 27 (2002): 121–60.

64. Mamigonian, "Do que 'o preto mina' é capaz," 74.

65. Luís Anselmo da Fonseca, *A escravidão, o clero e o abolicionismo*, edição fac-similar de 1887 (Recife: Editora Massangana, 1988), 185–96. The original document (page 187 of Fonseca) notes "slaves and *Africanos livres*." The majority of the latter group were former slaves (*Africanos libertos*) who labored in the port and who had paid for their freedom with income derived from their employment as sailors. See also Braz do Amaral, *História da Bahia do império à república* (Salvador: Imprensa Oficial do Estado, 1923), 172–73; Arnold Wildberger, *Os presidentes da província da Bahia* (Salvador: Typographia Beneditina, 1949), 321.

66. President Martins to Minister of Empire (Interior), Salvador, November 22, 1850, ANRJ/SPE, IJJ 9 339. See also Cunha, *Negros, extrangeiros*, 96–99.

67. "A indústria de saveiros," *O argos cachoeirano* (Cachoeira), November 9, 1850, 2.

68. "Cachoeiranos," *O argos cachoeirano*, October 9, 1850, 1; "Bahia: O primeiro passo a nacionalisação da indústria," *O argos cachoeirano*, November 6, 1850, 2; "As canoas na Cachoeira," *Voz da mocidade*, November 24, 1850, 2; *O argos cachoeirano*, January 25, 1851, 1; Dale T. Graden, "'This City Has Too Many Slaves Joined Together': The Abolitionist Crisis in Salvador, Bahia, Brazil, 1848–1850," in *The African Diaspora*, ed. Alusine Jalloh and Stephen E. Maizlish (Arlington: Texas A&M Press, 1996), 134–52.

69. Wildberger, *Os presidentes*, 321; Gorender, *O escravismo colonial*, 472–89.

70. Katia M. de Queirós Mattoso, *Bahia, século xix: Uma província no império*, trans. Yedda de Macedo Soares (Rio de Janeiro: Editora Nova Froneira, 1992), 531.

71. Ibid., 401.

72. "A Decision of the Emperor's Council of State of 1849," September 18, 1849, cited in Conrad, *Children of God's Fire*, 221.

73. President Wanderley to minister of justice, Salvador, October 24, 1854, ANRJ/SPE, IJ 1 711; President of Pernambuco Victor d'Oliveira to minister of

justice, Recife, July 28, 1851, ANRJ/SPE, IJ 1 824; President of Pernambuco Francisco Antônio Ribeiro to minister of justice, Recife, March 17, 1853, ANRJ/SPE, IJ 1 824; Jeffrey D. Needell, "The Abolition of the Brazilian Slave Trade in 1850: Historiography, Slave Agency and Statesmanship," *Journal of Latin American Studies* 33, no. 4 (November 2001): 700–11.

74. Needell, "Abolition of the Brazilian Slave Trade," 705.

75. "Sessão em 24 de Maio de 1851," *Anais do senado do império do Brasil* (Rio de Janeiro: Senado Federal, 1978) (hereafter cited as ASIB), 320.

76. "Sessão em 27 de Maio de 1851," ASIB, 387–88.

77. "Sessão em 2 de Julho de 1850," ASIB, 49.

78. João de Campos to first delegate Lúis Rodrigues Rocha, Santo Amaro, August 6, 1851, APEB/SACP 6184.

79. Mattoso, *Bahia, século xix*, 246.

80. Chief of Police Gama to president, Salvador, August 23, 1853, APEB/SACP, m. 5712.

81. Vice President of Alagoas Manuel Sobral Pinto to minister of justice, Maceió, Alagoas, July 22, 1852, ANRJ/SPE, IJ 1 360.

82. Chief of Police of Rio de Janeiro Alexandre Joaquim de Sequeira to minister of justice, Rio de Janeiro, January 16, 1854, ANRJ/Polícia, IJ 6 217.

83. Police delegate Reginaldo Gomes dos Santos to president of the Province of Espírito Santo José Bonifácio Nascentes d'Azambuja, São Matheos, Espírito Santo, October 13, 1851, ANRJ/SPE, IJ 1 732; Vilma Paraíso Ferreira de Almada, *Escravismo e transição: O Espírito Santo, 1850–1888* (Rio de Janeiro: Edições Graal, 1984), 165.

84. Chief of Police Gama to president, Salvador, August 19, 1852, APEB/SACP, m. 5709.

85. Francisco de Moura Rouzal to police subdelegate, second district, freguesia of Santo Antônio Alem do Carmo, Salvador, October 21, 1855, APEB/SACP, m. 6231.

86. APEB/SACP, packages 5702, 5704, 5707–01, 5708, 5709, 5712, 5714, 5718, 5721, 5723, 5730, 5747, 5753, 5781, 5782, 5788, 5793, 5794, 5800, 5804, 5809, 5811, 5818, 5828, 5832, 5836, 5846, 5854, 5860, 5866.

87. Porter to Lord Palmerston, Salvador, April 1, 1847, Public Records Office, Foreign Office, 84/679, as cited in Pierre Verger, *Trade Relations Between the Bight of Benin and Bahia from the 17th to 19th Century*, trans. Evelyn Crawford (Ibadan, Nigeria: Ibadan University Press, 1976), 379; for similar perspectives by other British observers, see 344 and 474.

88. Pierre Verger, *Notícias da Bahia: 1850* (Salvador: Corrupio, 1981), 213–32.

89. Paul E. Lovejoy, "The African Diaspora: Revisionist Interpretations of Ethnicity, Culture and Religion under Slavery," *Studies in the World History of Slavery, Abolition and Emancipation* II (1997): 1–19 (found on the Web at http://www.h-net.msu.edu).

Chapter Three

1. For descriptions of the War of the Triple Alliance against Paraguay, see Charles J. Kolinski, *Independence or Death! The Story of the Paraguayan War* (Gainesville: University of Florida Press, 1965); Júlio José Chiavenatto, *Genocídio americano: A guerra do Paraguai*, 2d ed. (São Paulo: Brasiliense, 1979); Wilma Peres Costa, *A espada de dâmocles: O exército, a guerra do Paraguai e a crise do império* (São Paulo: Editora HUCITEC, 1996); Dionísio Cerqueira, *Reminiscéncias da campanha do Paraguai, 1865–1870* (Rio de Janeiro: Biblioteca do Exército, 1980); Eduardo Silva, *Prince of the People: The Life and Times of a Brazilian Free Man of Colour*, trans. Mayra Ashford (London: Verso, 1993); Vera Blinn Reber, "A Case of Total War: Paraguay, 1865–1870," *Journal of Iberian and Latin American Studies* 5, no. 1 (July 1999): 15–40; Thomas L. Whigham, *The Paraguayan War*, Volume 1: *Causes and Early Conduct* (Lincoln: University of Nebraska Press, 2002); Hendrik Kraay, "Slavery, Citizenship and Military Service in Brazil's Mobilization for the Paraguayan War," *Slavery and Abolition* 18, no. 3 (December 1997): 228–56; Diego Abente, "The War of the Triple Alliance: Three Explanatory Models," *Latin American Research Review* 22, no. 2 (1987), 47–69. For a thorough review of the extensive historiography related to the war, see Hendrik Kraay and Thomas L. Whigham, eds., *I Die With My Country: Perspectives on the Paraguayan War, 1864–1870* (Lincoln and London: University of Nebraska Press, 2004).

2. Kraay, "Slavery, Citizenship and Military Service," 249.

3. For a concise description of the law, see Robert Conrad, *The Destruction of Brazilian Slavery, 1850–1888* (Berkeley: University of California Press, 1972), 91.

4. Richard Graham, *Britain and the Onset of Modernization in Brazil, 1850–1914* (Cambridge: Cambridge University Press, 1968), 171.

5. *Discussão da reforma do estado servil na camara dos deputados e no senado, 1871*, vols. I and II (Rio de Janeiro: Typographia Nacional, 1871).

6. Martha Abreu, "Slave Mothers and Freed Children: Emancipation and Female Space in Debates on the 'Free Womb' Law, Rio de Janeiro, 1871," *Journal of Latin American Studies* 28, no. 3 (October 1996): 567.

7. Ricardo Salles, *Guerra do Paraguai: Escravidão e cidadania na formação do exército* (Rio de Janeiro: Paz e Terra, 1990), 20. Reasons for the outbreak of the war are analyzed in Salles, 25–37.

8. León Pomer, *La Guerra del Paraguay: Gran negocio!* (Buenos Aires: Ediciones Calden, 1968); Eduardo H. Galeano, *Open Veins of Latin America: Five Centuries of Pillage of a Continent*, trans. Cedric Belfage (New York: Monthly Review Press, 1973; first published in Spanish in 1971); Júlio José Chiavenato, *Genocídio americano: A Guerra do Paraguai* (São Paulo: Brasiliense, 1979); and E. Bradford Burns, *The Poverty of Progress: Latin America in the Nineteenth Century* (Berkeley: University of California Press, 1980), 128–31.

9. This short analysis is based on Kraay and Whigham, "Introduction," in *I Die With My Country*, 13–17.

10. Afrânio Peixoto, *Breviário da Bahia* (Rio de Janeiro: Ministério da Educação e Cultura, 1980), 2, 196, offers an estimate of at least 18,330 soldiers sent from Bahia, followed by 11,467 from the Corte (city of Rio de Janeiro), 7,851 from the province of Rio de Janeiro, 7,136 from Pernambuco, and 6,504 from São Paulo province. See Braz do Amaral, *História da Bahia do Império à República* (Bahia: Imprensa Official do Estado, 1923), 250, for a higher estimate of 40,000 sent from Bahia. An official estimate of 14,495 troops sent from Bahia up until December 1869 is provided by the commander of Bahian forces Luiz José Monteiro, "Relatório do Comm.do das armas da Bahia," Salvador, January 1, 1869, ANRJ/SPE, IG 1 253.

11. Kraay, "Slavery, Citizenship and Military Service," 229, 241.

12. Kraay, "Slavery, Citizenship and Military Service," 231, table 1; Peter M. Beattie, *The Tribute of Blood: Army, Honor, Race, and Nation in Brazil, 1864–1945* (Durham, NC: Duke University Press, 2001), 39–40.

13. Hendrik Kraay, "Patriotic Mobilization in Brazil: The Zuavos and Other Black Companies," in Kraay and Whigham, *I Die With My Country*, 62.

14. Manoel R. Querino, *A Bahia de outrora*, 3d ed. (Salvador: Livraria Progresso Editora, 1955), 170–73; *O Alabama* (Salvador), March 18, 1865, 1; Silio Boccanera Junior, "A Bahia na guerra do Paraguai," *Revista do Instituto Geográfico e Histórico da Bahia* 72 (1945), 141–88.

15. *O Alabama*, March 18, 1865, 1.

16. Marcellino José Calunhas to president, Muritiba, February 20, 1865, APEB/SACP, m. 3669.

17. Antônio Mariano de Bomfim to president, Chique-Chique, October 1, 1865, APEB/SACP, m. 3669; General Paulo de Queiroz Duarte, *Os voluntários da pátria na guerra do Paraguai* (Rio de Janeiro: Biblioteca do Exército, 1981), I, 206–7.

18. President Almeida to president of council of ministers (Prime Minister), Salvador, January 23, 1865, ANRJ/SPE, IJ 1 176; Beattie, *Tribute of Blood*, 45–52.

19. Correspondence that describes such attacks include President Veloso to minister of justice, Fortaleza, Ceará, January 31, 1868, ANRJ/SPE, IJ 1 275; President Meira to minister of justice, Natal, Rio Grande do Norte, March 31, 1865, ANRJ/SPE, IJ 1 294; President Pereira to minister of justice, Maceió, Alagaos, December 29, 1866, ANRJ/SPE, IJ 1 364; President Fonseca to minister of justice, Curitiba, Paraná, November 13, 1868, ANRJ/SPE, IJ 1 546.

20. Antônio de Carvalho Pinto to Barão de São Lourenço, Tapéra, December 3, 1868, APEB/SACP, m. 3634. See also Chief of Police Doria to president, Salvador, March 23, 1868, APEB/SACP, m. 5800; Chief of Police Vianna to president, Salvador, May 19, 1868, APEB/SACP, m. 5800.

21. Sidney Chalhoub, *Cidade febril: Cortiços e epidemias na corte imperial* (São Paulo: Companhia das Letras, 1996), 133.

22. Francisco Antônio d'Althaide to president, Salvador, February 9, 1866, APEB/SACP, m. 3671.

23. "Uma data gloriosa." *A ordem* (Cachoeira, Bahia), August 1, 1885, 1.

24. President Almeida to president of council of ministers (Prime Minister), Salvador, January 23, 1865, ANRJ/SPE, IJ 1 176.

25. Antônio Augusto da Fonseca to minister of justice, Paranaguá, Parana, September 19, 1868, ANRJ/SPE, IJ 1 546.

26. Richard Graham, "Free African Brazilians and the State in Slavery Times," in *Racial Politics in Contemporary Brazil*, ed. Michael Hanchard (Durham, NC: Duke University Press, 1999), 31–36.

27. Marcelo Santos Rodrigues, "Os involuntários da pátria," in *Encontro de História Brazil-Paraguai I* (Salvador: IGHB; Academia Paraguaya de la Historia, 2001), 245.

28. Eduardo Silva, "O Príncipe Obá, a guerra do Paraguai e a abolição da escravatura," in *Encontro de História Brazil-Paraguai I* (Salvador: IGHB; Academia Paraguaya de la Historia, 2001), 98.

29. J. Watson Webb to Secretary of State Seward, Petrópolis, August 25, 1868, USNA, M 121:35.

30. Silva, "O Príncipe Obá," 90.

31. Rodrigues, "Os involuntários da pátria," 229–57; Marcelo Santos Rodrigues, "Os (In)Voluntários da Pátria" (MA thesis, Federal University of Bahia, 2001).

32. Manoel Pinto da Rocha to president, Alagoinhas, Bahia, July 15 and 22, 1867, APEB/SACP, m. 3629.

33. Chief of Police Assis to president, Salvador, February 1, 1869, APEB/SACP, m. 5804; President Baron of São Lourenço to minister of justice, Salvador, February 9, 1869, ANRJ/SPE, IJ 1 418; *Jornal da Bahia* (Salvador), February 6, 1869, 1. See also Salles, *Guerra do Paraguai*, 81.

34. Mundinha Araújo, *Insurreição de escravos em Viana, 1867* (São Luis: SIOGE, 1994), 90.

35. Illegible to minister of justice, Belo Horizonte, May 28, 1867, ANRJ/SPE IJ 1 779.

36. Mário Maestri, "Pampa negro: Quilombos no Rio Grande do Sul," in *Liberdade por um fio: História dos quilombos no Brasil*, orgs. João José Reis and Flávio dos Santos Gomes (São Paulo: Companhia das Letras, 1996), 320; Roger Kittleson, "The Paraguayan War and Political Culture: Rio Grande do Sul, Brazil, 1865–1880," in Kraay and Whigham, *I Die With My Country*, 113.

37. Hebe Maria Mattos de Castro, *Das cores do silêncio: Os significados da liberdade no sudeste escravista; Brasil, século xix* (Rio de Janeiro: Arquivo Nacional, 1995), 98–115, 238–39.

38. Silva, "O Príncipe Obá," 96.

39. Júlio José Chiavenato, *Os voluntários da pátria (e outros mitos)* (São Paulo: Global Editora, 1983), 29–36; U.S. diplomat J. Watson Webb to Minister of Foreign Affairs José Maria Silva Paranhos, Rio de Janeiro, August [date illegible], 1868, AHI/Notas, 280/3/11. For a description of violent reactions among potential recruits in Argentina, see José Alfredo Fornos Peñalba, "Draft Dodgers, War Resisters and Turbulent Gauchos: The War of the Triple Alliance Against Paraguay," *The Americas* 38, no. 4 (April 1982): 470–76; George Reid Andrews, *The Afro-Argentines of Buenos Aires, 1800–1900* (Madison: University of Wisconsin Press, 1980), 113–37.

40. Querino, *A Bahia de outrora*, 183.

41. Chief of Police Galeão to president, Salvador, September 3, 1866, APEB/SACP, m. 5793.

42. *O Alabama*, February 23, 1869, 1; Chief of Police Galeão to president, Salvador, October 18, 1867, APEB/SACP, m. 5794.

43. Chief of Police Galeão to president, Salvador, July 10, 1867, APEB/SACP, m. 5794; Chief of Police P. F. Guimarães to Comm. das Armas Marechal de Campos, Salvador, June 16, 1865, APEB/SACP, m. 5785; Chief of Police Galeão to president, Salvador, October 18, 1867, APEB/SACP, m. 5794; Chief of Police Assis to president, Salvador, January 31 and April 22, 1870, APEB/SACP, m. 5809.

44. Police delegate to president, Salvador, July 18, 1866, APEB/SACP, m. 2996.

45. Chief of Police Assis to police delegates of the province, Salvador, April 20, 1869, APEB/SACP, m. 5869.

46. Romão de Aquino Gomes to president of Bahia, Salvador, January 23, February 3, March 5, March 16, and September 23, 1868, APEB/SACP, m. 3671.

47. Katia M. de Queirós Mattoso, *Bahia, século xix: Uma província no império*, trans. Yeda de Macedo Soares (Rio de Janeiro: Editora Nova Fronteira, 1992), 48.

48. Cezar Muniz, "Os mendigos," *O Alcáçar* (Salvador), January 1, 1871 (written in 1867), 6; author's translation.

49. Chief of Police Assis to president, Salvador, September 10, 1870, APEB/SACP, m. 5809. See also *O Alabama*, July 20, 1867, 1; Chief of Police Assis to president, Salvador, September 5, 1868, APEB/SACP, m. 5800; Chief of Police Espinheira to president, Salvador, May 11, 1872, APEB/SACP, m. 5818.

50. *O Alabama*, February 10, 1869, 2.

51. Luís Anselmo da Fonseca, *A escravidão, o clero e o abolicionismo*, edição fac-similar de 1887 (Recife: Editora Massangana, 1988), 204–9; José Alvares do Amaral, *Resumo cronológico e noticioso da província da Bahia*, 2d ed. (Salvador: Imprensa Official do Estado, 1922), 475.

52. "Aviso" *O Tribuno* (Recife), September 18, 1866, 5.

53. Graham, *Britain and the Onset of Modernization*, 29.

54. Chief of Police Bittencourt to police delegate of the first district, Salvador, January 15, 1865, APEB/SACP, m. 5784.

55. Bittencourt to president, December 16, 1864, APEB/SACP, m. 5782.

56. João José Reis and Eduardo Silva, *Negociação e conflito: A resistência negra no Brasil escravista,* 2d ed. (São Paulo: Companhia das Letras, 1999), 71–75.

57. Chief of Police Bittencourt to president, Salvador, December 16, 1864, APEB/SACP, m. 5782.

58. Police subdelegate [Illegible] of Conceição da Praia to chief of police, Salvador, June 28, 1871, APEB/SACP, m. 6241.

59. Anna Amélia Vieira Nascimento, *Dez freguesias da cidade do Salvador* (Salvador: FCEB/EGB, 1986), 65, 95–97.

60. Police delegate José Mattos to vice president, Campos, May 15, 1870, APERJ, collection 96, m. 4, pasta 1; Commandante Fabiano Pereira Santos to president, Rio de Janeiro, August 14, 1870, APERJ, collection 99, pasta 13, m. 24; Warren Dean, *Rio Claro: A Brazilian Plantation System* (Stanford, CA: Stanford University Press, 1976), 124–32; Flávio dos Santos Gomes, *Histórias de quilombolas: Mocambos e comunidades de senzalas no Rio de Janeiro, século xix* (Rio de Janeiro: Arquivo Nacional, 1995), 329–31. *Insensato* could also be translated as foolish, or unreasoning.

61. Clovis Moura, *Rebeliões da senzala: Quilombos, insurreições, guerrilhas* (Rio de Janeiro: Conquista, 1972), 204–5.

62. President Barros to minister of justice, São Paulo, December 15, 1869, ANRJ/SPE, IJ 1 525.

63. Vice President Vicente da Motta to minister of justice, São Paulo, April 28, 1871, ANRJ/SPE, IJ 1 527. See also Robert Wayne Slenes, "The Demography and Economics of Brazilian Slavery, 1850–1888" (PhD dissertation, Stanford University, 1975), 133, 549–50.

64. For a few representative documents, see President Francisco Castro to minister of justice, Recife, March 13, 1866, ANRJ/SPE, IJ 1 336; President Joaquim do Carmo to president of the council of ministers, Victoria, February 11, 1865, ANRJ/SPE, IJ 1 437; Vice President Dionysio Rezende to minister of justice, Victoria, September 24, 1870, ANRJ/SPE, IJ 1 439; President Franklin Menezes to minister of justice, São Luis, August 21, 1867, ANRJ/SPE, IJ 1 233; President José Maya to minister of justice, São Luis, June 16, 1871, ANRJ/SPE, IJ 1 236; Chief of Police José Danin to vice president, Belém, May 24, 1866, ANRJ/SPE, IJ 1 208; Vice President da Cunha to minister of justice, Porto Alegre, July 1, 1868, ANRJ/SPE, IJ 1 591. See also Matthias Rohrig Assunção, "Quilombos Maranhenses," in Reis and Gomes, *Liberdade por um fio*, 450–54; Araújo, *Insurreição de escravos em Viana, 1867*; Kittleson, "Paraguayan War," in Kraay and Whigham, *I Die With My Country*, 106–13.

65. José Murilo de Carvalho, *Teatro de sombras: A política imperial* (Rio de Janeiro: Editora UFRJ, Relume-Dumará, 1996), 301, n. 43.

66. *Discussão da reforma do estado servil na camara dos deputados e no senado: 1871* (August 1 to September 27), vol. II (Rio de Janeiro: Typographia Nacional, 1871), 495–96; Joaquim Nabuco, *Abolitionism: The Brazilian Antislavery Struggle*, trans. Robert Conrad (Urbana: University of Illinois Press, 1977), 53. See also Sidney Chalhoub, "Slaves, Freedmen and the Politics of Freedom in Brazil: The Experience of Blacks in the City of Rio," *Slavery and Abolition* 10, no. 3 (December 1989): 82; and "Trabalhos da conferência abolicionista de Paris em 1867," *O Abolicionista* (Salvador), July 31, 1871, 6–7.

67. "Reforma do estado servil: Discurso proferido no senado,' in *Estudos sobre a escravidão negra*, II, ed. Leonardo Dantas Silva (Recife: Editora Massangana, 1988), 267–68, 278–79. See also Emilia Viotti da Costa, *Crowns of Glory, Tears of Blood: The Demerara Slave Rebellion of 1823* (New York: Oxford University Press, 1994).

68. *Discussão da reforma*, 1871, vol. II, 537–38.

69. Baron of Cotegipe to Rio Branco, Rio de Janeiro, March 11, 1871, AHI, box 313, package 1, pasta 1.

70. Carvalho, *Teatro de sombras*, 282.

71. See the chapter entitled "The Negro Abolitionist Movement" in Arthur Ramos, *The Negro in Brazil*, trans. Richard Pattee (Washington, DC: The Associated Publishers, 1939), 66–79; and Dorothy B. Porter, "The Negro in the Brazilian Abolitionist Movement," *The Journal of Negro History* 27, no. 1 (January 1952): 54–80. For the United States after 1830, see Herbert Aptheker, *The Negro in the Abolitionist Movement* (New York: Atheneum, 1941); William S. McFeely, *Frederick Douglass* (New York: Touchstone, 1991); and Jane H. Pease and William H. Pease, *They Who Would Be Free: Blacks' Search for Freedom, 1830–1861* (Urbana: University of Illinois Press, 1990).

72. Gama used the term *Africana livre* to describe his mother in a letter he wrote in July 1880, suggesting that she was a freedwoman (*Africana liberta*). See Elciene Azevedo, *Orfeu de carapinha: A trajetória de Luiz Gama na imperial cidade de São Paulo* (Campinas, SP: Editora da Unicamp, 1999), 36.

73. Robert Krueger, "Luís Gama: Racism, Struggle and Canon" (paper presented at the 2000 meeting of the Latin American Studies Association in Miami, Florida) (available online).

74. Azevedo, *Orfeu de carapinha*, 66.

75. Ibid., 69.

76. *Diabo Coxo*, September 3, 1865, cited in Azevedo, *Abolitionism*, 136–37, n. 12.

77. Luiz Gama, "Luiz Gonzaga Pinto da Gama," *Correio Paulistano*, November 10, 1871, cited in Azevedo, *Orfeu de carapinha*, 131, 134.

78. President Barros to minister of justice, São Paulo, December 15, 1869, ANRJ/SPE, IJ 1 525; emphasis in the original.

79. James H. Kennedy, "Luiz Gama: Pioneer of Abolition in Brazil," *The Journal of Negro History* 59, no. 3 (July 1974): 263; Luiz Luna, *O negro na luta contra escravidão* (Rio de Janeiro: Editora Leitura, 1968), 190–91; Celia Maria Marinho de Azevedo, "Quem precisa de São Nabuco?," *Estudos Afro-Asiáticos* 23, no. 1 (2001): 85–97.

80. Cited in Silva, *Prince of the People*, 121.

81. Silva, *Prince of the People*, 73.

82. Silva, "O Príncipe Obá."

83. Silva, *Prince of the People*, 123–24. Dom Obá's words were published in *O Carbonário*, September 8, 1882, and June 8, 1883.

84. See Vivaldo da Costa Lima, "Um boicote de Africanas na Bahia do século dezenove" (paper presented at the Seminário de Tropicologia: trópico e história social, in Recife in 1988). The essay can be read online at http://www.tropicologia.org.br/conferencia/1988boicotes_africanos.html.

85. *O Alabama*, September 10, 1871, 2.

86. *O Alabama*, July 10, 1869, 3.

87. Hendrik Kraay, "Between Brazil and Bahia: Celebrating *Dois de Julho* in Nineteenth-Century Salvador," *Journal of Latin American Studies* 31, no. 2 (May 1999): 255–86.

88. *O Alabama*, January 23, 1869, 7; and April 22, 1870, 5.

89. *O Alabama*, November 10, 1869, 2. See also Dale T. Graden, "'So Much Superstition Among These People!': *Candomblé* and the Dilemmas of Afro-Bahian Intellectuals, 1864–1871," in *Afro-Brazilian Culture and Politics: Bahia, 1790s–1990s*, ed. Hendrik Kraay (Armonk, NY: M. E. Sharpe, 1998), 57–89.

90. President Luís Almeida to president of the council of ministers, Salvador, February 23, 1865, ANRJ/SPE, IJ 1 176.

91. "A lei no. 2040 de 28 de setembro de 1871," *O Alabama*, October 17, 1871, 1.

92. Satyro de Oliveira Dias, *O Duque de Caxias e a guerra do Paraguay: Estudo crítico-histórico* (Bahia: Typographia do *Diário*, 1870), 43–48.

93. Dias, *O Duque de Caxias*, 49. Manoel Bonfim shares such views in *O Brasil nação: Realidade e soberania Brasileira*, 2d ed. (Rio de Janeiro: Topbooks, 1996), 269–79.

94. Chief of Police Assis to president, Salvador, June 13, 1869, APEB/SACP, m. 5804.

95. Lúcia Maria Bastos Pereira das Neves and Humberto Fernandes Machado, *O império do Brasil* (Rio de Janeiro: Nova Fronteira, 1999), 410.

96. Thanks to Thomas Whigham for estimates of mortality rates and the financial costs of the war.

97. Abreu, "Slave Mothers"; Robert Conrad, *The Destruction of Brazilian Slavery, 1850–1888* (Berkeley: University of California Press, 1972), 70–89; Ricardo Salles, *Nostalgia imperial: A formação da identidade nacional no Brasil do segundo reinado* (Rio de Janeiro: Topbooks, 1996), 158–70.

98. "A lei no. 2040 de 28 de setembro de 1871," *O Alabama*, October 17, 1871, 1; emphasis in the original.

Chapter Four

1. Lizir Arcanjo Alves, org., *O ginásio baiano de Abílio César Borges: Antologia* (Salvador: Instituto Geográfico e Histórico da Bahia, 2000); Anísio Teixeira, "Um educador: Abílio César Borges," *Revista Brasileira de Estudos Pedagógicos* (Rio de Janeiro) 18, no. 47 (July/December 1952): 150–55; Xavier Marques, *Vida de Castro Alves*, 3d ed. (Rio de Janeiro: Topbooks, 1997), 35–47.

2. Antônio de Castro Alves, *The Major Abolitionist Poems: Antônio de Castro Alves*, ed. and trans. Amy A. Peterson (New York: Garland Publishing, 1990), xiii–xiv.

3. Jorge Amado, *ABC de Castro Alves*, 3d ed. (São Paulo: Martins, no date), 86.

4. Mário Maestri, *A segunda morte de Castro Alves: Genealogia crítica de um revisionismo* (Passo Fundo, Rio Grande do Sul: Editora Universitária da Universidade de Passo Fundo, 2000), 22–23. See also Maestri, "Castro Alves: Genealogia crítica de um revisionismo," *Continente Sul Sur* (Porto Alegre) 9 (November 1998): 293–320.

5. For a helpful overview of Castro Alves's travels, see Afrânio Peixoto, *Castro Alves: O poeta e o poema*, 5th ed. (São Paulo: Companhia Editora Nacional, 1976), 3–69.

6. This translation is by Madeleine Picciotto, "Workers and Slaves: The Rhetoric of Freedom in the Poetry of Walt Whitman and Antônio de Castro Alves" (PhD dissertation, Princeton University, 1985), 176.

7. Edison Carneiro, *Castro Alves: Uma interpretação política*, 2d ed. (1947; reprint, São Paulo: Andes, 1958), 178.

8. Thomas Braga, "Castro Alves and the New England Abolitionist Poets," *Hispania* 67, no. 4 (December 1984): 592.

9. Carneiro, *Castro Alves*, 66–68.

10. Chief of Police Galeão to president, Salvador, September 5, 1866, APEB/SACP, m. 5793.

11. *O Abolicionista* (Salvador), July 31, 1871, 1.

12. Picciotto, "Workers and Slaves," 175; Eliane Zagury, *Castro Alves: Tempo, vida, e obra* (Rio de Janeiro: Editorial Bruguera, 1971), 15–16.

13. "Espumas flutuantes," *O Alcáçar* (Salvador), January 1, 1871, 2.

14. David T. Haberly, *Three Sad Races: Racial Identity and National Consciousness in Brazilian Literature* (Cambridge: Cambridge University Press, 1983), 56–57.

15. Recent versions of *Os escravos* do not include the epic poem *A Cachoeira de Paulo Affonso*, which was included in the 1883 edition. See Castro Alves, *Os escravos* (São Paulo: Martins, 1972); and Alves, *Major Abolitionist Poems*. There is no English translation in a single volume of the poems that compose *Os escravos*.

16. Translation by Picciotto, "Workers and Slaves," 178.

17. Peixoto, *Castro Alves*, 116.

18. Carneiro, *Castro Alves*, 82; Sud Mennucci, *O precursor do abolicionismo no Brasil (Luís Gama)* (São Paulo: Companhia Editora Nacional, 1938); Robert

Edgar Conrad, *Children of God's Fire: A Documentary History of Black Slavery in Brazil* (Princeton, NJ: Princeton University Press, 1983), 467–69.

19. Translation by Picciotto, "Workers and Slaves," 234–36.

20. Translation by Thomas Braga in "Castro Alves," 587.

21. Translation by Amy A. Peterson in Alves, *Major Abolitionist Poems*, 15.

22. Haberly, *Three Sad Races*, 62; Carneiro, *Castro Alves*, 82–89.

23. President of Pernambuco Conde de Baependy to British Consul Bentinck W. Doyle, Recife, October 17, 1868, AHI, Ministerio da Justiça, 301/2/5. The document notes that the president had received word from British informants that there had been a landing on September 26, 1868, of 240 slaves on the island of Santo Aleixo along the southern coast of the province. There was also information of an expected landing of slaves sometime in the next month of December.

24. Robert W. Slenes, "The Brazilian Internal Slave Trade, 1850–1888: Regional Economies, Slave Experience, and the Politics of a Peculiar Market," in *The Chattel Principle: Internal Slave Trades in the Americas*, ed. Walter Johnson (New Haven, CT: Yale University Press, 2004), 330–31.

25. *Correio Paulistano* (São Paulo), August 1, 1869, 1–2; *Jornal da Tarde* (Rio de Janeiro), June 23, 1870, as cited in Castro Alves, *Os escravos*, edição facsimile of the 1921 edition (Rio de Janeiro: Francisco Alves, 1988), 149.

26. Myriam Fraga, *Leonídia: A musa infeliz do poeta Castro Alves* (Salvador: Casa de Palavras; Fundação Jorge Amado, 2002), 199.

27. Pedro Calmon, *Castro Alves: O poeta e a obra* (Rio de Janeiro: J. Olympio, 1973), 246, 252.

28. For insightful essays about Palmares, see articles by João Reis and Flávio Gomes, Pedro Paulo de Abreu Funari, Richard Price, Ronaldo Vainfas, and Silvia Hunold Lara in João José Reis and Flávio dos Santos Gomes, orgs., *Liberdade por um fio: História dos quilombos no Brasil* (São Paulo: Companhia das Letras, 1996), 9–109.

29. Translation by Picciotto, "Workers and Slaves," 238–39.

30. R. K. Kent, "Palmares: An African State in Brazil," *Journal of African History* 6, no. 2 (1965): 163.

31. The manuscript was never published in Nabuco's lifetime. In 1924, his widow gave the manuscript to the Instituto Histórico e Geográfico Brasileiro in Rio de Janeiro. In 1949, "A escravidão" was published in the *Revista do Instituto Histórico e Geográfico Brasileiro* 204 (July–September 1949), 3–106 (hereafter *RIHGB*). A more recent edition appeared as an essay in Leonardo Dantas Silva, org., "A escravidão" (Recife: Fundação Joaquim Nabuco, 1988).

32. Nabuco, "*A escravidão*," *RIHGB* 204 (1949), 90.

33. Carneiro, *Castro Alves*, 89.

34. Ibid., 89.

35. Translated by Thomas Braga, "France in the Poetry of Castro Alves," *Modern Language Studies* 16, no. 3 (1986): 128.

36. Jonas Correia, "Sentido heróico da poesia de Castro Alves," *RIHGB* 295 (August–June 1972): 200; Marques, *Vida de Castro Alves*, 133–35.

37. Translated by Braga, "France in the Poetry of Castro Alves," 129.

38. It was published on July 5, 1870, as cited in Calmon, *Castro Alves*, 248.

39. Emilio Federico Moran, *Rui e a abolição*, trans. Carly Silva (Rio de Janeiro: Fundação Casa de Rui Barbosa, 1983), 35.

40. Rui Barbosa, "A emancipação progride," in *Obras selectas de Rui Barbosa*, vol. 6 (Rio de Janeiro: Fundação Casa de Rui Barbosa, 1956), 13–17, cited in Picciotto, "Workers and Slaves," 159–60.

41. *O abolicionista* (Salvador), April 30, 1871, 1–2.

42. Francesca Miller, *Latin American Women and the Search for Social Justice* (Hanover, NH: University Press of New England, 1991), 96.

43. *Discussão da reforma do estado servil na camara dos deputados e no senado, 1871*, vol. I (Rio de Janeiro: Typographia Nacional, 1871), 127, 155.

44. Haberly, *Three Sad Races*, 64.

45. See Maestri, "Castro Alves," 305–13; Maestri, "A segunda morte," 56

46. Manoel Bomfim, *O Brasil nação: Realidade da soberania brasileira*, 2d ed. (Rio de Janeiro: Topbooks, 1996), 356–57, 364, 360; see all of 351–91.

47. Maestri, "Castro Alves," 313.

48. "Os proprietários e a emancipação," *O abolicionista*, July 31, 1871, 3.

49. Calmon, *Castro Alves*, 290.

50. "Decennario de Castro Alves," *A Illustração Bahiana* (Salvador), July 1881, 2–3; and "Discurso pronunciado na Faculdade de Medicina, por occasião de commemorar-se o decennario de Castro Alves, por Antônio da Cruz Cordeiro Junior," *A Illustração Bahiana*, July 1881, 5–6; *Homenagem do grémio litterário Castro Alves ao laureado poeta Bahiano Antônio de Castro Alves: 10 de Julho de 1881* (Rio de Janeiro: Typographia Nacional, 1881).

51. Braga, "France in the Poetry of Castro Alves," 122. See *Monumento a Castro Alves: Adeus, meu canto, introdução do poema Os escravos; Recitada no concerto realisado no Theatro São João a 28 de setembro de 1894* (Bahia: Typographia *Diário da Bahia*, 1894); and the statement entitled "Os intelectuais Brasileiros e Castro Alves," signed on March 14, 1947, to celebrate the centenary of the poet's birth in Carneiro, *Castro Alves*, 187–93.

52. Carneiro, *Castro Alves*, 22.

53. Celia M. Azevedo, *Abolitionism in the United States and Brazil: A Comparative Perspective* (New York: Garland Publishing, 1995), 63.

Chapter Five

1. Zeca Ligièro, "Candomblé is Religion-Life-Art," in Phyllis Galembo, *Divine Inspiration: From Benin to Bahia* (Albuquerque: University of New Mexico Press, 1993), 102; Rachael E. Harding, *A Refuge in Thunder: Candomblé and Alternative Spaces of Blackness* (Bloomington: Indiana University Press, 2000), 38–39. Thanks to Dr. Harding for sending me a copy of her dissertation while I was writing this book.

2. Pierre Verger, *Notas sobre o culto aos orixás e voduns na Bahia de Todos os Santos, no Brasil, e na antiga costa dos escravos, na África*, trans. Carlos Eugênio Marcondes de Moura (São Paulo: Editora da Universidade de São Paulo, 1999), 24.

3. Rachel Harding offers a helpful overview of studies of Candomblé in *A Refuge in Thunder*. For other descriptions of Bahian Candomblé, see Jorge Amado, *Jubiabá* (1935; reprint, Lisbon: Livros do Brasil, 1977); Jorge Amado, *Tent of Miracles*, trans. Barbara Shelby (New York: Alfred A. Knopf, 1971; originally published as *Tenda dos milagres: Romance* [São Paulo: Martins, 1969]); Lindsay Hale, "Hot Breath, Cold Spirit: Performance and Belief in a Brazilian Spirit Religion" (PhD dissertation, University of Texas, 1994); Angela Luhning, "'Acabe com este santo, Pedrito vem aí': Mito e realidade da perseguição policial ao *candomblé* baiano entre 1920 e 1942," *Revista USP* 28 (December 1995–February 1996): 194–220; Joseph M. Murphy, *Working the Spirit: Ceremonies of the African Diaspora* (Boston: Beacon Press, 1994), 44–80; Abdias do Nascimento, *Orishas: The Living Gods of Africa in Brazil* (Rio de Janeiro: IPEAFRO, 1995); Mikelle Smith Omari, *From the Inside to the Outside: The Art and Ritual of Bahian Candomblé* (Los Angeles: Museum of Cultural History, UCLA, 1984); James W. Wafer, *The Taste of Blood: Spirit Possession in Brazilian Candomblé* (Philadelphia: University of Pennsylvania Press, 1991); J. Lorand Matory, " Imagining Nations and Races—The English Professors of Brazil: On the Diasporic Roots of the Yoruba Nation," *Comparative Studies in Society and History* 41, no. 1 (1999): 72–103; João José Reis, "Candomblé in Nineteenth-Century Bahia: Priests, Followers, Clients," *Slavery and Abolition* 22, no. 1 (April 2001): 116–34.

4. Harding, *Refuge in Thunder*, 46; Pierre Verger, *Notícias da Bahia, 1850* (Salvador: Corrupio, 1981), 227; João José Reis, "Magia jeje na Bahia: A invasão do calundu do Pasto de Cachoeira, 1785," *Revista Brasileira de Historía* 8, no. 16 (1988): 60–61; João José Reis, "Nas malhas do poder escravista: A invasão do

candomblé do Accú na Bahia, 1829," *Religião e Sociedade* 13, no. 3 (1986): 108–27. This same article is included in João José Reis and Eduardo Silva, *Negociação e conflito: A resistência negra no Brasil escravista* (São Paulo: Companhia das Letras, 1989), 32–61.

5. See Verger, *Notas sobre o culto*, 41–79.

6. Fortunato d'Andrade to chief of police, Salvador, September 17, 1877, APEB/SACP, m. 6245. Helpful insights with regards to African divination and the tensions it provoked in colonial Brazil are provided in James H. Sweet, *Recreating Africa: Culture, Kinship, and Religion in the African-Portuguese World, 1441–1770* (Chapel Hill: University of North Carolina Press, 2003), 119–230.

7. *O Alabama*, March 6, 1867, 2.

8. Subdelegate of the parish of Pilar Manoel Francisco Borges Leitão to chief of police, Salvador, April 4, 1853, APEB/SACP, m. 6230.

9. See, for example, João José Reis, "'The Revolution of the *Ganhadores*': Urban Labour, Ethnicity and the African Strike of 1857 in Bahia, Brazil," *Journal of Latin American Studies* 29, no. 2 (May 1997): 355–93.

10. Police subdelegate of the parish of Sé Joaquim Antônio Moutinho to chief of police, Salvador, November 4, 1855, APEB/SACP, m. 6231.

11. For a description of Imperial Decree of December 14, 1830 which allowed for a penalty of eight days in jail for illegal travel at night, see *Legislação da província da Bahia sobre o negro: 1835–1888* (Salvador: FCEB, 1996), 21. For one example of many "resolutions" of the provincial assembly against *batuques*, see "*Resolução de 15 de junho de 1855*," in *Legislação*, 126.

12. Inspector Francisco de Moura Rozal of Santo Antônio to police subdelegate, Salvador, October 21, 1855, APEB/SACP, m. 6231.

13. Chief of Police A. M. de Aragão e Mello to president, Salvador, February 10, 1859, APEB/SACP, m. 5730.

14. Reis and Silva, *Negociação e conflito*, 45–47.

15. Police delegate F. C. Raiz de Castro to secretary of police, Salvador, April 29, 1859, APEB/SACP, m. 5726.

16. "A Pedido," [sic] *O Alabama*, December 11, 1866, 3; *O Alabama*, March 6, 1867, 2–3; Chief of Police A. Ferreira Espinheira to Subdelegate of 2d district of Santo Antônio, Salvador, April 17, 1873, APEB/SACP, m. 5819. See also a description of white participants in Candomblé from Xavier Marques, *O feitiçeiro* (São Paulo: GRD INL, 1975; originally published with title of *Boto & Cia* in 1897), in Giorgio Marotti, *Black Characters in the Brazilian Novel*, trans. Maria O. Marotti and Harry Lawton (Los Angeles: UCLA Center for Afro-American Studies, 1987), 138.

17. *O Alabama*, June 29, 1864, 1.

18. Police delegate João Joaquim da Silva to president, Salvador, March 27, 1848, APEB/SACP, m. 3113.

19. Police subdelegate in parish of Santo Antônio João de Azevedo Piapitinga to chief of police, Salvador, April 26, 1862, APEB/SACP, m. 6195.

20. *Legislação da província da Bahia sobre o negro*, 130.

21. Subdelegate Piapitinga to chief of police, Salvador, May 16, 1862, APEB/ SACP, m. 6195.

22. Katia M. de Queirós Mattoso, *Bahia, século xix: Uma província no império*, trans. Yeda de Macedo Soares (Rio de Janeiro: Editora Nova Fronteira, 1992), 453–54.

23. João José Reis, "Quem manda em Salvador? Governo local e conflito social na greve de 1857 e no motim de 1858 na Bahia," in *O município no mundo Português: Seminário internacional* (Funchal, Madeira: Centro de Estudos de História do Atlântico, 1998), 665–76.

24. APEB/SACP, m. 5723.

25. Chief of Police J. B. Madureira to president, Salvador, March 1 and March 11, 1858, APEB/SACP, m. 5723; Chief of Police Leão to president, Salvador, June 18, 1858, APEB/SACP, m. 5723.

26. Baron of São João do Principe to president of the Province of Rio de Janeiro, Rio de Janeiro, June 15, 1859, APERJ, collection 174, maço 49, pasta 22; emphasis in the original.

27. Police delegate Justiniano Baptista Madureira to chief of police of the province of Rio de Janeiro, Rio de Janeiro, December 13, 1858, APERJ, collection 100, pasta 15, maço 26. For a helpful analysis of slave resistance in the interior of the province of Rio de Janeiro at the end of the 1850s, see Flávio dos Santos Gomes, *Histórias de quilombolas: Mocambos e comunidades de senzalas no Rio de Janeiro, século xix* (Rio de Janeiro: Arquivo Nacional, 1995), 99–109.

28. Robert Edgar Conrad, *World of Sorrow: The African Slave Trade to Brazil* (Baton Rouge: Louisiana State University Press, 1986), 173–74.

29. See Gilberto Freyre, *The Masters and the Slaves: A Study in the Development of Brazilian Civilization*, trans. Samuel Putnam (Berkeley: University of California Press, 1986); Richard Graham, *Patronage and Politics in Nineteenth-Century Brazil* (Stanford, CA: Stanford University Press, 1990).

30. Chief of Police J. P. da Silva Moraes to president of the Tribunal Manoel Messias de Leão, Salvador, March 4, 1861, APEB/SACP, m. 5742.

31. *O Alabama*, September 2, 1868, 1.

32. *O Alabama*, December 24, 1870, 5.

33. *O Alabama*, September 23, 1864, 1–2.

34. Reis and Silva, *Negociação e conflito*, 37–40, discusses the reactionary stance of president of the province Conde da Ponte and the more open response of the president of the province Conde dos Arcos to Candomblé in the late 1820s.

35. See *Legislação da província*, 126–50, covering the years June 1855 to May 1883.

36. *O Alabama*, May 13, 1869, 2. For one of many examples of descriptions that specifically note *licenças* (licenses, permits) signed by the police, see *O Alabama*, July 17, 1869, 3.

37. *O Alabama*, March 6, 1867, 2–3.

38. Donald Pierson, *Brancos e prêtos na Bahia*, 2d ed. (São Paulo: Companhia Editora Nacional, 1971), 307.

39. Mieko Nishida, "From Ethnicity to Race and Gender: Transformations of Black Lay Sodalities in Salvador, Brazil," *Journal of Social History* 32, no. 2 (winter 1998): 329–48.

40. *O Alabama*, July 27, 1865, 2.

41. Roger Bastide, *O candomblé da Bahia: (rito Nagô)*, trans. Maria Isaura Pereira de Queiroz, 3d ed. (São Paulo: Editora Nacional, 1978), 89–90. Thanks to Randy Matory for offering helpful insights about the New Yam Festival.

42. *O Alabama*, March 6, 1867, 2–3.

43. *O Alabama*, November 24, 1871, 4.

44. *O Alabama*, March 6, 1867, 2–3. See Dale T. Graden, "'So Much Superstition Among These People!': Candomblé and the Dilemmas of Afro-Bahian Intellectuals, 1864–1871," in *Culture and Politics in Nineteenth- and Twentieth-Century Afro-Bahia*, ed. Hendrik Kraay (New York: M. E. Sharpe, 1998), 70–71.

45. *O Alabama*, November 21, 1871, 3.

46. *O Alabama*, October 8, 1868, 1.

47. *O Alabama*, November 11, 1871, 4.

48. Reginaldo Prandi, *Herdeiras do axé* (São Paulo: Editora Hucitec, 1996), 38–39.

49. The definition is by André Malvar from the Catholic University of Salvador in "Candomblé recepciona calouros," *Correio da Bahia* (Salvador), February 22, 2000, 3.

50. *O Alabama*, February 18, 1864, 1.

51. *O Alabama*, May 2, 1867, 2–3.

52. *O Alabama*, May 6, 1869, 3–4.

53. *O Alabama*, April 19, 1866, 1–2.

54. *O Alabama*, January 26, 1864, 1.

55. *Dicionário de Português-Inglês* (Porto: Porto Editora LDA., 1983), 510.

56. "A Pedido," [sic] O *Alabama*, December 11, 1866, 2–3.

57. Um que não gosta, "Ao Illm. Sr. Dr. chefe de polícia," O *Alabama*, November 18, 1864, 4.

58. O *Alabama*, February 10, 1869, 2.

59. O *Alabama*, January 11, 1868, 1.

60. O *Alabama*, February 10, 1869, 2.

61. Paul E. Lovejoy, "Background to Rebellion: The Origins of Muslim Slaves in Bahia," *Slavery and Abolition* 15, no. 2 (August 1994): 157, 170.

62. O *Óculo Mágico* (Salvador), October 11, 1866, cited in Ana de Lourdes da Costa, "EKABÓ: Trabalho escravo, condições de moradia e reordenamento urbano em Salvador no século xix" (MA thesis, Federal University of Bahia, 1989), 134.

63. Chief of Police Carvalho to president, Salvador, August 8, 1877, APEB/SACP, m. 5836.

64. Lisa A. Lindsay, "'To Return to the Bosom of their Fatherland': Brazilian Immigrants in Nineteenth-Century Lagos," *Slavery and Abolition* 15, no. 1 (April 1994): 25. For insightful perspectives describing the return of Africans from Brazil to West Africa and extensive bibliography, see José C. Curto and Renée Soulodre-La France, "Introduction: Interconnections between Africa and the Americas during the Era of the Slave Trade," in *Africa and the Americas: Interconnections During The Slave Trade*, eds. José C. Curto and Renée Soulodre-La France (Trenton, NJ: Africa World Press, 2005), 1–11.

65. Matory, "Imagining Nations," 96.

66. Ibid., 83, 85.

67. Harding, *Refuge in Thunder*, 157.

68. Matory, "Imaging Nations," 74.

69. Maria Helena Machado, O *plano e o pânico: Os movimentos sociais na década de abolição* (Rio de Janeiro: Editora da UFRJ, EDUSP, 1994), 91–107.

Chapter Six

1. Carlos Eugênio Líbano Soares and Flávio Gomes, "'Com o pé sobre um vulcão': Africanos Minas, identidades e a repressão antiafricana no Rio de Janeiro (1830–1840)," *Estudos Afro-Asiáticos* 23, no. 2 (2001), 346; João José Reis, *Slave Rebellion in Brazil: The Muslim Uprising of 1835 in Bahia*, trans. Arthur Brakel (Baltimore, MD: Johns Hopkins University Press, 1993), 222.

2. Kátia M. de Queirós Mattoso, Herbert S. Klein, and Stanley L. Engerman, "Trends and Patterns in the Prices of Manumitted Slaves: Bahia, 1819–1888," *Slavery and Abolition* 7, no. 1 (May 1986): 61; Robert W. Slenes, "The Brazilian Internal Slave Trade, 1850–1888: Regional Economies, Slave Experience, and the

Politics of a Peculiar Market," in *The Chattel Principle: Internal Slave Trades in the Americas*, ed. Walter Johnson (New Haven, CT: Yale University Press, 2004), 327–29, 333–37.

3. Slenes, "The Brazilian Internal Slave Trade," 331; Robert Edgar Conrad, *World of Sorrow: The African Slave Trade to Brazil* (Baton Rouge: Louisiana State University Press, 1986), 179, 181.

4. See Erivaldo Fagundes Neves, "Sampauleiros traficantes: Comércio de escravos do alto sertão da Bahia para o oeste cafeeiro paulista," *Afro-Ásia* 24 (2000): 97–128; Chief of Police F. A. de Castro Loureiro to police subdelegates, Salvador, October 21, 1880, APEB/SACP, m. 5869.

5. Slenes, "The Brazilian Internal Slave Trade," 341–42.

6. Herbert S. Klein, "The Internal Slave Trade in Nineteenth-Century Brazil: A Study of Slave Importations into Rio de Janeiro in 1852," *Hispanic American Historical Review* 51, no. 4 (1971): 572; Robert Conrad, *The Destruction of Brazilian Slavery, 1850–1888* (Berkeley: University of California Press, 1972), 61; Neves, "Sampauleiros traficantes," 102.

7. Klein, "Internal Slave Trade," 571; Richard Graham, "Nos tumbeiros mais uma vez? O comércio interprovincial de escravos no Brasil," *Afro-Ásia* 27 (2002): 136.

8. "Escravos despachados para Rio de Janeiro, mediante o imposto de exportação," *O Monitor* (Salvador), July 1, 1877, to October 2, 1877.

9. Sandra Lauderdale Graham, "Slavery's Impasse: Slave Prostitutes, Small-Time Mistresses, and the Brazilian Law of 1871," *Comparative Studies in Society and History* 33, no. 4 (1991): 671–72, 680–81.

10. *Annaes da Assembléia Legislativa Provincial da Bahia: Sessões do anno de 1880* (Bahia: Typographia do *Diario da Bahia*, 1880), 263.

11. Ibid., 264.

12. Ibid., 211; Consul Richard Edes to William Hunter, Salvador, December 15, 1879, USNA, T 331:4; C. C. Andrews to William Hunter, Rio de Janeiro, April 14, 1884, T 172:25; Michiel Baud and Kees Koonings, "*A lavoura dos pobres*: Tobacco Farming and the Development of Commercial Agriculture in Bahia, 1870–1930," *Journal of Latin American Studies* 31, no. 2 (May 1999): 287–329; Mary Ann Mahony, "'Instrumentos necessários': Escravidão e posse de escravos no sul da Bahia no século xix, 1822–1899," *Afro-Ásia* 25–26 (2001): 95–139; B. J. Barrickman, "Até a véspera: O trabalho escravo e a produção de açúcar nos engenhos do Recôncavo baiano (1850–1881)," *Afro-Ásia* 21–22 (1998–99): 177–237; Eul-Soo Pang, *O engenho central do Bom Jardim na economia baiana: Alguns aspectos de sua história, 1873–1891* (Rio de Janeiro: AN/IHGB, 1979).

13. "A exportação de escravos," *O Monitor*, June 27, 1876, 1.

14. Robert W. Slenes, "The Demography and Economics of Brazilian Slavery: 1850–1888" (PhD dissertation, Stanford University, 1976), 207–8, 366–68.

15. Conrad, *World of Sorrow*, 186; Evaldo Cabral de Mello, "O norte, o sul e a proibição do tráfico interprovincial de escravos," in *Estudos sobre a escravidão negra*, vol. I, ed. Leonardo Dantas Silva (Recife: Editora Massangana, 1988), 508–10.

16. Conrad, *Destruction of Brazilian Slavery*, 170–71.

17. Paula Beiguelman, *A formação do povo no complexo cafeeiro: Aspectos políticos*, 2d ed. (São Paulo: Pioneira, 1977), 33–38.

18. Celia Maria Marinho de Azevedo, *Onda negra, medo branco: O negro no imaginário das elites, século xix* (Rio de Janeiro: Paz e Terra, 1987), 112–13; Richard Graham, "*Another Middle Passage?*: The Internal Slave Trade in Brazil," in *The Chattel Principle: Internal Slave Trades in the Americas*, ed. Walter Johnson (New Haven, CT: Yale University Press, 2004), 303–11; Slenes, "Brazilian Internal Slave Trade," 352–56.

19. Judge Eduardo Lindahiba de Mateos to president, Barra Mansa, Rio de Janeiro, June 22, 1876, APERJ, collection 82.

20. Petition signed by more than eight hundred *fazendeiros* from Nova Friburgo, Sapucaia, Magdalena, and Cantagallo to president, December 28, 1877, APERJ, collection 174, maço 50, pasta 22.

21. Maria Helena Machado, *O plano e o pânico: Os movimentos sociais na década da abolição* (São Paulo: Editora UFRJ/EDUSP, 1994).

22. Marcelo Santos Rodrigues, "Os involuntários da pátria," in *Encontro de História Brazil-Paraguai I* (Salvador: IGHB; Academia Paraguaya de la Historia, 2001), 238.

23. Chief of Police A. B. F. de Carvalho to police subdelegates, Salvador, May 4, 1877, APEB/SACP, m. 5869.

24. Graham, "*Another Middle Passage?*" 315.

25. Richard Graham writes that "the abolitionist movement was centered in the cities of Rio de Janeiro and São Paulo, not in the Northeast" (Graham, "*Another Middle Passage?*" 323, n. 77).

26. See Isabel Cristina Ferreira dos Reis, *Histórias de vida familiar e afetiva de escravos na Bahia do século xix* (Salvador: Centro de Estudos Baianos, 2001), 47–90.

27. Walter Johnson, *Soul by Soul: Life Inside the Antebellum Slave Market* (Cambridge, MA: Harvard University Press, 1999), 20.

28. Chief of Police Magalhães to president, Salvador, April 6, 1876, APEB/SACP, m. 5828; Magalhães to president, Salvador, September 21, 1876,

APEB/SACP, m. 5832; Chief of Police Carvalho to police subdelegates of Salvador, Salvador, June 8, 1877, APEB/SACP, m. 5869.

29. Jacob Gorender, *A escravidão reabilitada* (São Paulo: Editora Ática, 1990), 158–59. emphasis in the original.

30. Chief of Police Espinheira to president, Salvador, August 1, 1871, APEB/SACP, m. 5811.

31. Katia M. de Queirós Mattoso, *Bahia, século xix: Uma província no império*, trans. Yeda de Macedo Soares (Rio de Janeiro: Editora Nova Fronteira, 1992), 454.

32. President Barão Homem de Mello to Minister of Empire (Interior), Salvador, March 30, 1878, ANRJ/SPE, IJ 9 349.

33. President Mello to minister of justice, Salvador, June 4, 1878, ANRJ/SPE, IJ 1 427.

34. Jailton L. Brito, *A abolição na Bahia, 1870–1888* (Salvador: Centro de Estudos Baianos, 2003), 133–44.

35. Chief of Police Magalhães to president, Salvador, August 5, 1876, APEB/SACP, m. 5832; Chief of Police Carvalho to president, Salvador, April 16 and May 3, 1877, APEB/SACP, m. 5832.

36. APEB/Justiça, package 2594, process 2, Salvador, 1873.

37. Teodoro Sampaio, "O abolicionismo," unpublished manuscript, Instituto Geográfico e Histórico da Bahia (hereafter IGHB), I, 8.

38. Brito, *A abolição na Bahia*, 64.

39. Conrad, *Destruction of Brazilian Slavery*, 214; Barrickman, "Até a véspera," 194.

40. Walter Fraga Filho, "Histórias e reminiscências da morte de um senhor no Recôncavo," *Afro-Ásia* 24 (2000): 182. The document is from 1882, but it depicts the common experience of slaves from the interior of the province visiting Salvador in the 1870s and earlier.

41. Chief of Police Espinola to president, Salvador, May 29, 1874, APEB/SACP, m. 5824.

42. Police delegate (illegible) to chief of police A. Ferreira Espinheira, Inhambupe, September 7, 1871, APEB/SACP, m. 6208; Police delegate to Espinheira, Matta de São João, November 20, 1871, APEB/SACP, m. 5818; Police delegate Angelo José de Sá to chief of police, Abrantes, January 9, 1872, APEB/SACP, m. 6209; Police subdelegate to chief of police, Rica do Passo, March 29, 1877, APEB/SACP, m. 6245.

43. Police delegate Claudeo de Araujo Goes to chief of police, Nazareth, June 18, 1876, APEB/SACP, m. 6213.

44. Hebe Maria Mattos de Castro, *Das cores do silêncio: Os significados da liberdade no sudeste escravista; Brasil, século xix* (Rio de Janeiro: Arquivo Nacional, 1995), 181; Maria Helena P. T. Machado, *Crime e escravidão: Trabalho, luta e resistência nas lavouras paulistas, 1830–1888* (São Paulo: Editora Brasiliense, 1987), 90–94.

45. *A república* (Rio de Janeiro), September 14, 1872, 1. Thanks to Hendrik Kraay for bringing this article to my attention.

46. Police delegate Ireneo de Mascarvenhas Nogueira to chief of police, Taperoá, June 29, 1872, APEB/SACP, m. 6209.

47. Police delegate Dr. Ulises Leonesi Dantas to president, São Francisco do Conde, September 5, 1878, ANRJ/SPE, IJ 1 427.

48. Police delegate Dantas to president, São Francisco do Conde, September 12, 1878, APEB/SACP, m. 2998.

49. President Mello to Minister of Empire (Interior), Salvador, September 24, 1878, ANRJ/SPE, IJ 9 349.

50. David Eltis, *The Rise of African Slavery in the Americas* (Cambridge: Cambridge University Press, 2000), 284.

51. Hendrik Kraay, *Race, State, and Armed Forces in Independence-Era Brazil: Bahia (1790s–1840s)* (Stanford, CA: Stanford University Press, 2002), 4. An extensive historiography focuses on ties between expanding capitalism in Brazil in the nineteenth century and abolition. Important works include Roger Bastide and Florestan Fernandes, *Brancos e negros em São Paulo*, 2d ed. (São Paulo: Companhia Editôra Nacional, 1959); Fernando Henrique Cardoso and Octávio Ianni, *Côr e mobilidade social em Florianópolis: Aspectos das relações entre negros e brancos numa comunidade meridional* (São Paulo: Companhia Editôra Nacional, 1960); Fernando Henrique Cardoso, *Capitalismo e escravidão no Brasil meridional: O negro na sociedade do Rio Grande do Sul* (São Paulo: Difusão Européia do Livro, 1962); Octávio Ianni, *As metamórfoses do escravo: Apogeu e crise da escravatura no Brasil meridional* (São Paulo: Difusão Européia do Livro, 1962); Emília Viotti da Costa, *Da senzala à colônia* (São Paulo: Difusão Européia do Livro, 1966); Richard Graham, "Causes for the Abolition of Negro Slavery in Brazil: An Interpretative Essay," in *Hispanic American Historical Review* 46 (1966): 123–38; Richard Graham, *Britain and the Onset of Modernization in Brazil, 1850–1914* (Cambridge: Cambridge University Press, 1968); Beiguelman, *A formação do povo*.

52. See Lilia Moritz Schwarcz, *O espetáculo das raças: Cientistas, instituições e questão racial no Brasil, 1870–1930* (São Paulo: Companhia das Letras, 1993); Sidney Chalhoub, *Cidade febril: Cortiços e epidemias na corte imperial* (São Paulo: Companhia das Letras, 1996), 92–93; and E. Bradford Burns, *A History*

of Brazil, 3d ed. (New York: Columbia University Press, 1993), 157–71.

53. Manoel Pinto de Aguiar, "Notas sôbre o 'enigma baiano,'" *Planejamento* 5, no. 4 (October/December 1977): 129; Eduardo Carigé, *Geographia, physica e política da província da Bahia* (Bahia: Imprensa Económica, 1882), 40.

54. Satyro de Oliveira Dias, *O Duque de Caxias e a guerra do Paraguay: Estudo crítico-histórico* (Bahia: Typographia do *Diário*, 1870), 12.

55. Dr. Polycarpo Lopes de Leão, *Como pensa sobre o elemento servil* (Rio de Janeiro: Typographia Perseverança, 1870), 7–9.

56. Eliana Bittencourt Dumêt, *O semeador de idéias: O pensamento, a vida e a obra de Luiz Tarquínio, um empresário de idéias revolucionárias em pleno século xix* (São Paulo: Editora Gente, 1999), 17–20.

57. Cincinnatus (Luís Tarquínio), *O elemento escravo e as questões económicas do Brazil* (Bahia: Typographia dos Dois Mundos, 1885); Dumêt, *O semeador*, 95–102.

58. Anyda Marchant, *Viscount Mauá and the Empire of Brazil: A Biography of Irineu Evangelista de Sousa (1813–1889)* (Berkeley: University of California Press, 1965).

59. Dumêt, *O semeador*, 73–83.

60. Brito, *A abolição na Bahia*, 109–10.

61. Leão, *Como pensa sobre o elemento servil*, 12–13.

62. Ibid., 9.

63. Brito, *A abolição na Bahia*, 106–7.

64. D. T. Haberly, "Abolitionism in Brazil: Anti-Slavery and Anti-Slave," *Luso-Brazilian Review* 9, no. 2 (1972): 30–46.

65. Celia Maria Marinho de Azevedo, "Batismo da liberdade: Os abolicionistas e o destino do negro," *História: Questões e debates* 9, no. 16 (January 1988): 52; Celia Maria Marinho de Azevedo, "Quem precisa de São Nabuco?," *Estudos Afro-Asiáticos* 23, no. 1 (2001): 85–97; Machado, *O plano e o pânico*, 54; Castro, *Das cores do silêncio*, 236, 251.

66. Eul-Soo Pang, "Modernization and Slavocracy in Nineteenth-Century Brazil," *Journal of Interdisciplinary History* 9, no. 4 (spring 1979): 681.

67. *Cartas de Vindex ao Dr. Luis Alvares dos Santos publicadas no Diário da Bahia* (Bahia: Typographia do *Diário*, 1875), 19, 15.

68. Conrad, *Destruction of Brazilian Slavery*, 135; Lana Lage da Gama Lima, *Rebeldia negra e abolicionismo* (Rio de Janeiro: Achiamé, 1981), 97–100.

69. Sampaio manuscript, "O abolicionismo," IGHB, I, 8.

70. Conrad, *Destruction of Brazilian Slavery*, 137–41.

Chapter Seven

1. Luís Anselmo da Fonseca, *A escravidão, o clero e o abolicionismo*, edição fac-similar de 1887 (Recife: Editora Massangana, 1988), 135.

2. See note 8 in introduction, along with Jacob Gorender, *A escravidão reabilitada* (São Paulo: Editora Ática, 1990). For historiographic essays, see Ciro Flamarion Cardoso, org., *Escravidão e abolição no Brasil: Novas perspectivas* (Rio de Janeiro: Jorge Zahar Editor Ltda., 1988), 73–110; and João José Reis, "Abolicionismo e resistência escrava," *Revista da Bahia* 14 (September/November 1989): 13–20.

3. Chief of Police Carvalho Albuquerque to police delegate in Nazareth, Salvador, June 14, 1882, APEB/SACP, m. 5852; Albuquerque to delegates in several interior towns, Salvador, May 23, 1882, APEB/SACP, m. 5852.

4. J. A. Gomes to police delegate in Nazareth, Salvador, January 25, 1883, APEB/SACP, m. 5856.

5. Unpublished notes, AMHN, Wanderley Pinho collection (hereafter WPC), Box 2, Document 9.

6. João da Silva Campos, "Tradições Bahianas," *Revista do Instituto Geográfico e Histórico da Bahia* (hereafter *RIGHB*) 56 (1930): 377–78.

7. Walter Fraga Filho, "Histórias e reminiscências da morte de um senhor no Recôncavo," *Afro-Ásia* 24 (2000): 184–98.

8. Arnold Wildberger, *Os presidentes da província da Bahia* (Salvador: Typographia Beneditina, 1949), 325.

9. Police delegate to chief of police Magalhães, Viçosa, January 27, 1876, APEB/SACP, m. 6164.

10. Police delegate at Colônia Leopoldina to chief of police, Viçosa, September 4, 5, 7, and 23, 1882, APEB/SACP, m. 6219; Fermino Bernardo de Mottas to president, Viçosa, September 20, 1882, APEB/SACP, m. 2638.

11. José Alípio Goulart, *Da fuga ao suicídio* (Rio de Janeiro: Editora Conquista, 1972), 164–65.

12. José Machado Pedreira to president, Viçosa, May 7, 1884, APEB/SACP, m. 2638.

13. Leon F. Litwack, *North of Slavery: The Negro in the Free States, 1790–1860* (Chicago: University of Chicago Press, 1961); Benjamin Quarles, *Black Abolitionists* (New York: Oxford University Press, 1969); R. J. M. Blackett, *Building an Anti-Slavery Wall: Black Americans in the Atlantic Abolitionist Movement* (Baton Rouge: Louisiana State University Press, 1983).

14. Manuel Raimundo Querino, *The African Contribution to Brazilian Civilization*, trans. E. Bradford Burns (Tempe: Arizona State University, Center for Latin American Studies, 1978), 1. See also Manoel R. Querino, *As artes na*

Bahia: Escorço de uma contribuição histórica, 2d ed. (Bahia: Oficinas do *Diário da Bahia,* 1913).

15. R. Magalhães Junior, *A vida turbulenta de José do Patrocínio* (Rio de Janeiro: Editora Sabiá, 1969); José do Patrocínio, *Campanha abolicionista: Coletânea de artigos* (Rio de Janeiro: Fundação Biblioteca Nacional, 1996); Club dos libertos contra a escravidão, *Homenagem a José do Patrocíncio* (Rio de Janeiro: Typographia Central de Evaristo Rodrigues da Costa, 1883); Confederação Abolicionista, *Conferência pública do jornalista José do Patrocínio de 17 de Maio de 1885* (Rio de Janeiro: Typographia Central de Evaristo Rodrigues da Costa, 1885).

16. Osvaldo Orico, *O tigre da abolição* (Rio de Janeiro: Gráfica Olímpica Editora, 1953), 99–102.

17. Robert Conrad, *The Destruction of Brazilian Slavery, 1850–1888* (Berkeley: University of California Press, 1972), 176–82, 186–89.

18. "The Ceará Festival" in Trail to Frelinghuysen, Rio de Janeiro, May 21, 1884, USNA, m. 121:48, 16–23; *25 de Março: O Ceará no Rio de Janeiro* (Fortaleza: n.p., 1884).

19. President of Ceará Domingo Raiol to president of the Council of Ministers João Paranaguá, Fortaleza, January 20, 1883, Arquivo Histórico do Museu Imperial (Petrópolis), DPP-20.1.883-Rai.c, 1–7.

20. "Eduardo Carigé," *RIGHB* 27, no. 36 (1910): 198–200; "Discurso de Dr. Theodoro Sampaio," *RIGHB* 11, no. 42 (1916): 98–102. See Eduardo Carigé, *Chorographia bahiana* (Bahia: Typographia Dos Dois Mundos, 1884).

21. Dr. Ruy Barbosa, *Decennario de Castro Alves: Elogio do poeta* (Bahia: Typographia *Diário da Bahia,* 1881).

22. Xavier Marques, "Castro Alves no decénio de sua morte," *RIGHB* 54 (1928), 185–91; "Decennario de Castro Alves," *O Monitor* (Salvador), July 16, 1881, 1; "Decennario de Castro Alves," *A Illustração Bahiana* (Salvador) July 1881, 2.

23. Marquês de Paranaguá to José Saraiva, Salvador, July 4, 1881, AMHN, WPC, Box 5, folder 46.

24. Rebecca Baird Bergstrasser, "The Movement for the Abolition of Slavery in Rio de Janeiro, Brazil, 1880–1889" (PhD dissertation, Stanford University, 1973), 113–20.

25. Fonseca, *A escravidão,* 239–54; Teodoro Sampaio manuscript, "O abolicionismo," IGHB, II, 6.

26. Chief of Police Gomes to president, Salvador, April 12, 1883, APEB/SACP, m. 5854.

27. Sampaio manuscript, "O abolicionismo," IGHB, II, 29–36.

28. "Homenagem ao Amazonas Livre," *Gazeta da Tarde* (Salvador), September 13–14, 1884, 2.

29. Sampaio manuscript, "O abolicionismo," IGHB, II, 10.

30. AMNH, WPC, box 5, document 21. Carigé wrote about his experiences (and from which this document is derived) in the *Diário da Bahia* (Salvador), September 29, 1888.

31. Police delegate Guimarães to chief of police, Alagoinhas, October 10, 1884, APEB/SACP, m. 6249.

32. Sampaio manuscript, "O abolicionismo," IGHB, II, 23.

33. Chief of Police Devoto to president, Salvador, February 10, 1885, APEB/SACP, m. 5860.

34. Eduardo Carigé (on behalf of the supplicant Pureina) to president, Salvador, April 18, 1887, APEB/SACP, m. 2897.

35. José Pedro da Silva Lobo to chief of police, Bonfim, July 7, 1886, APEB/SACP, m. 6250.

36. Seventy-seven persons to president Muritiba, March 11, 1885, seventeen persons to president, Camamú, November 16, 1886, APEB/SACP, m. 3136; Judge Rocha to president, Alcobaça, September 3, 1887, APEB/SACP, m. 2231; "A questão actual," *O Tempo* (Cachoeira), April 18, 1888, 1. For a description of similar incursions into the province of Rio de Janeiro by the abolitionist Luiz Alves de Lacerda, see Police delegate Antônio Alves da Cruz Filho to chief of police, Campos, October 8, 1886, APERJ, collection 80. See also José Honório Rodrigues, "A rebeldia negra e abolição," *Afro-Ásia* 6–7 (1968): 101–17.

37. APEB/Justiça, package 5273, process 2, Salvador, 1880.

38. APEB/Justiça, package 5512, process 3, Salvador, 1887.

39. Emilio Federico Moran, *Rui e abolição*, trans. Carly Silva (Rio de Janeiro: Fundação Rui Barbosa, 1973), 38.

40. Ibid., 38–39, 45, 60–61.

41. João José Reis, "De olho no canto: Trabalho de rua na Bahia na véspera da abolição," *Afro-Asia* 24 (2000): 201–2.

42. Fonseca, *A escravidão*, 141. See also *Cartas de Vindex ao Dr. Luiz Alvares dos Santos publicadas no Diário da Bahia* (Bahia: Typographia do *Diário*, 1875), 2.

43. "Discurso aos parachianos do Mares," *O Abolicionista* (Salvador), March 1, 1872, 2–4.

44. Fonseca, *A escravidão*, 342.

45. Josiella Pedreira to president, Viçosa, May 5, 1886, APEB/SACP, m. 2638.

46. Conrad, *Destruction of Brazilian Slavery*, 213. See also Joseli Maria

Nunes Mendonça, *Entre a mão e os anéis: A lei dos sexagenários e os caminhos da abolição no Brasil* (Campinas: Editora da Unicamp, 1999).

47. "Grande e Importante Festival Abolicionista no Polytheama," *Gazeta da Tarde* (Salvador), September 13–14, 1884, 3.

48. "Noticiário," *O Guarany* (Cachoeira) July 7, 1885, 1.

49. Brito, *A abolição na Bahia*, 97–98.

50. "Victoria Abolicionista," [sic] *O Asteróide* (Cachoeira), March 7, 1888, 1–2.

51. Castro Alves, "Carta ás senhoras bahianas," *O Abolicionista*, April 30, 1871, 1–2.

52. See, for example, *O Alabama*, May 17, 1887, 3; "As Excellentissimas Matronas Cachoeiranas, e ao Bello Sexo em Geral," *O Asteróide*, November 11, 1887, 2.

53. Rui Barbosa, "Pelos escravos! As Senhoras Bahianas," *Diário da Bahia*, August 15, 1875, (no page citation), later published in the second part of Barbosa, *Decennario de Castro Alves*.

54. Fonseca, *A escravidão*, 170–76; Gilberto Freyre, *Order and Progress: Brazil from Monarch to Republic*, trans. Rod W. Horton (Berkeley: University of California Press, 1986), 128–33. Although Bahian historian Jailton Lima Brito questions this opinion, it does appear that the number of outspoken activists remained small up to 1887. See Jailton L. Brito, *A abolição na Bahia, 1870–1888* (Salvador: Centro de Estudos Baianos, 2002), 61–79.

55. *Diário da Bahia*, March 27, 1887.

56. Antônio Lúis de Carvalho to Cotegipe, Salvador, April 6, 1887, AIHGB, CC, 883/89; Aurélio Ferreira Espinheira to Cotegipe, Salvador, July 28, 1887, AIHGB, CC, 892/45; Domingos Guimarães to Cotegipe, Salvador, May 3, 1888, AIHGB, CC, 897/106.

57. "Discurso de Dr. Teodoro Sampaio," 98–102; Robert Brent Toplin, *The Abolition of Slavery in Brazil* (New York: Athenuem, 1972), 91–92.

58. AMHN, WPC, box 5, folder 21. See also the list of the names of Bahian lawyers and nineteen Brazilian judges who helped the abolitionist cause in "A legislação escravocrata e a magistura," *Jornal do Comércio* (Rio de Janeiro) February 6, 1938.

59. Elpidio de Mesquita, *Africanos livres* (Salvador: Typographia Dos Dois Mundos, 1887), 31. In this instance Mesquita defines an Africano livre as any African slave transported to Brazil after the 1831 law.

60. APEB/Justiça, package 4321, process 5, Cachoeira, 1887.

61. "Capitães do matto e o povo," *O Asteróide*, October 25, 1887, 2; "Pode, quer e deve," *O Asteróide*, November 8, 1887, 1; "A Bahia escravocrata," *O*

Asteróide, November 25, 1887, 1; "Barbaridade," *O Asteróide*, January 17, 1888, 1; "O escravigismo em Santo Amaro," *O Asteróide*, January 20, 1888, 1; "A monarchia e o abolicionismo," *O Asteróide*, February 14, 1888, 1; "Um thug," *O Asteróide*, April 3, 1888, 2.

62. APEB/Justiça, package 4321, process 5, Cachoeira, 1887.

63. "Ao consciencioso jury," *O Asteróide*, February 22, 1888, 2; "Liberdade Cachoeiranos!! . . . Liberdade!!," *O Asteróide*, February 22, 1888, 1; "Victória abolicionista," [sic] *O Asteróide*, March 7, 1888, 1–2.

64. APEB/Justiça, package 3531, process 8, Salvador, 1887.

65. Cotegipe to Guimarães, Rio de Janeiro, March 29, 1887, AIHGB, CC, 897/106.

66. Guimarães to Cotegipe, Salvador, March 8, 1887, AIHGB, CC, 897/106; emphasis in the original.

67. Guimarães to Cotegipe, Salvador, May 3, 1888, AIHGB, CC, 897/106; emphasis in the original.

68. *Manifesto que vai ser apresentado ao corpo legislativa pela sociedade abolicionista bahiana* (Rio de Janeiro: Typographia de G. Leuzinger e Filhos, circa 1887); emphasis in the original.

69. Magalhães Junior, *A vida turbulenta*, 119.

70. "Aos martyres da liberdade!!!," *O Asteróide*, October 8, 1887, 3.

71. Sampaio manuscript, "O abolicionismo," IGHB, II, 10–20.

72. "A monarchia e o abolicionismo," *O Asteróide*, February 14, 1888, 1.

73. "Miscellanea," *O Asteróide*, April 11, 1888, 2; "Os escravos devem fugir!," *O Asteróide*, April 6, 1888, 1; "Aos escravos," *O Asteróide*, April 18, 1888, 1.

74. "Colonização nacional," *O Asteróide*, November 22, 1887, 1.

75. Um espreitador, "Pedido justo," *O Asteróide*, April 27, 1888, 2–3.

76. "A Bahia escravocrata," *O Asteróide*, November 25, 1887, 1.

77. "O escravagismo em Santo Amaro," *O Asteróide*, January 20, 1888, 1–2.

78. "José Mariano," *O Faisca* (Salvador), February 14, 1886, 138.

79. *O Faisca*, June 13, 1886, 270. See also "Noticiário," *O Guarany*, July 7, 1885, 1.

80. See *Cartas de Vindex*, 75–76, 82–86.

81. "Como Adultera-se Os Factos," *O Asteróide*, October 21, 1887, 1–2

82. "Liberalismo conservador," *O Guarany*, December 11, 1884, 2.

83. "A immigração," *O Tempo*, March 10, 1888, 1.

84. *O Guarany*, May 16, 1878, 2.

85. Beatriz Góis Dantas, *Vovó nagô e papai branco: Usos e abusos da África no Brasil* (Rio de Janeiro: Edições Graal, 1988).

86. M. S. F., "Verdadeira Philantropia," *O Guarany*, November 29, 1884, 2.

87. Os abolicionistas conscienciosos, "Aos escravos," *O Tempo*, April 4, 1888, 2; "Cruel expectativa!" *O Tempo*, April 14, 1888, 2.

88. Hebe Maria Mattos de Castro, *Das cores do silêncio: Os significados da liberdade no sudeste escravista, Brasil, século xix* (Rio de Janeiro: Arquivo Nacional, 1995), 249–56. For background of newspaper coverage of slaves and African descendants in the city of São Paulo, see Lilia Moritz Schwarcz, *Retrato em branco e negro: Jornais, escravos e cidadãos em São Paulo no final do século xix* (São Paulo: Editora Schwarcz, 1987).

89. "Um documento valioso," *O Asteróide*, March 27, 1888, 1.

90. "Festa abolicionista," *O Tempo*, April 18, 1888, 2; "A Cachoeira libertase," *O Asteróide*, April 18, 1888, 1. See also "Emancipação no Iguape," *O Tempo*, April 28, 1888, 1.

91. Egas Moniz Barreto to Cotegipe, Bahia, April 2, 1888, AIHGB, CC, 874/6; Baron Pojúca to Cotegipe, Bahia, April 29, 1888, AIHGB, CC, 884/64.

92. João Ferreira to Cotegipe, Santo Amaro, October 27, 1888, AIHGB, CC, 925/111.

93. Guimarães to Cotegipe, Salvador, April 9, 1887, AIHGB, CC, 197/111. See also President Mello to Cotegipe, Salvador, August 25, 1887, AIHGB, CC, 912/123.

94. "A imprensa da capital e o abolicionismo," *O Asteróide*, February 18, 1888, 1; Reis, "De olho no canto," 201.

95. Guimarães to Cotegipe, Salvador, January 4, 1888, AIHGB, CC, 28/133.

96. Several vivid descriptions are available in the Cotegipe collection; see, for examples, Antônio Bastos to Cotegipe, Bahia, October 2, 1887, AIHGB, CC, 878/133; and João Ferreira to Cotegipe, Bahia, April 3, 1888, AIHGB, CC, 925/119.

97. Poster sent from the engenho Cassarangongo to Cotegipe, Bahia, April 12, 1888, AMHN, WPC, box 67; emphasis in the original.

98. David Waldstreicher, *The Struggle Against Slavery: A History in Documents* (New York: Oxford University Press, 2001), 105–7; Seymour Drescher, "Brazilian Abolition in Comparative Perspective," in *The Abolition of Slavery and the Aftermath of Emancipation in Brazil*, ed. Rebecca J. Scott (Durham, NC: Duke University Press, 1988), 47–48.

99. Police subdelegate Francisco Parassú to Police Chief Guimarães, Pirajá, March 26, 1888, APEB/SACP, m. 6253.

100. "Bravo Mil Vezes Bravo," *O Asteróide*, May 11, 1888, 2.

101. "A Bahia Escravocrata," *O Asteróide* November 25, 1887, 1; "Últimas palavras," *O Tempo*, May 16, 1888, 1.

102. "Grande enthusiasmo," *O Asteróide*, May 19, 1888, 1–2.

103. "Manifestação honrosa," *O Asteróide*, June 6, 1888, 1.

104. AMNH, WPC, box 3, document 117 contains a copy of the pastoral letter dated May 13, 1888. The letter was subsequently published in the *Diário da Bahia*, May 18, 1888 (page not cited).

105. José Garcia Pacheco da Aragão Junior, "O 50 anniversário da lei da abolição," *Annaes do Arquivo Público do Estado da Bahia* 27 (1941): 527–30.

106. *Programme of the Festivities in Honor of the Brazilian Slavery Emancipation*, cited in David Brion Davis, *Slavery and Human Progress* (New York: Oxford University Press, 1984), 298, 361 n. 111.

107. Davis, *Slavery and Human Progress*, 298–99; Suzanne Miers, *Britain and Ending the Slave Trade* (New York: Africana Publishers, 1975).

108. Chief of Police Gomes to president, Salvador, May 2, 1883, APEB/SACP, m. 5854.

109. Cleber da Silva Maciel, *Discriminações raciais: Negros em Campinas, 1888–1921* (Campinas: Editora da Unicamp, 1987); L. A. Costa Pinto, *O negro no Rio de Janeiro: Relações de raças numa sociedade em mudança*, 2d ed. (1953; reprint, Rio de Janeiro: Editora UFRJ, 1998); Antônio Sérgio Alfredo Guimarães, *Racismo e anti-racismo no Brasil* (São Paulo: Editora 34, 1999); Michael Hanchard, ed., *Racial Politics in Contemporary Brazil* (Durham, NC: Duke University Press, 1999).

Chapter Eight

1. Cid Teixeira, *Bahia em tempo de província* (Salvador: Fundação Cultural do Estado da Bahia, 1985), 191–93; Américo Jabobina Lacombe et al., *Rui Barbosa e a queima dos arquivos* (Rio de Janeiro: Fundação Casa de Rui Barbosa, 1988), 42.

2. *Livro da sociedade 13 de Maio*, 1, located at the Archive of the Instituto Geográfico e Histórico da Bahia (AIGHB).

3. *Sociedade Educadora Treze de Maio: Estatutos approvados em sessão de 14 de Julho de 1896* (Bahia: Typographia Diário da Bahia, 1896).

4. "Mappa da escola nocturna 'Machado Portella' da 'Sociedade Educadora Treze de Maio': Relatório do mez do Novembro do anno de 1899," in *Livro da sociedade 13 de Maio*, AIGHB.

5. Burke to Wharton, Salvador, May 31, 1889, USNA, T 331:5.

6. Katia Maria de Carvalho Silva, "O *Diário da Bahia* e o século xix" (MA thesis, Federal University of Bahia, 1975); Weaver to Hunter, Salvador, June 15, 1885, USNA, T 331:5; Burke to Wharton, Salvador, August 12, 1890, USNA, T 331:6.

7. Manuel Raimundo Querino, *The African Contribution to Brazilian Civilization*, trans. E. Bradford Burns (Tempe: Arizona State University, Center for Latin American Studies, 1978), 2.

8. José Raimundo Fontes, "Manifestações operárias na Bahia: O movimento grevista, 1888–1930" (MA thesis, Federal University of Bahia, 1982), 55–56.

9. João José Reis, "A greve negra de 1857 na Bahia," *Revista USP* 18 (June–August 1993): 8–29; and see Leon F. Litwack, *Been in the Storm so Long: The Aftermath of Slavery* (New York: Alfred A. Knopf, 1979), 441; Francisco Scarano, "Labor and Society in the Nineteenth Century," in *The Modern Caribbean*, eds. Franklin W. Knight and Colin A. Palmer (Chapel Hill: University of North Carolina Press, 1989), 83; Peter Linebaugh and Marcus Rediker, *The Many-Headed Hydra: Sailors, Slaves, Commoners, and the Hidden History of the Revolutionary Atlantic* (Boston: Beacon Press, 2000).

10. Burke to Wharton, Salvador, March 25, 1891, USNA, T 331:6.

11. For descriptions of the Bahian political elite after 1889, see Consuelo Novais Sampaio, *Partidos políticos da Bahia na primeira república: Uma política de acomodação*, 2d ed. (Salvador: EDUFBA, 1998); Eul-Soo Pang, *Bahia in the First Republic: Coronelismo and Oligarchies, 1889–1934* (Gainesville: University of Florida Press, 1979); Dain Borges, *The Family in Bahia, Brazil, 1870–1945* (Stanford, CA: Stanford University Press, 1992); Dain Borges, "Salvador's 1890s: Paternalism and Its Discontents," *Luso-Brazilian Review* 30, no. 2 (winter 1993): 47–57.

12. Archive of the Centro Operário of the State of Bahia, *Acts of the General Directory*, May 6, 1894, 1.

13. Several authors have written about the unionization of black workers and social tensions in cities after 1889 and into the early part of the twentieth century. See Sheldon Leslie Maram, *Anarquistas, imigrantes, e o movimento operário Brasileiro, 1889–1920* (Rio de Janeiro: Paz e Terra, 1979); Boris Fausto, *Trabalho urbano e conflito social, 1890–1920* (São Paulo: Difel, 1977); Paulo Sérgio Pinheiro and Michael M. Hall, *A classe opéraria no Brasil, 1889–1930*, 2 vols. (São Paulo: Editora Alfa Omega, 1979); George Reid Andrews, *Blacks and Whites in São Paulo, Brazil, 1888–1988* (Madison: University of Wisconsin Press, 1991); Teresa Meade, "'Living Worse and Costing More': Resistance and Riot in Rio de Janeiro, 1890–1917," *Journal of Latin American Studies* 21, no. 2 (May 1987); José Murilo de Carvalho, *Os bestializados: O Rio de Janeiro e a república que não foi* (São Paulo: Companhia das Letras, 1987); Sidney Chalhoub, *Trabalho, lar e botequim: O cotidiano dos trabalhadores no Rio de Janeiro da belle epoque* (São Paulo: Brasiliense, 1986); William H. Harris, *The Harder We Run: Black Workers since the Civil War* (New York: Oxford University Press, 1982).

14. Teixeira, *Bahia em tempo*, 207–9.

15. Peter Fry, Sérgio Carrara and Ana Luiza Martins-Costa, "Negros e brancos no carnaval da velha república," in *Escravidão e invenção de liberdade: Estudos sobre o negro no Brasil*, ed. João José Reis (São Paulo: Editora Brasiliense, 1988), 244–45; Hildegardes Vianna, "Do entrudo ao carnaval na Bahia," *Revista Brasileira de folclore* 13 (September/December 1965): 283–98.

16. *Jornal de Notícias* (Salvador), February 19, 1896.

17. *Jornal de Notícias*, January 22, 1902; cited in Kim D. Butler, *Freedoms Given, Freedoms Won: Afro-Brazilians in Post-Abolition São Paulo and Salvador* (New Brunswick, NJ: Rutgers University Press, 1998), 181.

18. Fry et al., "Negros e brancos," 250–52; Butler, *Freedoms Given, Freedoms Won*, 174–85.

19. Nina Rodrigues, *Os africanos no Brasil*, 5th ed. (São Paulo: Companhia Editora Nacional, 1977), 238–52.

20. Butler, *Freedoms Given, Freedoms Won*, 201. For a description of the annual homage to Yemanjá, see Licídio Lopes, *O rio vermelho e suas tradições* (Salvador: Fundação Cultural do Estado da Bahia, 1984), 58–66; and for the ways in which race and class intersected during the huge celebrations each July 2, see Wlamyra R. de Albuquerque, *Algazarra nas ruas: Comemorações da independência na Bahia (1889–1923)* (Campinas, SP: Editora da Unicamp, 1999); and Hendrik Kraay, "'Frio como a pedra de que se há de compor': Caboclos e monumentos da Independência na Bahia, 1870–1900," *Tempo* (Rio de Janeiro) 7, no. 14 (January 2003): 51–81.

21. See Joseli Maria Nunes Mendonça, *Entre a mao e os anéis: A lei dos sexagenários e os caminhos da abolição no Brasil* (Campinas: Editora da Unicamp, 1999); Hebe Maria Mattos de Castro, *Das cores do silêncio: Os significados da liberdade no sudeste escravista, Brasil, século xix* (Rio de Janeiro: Arquivo Nacional, 1995); Maria Helena Machado, *O plano e o pânico: Os movimentos sociais na década da abolição* (Rio de Janeiro: Editora da UFRJ, EDUSP, 1994). Other perspectives are provided in Ademir Gebara, *O mercado de trabalho livre no Brasil (1871–1888)* (São Paulo: Brasiliense, 1986); Lúcio Kowarick, *Trabalho e vadiagem: A origem do trabalho livre no Brasil* (São Paulo: Brasiliense, 1987).

22. Eric Foner, *Nothing but Freedom: Emancipation and Its Legacy* (Baton Rouge: Louisiana State University Press, 1983), 6.

23. Moniz Barreto de Aragão to Cotegipe, Bahia, May 20, 1888, AIHGB, CC, 5/9; emphasis in the original.

24. Arístides Novis to Cotegipe, Bahia, May 16, 1888, AIHGB, CC, 49/23.

25. Angelo Domingues Monteiro to president, Caravellas, June 3, 1888, APEB/SACP, m. 2986.

26. Isaias Alves, *Matas do sertão de baixo* (Bahia: Reper, 1967), 48.

27. Lopes, *O rio vermelho*, 69.

28. Eduardo Carigé to president, Bahia, October 8, 1888, APEB/SACP, m. 2901.

29. For helpful studies of the education of freedpersons in the U.S. South, see Robert C. Morris, *Reading, 'Riting, and Reconstruction* (Chicago: University of Chicago Press, 1981); James D. Anderson, *The Education of Blacks in the South, 1860–1935* (Chapel Hill: University of North Carolina Press, 1988); Leon F. Litwack, *Trouble in the Mind: Black Southerners in the Age of Jim Crow* (New York: Alfred A. Knopf, 1998), 52–113.

30. Alexander Augusto d'Azevedo Leitão e Gotha (on behalf of Quintino José da Silva) to president, Bahia, November 8, 1888, APEB/SACP, m. 2751.

31. APEB/Judicial section, Villa de São Francisco do Conde, package 2441, process 8, 1895.

32. João Theo de Almeida to president, Barracão, Bahia, October 13, 1888, APEB/SACP, m. 2244.

33. APEB/Judicial section, maço 7034, process 4, Santo Amaro, 1907.

34. Foner, *Nothing but Freedom*, 18, 72.

35. Arístides Novis to Cotegipe, Bahia, May 30, 1888, AIHGB, CC, 49/25; Novis to Cotegipe, Bahia, June 16, 1888, AIHGB, CC, 49/27; Novis to Cotegipe, Bahia, August 25, 1888, AIGHB, CC, 49/28; Moniz Barreto de Aragão to Cotegipe, Bahia, June 16, 1888, AIHGB, CC, 5/10.

36. Novis to Cotegipe, Bahia, October 6, 1888, AIGHB, CC, 49/29; José Teixeira Duque Estrada to Cotegipe, Bahia, June 26, 1888, AIHGB, CC, 21/159.

37. Novis to Cotegipe, Bahia, May 30, 1888, AIHGB, CC, 49/25; Novis to Cotegipe, Bahia, June 20, 1888, AIHGB, CC, 49/26.

38. A. Carvalho (illegible, but based on handwriting most likely Anfilófio Botelho Freire de Carvalho) to Dr. Araújo Pinho, Bahia, May 21, 1888, AIHGB, WPC, box 28 (not catalogued).

39. Description of a lecture given by Artur Neiva in August 1938, AMHN, WPC, box 10. See also Castro, *Das cores do silêncio*, 285–306; George Reid Andrews, "Black and White Workers: São Paulo, Brazil, 1888–1928," in *The Abolition of Slavery and the Aftermath of Emancipation in Brazil*, ed. Rebecca J. Scott (Durham, NC: Duke University Press, 1988), 107–9. For analyses of the negotiations after emancipation in other plantation regions, see Litwack, *Been in the Storm*; Foner, *Nothing but Freedom*; Rebecca J. Scott, *Slave Emancipation in Cuba: The Transition to Free Labor, 1860–1899* (Princeton, NJ: Princeton University Press, 1985), 201–78; Rebecca J. Scott, "Defining the Boundaries of Freedom in the World of Cane: Cuba, Brazil, and Louisiana

after Emancipation," *American Historical Review* 99, no. 1 (February 1994): 70–102.

40. Domingos José Brandão to president, Bahia, May 25, 1889, APEB/SACP, m. 3007.

41. Moniz Barreto de Aragão to Cotegipe, Bahia, May 20, 1888, AIHGB, CC, 5/9.

42. For a discussion of the psychological aspects of subsistence farming and the relationship of small farming with family and community, see a review of the writings of Wendell Berry in Bill McKibben, "Prophet from Kentucky," *The New York Review of Books* 37, no. 10 (June 14, 1990): 30–34; Castro, *Das cores do silêncio*, 52–53, 111–14.

43. See Bert J. Barickman, *A Bahian Counterpoint: Sugar, Tobacco, Cassava, and Slavery in the Recôncavo, 1780–1860* (Stanford, CA: Stanford University Press, 1998), 44–96; Katia M. de Queirós Mattoso, *Bahia, século xix: Uma província no império*, trans. Yeda de Macedo Soares (Rio de Janeiro: Editora Nova Fronteira, 1992), 556–78; and Ira Berlin and Philip D. Morgan, eds., *Cultivation and Culture: Labor and the Shaping of Slave Life in the Americas* (Charlottesville: University Press of Virginia, 1993).

44. For a helpful analysis of similar transformations in the Caribbean and the U.S. South, see Sidney W. Mintz, "Slavery and the Rise of Peasantries," in *Roots and Branches: Current Directions in Slave Studies*, ed. Michael Craton (Toronto: Pergamon Press, 1979), 213–42; Edward Magdol, *A Right to the Land: Essays on the Freedmen's Community* (Westport, CT: Greenwood Press, 1977); Ira Berlin, ed., *The Wartime Genesis of Free Labor: The Lower South* (New York: Cambridge University Press, 1990); W. E. B. Du Bois, *Black Reconstuction in America, 1860–1880* (1935; reprint, New York: Atheneum, 1969), 75.

45. Lydio Nunes Bahiense et al. to Cotegipe, Bahia, August 7, 1888, AIHGB, CC, 77/50; emphasis in the original.

46. Dr. Candido Figueiredo et al. to Cotegipe, Bahia, July 16, 1888, AIHGB, CC, 77/47.

47. Moniz Barreto de Aragão to Cotegipe, Bahia, June 16, 1888, AIHGB, CC, 5/10.

48. The low estimate is provided by Angelina Garcez, "O econômico no movimento de Canudos," *Revista do Instituto Geográfico e Histórico da Bahia* 94 (January/December 1998): 195–96. The higher estimate can be found at the web site organized by Antônio Olavo *A História de Canudos,* http://www.portfolium.com.br/canudos

49. T. Gaudenzi, *Memorial de Canudos* (Salvador: Fundação Cultural do Estado da Bahia, 1993), 19.

50. Ibid., 17.

51. Lino [illegible] Lima to president, Inhambupe, November 5, 1886, APEB/SACP, m. 2416.

52. Edmundo Moniz, *Canudos: A guerra social*, 2d ed. (Rio de Janeiro: Elo Editora, 1987), 71.

53. Walnice Nogueira Galvão, "Piedade e paixão: Os sermões do Conselheiro," in *Brevário de Antônio Conselheiro*, orgs. Walnice Galvão and Fernando da Rocha Peres (Salvador: EDUFBA, 2000), 16.

54. José Calasans, *Antônio Conselheiro e a escravidão* (Salvador: S. A. Artes Gráficas, n.d.); José Calasans, "Antônio Conselheiro e os escravos," *A Tarde* (Salvador), October 5, 1988, 6. An extensive bibliography is provided in Robert M. Levine, *Vale of Tears: Revisiting the Canudos Massacre in Northeastern Brazil, 1893–1897* (Berkeley: University of California Press, 1992). See also *Revista USP: Dossiê Canudos* (December–February 1993–94); and Roberto Pompeu de Toledo, "O legado do Conselheiro," *Veja*, September 3, 1997, 64–87. For photographs of the war against Canudos, see Antônio Olavo, *Memórias fotográficas de Canudos* (Salvador: Impressora Rocha, 1989).

55. Cited in Levine, *Vale of Tears*, 140. See also Consuelo Novais Sampaio, *Canudos: Cartas para o barão* (São Paulo: Edusp/Imprensa Official, 1999).

56. For comments about beheadings supposedly practiced by both sides in the conflict, see Oliveiros Litento, *Canudos: Visões e revisões* (Rio de Janeiro: Biblioteca do Exército Ed., 1998), 140.

57. Antônio Olavo, org., *Histórico e relatório do Comitê Patriótico da Bahia, 1897–1901* (Salvador: Portfolium Editora, 2002).

58. Olavo, *Memórias fotográficos*, no page, listed under the Chronology in part IV.

59. Levine, *Vale of Tears*, 215.

60. The estimate of 115 is based on the number of quilombos represented at the "Encontro Estadual de Comunidades Quilombolas" in April 2005 in Salvador, Bahia. Much higher estimates, not substantiated by scholarly research, are cited in Larry Rohter, "Former Slave Havens in Brazil Gaining Rights," *The New York Times*, January 23, 2001, 1. The author suggests, "In total, 724 *quilombos*, some dating back to the seventeenth century, have been identified across Brazil and are seeking formal recognition of their status. The largest single concentration of such communities, 259, is in Bahia."

Conclusion

1. Ruth Landes, *The City of Women* (1947; reprint, Albuquerque: University of New Mexico Press, 1994).

2. Eduardo Silva, "O Príncipe Obá, a guerra do Paraguai e a abolição da escravatura," in *Encontro de História Brasil-Paraguai I* (Salvador: IGHB; Academia Paraguaya de la Historia, 2001), 96.

3. George Reid Andrews, *Afro-Latin America, 1800–2000* (New York: Oxford University Press, 2004), 53–84; John Hope Franklin and Alfred A. Moss Jr., *From Slavery to Freedom: A History of African Americans*, 8th ed. (Boston: McGraw Hill, 2000), 220–44.

4. Antônio Olavo, org., *Histórico e Relatório do Comitê Patriótico da Bahia, 1897–1901* (Salvador: Portfolium Editora, 2002), 54–55.

5. Martha Abreu, *O império do divino: Festas religiosas e cultura popular no Rio de Janeiro, 1830–1900* (Rio de Janeiro: Nova Fronteira; São Paulo: Fapesp, 1999), 385.

6. Celia M. Azevedo, *Abolitionism in the United States and Brazil: A Comparative Perspective* (New York: Garland Publishing, 1995), xxii.

Index

Page numbers in bold type indicate illustrations.

abadás, 23

ABC de Castro Alves (Amado), 98

Aberdeen Act, 4

abolition: importance of courts to, 176, 178; police harassment of organizers and participants, **185**

Abolitionist Confederation, 165

Abolitionist Festival, 167

abolitionist societies, 13, 79, 81, 82, 96, 146–47, 162

Abolitionist Society of Cachoeira, 172

Abreu, Martha, 229

Adriano (*ingênio*), 177

Africa, 1, 3, 6–12, 18–20, 22, 24, 28, 32, 36, 42, 48, 74, 123, 128, 133; Bahia and slave imports from, xviii–xix; and Candomblé, 103; deterring influence and culture of, 107

African Embassy, 204

African Merrymakers, 204

Africanos livres, xxi

Africans: late-night meetings of, 114; returning to Africa following Malês Revolt, 129–30; Yorubas, 23, 24, 76

The Africans in Brazil (Rodrigues), 206

African straw, 112

Aguirre, Atanasio Cruz, 55

Alagoinhas, Brazil, 168

Almeida, Candido Mendes de, 72

Almeida, Luis Antonio Barbosa de, 79

Alves, Constancia, 194

Alves, Rodrigues, 84

Amado, Jorge, 84, 98

Americano, Arthur, 165

Andrada, Mario de, 97

Andrada e Silva, José Bonifácio de, xxiv

Andrade, Ignacio Dias de, 67

Anthony the Counselor, xxiii–xxiv, 216

anti-slave trade law, 37

Aragão, Edmundo Ferrão Moniz de, 220

Aragão, Muniz Barretto de, 188, 216

Araújo, Antonio de, 209

Araújo, José Tomás Nabuco de, 71–72

Argentina, 53, 55, 56

Argolo, Alexandre Gomes, 150

Argolo, Anna, 178

Argolo, João, 178, 179

assassinations, xviii, 29, 35, 70, 141, 150–51, 187, 226

Assis, A. Cicero de, 64, 65

Association for the Friends of Slaves, 172

Audouard, M. F. M., 10

Augusto, Miguel, 123

Azevado, Celia Maria Marinho de, 140, 157

Azevado, Elciene, 74

Bahia: causes for end of slavery in, 226–27; disintegration of slave regime, 215; drought in, 214; establishment of Workers

Protective Association, 202; first railroad line in, 152; labor movement in, 201; map of, 217; patriotism in, 57; use of violence in recruitment of military forces, 59
Bahia, Torquato, 194
Bahian Abolition Society, 180
Bahian Liberating Society, 165–66, 167, 171, 177, 178, 178–79, 180
Baianos, Zuavos, 60
Baptist Revolt, 72
Barbosa, Rui, 84, 95, 165, 170, 171, 175, 184
Barros Jr., João Antonio, 59
Barroso, Romualdo Maria de Seixas, 172
batuques, 108–9, 111
Bay of All Saints, xix, 23, 34
Bedthell, Leslie, 22
"The Beggars" (Gomes), 64–65
Bento, Antônio, 228
Bittencourt, Carlos Machado, 222, 229
"Bloodless Goddess" (Castro Alves), 94
Bomfim, Manoel, 97
Bom Jesus da Cruz, 39
Bonfim festival, 191, 194
Borges, Abílio César, 83
Braganza family, xix
Branco, Manoel Alves, 11
Brazilian Emancipation Committee, 195
Brazilian Institute of History and Geography, 93
The Brazilian Nation: Reality of Brazilian Sovereignty (Bomfim), 97
British West Africa Squadron, xvi, xxi, 1, 4, 37
Britto, Joaquim Marcellino de, 28
Bruderer family, 153
Bulcão, Joaquim Ignacio de Siqueira, 176, 177
Burke, David, 200, 201
Burns, E. Bradford, 55

Caboto, Lino, 166
Cachoeira, Brazil, 25, 146, 187, 193, 194
Calasans, José, 219, 220
Calisco (slave), 176, 177
Câmara, Eugênia, 90
Camizão, 62
Campos, João da Silva, 161
Candomblé, xxii, 44, 47, 103–31; and abolition, 128–31; and Carnival, 205; Castro Alves and, 99; and Catholic doctrines, 122; disruption of police, 118; and efficient cultivation and availability of food crops, 111; as form of resistance to slavery, 103; and police sweeps, 107; and slave resistance, 126; as social organization for understanding the world, 125; as a spreading cancer, 116; as symbol of African subversion, 104
Canning, George, xvi
Canudos, 216–23, xxiv
capitalism: and antislavery legislation, 54; loss of credibility and legitimacy of slavery, 156; and spread of abolitionist ideals, 152
Capitalism and Slavery (Williams), xvi, xvii
Cardos, Passos, 176
Cardoso, Antônio Pereira, 73
Cardoso, Sergio, 166
Carigé, Eduardo, 14, 163, 164, 165, 166, 167, 170, 171, 178, 180, 181, 184, 194, 196, 199, 220, xxiv; and Victoria, 208–9
Carigé Club, 194
Carneiro, Edison, 85, 93, 97
Carneiro da Silva Rego, João, 25
Carneiro Leão, Honório Hermeto, 40, 41
Carnival, 203–6
Carnival clubs, 204–5
Carolina (slave), 195

Carvalho, Amphilophio Botelho
    Freire de, 176
Carvalho, Anfilofio, 212–13
Carvalho, Francisco Pires de, 168
Carvalho, José Murilo de, 22, 71
Castro, Moreira do, 139
*Castro Alves (1847–71): A Political
    Interpretation* (Carneiro), 93
Castro Alves, Antonio Frederico de,
    83–99, 164, 165, 166, 171, 175,
    xxii; brought abolitionist debate
    to forefront of politics, 84; and
    establishment of abolitionist
    so-ciety, 96; poems calling for
    an immediate end to slavery,
    85; as "poet of the slaves,"
    86; publishes his "Letter to the
    Women of Bahia," 95; reached
    large audiences through public
    readings, 86
Castro de Araújo, Ubiratan, xx
Catholic brotherhoods, 119–20
Catholic Church, 99, 118, 195;
    attitude toward Candomblé,
    103; Candomblé erodes
    influence of, 119; and exorcism,
    123; reactionary position with
    regard to abolition, 87; and
    recognition of mixed-race
    brotherhoods, 39; unwillingness
    to speak out on behalf of slaves,
    171
Caxias, Duke of, 80
Ceará, Brazil: first province to end
    slavery, 164
Central Emancipation Society, 165
Chalhoub, Sidney, 58
Chiavenato, Júlio José, 55
Chichôrro da Gama, A. C. P., 13,
    35–36
cholera, 11, 12, 13, 106, 108
citizen's patrol, 34, 49
Clapp, João, 228
Clarkson, Thomas, xv–xvi
Claudio (African freedman), 28
Closing of the Basket, 123

Cloth Factory of Boa Viagem, 154,
    155
Club Carigé, 182
Commercial Abolitionist Society, 146
Committee for Effecting the
    Abolition of the Slave Trade, xv
Communist Manifesto, 117
condoreirismo, 84
conductors (in labor unions), 65
Conrad, Robert, 173
Conselheiristas, 220–23, 229
Convent of Carmo, 148
Costa, Lucio Jeronimo da, 35, 49
Costa, Silvestre José da, 170
Cotegipe, Baron of, 72, 166–67, 179,
    182, 184
Counselheiro, Antônio. *See* Maciel,
    Antonio Vicente Mendes
courts, 42, 44, 67, 74, 143, 144, 160,
    171, 175–76, 178, 179, 209, 210
Cranotick, Vincent D., 12
crioulo: defined, xxv
Cruz, Roque Jacinto da, 163, 165–66,
    171
Cuba, 5, 130
Curralinho, Brazil, 90

da Cunha, Euclides, 97
d'Almeida, Albino Antonio, 31
Damião (slave), 178, 179
dancing and drumming:
    accommodation to, 111
Dantas, Manoel Pinto de Souza, 171,
    183
Davis, David Brion, xvii
deportation, 28, 30, 31, 48, 49;
    threat of, 115
Dias, Satyro de Oliveira, 80, 153
diseases and epidemics, 1, 9–13, 15,
    43, 49, 81, 90, 106, 108; and
    Paraguayan War, 58
documents: destruction of, 199;
    translation of foreign language,
    29, 30, 30–31, 105
Drescher, Seymour, xvii
drought, 191, 200, 214

The Duke of Caxias and the War with Paraguay: A Critical Study (Dias), 80, 153
Duling, Thomas, 5, 6

emancipation fund, 54
Emygdio (African freedman), 170
engenhos, 12, 43, 150, 207, 192, 212; fleeing from, 61
epidemics. *See* diseases and epidemics
Equiano, Olaudah, xvii
Eutherpe Philharmonic Society, 148

Faria, Maria da Paixão Gomes, 174
Feira, Lucas da, 187
Feira de Santana, Brazil, 27
feitiço, 104, 110, 114, 126–27
Felicidade (African freedwoman): deportation of, 36
feminists, 171
Fernandes, Alexandre, 194
Filho, Walter Fraga, 161
The First Burlesque Ballads of Getuliano (Gama), 74
Foner, Eric, 211
Fonseca, Joaquim de Aquino, 165
Fonseca, Luís Anselmo da, 14, 159, 163, 168, 171, 194, 199
food riot of 1858, 113
Fortaleza, Brazil, 21, 218, 227
Fox, Charles, xvi
freedpersons, 9, 19, 24, 27, 28, 29, 43, xxi; arrested on suspicion of planning an insurrection, 67; arrests of, 35; capacity to organize, 106; distinction from slaves lessened, 62; harassment of, 31; hiding with slaves, 64; lived like slaves, 48; role in Malês Revolt, 48; tax on, 31; working on plantations, 212
Freeman, John, 8
free workers, 140, 189; maintaining controls over, 156; treated like slaves, 61

Galeano, Eduardo, 55
Galeao, C. V. de Almeida, 63
Galvão, Cândido de Fonseca, 76–77
Gama, Luís, xxiii, 44, 73–76, 84, 87, 133, 166, 196; legal defense of slaves, 76; statue of, 73
Gertrudes, Valeriana Maria, 106
Gillmer, John, 6
Ginásio Baiano, 83, 84
Golden Law of May 1888, 196
Gomes, Flávio, 29, 31
Gomes, Romão de Aquino, 64
Gomes, Torquato Teixeira, 209
Gonzaga (Castro Alves), 165
Gordon, George, 6
Gorender, Jacob, xxi, 144
Graham, Richard, 142
Great Britain: interception of slave transporting ships, 14; as symbol of beneficence, 8; treaty with Brazil, 18
Guimarães, Domingos, 179, 191
Guimarães, Joaquim Antonio, 28

Haberly, David, 97, 157
Haitian Revolution, xviii, xxi, 2, 72
Harding, Rachel, 130
"Hidden History of the Revolutionary Atlantic" (Lindbaugh and Rediker), 14
Horta, Constança da S., 106
How to Think About the Servile Element (Leão), 153, 156
Hudson, James, 6
Humanitarian Abolitionist Society, 146

Ilê Aiyê, 230
ingênuo, 176, 177
Intertropical Parasitic Diseases (Victorino), 154
inversions: gender and racial hierarchy, 115
Islam, 24, 27, 28, 29, 31, 36, 47, 49, 72, 105

Jambeiro, Rafael José, 160
Jesus, Manoel Casemiro de, 210–11
Jesus, Maria Antonia de, 210
João VI, xix, 1
Junqueira, João José de Oliveira, 96
Justino (slave), 168

Kraay, Hendrik, 25

Lagos entourage, 130–31
Landes, Ruth, 227
land reform, 33
Law of the Free Womb, xxi, xxiii,
    53, 54, 71, 72, 76, 80, 82, 141,
    148, 157, 158, 173, 177; and
    death of Castro Alves, 98; and
    disappearance of abolitionist
    societies, 147; and writings of
    Castro Alves, 83
Law of the Sixty Year Olds, 173
League of Bahaian Workers, 201
Leão, Polycarpo Lopes de, 153, 156
"Letter to the Women of Bahai"
    (Castro Alves), 175
liberals: repression of, 26
liberated Africans, 110
Liberated Africans (Mesquita), 176
Liberia, 28
libertos, xxi
Lima, Joaquim Manoel Roiz, 202
Lindbaugh, Peter, 14
Lisbôa, Frederico, 165, 168, 199
Lobato, Francisco Vigario, 26
Lopes, Licídio, 208
López, Francisco Solano, 55
Lucas (escaped slave), 27;
    deportation of, 36
Lucas, João, 161
Luís (slave), 188
Lyceum of Arts and Trades, 163

Maceió, Brazil, 21
Machado, Maria Helena, 131
Machado Portella, Manoel do
    Nascimento, 200
Machado Portella School, 200

Maciel, Antonio Vicente Mendes,
    216–22
macumba ceremony, 115
Magalhães, João de Moura, 34, 35,
    37
Mahim, Luísa Matheu, 73
Malê contamination, 29
Malês Revolt, xx–xxi, 18–19, 22–33,
    26, 45, 72, 73, 98, 130, 133;
    and persecution of African
    freedpersons, 106
Mamigonian, Beatriz Gallotti, 37
manioc flour, 113, 145–46, 191, 200,
    214
Mann, Horace, 83
manumission, 146, 151–52, 167,
    174, 175, 187, 189, 190, 193,
    196
Maragogipe, Brazil, 214
Mariano, José, 184
Marinho, Frederico, 195
Marinho de Azevedo, Celia Maria,
    xxiv
Martins, Anna Francisca da Rocha,
    195–96
Martins, Cicero Dantas, 220
Martins, Francisco de Souza, 25
Martins, Francisco Gonçalves, 10,
    38, 65–66; participation in slave-
    smuggling ring, 89
Martins, Julião Augusto de Serra,
    229
Martins, Raimundo Mendes, 176
Matory, Randy, 130
Matos, Isaias Guedes de, 176
Mattos, José Francisco de, 70
Mauá, Baron of, 154
May 13th Society, 199, 200
Mello, Barão Homem de, 145, 151
Mendes, Cesário Ribeiro, 169, 174,
    176, 177
Mesquita, Elpidio de, 176
Moreno, Tati, 120
Muniz, Sabino Francisco, 44
Muslims. *See* Islam

Nabuco, Joaquim, 76, 84, 93, 157, 170, 174, 180, 194
Nagô African freedpersons, 37; exodus from Salvador, 29
Nagô Malês, 27
Nagôs, 30–31
Needell, Jeffrey D., 40
"Negroes in the Bottom of a Slave Ship" (illustration), 9
Nepomuceno, João, 194
New Burlesque Ballads (Gama), 74
newspapers, 76; *O Abolicionista*, 95, 175; *Actualidade*, 182; *O Alabama*, 78–80, 89, 118, 121, 123, 125, 126, 127, 147, 178, 228; *O Asteróide*, 182, 183, 193, 194; *O Balão*, 182; *O Brasil*, 6; *Correio da Tarde*, 6; *Correio Paulistano*, 89; *Diablo Coxo*, 76; *Diário da Bahia*, 66, 95, 170–71, 172, 194, 228; *O Faisca*, 184, 185, 202; *A Gargalhada*, 182; *Gazeta da Tarde*, 165, 166, 179, 181, 228; *O Guarany*, 187; *Illustração Bahiana*, 182; *A Independência*, 170; *O Iparanga*, 76, 170; *Jornal da Tarde*, 89, 176; *Jornal de Notícias*, 205; *O Lábaro*, 182; *A Lanterna*, 182; *O Monitor*, 165; *O Oculo Mágico*, 128; *O Polichinelo*, 76; *O Popular*, 183; *A Província*, 162; *O Radical Paulistano*, 95, 170; *Renascimento*, 182; *O século*, 6; *O Socialista*, 182; *O Tempo*, 187; *O Trabalho*, 162
New Yam Festival, 121, 122
Nogueira, Artur, 213–14
Nossa Senhora do Boqueirão, 39

Obá II, 77
O Cabrião, 76
Ogam, 117
Oliva, Anna Maria de Jesus, 150
orixás, 103, 120, 125

"O século" (Castro Alves), 85
Ouseley, William Gore, 17

Palmares (quilombo), 93
Paraguay, xxiii, 53, 55, 56
Paraguayan War, 53, 127; dissatisfaction with, 57–58; dissatisfied veterans of, 65; recruiters attacked, 58; veterans attempt to displace slaves in labor market, 65
Paranhos, José Maria da Silva, 82
Party of Order, 40
Passos, Manuel Benico dos, 163
Patrocínio, José Carlos do, 163–64, 166, 180, 181
Paulistano Radical Club, 75
Pedras Brancas, 62–63
Pedreira (judge), 172–74
Pedro II, xix–xx, 39, 41, 53, 82, 95, 145, 147, 182
Penna, Afonso, 84
Pereira, Arsenio, 194
Pereira, Francisco Sodre, 151
Pereira de Vasconcelos, Bernardo, 40
Philanthropic Society, 13, 48
Phillips, James, xvi
Piapitinga, João de Azevedo, 110–11
Pierson, Donald, 119
Pinheiro de Vasconcelos, Joaquim José, 27
Pitt, William, xvi
Placido (slave), 168
Polytheama Theater, 167, 202
Pomer, León, 55
popcorn cleansing, 124
Portugal, xix, xx, 1, 3, 79, 121, 156
Prandi, Reginaldo, 125
Provincial Law 9, 42
Provincial Law 344, 38

Queiroz, Eusébio de, 30–31, 40
Queiroz Law, 28, 34, 40, 41, 42, 44, 89, 226, 232
Querino, Manoel Raimundo, 162, 201, 202

quilombos, 22, 43, 62–63, 81, 90; proliferation of, 47; as refuges for slaves, 149

Ramos, Arthur, 97
Rebouças, André, 180
Recife, Brazil, 11, 21, 29, 84, 96, 163
Recôncavo, xix, xx, xxiii, 11, 23, 27, 34, 61, 64, 82, 138, 151, 168–69, 178, 183–84, 192; drought in, 111, overseers killed by slaves in, 150
red feijoada, 117
Rediker, Marcus, 14
Reis, João José, 24, 27
Republican Party, 81, 99
Rio Branco, Viscount of, 82
Rio Branco Law, 53
Rio de Janeiro, Brazil, xviii–xxiii, 3, 6, 7, 9, 19–22, 28–31, 66, 73, 90, 115, 133–34, 141, 163–66, 227–29
Rocha, Antonio Carneiro, 157
Rodrigues, Raimundo Nina, 206
Rodrigues Torres, Joaquim José, 40
Romana (slave), 178
Rufino (African freedman), 29

Sabinada rebellion, 25, 26
Sailors Club, 181
Salles, Guillherme Pinto da, 172
Salles, Ricardo, 55
"Salute to Palmares" (Castro Alves), 90–92, 94; reviews of, 93
Salvador, Brazil, xviii–xix; exodus of Nâgo African freedpersons from, 29; free workers used in place of slave labor on public works project in, 39; kidnappings in, 63; Lacerda elevator, 153; laws seeking to expel African freedpersons from, 31; middle class in, 152; rebels gain control during Sabinada uprising, 25; record of deaths, 12; slave population in, 20, 69; slave revolts in, xx; slaves transported from, 135–36; streets patrolled by pedestrian guards, 42
Sampaio, Teodoro, 162
Santa Anna, Arístides Ricardo de, 148
Santa Anna, Geraldo Xavier de, 172, 207
Santa Cruz, Pamphilo da, 166, 168, 178, 179, 199
Santana, Arístides de, 125–26, 128
Santiago, Felipe, 131
Santo Amaro, Brazil, 42
Santos, Francisco Alvares dos, 14, 163
Santos, Luís Antonio dos, 144, 184
Santos, Manoel Emilio dos, 210
Santos, Otacilio, 176
São João Theater, 194
São Luís, Brazil, 21
São Mateus, Brazil, 12
São Paulo, Brazil, xxiii, 13, 21, 37, 44, 56, 66, 74, 76, 84, 131, 141–42, 188–89, 227
Second of July Emancipation Society, 13–14
Seventh of September Abolitionist Society, 96, 147
Seventh of September Liberating Society, 146
ships: *Ascension*, 8; *Bella Miquelina*, 4; *Dolphin*, 7; *Fire Fly*, 7; *Gouverneur Vandes El*, 43; *Grecian*, 4, 8; *Iberia*, 170; *Itapagipe*, 7; *Lucy*, 61; *Mary Adeline*, 7–8; *Mary E. Smith*, 12, 13; *Olinda*, 12; *Paraguassú*, 129; *Relâmpago*, 7, 44; *Rifles*, 5; *Saraiva*, 73; *Trent*, 166; *Três Amigos*, 4; *Ultimação*, 7, 44. See also slave ships
Sierra Leone, 130
Silva, Ambrosio Alba da, 144
Silva, Eduardo, 67
Silva, José de, 209
Silva, Theodoro Machado Freire Periera da, 72, 97
Silvestre (slave), 178, 179
Sinimbú, João Lins Cansação, 113

The Slave Element and the Economic Questions of Brazil (Tarquínio), 153

slave flight, 22, 45, 67–68, 70–71, 90, 94, 141, 143, 168, 189, 190, 193, 195, 226; reasons for, 160; upsurges in, 143; urban, 111

slave resistance, xvii–xviii, xx, 18, 42, 45, 54, 67, 70, 71; by individual initiative and by organized collective acts, 144

slave revolts: attempts to start, 131; fear of, 19, 22, 25, 26, 42, 67, 69

Slavery, the Church, and Abolition (Fonseca), 159, 171

slaves: abuse of, 147–48, 168, 169; and arrests, 45, 46, 47, 68, 142–43; attention to debates about emancipation, xxii; decrease in population of, 70, 187; distinction from free persons lessened, 62; escaped, 45, 70; excessive castigation of, 148; excessive taxes on imports of, 140; export tax on, 136; granted freedom to fight against Paraguay, 56; hiding with free persons, 64; indentured African colonists vs., 32–33; and Islam, 24, 29, 31, 47, 49, 72, 105; large-scale transfer of "difficult," 142; legislation to control, 31; and letters, 31; and lottery, 154; marginalization of, 66; Nâgo, 23–24; occupations by gender, 21; and opportunities created by war, 81; opposition to outflow of, 139; owners required to register, 54; as percentage of population in Salvador, 19; population in Bahia, 186; profound changes brought by freedom, 215; rise in price of, 134; and self-purchase of manumission, 54; and sharing

of knowledge, 149; and slave hunters, 193; as substitute military recruits, 136; and subversive news networks, 14; transfers with Bahia, 136; treaty outlawing transport of, 18

The Slaves (Castro Alves), 87, 98

"The Slave Ship and the Tragedy at Sea" (Castro Alves), xxiv, 88–89; and national prominence for Castro Alves, 90

slave ships: British interception of, xvi, 4, 14

slave trade: fear of resumption of, 89; internal, 133, 138–42; legal restrictions on traders, 3; popular and official opinion turns against, 19; suppression of, 1–15

smallpox, 58, 122, 200

Soares, Carlos Eugênio Libano, 29, 31

Soares de Sousa, Paulino José, 40, 40–41

Sodré, Jeronymo, 14, 157, 158

"Solitary Stanzas" (Castro Alves), 94–95

Sorocaba, São Paulo, 44

Sousa Ramos, José Ildefonso de, 18

Souza, Paula, 188–89

Spinola, Arístides de Sousa, 151, 167

Stowe, Harriett Beecher, 96, 172, 199

The Substitution of Slave Labor by Free Workers in Brazil (Velloso de Oliveira), 33

sugar production, xvii, xix, xx, 12, 61, 134, 138–39, 190, 216

A Summary View of the Slave Trade and of the Probable Consequences of Its Abolition (Phillips), xvi

Symbol of Liberty Club, 174

Tarquínio, Luís, 153–54; statue of, 155

Temistocles, Colonel, 189

terreiros, 103–31, 206; and commu-
  nal sharing, 115; and hiding men,
  127; and police permits, 118
Tindal, L. S., 9
"To America" (Castro Alves), 87
"Tragedy at Sea: The Slave Ship"
  (Castro Alves), xxiv
treaties, 3
Triple Alliance, 53, 54
tuberculosis, 90
Turner, Thomas, 10
Twenty-Fifth of June Liberating
  Society, 146
Tyler, Alexander, 5

Underground Railroad, 159, 164,
  168, 185
Union and Industry (labor union), 65
Urban Guard, 74
Uruguay, 53, 55

vaccination: of recruits, 59
Varela, José Pedro, 83
Vasconcelos, João Lucas do Monte
  Carmelo, 160
Velloso, Marcos Leão, 208
Velloso de Oliveira, Henrique, 33
Verger, Pierre, 4
Vianna, Luís, 84
Vianna, Vigario Rocha, 139
Viçosa, Brazil, 207
Victorino, Manoel, 14, 154, 194
Vinerote, José Antonio, 162
violence, 63, 99, 191, 206;
  perpetrated by slaves, 71, 160;
  and recruitment of military
  forces, 59; slaves' right to use,
  75
Vitória, Brazil, 21
"Voices of Africa" (Castro Alves), 88
Voluntários, 56–57

Wanderley, João Maurício, 28, 160
War of the Triple Alliance, 56; costs
  of, 81; disillusionment with, 80,
  82

Wetherell, James, 29
Wilberforce, Wilber, xvi
Williams, Eric, xvi–xvii
Wise, Henry A., 5
women, 27, 119; abolition and
  female emancipation, 95–96;
  abolitionist, 164, 174; African
  and Bahian-born black, 118;
  as priestesses of terreiros, 118;
  rights of, 154; role in overthrow
  of slavery, 227
Woodbury, John, 5
Workers Protective Association of
  Bahia, 202

yellow fever, 9–11, 43, 200
Yoruba Africans, 23, 24, 76

Zama, Arístides César, 151, 189